THE PLATONIC BIBLE

THE SOURCE OF ALL WESTERN SPIRITUALITY

JERRY DELL EHRLICH

PLATONIC TRADITION
P O BOX 80247
SAN DIEGO, CA 02138-0247

TELEPHONE 619-422-8701
FAX 619-422-8749
E-MAIL acachrprsjdehr@msn.com

Published by Platonic Tradition
P O Box 80247
San Diego, CA 92138-0247

Library of Congress Cataloging-in-Publication Data

Ehrlich, Jerry Dell
The Platonic Bible: The Source of all Western Spirituality.
Includes bibliographical references, glossary and index.

ISBN 978-0-9710000-3-2 $32.95

1. The Hebrew Scriptures, the Tanak. 2. The Christian Canon 3. The Christian Church takes Control of the Roman Empire. 4. Christian Europe. 5. Renaissnce, Reformation, and Dissent. 6. Plato, his Person and Philosophical Faith. 7. The Academy. 8. The Nature of God and Man. 9. The Cosmos. 10. Plato's Cardinal Virtues. 11. Human Intimacy. 12. Platonic Education. 13. Science and the Fine Arts. 14. Platonic Proverbs and Adages. 15. Platonic Love.

Library of Congress Control Number: 2007937798

10 9 8 7 6 5 4 3 2 1

Courtesy of the Boston Public Library

Plato

Also by Jerry Dell Ehrlich, M.Div., M.A., Ph.D.

Suicide in the Roman Empire:
An Historical, Philosophical, and Theological Study.
University Microfilms International
Ann Arbor, MI

Plato's Gift to Christianity:
The Gentile Preparation for and the Making of the Christian Faith
(A study that presents the enormous amount of Platonic concepts that are present in the Christian Canon)
ISBN 0-9710000-0-X

Building a Life by Carpenter Jesus:
The Divine Teacher's Seven Steps to Wholeness with Supplementary Wisdom from both Western Classical and Eastern Sages.
(A work that presents the familiarity of the ethical teachings of all the great teachers of the past that render to all men a common heritage)
ISBN 0-9710000-1-8

The Joy of Embracing God:
Humanity's Longing for the Eternal
(A thesis that reveals that all mankind, from its infancy, longed for a power that could offer an eternal existence to mortal humans)
ISBN 0-9710000-2-6

HYPATIA

PLATO AMICUS, MAGIS AMICA VERITAS

(PLATO IS A FRIEND, A GREATER FRIEND IS TRUTH)

"AN UNEXAMINED LIFE IS NOT WORTH LIVING"

PLATO'S SOCRATES

"AN UNEXAMINED FAITH IS NOT WORTH BELIEVING"

JERRY DELL EHRLICH

THE GREEK ALPHABET

Greek: capital, small, spelling in both captital and small				English: capital, small (lower case), and pronunciation		
Α	α	ΑΛΦΑ	αλφα	A	a	alpha
Β	β	ΒΕΤΑ	βετα	B	b	beta
Γ	γ	ΓΑΜΜΑ	γαμμα	G	g	gamma
Δ	δ	ΔΕΛΤΑ	δελτα	D	d	delta
Ε	ε	ΕΨΙΛΟΝ	εψιλον	E	e	epsilon (short e)
Ζ	ζ	ΖΕΤΑ	ζετα	Z	z	zeta
Η	η	ΕΤΑ	ετα	E	e	eta (long e)
Θ	θ	ΘΕΤΑ	θετα	TH	th	theta
Ι	Ι	ΙΟΤΑ	ιοτα	I	I	iota
Κ	κ	ΚΑΠΠΑ	καππα	K	k	kappa
Λ	λ	ΛΑΜΒΔΑ	λαμβδα	L	l	lambda
Μ	μ	ΜΥ	μυ	M	m	mu (mi)
Ν	ν	ΝΥ	νυ	N	n	nu (ni)
Ο	ο	ΟΜΙΚΡΟΝ	ομικρον	O	o	omicron (short o)
Π	π	Π Ι	πι	P	p	pi
Ρ	ρ	ΡΟ	ρο	R	r	rho
Σ	σ	ΣΙΓΜΑ	σιγμα	S	s	sigma
Τ	τ	ΤΑΥ	ταυ	T	t	tau (tai)
Υ	υ	ΥΨΙΛΟΝ	υψιλον	U (Y)	u (y)	upsilon (ipsilon)
Φ	φ	ΦΙ	φι	PH (F)	ph (f)	phi
Ξ	χ	ΞΙ	χι	Ch (K)	ch (k)	chi
Ψ	ψ	ΨΙ	ψι	PS	ps	psi
Ω	ω	ΩΜΕΓΑ	ωμεγα	O	o	omega (long o)

ABBREVIATIONS

ANF The Ante-Nicene Fathers. Editors A. Roberts and J. Donaldson. Revision and Notes by A.C. Coxe. Eerdmans Publishing Co. Grand Rapids, MI. 1963.

BS-P Bollingen Series LXXI. Plato. Editors Edith Hamilton and Huntington Cairns. Princeton U. Press. 1973.

CTHP Cambridge Texts in the History of Philosophy. Cambridge: Cambridge U. Press.

CTHPT Cambridge Texts in the History of Political Thought. Cambridge: Cambridge U. Press.

FCL Family Classical Library. A.J. Valpy, Henry Colburn and Richard Bentley. New Burlington St., London: 1830-1833.

GBWW Great Books of the Western World. Associate Editor, Mortimer J. Adler. Encyclopaedia Britannica, Inc. London. 1952.

LCL Loeb Classical Library. Harvard U. Press. Cambridge, MA.

NPNF Nicene and Post-Nicene Fathers. Eerdmans Publishing Co. Grand Rapids, MI. 1952.

OCD The Oxford Classical Dictionary. Edited by N.G.L. Hammand and H.H. Scullard. Clarendon Press. Oxford. 1970.

ODCC The Oxford Dictionary of the Christian Church. Edited by F.L. Cross. Oxford U. Press. N.Y. 1963.

CONTENTS

INTRODUCTION

The Judeo-Christian culture and religion which has been so prominent in Western Civilization in the past 1700 years, that those born within its scope of influence seem to accept the idea that one can not be religious or reach out to God except under its wings of influence, despite the fact that it has not only not brought peace and harmony to the Western World, but, on the contrary, has brought conflict, brutality, slavery, suppression of women, colonization of the weaker peoples of the earth, and constant wars, even within the Judeo-Christian faith itself. Also, it has hindered science and all its benefits, imposed guilt upon millions for natural pleasures, silenced and killed its critics, established control of politics and systems of morality that beg for their backing and/or forgiveness by means of the "magical sacraments", taught myths for history, overpopulated the earth at the expense of all other life, and, by in large, suppressed all knowledge and mental and physical activities that did not conform to its tyranny. It has even claimed to have taken the place of God and dictated who would enjoy the afterlife and who would be condemned to the hell and Satan which they have created for the very purpose of using them by the force of fear to control all people All three of the Abrahamic religions, Judaism, Christianity, and Islam have shown very little desire for peace and harmony and fairness to others when they themselves have had the power to enforce themselves upon another. They have created fictitious promises of God that not only permits their slaughter of others but imposes a duty upon them to kill off others who are occupying "their promised Holy Land." From Genesis to Revelation to the Koran, the believer has claimed the right and the duty to suppress or kill the uncircumsized goyim, the person who rejects Jesus, or the ones who do not accept Allah and Mohammed, His Prophet. Not only that, the three children of Abraham have chosen to kill and suppress each other, all claiming to be the favorite son, and the only son that has the truth. Wherever they are upon the earth, they spread their fear, their terror, and their arrogance It is easy to see that the Western World needs and new spiritual guidebook that can be open and honest and useful to humanity in the 21st Century. It will be one that applauds our differences, promotes dialogue in press and discussion, lets science better our future for the search for the knowledge that is necessary to enhance the health of our bodily lives and to control diseases, repair physical damage, and bring us the tools we need to lighten our load and to communicate to the others of the world. Likewise, it will teach how to take care of our earthly mother and how to share it with her other animals our beloved relatives and companions during our stay upon her soil.

The Platonic Bible uses the philosophy and cultural tradition that was established by Plato in his dialogues, teachings, and his disciples at the Academy in Athens which he established in 386BCE, and which helped and encouraged many people in every aspect of culture, life, spirit, mathematics, politics, science, psychology, education and all other facets of human life and activity for over 900 years before the "Christian" Emperor of Rome, Justinian, shut down all "pagan" temples and schools of philosophy of the ancient world. The teachers were declared heretics, the books were burned, and the temples, after being looted, were destroyed by the Christians, actions that sent Western Mankind into the dark ages for a thousand years before such knowledge was reborn in the Renaissance. The actions, methods, and effects of this brutality are presented in the first five chapters of this book so that the readers, who, in general, are not aware of such massive and deadly brutalization the Christian church forced upon others, and is not recognized.

After that brief critical history, the substance of the Platonic Tradition is presented and expanded in the rest of the book, that people may see the beauty, richness and depth of Plato's philosophy and come to recognize the names of so many great Platonists throughout the course of Western Civilization who tried to keep his way of thinking alive. Plotinus, a devout Platonist of the 3rd Century CE, stressing the spiritual side of the Platonic teachings stated (VI.9):

"To those desiring to see, we point to the path; our teaching is about the road and the traveling; the seeing is the very act of the one who has made this choice."

The Platonic Tradition projects its beautiful, scientific, and honest search for the truth without any brutal judgmentalism of other views. It likewise has no dogmas or stiff doctrines, or threats towards the hearer. It simply invites the hearer to join the banquet and the discussion of man's search for identity and happiness and justice. All the people brought into this discussion in this "Bible" did not necessarily see themselves as Platonists, but were, often without any knowledge of it, very well saturated with his thoughts that came to him or her by means of others who were well aware of their Platonic connection. But most of them were very happy to claim their Platonism.

Walter Burkert stated in his *Greek Religion:*

"Whoever reads Plato is fascinated by the encounter with an inexhaustibly rich mind who at the same time is one of the most refined master of Greek language. Plato is the first .philosopher whose entire work has survived and established forever the measure for what is to be philosophy...Since Plato there has been no theology which has not stood in his shadow."

Plato never becomes old because he taught us to always look forward in the search for knowledge, for God had equipped us with reason and longing for the truth in all matters. Idols, creeds, superstitions, and fears had to be boldly put aside that truth might appear, a truth that liberates, even if but for a moment, until another quest is undertaken. The joy of life is in knowledge of good and evil, knowledge of science, of physics, of chemistry, of psychology, of ecology, of botany and zoology, of the universe, of the beauty of the arts and the art of living happily. In such quests, when honestly undertaken for the sake of truth, mankind is constantly lifted upward toward the ever available access of the limitless abundance of knowledge that can enhance man's life in every field, for the sake of both body and soul. Science enhances and ennobles life in body and spirit, that both may find life's greatest goodness, and beauty and happiness. Dietrich Bonhoeffer's words are so very applicable to our situation today:

"The day will come, when men will be called again to utter the word of God with such power as will change and renew the world. It will be a new language, perhaps quite nonreligious, but liberating and redeeming -- it will shock people and yet overwhelm them by its power." (*Can Christianity Survive?* p 123)

While Platonism is a new language for many of the Abrahamic faiths, it certainly has its powerful religious element and does proclaim the Logos (Word) of God. Logos, that is, Reason, and it is a new rational way of approaching God and the human experience and its challenges and the hopes it has for its own future. Ancient "revelations" and many centuries old cemented dogmas condemn humanity's future, but reason and science open up the gates of the cosmos for all, and the wonder of life is uplifted to its highest levels of joy and happiness. That is true religion at work for the benefit of the believers. For 24 centuries the Platonic River of Spiritual and Materialistic Life have flowed through human history and watered humanity that it might grow into manhood, and even though there have been fanatical and superstitious impediments and barriers against its bounteous flow, the Platonic Tradition still has its force to enhance human life, and if it be fully liberated so that its charm can be actualized in the lives of the masses of the seeking and searching population then indeed humanity will enjoy its adulthood and be at harmony within itself and with the very depths of the universe itself. Let the many of humanity come and drink of these waters, and not shy away from them because "philosophy" is an "intellectual" term for only a few. The words of Paul Tillich in his *The Shaking of the Foundations* (p 60) are so appropriate:

"But the mark of real depth is its simplicity. If you should say, 'This is too profound for me; I cannot grasp it', you are self-deceptive. For you ought to know that nothing of real importance is too profound for anyone. It is not because it is too profound, but rather because it is too uncomfortable, that you shy away from the truth....The deep things must concern us always, because it matters infinitely whether we are grasped by them or not."

It is indeed uncomfortable to change religious language, but let that not stop the sincere thinker in his quest for the most beautiful life possible. It may be difficult to go against one's childhood thoughts or those of one's religious ambience, but let all hear the words of Emerson say with him:
"Life is a sincerity. In lucid intervals we say, 'Let there be an entrance opened for me into realities; I have worn the fool's cap too long'....We have been cheated of our reason, but those who were truly sane men have enjoyed a rich and related existence." *(Representative Men*, p 15)

ΑΛΦΑ

A

CHAPTER ONE THE TANAK

I. THE IMAGE OF GOD

A. FROM THE BOOK OF GENESIS

1a) Even though the Book of Genesis is a book of myths and legends and can not be used as actual history, it is possible to see the image of God that is portrayed by its authors and editors, which therefore could reflect ideas that were as late as Ezra, who was perhaps the final redactor of the different (probably four) strands of legends that were available to him in the middle of the Fifth Century BCE.

b) After the two mythical creation stories are presented, the reader is then presented with a difficult to understand fable that portends to tell him the cause of suffering and death. The basic idea is that man disobeyed his Creator and the Creator, having no tolerance at all for his creature, immediately curses the man and his wife and the ground they live on and cultivate for their food, and then determines that they will not benefit of the blessings of the garden initially given them to live in, including the tree of life and thus barring man from living forever.There is also the hint of polytheism in the story: the first creation story tells of Elohim (the gods) creating all and also the element of fear that God has **c)** and betrays when he said that man, after knowing good and evil is somewhat his equal, can live forever as "one of us": "Then Yahweh God said, "Look, man has become just like us for he knows good and evil; now, if he eats also of the tree of life he will live forever." Therefore, Yahweh God drove man out of the garden and placed cherubim and a blazing sword of fire to guard the garden of delight with its tree of life from man. If one looks closely at this myth it shows Yahweh and the Elohim as being very insecure in their positions of authority and power, which, of course, is ironic if they created the entire universe. All this punishment is put on man because man wanted to know the difference between good and evil. The Creators wanted, not a thinking and learning creature, but one of obedience only. The punishment shows of a Deity that has no charity, love or forgiveness for his new born creature.

d) Not much later the sons of the Elohim were attracted to the beauty of human females and had intercourse with them and produced mighty men. Now think of it, the sons of the Creators come to earth for sensual pleasure, but Yahweh is angry with mankind and curses them and limits their earthly life to 120 years. Shortly after (same chapter: Genesis 6), Yahweh is fed up with mankind and sends a flood to kill everyone except one family that he favored. All the people of the earth who had hopes, loves, and the joy of children were all killed because Yahweh was sorry he ever made man and was angry at the entire group. The "loving kindness" of Yahweh is not very evident throughout the book of Genesis, and, as a simple fact, throughout all of the established canon of the Tanak. That one family that survived, Noah's, soon displeased Yahweh again. Noah gets drunk and lies around naked in his tent, and when Ham accidentally walks in on him and tells his brothers, his son is cursed; not Ham himself but his son. Of course this is a myth created to justify Israel's invasion of the people of Canaan and the way they slaughtered all of the people--which will be handled later. But it does show an injustice of God that one man sins and another is punished, and his children forever.

e) In Chapter 11 of Genesis, Yahweh once again reveals his insecurity that mankind might compete with him in his power and again punishes them by confusing their language so that they are driven apart from one another. The story, to a modern man, is childish. Some men are building a tower as a show of strength so that invaders might be persuaded not to attack and also they would make a name for themselves so others would not seek to conquer them and take them into captivity. Seems normal. But Yahweh "comes down" to see what is happening, and fears that they may even be able to build this tower to heaven and that nothing that the gods could do would stop them. So Yahweh "confused their language" and scattered them to all parts of the earth. This action would break man's unity and be a source of conflict between them ever after.

2a) From Genesis 12 to the end of the Hebrew Canon Yahweh decided that he would bless only one part of humanity with a personal and covenantal relationship: Abraham's posterity. All others would be forever on the outside looking in at Yahweh's favors to the only people whom he would treat like a son. This partiality on behalf of the Creator and Father of all mankind, seems basically uncivilized -- something of a dead beat dad of our 21st Century morality: he gives birth to all, but supports only his chosen. While this was common in all ancient societies, and can therefore be understood, yet it is not suitable to be presented as God's will today. In that sense, such scriptures are a hindrance to a spiritual growth that extends equal love to all people. Mo Tzu was a near contemporary of Ezra, and he taught a universal love to be had by all the sons of men; he was perhaps the first to do so. Mo Tzu's teaching can therefore fit into the spiritual base of modern men, but an Abrahamic covenant with God to the exclusion of all other people can not. For a god who shows partiality for the benefit of only one group of people today is at best snobbish and at worst cruel.

b) Genesis also projects Yahweh as controlling childbirth, giving as he pleased to some and shaming other women by withholding fertility to others. "Yahweh has prevented me from bearing children" was to be the miserable cry of a disheartened Sarai (later Sarah). This is a common theme throughout the entire Tanak. Those who were unable to have children were considered "cursed". This, of course, was little compared to the brutality of the "Christian" witch hunts that took place in the late Renaissance era, but it still was a suffering that was needlessly imposed on the women: not only that they did not have children, but that Yahweh himself chose not to permit them to have children.

c) In 18th and 19th chapters of Genesis, it seems, in dealing with the people of Sodom and Gomorrah, Abraham was more charitable and concerned about the people than Yahweh was, who, of course, followed through on his anger and "brimstone and fire" upon the two cities so that none escaped. Imagine how many innocent people will die was the cry of Abraham, but Yahweh felt none but Lot and his wife and daughters worthy enough to be able to go on living.

Yes, the book of Genesis presents myths and legends, but that does not take away from the ugliness with which the character of God is presented. There are many more such things in both Genesis and the rest of the Tanak that fortify the image of God of the Judeo-Christian Bible as being outside the acceptable views of modern man. They follow.

B. YAHWEH'S CHOSEN PEOPLE: YAHWEH'S PARTIALITY

d) That Yahweh has chosen a "son" for himself and that "son" is the children of Abraham is perhaps the main theme to the entire Tanak. "You, O Israel, are my people, and I am your God" for "Of all the peoples of the earth I picked you", and "You shall be covenanted to me forever" and "You shall have no other gods beside me". It was to be an insoluble marriage and no other mates were permitted, for spiritual adultery was harlotry and was to be punished severely. The mindset of the prophets especially emphasized this fact, and, in a sense, Hosea, was to play the role in his life as an example of the misery Israel was causing Yahweh when it played the harlot with other gods. This mindset caused a great intolerance of all other peoples, all other theological systems and all the images and statues that others made to help them worship. Intermarriage between the circumcised and uncircumcised was idolatry and was punishable by death in some circumstances. Genesis 24:3-4, 27:46, 28:6 made such very clear: Abraham makes his servant, who would be in charge of Isaac, swear "Put your hand upon me and swear that you will not take a wife for my son from among the Canaanites, but..from my kindred." Rebekah concerned about Jacob declared "I am weary of my **3a)** life because of the Hittite women. If Jacob marries one of them my life will be worthless." Exodus 4:22, 19:4-6, 34:11-16 enforce the idea. Moses to Pharaoh "Thus says Yahweh: Israel is My first-born son. I have said to you, 'Let My son go, that he may worship me." "Now if you will obey me (Yahweh) faithfully and keep my covenant, you shall be my treasured possession among all the peoples." "Mark well what I command you this day. I will drive the Amorites, the Canaanites, the Hittites, the Perizzites, the Hivites and the Jebusites out of the land that lies before you. Beware of making a peace agreement with them, lest they mingle you with their worship. Tear down and destroy their altars, their pillars, and all sacred areas; for you must not worship another god, because my name is Jealous, for I am a jealous god. Do not play the harlot with them and their gods and do not marry their daughters for they

will lead you into harlotry." The Second Law, Deuteronomy 14:2 states, "You are a people consecrated to Yahweh your God, and Yahweh has chosen you to be his very own people out of all the peoples of the earth."
b) David's prayer goes "This is your greatness Lord Yahweh; there is none like you, and there is no god but You. Is there another people on earth like Israel, your own people. You have redeemed them, made them famous in the earth, driving out nations on their behalf. You have made Israel to be your people forever, and you are their God (2 Samuel 7:22ff). Faithfulness was to destroy all that was not Yahweh's. 2 King11:17-18 recorded "Jehoiada made an agreement with the king and the people by which the latter undertook to be the people of Yahweh. All the people then went to the temple of Baal and destroyed it, smashing and breaking its altars and images, and before the altars they killed the priest, Mattan."
c) So that is what it is to be the people of Yahweh--destroy and kill those who have a different theology! Psalm 2:7-9 states "Let me proclaim Yahweh's decree; as he has told it to me. 'You are my son and I am your Father as of today. Ask and I will give you the nations for your heritage, your rule shall reach the ends of the earth. With an iron scepter you will destroy them, and they will break in pieces like a dashed pottery." Yahweh will be quite ruthless and intolerant when he decides to bless his own people with the possessions and land of others. And there will be no limit to the vastness of the destruction--to the ends of the earth.
d) The prophets of Israel were just as dedicated to this call, if not more than the historians and the poets. The so called Third Isaiah, a rabid nationalist, declared: "The wealth of the nations shall be yours"(60:5). He continues (60:10-12)

> Foreigners shall rebuild your walls, their kings shall serve you:
> ...
> Ever shall your gates lie open, never shutting either day or night,
> in order that the nations can pour their wealth into the city,
> being carried by their kings.
> For the nation and kingdom that will not serve you shall perish,
> those nations shall be utterly laid waste.

This is the salvation of Yahweh? This is a light to the world? Only Israel could think so. The 61st chapter of Isaiah also declares that those aliens will do all the work that needs to be done, and Israel will consume the wealth of the nations. Isaiah ends his ministry with this prophecy: "All flesh shall come to worship Yahweh...And they shall go forth and look on the dead bodies of those that rebelled against Yahweh and his rule; and their worm will not die nor will their fire burn out, and they will be abhorred by all living flesh".

4a) During the Babylonian Captivity many of the Jews who had remained in Palestine had through the years intermarried with the local people. When Ezra came from Babylon to Palestine to start the rebuilding of Israel that was granted by the Persian king Cyrus, he found the situation "horrifying". He claimed to be ashamed to face Yahweh in prayer, but he soon took action. Families that were, as far as one can tell, happy and loving, but were of mixed faith or race, had to be broken up and the women and children of such were cast out to survive on their own. Is this once again proof of Yahweh's "loving kindness"? Ezra, before the action was declared, expressed the situation as follows:

> The leaders (of those left in Palestine) came to me and said "The people of Israel, including the Priests and Levites, have not separated themselves from the Palestinians who are steeped in abominations--Canaanites, Hittites, Perizzites, Jebusites, Ammonites, Moabites, Egyptians and Amorites--but have taken wives for themselves from these foreigners, and have sons by them. The **holy race** has been mixing with the natives of the countries, and the chief people have actually led the way for this." At his news I tore my garment and my cloak; I tore out hair from my head and beard and collapsed to the ground, being overcome.(Ezra 9:1-3)

b) Ezra then prayed to Yahweh pleading that he knew they had broken the covenant in which Yahweh had commanded "Give not your daughters to their sons, neither take their daughters for your sons, and never seek their peace and prosperity"(Ezra 9:12)

Ezra then went to work and preached and demanded that they separate from their wives and polluted children, and many obeyed. The 10th and last chapter of Ezra is a list of all those who "had married foreign women, and they put them away with their children" Family values does not extend to the unholy races of the world, at least in a mixed marriage with one of the holy race.

c) Nehemiah was Ezra's equal in racial purity, recording that the people stood up and confessed their sins of having entered into such unholy alliances and made an oath to separate and never again enter into such marriages. It was also declared that no Ammonite or Moabite could enter the assembly of God. "When the people heard the law they separated from Israel all those of foreign descent. Nehemiah prays that God remember him for the good he has done (13:14) and then proceeded to preach and curse those who had entered into such marriages--many of the children did not even know Hebrew anymore. "And I contended with them and cursed them and beat some of them and pulled out their hair (Ezra at least had pulled out his own hair), and I made them take an oath to God" pledging not to enter into such unholy unions in the future. The ethnic cleansing was accomplished. "Thus I cleansed them from everything foreign...Remember me, O my God, for good"(13:30). Amos (3:2) also reminded Israel that they were Yahewh's special people: "You only have I known of all the families of the earth." Zechariah (8:23) is not going to be outdone by the other "chosen people" advocates "Thus says Yahweh of hosts: In those days ten men from the nations of every tongue shall take hold of the robe of a Jew, saying 'Let us go with you, for we have heard that God is with you.'" But this is not enough,

d) "And the wealth of all the nations round about shall be collected (for Israel), gold, silver, and garments in great abundance...Then every one that survives of all the nations that have come against Jerusalem shall go up every year to worship the King, the Lord of hosts...If any nation does not go up every year...no rain shall fall upon that race...they will be struck by the plague that Yahweh sends to all the nations...On that day the bells on the horses shall be inscribed "Holy to Yahweh".(Zechariah 14).

Holy carries the sense of separateness in Hebrew. One must be totally separated from other cultures, religions, interracial marriages and keep the covenant of Yahweh, and then one will be "Holy to Yahweh", and member of the Chosen Race.

5a) C. YAHWEH GIVES HIS PEOPLE A PROMISED LAND

One of the more difficult myths to accept is the promise of God to give land to one people, but have to take it away from someone else in order that his favorite people could occupy it. But in the Yahwistic lore it is presented as if it actually was the will of God to do so, even if it meant slaughtering all the innocent people who were living in that land and had cultivated it and made it their home. Yet this is precisely the myth that the Israelites created to justify their slaughter of the Palestinians who resided there for some lengthy period of time. Over and above this, the myth presented Yahweh as a warrior god who would go before them and lead the killings of the local people, and even punish those who had hesitated to participate in such a horrible activity. This invasion of the land of Canaan is, along with the Exodus from Egypt, repeated over and over again in the Tanak as an example of the wonderful things that Yahweh did for his people. It is shamefully glorified. Let the Hebrew Scriptures speak for themselves.

Numbers 15:3, 11-12 declares Yahweh to be a tribal warrior:

> Yahweh is a man of war; Yahweh is his name...
> Who is like you, O Yahweh, among the gods?
> Who like you is so majestic in holiness.
> You do wonders that are terror inspiring.
> You extended your right hand and the earth swallowed them.

b) Thus did Yahweh to the Egyptians. But this can be accepted and understood as a kindness of Yahweh to a degree, for the Jews had been held in bondage doing the menial work that the Egyptians needed done. It was an act of liberation. But where then could Yahweh lead them? A difficult question, but after "40" years in the desert the die was cast, Canaan was to be taken by force, and Yahweh's wonderful works continued for his people. At Amalek, Joshua led the fighting and Moses held up his hand. "Whenever Moses held up his hand, Israel prevailed; and whenever he lowered his hand, Amalek prevailed. Moses became tired but Aaron and Hur helped his him hold up his hand (Ex 17:10-11)". Yahweh was not a happy winner: "I will utterly blot out the memory of Amalek from under heaven (Ex 17:14)". Yahweh encourages his people with assurance of his participation in blotting out the necessary people.

Ex 23:23 "When my messenger goes before you, and leads you to the Amorites, the Hittites, Perizzites, Canaanites, Hivites and the Jebusites, I will destroy them." The writer continues this assurance of Yahweh's participation:

> I will put forth the fear of me and in terror all the people you come to will panic and run. I will put forth a plague of hornets that will go before you and drive out the Hivites, Canaanites and Hittites. ...I will extend your borders from the Sea of Reeds to the Sea of Philistia, and from the desert to the Euphrates; for I will deliver the inhabitants of all that land into your power, and you will drive them out. You shall make no agreements with them or their gods. they are not to remain in the land, it is to be yours (Ex 23:27-33).

c) It will be a land of milk and honey (Ex 33:3), and it will be the gift of Yahweh for his people. The book of Numbers continues the invasion story, and God continues to help devastate the people of Canaan: (Nbs 21:3) "And Yahweh listened to the plea of Israel, and gave victory over the Canaanites, and Israel totally destroyed them and their cities." One village after another was utterly devastated--with the help of Yahweh. The local people were constantly killed or dispossessed of their land. (Nbs 31:7-9) "They warred against Midian, and keeping the command God gave Moses, they killed every male...and took captive the women and their little ones. They also took as booty all the cattle, the flocks, and all material goods." But this kindness of letting the women live brought the wrath of Moses and Yahweh, and for not killing the women also, and Yahweh sent a plague upon Israel. After suffering the plague Israel decided to obey Yahweh and were commanded to "kill every man among the little ones, all women who had had intercourse, but could take unto themselves the young virgin girls (they had not be defiled by having sex with the uncircumcised). Yahweh again makes it very clear to Moses that only a total cleansing of the land will do. (Nb 33:50)

> And Yahweh said to Moses when they were near the Jordan and In the vicinity of Jericho, "Tell the people of Israel that when they pass over the Jordan and into the land of Canaan, they must drive out all the inhabitants of the land, destroy all sculptured stones, all graven images, and then take the land as your possession and

> settle down in it, for this land I have given it to you as your possession.

d) After Israel had lived in Palestine for several hundred years, there still remained many of the locals who had survived the holocaust inflicted upon their ancestors. And this agitated the Reformer King, Josiah (640-609), and during his reign the book of Deuteronomy (Second Law) was either written or "found" and presented to him. His time was an unsettling time as Pharaoh Neco was rising in power in Egypt, Assyria was struggling to keep its power and Babylon was rising to challenge the entire Middle East. Israel was at the mercy of things beyond its control. But Hilkiah "found" the book that declared that if Israel keeps the covenant that it had made with Yahweh earlier, then Yahweh would be with them and protect them. Thus a new round of cleansing reform was called for. The book of Deuteronomy called for such actions as the following:

> You shall not make marriages with them, giving into marriage your sons or your daughters. For they will be turned away from serving me (Yahweh) and honoring other gods. Then my anger will be ignited against you and I will destroy you quickly. You shall destroy their altars, dash to pieces their pillars, and burn with fire their graven images (Dt 7:3-5).

> (Put back into Moses' mouth were these words) And you shall destroy all the peoples that Yahweh your God will give over to you, your eye shall not pity them, and you shall not serve their gods (Dt 7:16).

6a) Even if family members are involved in any kind of idolatry, they are to be killed by stoning. No mercy shall be shown to either your sons or your daughters for spiritual harlotry. No pity or tolerance shall be permitted. The evil must be stamped out (Dt 13). The message is always "Israel must expand to the promised borders and cleanse the land of all peoples who are not circumcised and their places of worship shall be utterly destroyed."

Throughout the books of Joshua and Judges, the conquests against the Canaanites, obviously some legendary, were described and adorned in heroism. But what remained was the utter brutality, lack of mercy, absence of tolerance, and the savage slaughtering of all those innocent people whose crime was unknowingly living in and cultivating a life in an area that Yahweh had decided to give to his chosen people. At Jericho all were killed except for the harlot who betrayed her people to survive. At Ai all the people were attacked until none survived or escaped. Against the Amorites Yahweh helped in the slaughter by throwing down great stones from heaven and killing more Amorites that the Israeli soldiers did. Joshua gets the sun to stand still to give the Israelites more time to kill whatever Amorites had survived the stones from heaven. Joshua had every person slaughtered in Makkedah, Lachish, Eglon, Hebron, Debir and Negeb where "he left none remaining, but utterly destroyed all that breathed (yes, every living creature), "as Yahweh the God of Israel had commanded" (Joshua 10).

b) The book of Judges presents a series of mop up operations as well as the struggle against the strong Philistine opposition. But again the same disrespect for innocent life continued. "The Danites (tribe of Dan) came to Laish, <u>to a quiet and unsuspecting people</u>, and killed them with the sword and burned down the city"(Jud 18:27). And, even though there are scores of more examples of bragging of such slaughters, one more will be sufficient. The tribe of Benjamin, after a civil war conflict with Israel, was short of women, so this was the advise of Israel to the Benjaminites--go and wage war and collect the virgins for your wives, but slaughter everyone else.

> Go and kill the inhabitants of Jabesh-gilead with your swords; also the women and the little ones. Do this: every male and every woman who has slept with a male you shall totally annihilate.

But they found only 400 virgins to ease some of the needs of the men of Benjamin. Want a young virgin wife--go kill her family and take her. Not quite fit for 21st Century morality.

D. YAHWEH'S STRICT DEMAND OF RITUALS AND LAWS

c) By far the most important ritual is that of circumcision for the male infants of the Jewish faith. Probably started in Egypt, Egyptians too practiced circumcision, while Israel was there on their 400 years stay, it was written backwards into Abraham's time and declared that all the seed of Abraham was to be circumcised as a sign of the covenant between Yahweh and Abraham's seed. At any rate the ritual was a standard barrier for the Israelites: there were the circumcised and the uncircumcised. The Greeks, who were much more open about nakedness both in the games and in the gymnasia, thought it was rather counter-productive to shelter the body with clothing if the sign of the covenant was circumcision, as, to them, a sign was to be visible to others to indicate something of importance. Make a sign and then hide it did not make much sense to them and it became a object of ridicule of the Jews among the Greeks. Nevertheless, among the Jews it was a sign upon their very bodies, indeed the very part of the body that channeled the seed of Abraham and planted it for the birth of the next generation. Here what is important is how important it was to the people of Israel, something very hard for others to understand (although Christians put the same great importance on the ritual of baptism which will be handled later in its proper place). In Genesis 34 the ritual seemed to be more important than **d)** justice, peace, and unity--not that the Israelites desired such. Shechem longed for Dinah, with whom he was intimate, and his father, Hamor asked that the Jews and the local Canaanites live in peace with one another and even intermarry to show the unity between them. But Jacob never intended such, but still acted like it was a good idea. He suggested that Hamor have all his men circumcised as a first step to unity and Hamor agreed and the process took place. However, afterwards when the Canaanites were sore from the procedure, Jacob's sons Simeon and Levi took swords into the village and killed all of Hamor's men. Of course this never happened as circumcision came later, but the slaughter of Hamon's village could have happened, although that too is doubtful. But the idea of the duplicity of Jacob's sons using circumcision, made a later story for educational purposes to show how important circumcision was to the later Israelites, more important than peace, unity, and justice with the uncircumcised. Exodus 12:48 states: "If a stranger who dwells with you would offer the Passover to Yahweh, all his males must be circumcised; then he shall be permitted to offer sacrifice; he shall then become as a citizen of the country. But no uncircumcised person may participate in the Passover." When Joshua was about to invade Canaan there was a mass circumcision on all the men who had evidently not kept the ritual during the stay in the wilderness, and no venture into war was to be undertaken without the sign of the covenant upon all the soldiers.

7a) The Passover itself was almost equal to circumcision, less in importance because circumcision happened only once in a life-time and could not be reversed. It was a sign for one's entire life. But the Passover was to be permanent in the sense that every year it was to be celebrated, for it marked Israel's liberation and perhaps, in a sense, Israel's birth as a nation. The celebration of the Passover also was to be an opportunity for the family to teach the children of the liberation from Egypt--an act that is constantly referred to the Tanak. "And you shall explain to your son on that day, 'It is because of what Yahweh did for me when I went free from Egypt'"(Ex 13:8). The Passover itself in ancient Egypt sounds a little too fictitious as do all the plagues, but within it is another ritual that supposedly made the difference of life or death: the blood on the door posts. Did the spirit of Yahweh not know who was Jewish or not?

b) It also seems a little too ritualistic to believe that Joshua marched around Jericho six days and had trumpets blown so that the seventh day the walls would fall down. This conquering of Jericho is a well adorned legend, but what is significant is that ritual again played such a big role. Likewise the entire animal sacrificial system, besides being simply a way to provide food for the priests, seemed to be a system by which the people actually felt their sins had been removed. Many ancient cultures also had animal sacrifices to the gods, but the careful division of clean and unclean animals and the males and female division and the exclusion of any blemished animal, all seem to be a ritualistic overload. It also is strange that the good and unblemished animals would be sacrificed while the inferior and blemished ones were left to reproduce the next generation--a survival of the most unfit. The right of primogeniture which was probably, and still today, an almost universally practiced right within families and even in law. But it is childish to think that the first born is automatically the best or most responsible of one's children. Rebekkah recognized this and took matters into her own hand by means of deception to a blind and near helpless Isaac. Rebekkah had to lie and deceive her dying husband to overcome such a poor ritual by law or at least by custom. During Isaiah's confrontation with Yahweh he pleads his sinfulness and claims not to be worthy of the call of his God. However, Yahweh has a ritual ready:

> Then one of the seraphs flew to me, holding in his hand a live coal which he had taken from the altar with a pair of tongs. With this he touched my mouth and said: "See now, this has touched your lips, your sin is taken away, your iniquity is purged." (Is 6:6-7)

There is no doubt that psychologically ritual throughout all ages and all peoples have played a role in instruction and a feeling of rebirth. But that it actually forgives sins seems immoral. It becomes a Deus ex machina or an ex opere operato. That is, it seems to make a machine of God that by the mere fact of the ritual performed something magic or spiritual has happened.

E. YAHWEH'S WRATH AND MOODY EMOTIONS

c) While it is always necessary that when speaking of the Deity or any absolute metaphysical reality the employment of anthropomorphisms and metaphors will play a major role in our verbal expressions, it is still necessary to try to understand in human terms the images and representations of our words when trying to convey a thought to another. Platonic thought put the Deity beyond passions as we know them, but, in contrast, the Hebrew Scriptures are full of such passions and moods that it attributes to Yahweh. Many of them such as insecurity of the Deity, Yahweh's wrath at both major and minor infractions of the given law or covenant, Yahweh's loss of memory, his brutality, his partiality, his violent punishments upon his creatures, and his remorse or repentance of his own actions when his passions subsides and he comes to his better self are symbolic of a god who is no more than a big overgrown brute in the neighborhood who is controlling, threatening, and violent when he does not get his own way. Such passions are often projected into the nature of Yahweh by the Hebrew Scriptures, the Tanak.

d) First let us look at the brutality of some of Yahweh's laws that are required to be kept to remain within the covenantal relationship with him. Exodus 21:17 "Whoever curses his father or mother shall be put to death". This is very harsh, when after all, Yahweh himself has cursed his creatures and punished them many times. The approval of slavery is also a cause of some brutal laws such as Exodus 21:20-21 "When a man strikes his slave, male or female, with a rod and the slave dies immediately, he shall be punished. But if the slaves survives at least a day, the slave owner is not to be punished for the slave was his property." Exodus 22:18-20 reads: "You shall not permit a sorceress to live. Whoever lies with a beast shall be put to death. Anyone who sacrifices to any god except Yahweh, shall be totally destroyed." Exodus 35:2 declares that anyone who does any work at all on the Sabbath shall be put to death." The sacrificial food for Yahweh must be held extremely sacred and thus "Every person who eats of the fat of an animal of which an offering by fire is made to Yahweh shall be exiled from the people."(Lev 7:25). In Leviticus 20 there is a series of brutal laws for those who trespass against them. As to adultery, "both the adulterer and adulteress shall be put to death"; "If a man lies with a man as with a woman, both of them have committed and abomination; they shall be killed"; "If a man takes a wife and her mother also, it is wickedness; they shall be consumed in fire"; "If a man lies with a beast; both he and the beast shall **8a**) be killed". Yahweh does not want any sacrifices or offerings from "blemished" people: "None of your descendants throughout their generations shall approach the altar to make an offering of bread to God."(Lev 21:16). For "because he has a blemish, he may not profane my (Yahweh's) sanctuaries" (Lev 21:23). "He who dishonors the name of Yahweh shall be executed, the entire congregation shall stone him" (Lev 24:16). And Yahweh gives Israel this threat:

> But if you will not listen to me and will not do all these commandments...then this is what I will do to you: I will put you into a state of constant terror, you will be chronically sick, your eyes will waste away, and life itself will slip away from you. You will sow for food, but your enemies will eat it, and those you hate will rule over you. Then if you still do not obey my commandments, I will punish you sevenfold for your sins (Lev 26:14-18).

b) Even Moses is not spared Yahweh's moody wrath, for after calling him to lead Israel to freedom, he attacks Moses seeking to kill him because he has not circumcised his son. Yahweh has called Moses to go back to Egypt to liberate his people, but "At a lodging place on the way Yahweh met him and sought to kill him. Then Zipporah took a flint and cut off her son's foreskin, and touched Moses' feet with it...So Yahweh then let him alone"(Ex 4:24-25).

c) One of the most distasteful images of Yahweh is his constant hardening of Pharaoh's heart and then punishing him and the Egyptian people because Pharaoh's heart is hardened against him. This happens over and over again in the Seventh through the Eleventh Chapters of Exodus. How can this in any way represent Divine Justice and Mercy? It can not, for Yahweh has set the entire scene up to display his power and glory. Yes, Yahweh plays with Pharaoh and his game is to destroy the crops and cattle and the first born children of the Egyptians.

> Then Yahweh said to Moses "Go to Pharaoh, for I have hardened his heart and his servants' hearts, that I can display these signs among them, and you, Moses, can tell your children and grand-children how I have made sport of the Egyptians and what signs I have done in their midst: for the purpose that you may know that I am Yahweh". (Ex 10:1-2).

d) One anthropomorphism that is rather perplexing is that after 430 years in Egypt doing heavy work and being oppressed by the Pharaohs, God remembered his covenant with Abraham, Isaac, and Jacob. To imply that God could forget his choice of one people to love and then leave them in virtual slavery for over 400 years, that is bad enough. But then to present Yahweh as exploding with anger every time Israel forgets one of his commandments seems to present God as inconsistent at best or, at worst, very self-centered: so self-centered that he would forget to keep his covenant with his special "son" by choice and adoption (Ex 2:24). Such a situation makes Yahweh's punishment for law breaking all the more difficult to understand.

9a) It also appears that at times human beings were more gentle and more logical than Yahweh. As previously mentioned Abraham seemed more gracious towards the Sodomites than Yahweh. Also Moses twice counseled Yahweh against unreasonable punishment against his own people, Israel. David became angry with God when he killed one who tried to stabilize the ark when it was about to fall to the ground.

> And Yahweh said to Moses, "How much longer will this people dishonor me? How long will they not trust in me, despite all the miracles I have done in their midst? I will first hit them hard with the pestilence and then I shall disown them. But you, Moses, I will make of you a better nation than they." But Moses said to Yahweh, "But when the Egyptians hear about this failed covenant, especially after you with all your power brought your people out from among them...they will say it was because you, O Yahweh, were not able to bring the people into the promised land that you had sworn to give them, so you slaughtered them instead...It is better that you pardon them and fulfill the covenant promise"...(Yahweh then agrees with Moses and says, "I have pardoned them according to your reasoning" (Nb 14:13-20).

b) David's anger against Yahweh would certainly seem justified, as the action of Yahweh seemed loaded with uncalled for wrath and stemming from a strong ego. It was at a happy time when David and all Israel were making merry before God with all their might, singing and playing music upon instruments. As the were journeying,

> They came to the threshing floor of the Chidon, and Uzza put out his hand to hold the Ark of God from falling because the oxen had stumbled. Yahweh was incensed at Uzza, and struck him down because he had laid a hand on the Ark; and so Uzza died there in front of God. David was angry because Yahweh had burst out in anger against Uzza (I Chr 13-9-12).

c) Uzza was trying to protect the holy Ark from falling to the ground and be soiled and possibly even suffering damage, and his reward was to be killed by Yahweh for not keeping his hands off of the holy Ark. Most decent men would have honored Uzza, but Yahweh in all his holiness thought more of his commandments than a deed that was done to honor him and his Ark. Even David, a man of blood himself, saw this killing as wrong and totally unjustified.

Another story to show Yahweh's moodiness and ego-centered wrath against humankind when someone breaks one of his laws is the story recorded in 2 Kings 17. The king of Assyria, when he conquered a certain people would take them out of their ancestral setting and move them to another part of their conquered world. He brought some people from Babylon and other places to settle them in Canaan, now claimed by Israel. These unsuspecting people who had probably never heard of the law code of Yahweh, were punished by Yahweh for being on holy ground without living according to his laws and commandments, therefore "Yahweh sent lions among them which killed some of the dispersed people." This is the Lord of creation who sends rain upon the just and the unjust? He controls the world and all is his, but he reacts viciously and unjustly to the innocent because they have been forced to live in an area where they unknowingly did not do what Yahweh wanted them to do.

d) The final illustrative story of the many that could be chosen has to do with some Israelites who went off and had sex with a non-Israelites and even participated in their religious rituals. So Yahweh demanded that the chiefs of those involved should all be hanged, which they were. One Israelite evidently cared dearly for his Midianite woman and brought her home to his family "in the sight of Moses and the whole people of Israel while they were repenting". Then Phinehas the priest, went into action. He took a spear, went into the man's family's dwelling and pierced both the man and the woman through their bodies so that they died. That stopped the plague that God had sent upon the Israelites, for God had now considered it an act of atonement. For Phinehas "was jealous for his God, and made atonement for the people of Israel" (Nb 25). But before Phinehas did his "glorious" deed, Yahweh's plague had killed 24,000 Israelites. But this killing of a man and woman who wanted to live together served as an atonement for all of Israel. A man in love must take care that the woman will be approved of by God or else thousands will die in a plague. This is brutal far beyond human wisdom.This seems all the more ridiculous since Moses himself had married a Midianite priest's (Jethro's) daughter, Zipporah, who later saved Moses' life when Yahweh attacked him for not having circumcised their child (Ex 2:21 & Ex 4:25).

10a) So much then for Yahweh's wrath, brutality, and moodishness in his dealings with his people of Israel as well as with others who were not in a covenant relationship with him. The impressions and images of these stories are simply not appropriate in the education of children today for they must be shown a God with an entirely different face if they are to love him as a Heavenly Father and they are certainly not of any value for any rational person of the 21st Century.

II. MYTHS

b) In this present century the myths of old must, at least, be considered as myths and not as recorded history and foolishly "defended" by pseudo-science for the purpose of trying to maintain the outdated idea that the Judeo-Christian Bible is inspired by God, even word for word, to such a degree that all myths are actually real history and must be taught as such. Myths certainly can serve a purpose in instruction and may always be with us as human thinkers and dreamers. But they must be taught to be what they actually are, myths, not historical or scientific material for instruction or doctrine. Without doubt the first 13 chapters of Genesis are mythical, reflecting similar myths from other ancient societies and most likely borrowed from the myths of the Fertile Crescent which were written long before the ones found in Genesis. The book of Genesis is made up from different strands of mythical and legendary sources and that is why there are two creations stories that do not agree with each other as well as two flood stories, intermingled with **c**) each other by a much later redactor, that also do not agree with each other. In our approach to any story that speaks before the more verifiable "historical" age, one will always find stories of myth and legend. He may find a story of virtue there or he may find an atrocious story there that has neither truth nor virtue to it. The mythological genealogies of all the races of the earth of Genesis 10 leaves out the existence of all Asian people, that is not offensive if one understands them to be mythical, but very offensive if they are presented as true history. The book of Esther is so far away from historical truth that the only real decision a reader must make is to what category it fits: myth or legend. Similar criticism can be said of the book of Daniel, which will be discussed in another section. Ancient writings must be carefully and rationally interpreted, and it must also be remembered that they were created by people who lived with a much different world-view than mankind has today. Later in this book some myths, fables, and legends will appear, but they will appear as such and not as history or science, and it will be up to the reader to decide if he is going to find any value to them, and if so how he is going to use them for his own life or for the instruction of his or her children.

III. HISTORICAL INACCURACIES IN THE TANAK

d) This is a difficult section to present because of the mixture of exaggerated legends, myths, post-facto prophecies, inconsistencies, contradictions, and the basic historical inaccuracies that are spread throughout the Tanak. However, an attempt will be made to separate the fine distinctions among these overlapping stories. This section will look at some of the stories that are in all seriousness presented as historical happenings and the particular events present within each one. Anachronisms abound. Genesis 21:34 has Abraham (c 1700 BCE) dwelling in the land of the Philistines who came into such territory only in 1200 BCE. Therefore, he never really met any Philistines: this also makes Genesis 10:14 out of place with historical reality. The Passover story has so many exaggerated legendary and miraculous events in its presentation of the exodus story that, other than the fact that the Jews were in Egypt and found themselves in an undesired position and left Egypt, all the particular events described, especially the magic of Moses staff turning into the conquering serpent, are certainly non historical in nature. Yet this "event" and all of the adorned legendary happenings that are claimed to have taken place are celebrated every year within the Jewish and Christian faiths. Many of the laws of Exodus 20:22--23:33 are laws for an existing agricultural society while the Jews were still in the desert: they were written and put back into Moses' mouth after the conquering of Canaan.

11a) When one has a record of events and one event is impossible to follow a preceding event, then one can be assured of an historical inaccuracy. Such takes place in the legendary tale of the plagues in Egypt in the Exodus story: Ex 9:6 states that all the cattle of the Egyptians died in that particular "event", yet another "event plague" that happened shortly thereafter claims to have killed all the first born of the cattle--what cattle? They are all already dead--alittle beyond being able to reproduce.

b) Luther said that they prophets often erred. Isaiah declared: "An oracle concerning Damascus: Behold, Damascus will cease to be a city, and will become a pile of ruins. Her cities will be desolate forever" (Is 17:1-2). Of course, Damascus is well and alive in 2007 CE. Isaiah had a difficult time in making good on his prophecies, for in trying to comfort his people not to fear the Egyptians, he declared:

> And the waters of the Nile river will be no more, and its river bed will be parched and dry; its watering canals will smell of death, and all its tributaries will be dried up as well. Neither reeds nor rushes will survive. All that surrounds the Nile will be dry and nothing planted will grow, all life dependent upon it will never be again. (Is 19:5-7).

c) This also never happened and Egypt today is still "the gift of the Nile". Isaiah then declared that Egypt would be totally converted to the worship of Yahweh, and it never happened (Is 19:19-22). But the Middle-East is not enough for Yahweh's wrath and control: the entire earth will be under his curse, dry up, be desolate, "utterly laid waste and totally despoiled", and few people will be left alive after Yahweh's actions (Is 24:1-7). In fact about this time and thereafter new nations of Medes and Persians were developing a wonderful culture, one that would eventually conquer Israel itself. Joel, also trying to comfort his contemporaries, declared that "Jerusalem shall be holy and strangers shall never again pass through it" (Joel 3:17)--(He missed of course, as Persians, the Greeks, and the Romans, not only passed through Jerusalem, but conquered it and controlled it for centuries). Zechariah likewise did not have much historical foresight when he predicted that Judah would defeat the up and rising Greeks (9:13). And perhaps Jonah ought not be here because of it obvious fictional character, yet it does declare the size of Nineveh to be many times larger than it ever was both geographically and population wise. Jonah claimed it was three days journey (perhaps 60 miles) in width--it was only one and a half miles wide; and a population that had 120,000 children under the age of three, which would amount to several million people (in Europe in 1500 CE there were only 5 cities with over 100,000 people total and the largest one in Germany was Augsburg with 35,000 inhabitants). While exaggerations are great in many ancient works, especially in fictional works and exaggerated works put out by egoistic kings, nevertheless, to proclaim a work an inspired work of God with no inaccuracies in it and then to find it a grossly exaggerated story, leaves one with the opinion that this may not be a reliable historical presentation.

In 2 Chronicles 14 it is said that Yahweh defeated the Ethiopians in which they were fighting against Asa and Judah. This is an entirely imaginary and fictional battle.

IV. CONTRADICTIONS AND INCONSISTENCIES

d) Because of the similar nature of contradictions and inconsistencies they have both been brought together in this section. The reader will easily see the difficulties involved in trying to make such statements logical or harmonious.

Genesis 2:24 stated an, perhaps, overly ideal state of human unions when it declared, after the "making of Adam and Eve": "Hence a man leaves his father and mother and clings to his wife, so that they become one flesh".Yet, in reading the rest of the Tanak one would think the statement would be something like this: "All the leaders of the people, especially patriarchs and kings, shall breed with as many women as possible so that the nation shall be as numerous as the stars of the sky". For, in reality nearly all the anointed ones of Yahweh (the messias or christs) who served the people of Israel seemed to follow a form of polygyny (one man, many women for marriage). Abraham, the father of Israel, became one flesh with Sarah, Hagar, Keturiah, and his "concubines" (Gen 25:1-6). Jacob married sisters, Leah and Rachel, and **12a**) had children also with the maids Bilhah and Zilpah. Many of the "judges"of Israel also had many children, far beyond the ability of one woman. Ibzan had 30 sons and 30 daughters. Abdon had 40 sons and had 30 grandsons. Samson united with a harlot in Gaza and then he had a splendid time with Delilah who cut his hair--he should have stayed with the harlot of Gaza. David did quite well for himself: Abigail, Ahinoam, Michal (Saul's daughter), Maacah, Haggith, Abital, Eglah, Bathsheba who was Uriah's wife and he was killed by the cunning of David, at least 10 concubines, and 2 Sam 5:13 adds "And David took more concubines and wives after he came from Hebron." Of course the all time champion is Solomon: "He had seven hundred wives and princesses, and three hundred concubines" and he clung to these in love (I Kings 11:1-4). Of course there is a good chance that Genesis 2 was written after the time of the David and Solomon, nevertheless today very few Jews or Christians have many women living with them in sexual union.

b) In a lighter way it is claimed by the Psalmist that Yahweh, who keeps his eye on Israel, neither slumbers nor sleeps (121:3-4). Yet it is also said, as aforementioned, that he had forgotten Israel for more than 400 years while they struggled in poverty doing hard work in Egypt. In a much sadder way it seems illogical that Moses would lead the slaughter of the Midianites (Nb 25) when he had been sheltered by a Midianite priest, Jethro, and even married his daughter (Ex 2:15ff). How could Moses say basically: "Thanks for sheltering me and protecting me from Pharaoh's wrath when he tried to kill me, and thanks for giving me Zipporah as a wife--she was wonderful, but now I have an army with me and I am going to slaughter all of you."

c) Deuteronomy 9 gives an unconditional promise and in Deuteronomy 11 he makes it conditional. Dt 9:3 states:

> So know that Yahweh goes before you into the land as a devouring fire and he will bring them down and destroy them for you. You will drive them out of the land and make them come to nothing, in accordance with his pledge to you.

Dt 11:22-23 states:

> <u>If</u> you will be careful to all that I have commanded you to do, loving Yahweh your God, keeps all his statutes, and clinging to him, <u>then</u> Yahweh will push out from the land all these nations and you will replace peoples more numerous and stronger than yourselves.

That is a big difference and a big if.

d) Now just how tall was Solomon's temple? After all it was the glory of Israel. I Kings 6:2 says: "Yahweh's house that Solomon built was 60 cubits long, 20 cubits wide, and <u>30 cubits high</u>. It is 60 cubits long, 20 cubits wide, and <u>120 cubits high</u> in 2 Chr 3:3-4. In general the books of Kings and the books of Chronicles had different opinions about many things. Asa was a good man in Kings "The heart of Asa was totally faithful to Yahweh all his days" (1 Kings 15:14). But in 2 Chronicles there are two conflicting views of Asa, the first echoing the statement in First Kings, that Asa's heart was without blame all his days (2 Chr 15:17). However, in the next chapter, 16, the prophet Hanani has this to say to Asa:

> Because you relied on the king of Syria, and did not rely on Yahweh your God, the army of the king of Syria has escaped you....You have acted like a fool, therefore, henceforth you shall have wars.

13a) Asa was not too happy with his critic and put him into prison. Yet the narrator goes on being critical himself of Asa: "In his 39th year as king he had a foot disease, and it became serious, yet he still would not call upon Yahweh, but sought help from the physicians." Now that is old time religion: against both military alliances and the help of physicians when suffering from a disease when all one has to do is call upon Yahweh. Besides it was an insult to Yahweh for Asa to turn to man for help when he has a God. But the inconsistency was that Asa was faithful to the death in the book of Kings, but turned to man, despising God's help in the book of Chronicles.

b) Deuteronomy states a law of fairness, i.e. the sinner shall die for his own sin: "The fathers shall not be put to death for the children, nor shall the children be killed for their fathers: each person shall be put to death for his own sin"(Dt 24:16). Yet David's child from by his adulterous sex with Bathsheba died because of David's sin and the death was decreed by Yahweh. Jeroboam sinned in Yahweh's sight and Yahweh had his child die because of the father's sin (1 Kg 14:17). And Canaan was cursed by Yahweh because of his father's, Ham's, sin (Gn 9:20-27), and all of Canaan's posterity was also cursed to be slaves of the Israelites. Finally, Yahweh will punish also the posterity of the Assyrians for the sins of their fathers: "May the posterity of evil doers never be heard from again. Prepare slaughter for their sons because of the guilt of the fathers"(Is 14:20-21). Isaiah hears Yahweh make a similar threat to the Moabites: "I will kill your posterity at its roots and any remnant I will slaughter"(Is 14:30).

c) Yahweh set up an elaborate sacrificial system of animals, making sure they were without blemish, male, and of the correct animal type for the appropriate sin to be forgiven. Then with the shedding of that blood man would be forgiven. This was good for the priest because it gave them plenty of meat to eat. But the prophets, never too close to the priests, often declared such sacrifices as worthless. Isaiah is a good example, Yahweh speaking through Isaiah: "What do I care about your many sacrifices? I have had enough of your fat beasts: your rams and your bulls and your sheep--I have no desire for them at all"(Is 1:11).

At the creation nakedness was natural but in Noah and afterwards it was shame.

d) The death of Saul had mixed reporting. Saul did not want to be captured by the Philistines and paraded before their masses for that would shame his God, Yahweh. He therefore decided to die first. He asked his armor-bearer to kill him, but the offer was refused. So Saul fell on his own sword and when the armor-bearer saw that he was dead he killed himself in order to die with his king. This was reported in 1 Sam 31:1-5. But the very next chapter in the Bible 2 Samuel Chapter One states that an Amalekite killed him. Of course the story, even though believed by David, could have been a lie by the Amalekite who might have been hoping for a reward: he received one, death. Therefore, this may simply be two true stories and not a contradiction, but, as the narrator stated, David did believe the Amalikite's story.

14a) The census that David took is certainly a true contradiction: "Yahweh was wrathful towards David and commanded him to take a census" (2 Sam 24:1). But afterwards David felt he had sinned and Yahweh agreed and sent a plague to kill some of his chosen people because of David's sin, that Yahweh himself had commanded him to do (2 Sam 24:15). This didn't make sense to the Chronicler who changed the story and said that "Satan" inspired David to take the census. This is evidence of the late dating of Chronicles (1 Chr 21:1).

V. POST-FACTO PROPHECIES

b) The entire Tanak is loaded with post-facto prophecies; events are, of course, more reliable to predict once they have taken place. Throughout the Torah (Pentetuch or The Books of Moses) there are many prophecies put back into old legends that "predict" Israel's conquering of the promised land. They were probably written during or after the reign of David, about 500 years after Israel had already entered Canaan. Such a post-facto prophecy that was put back into the life of Abraham that spelled out the entire future of his people, that they would be sojourners who would be oppressed in a foreign land to the point of slavery for more than 400 years, but also promised that they would be given the land of Canaan, from the land of Egypt to the Euphrates River as their promised land (Gen 15:12-20). This was made up to justify to the people that the land they invaded by slaughtering the local inhabitants was really their land to begin with, by the promise of Yahweh. The entire **c**) book of Deuteronomy is constantly repeating this same promise of Yahweh that the land is holy to Yahweh and he wills it to be for his chosen race. Deuteronomy (32) includes Moses' blessings for each of the tribes and the land each would have after the conquest of Canaan. Of course, since the conquest had already happened, it can put into Moses' mouth very accurate "prophecies". 1 Kings 9:6 reflects the time of the Babylonian captivity and seeks to say, "Well, God told David that if his people will not obey all the laws and commandments of Yahweh their country would end up in ruins." Jeremiah (25:12) likewise "predicts" that the coming Babylonian captivity will last 70 years, after which Yahweh will raise up a nation of Caldeans that will take down Babylon and the Jews will be able to return again to Palestine. The absolutely most obvious tale of post-facto "prophecy" is the Book of Daniel. Written about 160-155 BCE the Book of Daniel is the first of the many books written as an "apocalyptic" revealing secret knowledge of what is going to happen in the future: I Enoch and the Christian Book of Revelation are similar books. Daniel tries to present to the reader that Daniel foretold the coming of all the events up to 160 BCE when it was actually written. It is a fantasy story about Daniel and his friends in Babylon under the rule of **d**) Nebuchadnezzar. They miraculously survived fire and the lions and Daniel, as Joseph in Egypt and Mordecai in Persia, rose in rank second only to the kings they served--none of it ever happened to any of them. He foretells the destruction of four kingdoms in the future: they represent the Babylonian, Median, Persian, and Greek all of which will be destroyed and then The Great God of Heaven will set a great kingdom that will last forever. This is the point at which the author actually had to "prophesy" something that had not yet happened. Well Rome, who worshiped Jupiter and his fellow gods came in and lasted for some time but not forever, and it never gave Yahweh, the God of Heaven, his due. The Book of Daniel also had a problem getting history correct. He spoke of Belshazzar as the son of Nebuchadnezzar and repeats the mistake five times: Belshazzar was actually the son of Nabonidus, and three more kings ruled between the two of them. In short the author skipped four generations to falsely claim that Belshazzar was the son of Nebuchadnezzar. To think that a man was "inspired by God" to foretell the future, one would think that he was able to get the past that had already happened correct. Yet the Books of Daniel in the Tanak and Revelation in the Greek Christian scriptures are constantly quoted for the most ridiculous teachings and doctrines of the modern "voices of prophecy". Also in the Book of Daniel as well as the Book of Esther, Persia is presented in a way that is just the opposite of the general course of behavior for them. They had a benign and kind reign as shown in Ezra and Nehemiah who were released and aided by the Persians to restore their homes and temple again in Jerusalem. The setting is presented this way in *Plato's Gift to Christianity* from whom this long quotation is taken:

15a) "Daniel is a compilation of stories and visions that were projected back into history to the person of a Daniel of Israel's past, in order to encourage the Jewish people in their rebellion: "We can overcome the Greeks just as Daniel overcame impossible situations and even prospered with the help of God, because he was faithful to Him.' That was the theme of the various stories and visions: they were fictitious, written by several different people. Most were probably written in Aramaic, but show some Hellenistic influences in four ways: the use of general names for God, a stress on wisdom, references to and the hope of eternal life, and the named angels, Michael and Gabriel. Various authors are indicated by the different names for God. Chapters One and Nine use ELOHIM (3 times and also in Chapters Ten and Eleven); only ELAH is used in Chapters Two and Six; Chapters Nine and Eleven use EL, but only a total of three times; Chapter Seven uses only ELYON (the Most High); and only Chapter Nine uses Yahweh (six times). Since Chapter Nine also has a strong emphasis on the sins of Israel, the covenant and the Mosaic Law, it is certainly a separate work by a Yahwist. But the rest of the book uses names that are universally used by Semitic society; in fact ELYON is from a Canaanite term for God. Secondly, Hellenisation is sown by the stress on wisdom and the benefits reaped by the wise: 1:4, 17,20. 2:14,20,21,24,30. 4:18. 5:12. 9:22, and 12:3. Thirdly, the reference to everlasting life, and its being based on wisdom and righteousness, 12:2-3. And lastly, the angels of the Lord are being named with their own identities and personalities: Gabriel (God is mighty) 8:`16 and 9:21; and Michael (Who is like God?) 10:13,21 and 12:1. Greek and Platonic influences are undeniable."(*Plato's Gift to Christianity*, pp 151-152)

All of this makes it very evident that there was no way in which this Book of Daniel was written before the arrival of the Greek influence upon the Jewish people.

VI. "ADORNED" LEGENDS

b) Genesis 16-50 is a series of exaggerated stories about the Patriarchs of Israel and they can be so easily detected it is not necessary here to enumerate them. Yet a few are in order: Abraham's wealth 16; and Isaac's wealth 26:12; story of Isaac's blessing given to Jacob instead of Esau; lives of the earliest men living past 900 years and even the patriarchs--Abraham 175 years, Isaac 180, Jacob 130, Joseph 110, and Moses 120. While these are closer to reality than 900 years of the earliest men, it is still far beyond what any scientific study would permit. Joseph's ability to interpret dreams and his rise to be second only to the Pharaoh in Egypt is well adorned. It is doubtful that Pharaoh's daughter would go against the law of her father and protect a Hebrew baby found in a basket in the Nile (sounds borrowed from the Marduk legend). How would a large gathering of Hebrews be possible in Exodus 4:29 if they were slaves and the Egyptians already had a fear of them? The story of Hagar the Harlot of Jericho sounds too good to be true for the Israelites (Jos 2). It likewise seems quite exaggerated that an untrained group of men just coming out of the desert could defeat a well trained army that had 900 chariots of iron (Jud 4:12ff). Again, it doesn't seem to be historical reality that Gideon could fight an army of 120,000 men and kill all but 15,000 of them in his victory over them (Jud 8:10). Gideon's 70 sons sounds like a well-rounded exaggerated number--70 was often used this way. Then there is Samson's killing a 1000 Philistines (who had iron swords) with the jaw born of an ass; and then when he is trapped in Gaza, he waits until it is night then he "got up and took the doors of the gate of the city as well as the two door posts, put them on his shoulders and carried them to the top of the hill--all this without disturbing those waiting for him outside the city (Jud 16:3). But his strength was in his hair and through his own stupidity unknowingly had his hair cut. Again, numbers are a problem when the narrator claims that Israel was able to put together an army of 400,000 men with swords. The next will be the self-praise of David in 2 Samuel 22 where he claims: that he was pure and blameless before Yahweh, he could leap over a wall, he pursued his enemies and destroyed them, and takes pleasure that "I beat them to pieces so that they were like the dust of the earth, and crushed them and stamped them down into the mire of the earth." Perhaps a king's poetic license.

c) Finally it is necessary to look at the legendary rule of king Solomon which makes the legend of Camelot sound like authentic history. He prays for wisdom and receives so much wisdom that people from the ends of the earth come to hear him, and, as with the Queen of Sheba, to deposit a great wealth of gold before him. It is declared that he would be the wisest man ever to walk the earth, yet this wisest of men, betrays the God who gave him these blessings by marrying many foreign **d)** women and building places of worship for their "foreign" gods, overtaxing the people so severely that after his reign a civil war broke out and destroyed the Israelite unity for the rest of ancient history, betrayed his choice of wisdom over wealth by taking in enormous sums of money by taxes, alliances and awards that he could have enough to build the temple where everything seemed to be gold and also a palace that took him six years longer to build than the temple so that he could house all his wives and concubines. He probably would have destroyed husbandry in Israel if the exaggerations of his sacrifices were any where near to be true: for what purpose would he sacrifice 22,000 oxen and 120,000 sheep for a festival? I Kings 1-9 rightly criticizes him for all these things done by his foolishness and concludes: "So Solomon did what was evil in the sight of Yahweh...and Yahweh express his wrath towards Solomon." There actually was very little common sense in his reign filled with egoism, folly, lust for women and wealth, and without much care for his shepherds, neatherds, his tax payers, and the mandates of his own religion.

VII. WOMEN

16a) Women, of course, were not valued as much as men, nor girls as much as boys, not only in Ancient Israel but throughout the ancient world in general. To understand the spirit of the Ancient Hebrew, to be fair, he must be judged against his contemporaries, not by the standards of the year 2000 CE. However, if we are looking for spiritual guidance from a book in 2000 CE, it is necessary that it not be a step backwards from where women are today in today's society in the Western World. If the Hebrew scriptures claim validity for a spiritual canon or measuring stick for the morality of today's living, then it must, like all cultures, be compared with the culture of today. How often we have heard something like this: "The Bible says a woman should...etc." If that is done, then the Judeo-Christian Bible must be judged by its ability or inability to lift up woman's status to equality with man's status. Plato, far ahead of his and all ancient cultures of his time, demanded in his Republic that both in the priesthood and in the guardians--like the congress in the USA--be of sexually equal numbers. However, Plato's Republic was rejected both in Athens and Syracuse, and his thoughts of such equality were rejected in general by all ancient cultures with a partial exception of the Todas and Spartans who were half way between the ancient cultures and Plato.

b) In the Hebrew Tanak woman's place would not at all be a cause of envy to today's woman in the Western World. First of all, she is created as an afterthought to be a helper for man, man being the initial focus of creation. They both "sin" but she is to be subjected to him: "He shall rule over you" (Gen 3:16). The Ten Commandments make her part of man's property that ought not to be coveted by another man (Ex 20:17). A man can sell his daughter as a slave (Ex 21:7). A woman is declared unclean and thought of as being in a state of sin when she bears a child, either male or female: she must then "bring two offerings, a burnt offering and a sin offering, and the priest shall make atonement for her and she shall be clean" (Lev 12:6-8). This relates to Lev 18:19: "You shall not come to a woman sexually while she is in her menstrual uncleanness."

c) A gross double standard is shown in the divorce decree that "Moses" gave to Israel in the book of Deuteronomy, chapter 24:1-4.

> If a man takes a woman and possesses her as a wife and then finds something unpleasing about her, and writes out a bill of divorce, and hands it to her and sends her out of the house, and she goes (as if she had any choice), and gets married again, and again is divorced because the husband dislikes her and he sends her out of his house--or even if the second husband dies, then the first husband, who sent her away, shall not bring her back and remarry her, for she has been defiled. For that is an abomination before Yahweh, and you shall not bring such guilt upon the people of the land.

A man can marry and remarry at will, have several wives in marriage, and still can have lovers, concubines, and see harlots and not bring guilt and abomination upon the people, but a woman is defiled once she has sexual contact with another man, even if she marries him, and can not return to the first husband who, after divorcing her and sending her out of the house, may have reconsidered her value. After divorce or even the death of her husband a woman in actuality and also in law is usually considered defiled. Such a law or custom is the abomination!

d) In Judges eleven, a non too brilliant Jephthah makes a foolish vow to Yahweh which ends up with his "having to sacrifice to death" his only child, his daughter. The entire issue of making vows to God is stupid anyway and is an insult to God that he can act in partiality because of some vow. Yet Jephthah made a vow, sacrificed his daughter, and kept peace with a Yahweh that would not relieve him of his vow. Jephthah is stupid, Yahweh is uncompromising, and a lovely young girl is sacrificed to death. Where is the wisdom of the Tanak and where is the "loving kindness" of Yahweh?

17a) In Judges 19 an old man sheltered another man, and the local men pounded on his door demanding the man to be given to them, but instead he offered his virgin daughter and his concubine that they could be raped

and used as pleased in order to spare the sheltered man. So the men took the concubine and used her all night and, after she made her way back to the doorstep, she died. The story is not unsimilar to the one about Lot in Sodom. But the backbone of both stories is that man is to be sheltered at all costs, but woman can be disposed of. It was a brutal custom and a sickly concept. Woman also is the general representation of the spiritual harlotry of Israel--Israel like an unfaithful woman and Yahweh as the faithful man having to put up with this worthless and unthankful woman who plays the harlot with other gods (Hosea, Isaiah 51 and Jeremiah 3).
b) The Book of Proverbs can not seem to warn its male hearer enough about the loose woman at the corner: she is a thief who will cause you poverty and even death: "for her house sinks down to death, and her paths to the shades; none who go to her come back nor come to life again"(Prv 2:16-19). Man must be kept from the "evil woman, from the smooth tongue of the adventuress"..."do not desire her beauty in your heart" for it all leads to evil (Prv 6). Proverbs chapters 2, 5, 6, 7, ll, and 23 advise is given against the evil they may bring to men. And "a continual dripping on a rainy day and a contentious woman are alike" the 28th Chapter throws in. On top of this, in the Tanak, especially the books of Genesis and the Histories when speaking of children seldom count the women, for "children" almost meant "boys". They seldom show up in genealogies. Jacob had 12 sons and no girls--until Dinah gets into trouble by going out on the town and getting sexually involved with someone not of the tribe of Israel. Otherwise she would have never been mentioned. Gen 35:22-26:

> Now the sons of Jacob were twelve: The sons of Leah: Reuben, Simeon, Levi, Judah, Issachar, and Zebulun. The sons of Rachel: Joseph and Benjamin. The sons of Bilhah, Rachel's maid: Dan and Naphtali. The sons of Zilpah Leah's maid: Gad and Asher. These are the sons of Jacob who born to him in Paddan-aram.

c) Even though Dinah went out and got into trouble to be noticed, she still did not make the genealogy; after all, she was only a woman.

VIII. MIRACLES AND SIGNS

d) The Tanak is full of miracles and signs that are presented to prove Yahweh's power, encourage the people, aid Israel, or strengthen a leader's position and prove his calling from Yahweh. "Show me your powers and then I shall follow you" the people of Israel seemed to demand. Sometimes they are proclaimed to show that nothing is impossible for Yahweh if one believes He will take care of the believer. Certainly when Sarah has a child at age 99 there is evidence of a higher power than the natural order at work. Manna appears daily in the wilderness to feed more than a million people--for forty years. Moses held up his hand and Joshua succeeded in battle, but if the hand came down, then Joshua would start losing the battle (Ex 17). Mount Sanai was hidden in smoke because Yahweh descended within a fire (Ex 19:18). Balaam's ass can speak and communicate to Balaam (Nb 22:28). Moses' life is filled with miracles and he also played a role in the opening of the Reed Sea so that the Israelites could escape Egypt. Joshua opened, or stopped the flow of the Jordan River so that all Israel could pass over into Canaan (Jos 3). But the biggest miracle of Joshua, with the help of Yahweh, was cosmic: he made the sun stand still so that Israel had enough time to kill all of their enemies, the Amorites:

18a)

> He (Joshua) said while all Israel was watching, "Sun, you stand still...and the sun stopped moving and stayed in its same place until Israel took vengeance on its enemies." (Jos 10:12-13)

The narrator continues: "Is this not written in the Book of Jashar? The sun remained in the middle of heaven and did not move for an entire day. There was never a day like it before or after." (Jos 10:13-14). Of course this is mentioned by no other culture, which would be quite strange, especially in Babylon where the magi always looked to the heavens. Miracles abounded for ancient Israel that never have happened again in human society, and they have never been believed by the philosophers of old who relied on logic, mathematics, and science. But they continued to be believed in Israel for an angel of Yahweh came to the Assyrian army that was threatening Israel and slaughtered 180,000 Assyrian soldiers (2 Kings 19:35). When Solomon dedicated the temple in Jerusalem heaven responded by sending down fire to burn the offerings and sacrifices and the entire temple glowed with the glory of Yahweh (2 Chr 7:1).

b) Perhaps of interest to Christians is the claim that between Elijah and Elisha all the types of miracles credited to Jesus in the Gospels were done, thus making Jesus' miracles simply a replay of the two prophets. Elijah's miracles will be presented first. I Kg 17:8-16 provides food for a widow during a famine from a lone jar of meal and a cruse of oil. They were used daily without diminishing until the rains came and the earth produced food. In the same 17th Chapter Elijah raises a dead child and returned him to a bereaved mother who then proclaimed to Elijah, "Now I know that you are a man of God." At Mount Carmel during a face off with the priests of Baal, Elijah is able to get Yahweh to bring down fire from heaven and consume offerings that had been saturated by water. But the moody Elijah went off to moan and grown, but Yahweh sent an angel to minister to him with food for forty days and nights (I Kg 19:4-8). King Ahaziah was upset with Elijah for predicting his death and sent 50 soldiers to arrest Elijah, but he was able to call down fire from heaven that killed them all (James and John once asked Jesus to do similar to a village that had not accepted them: Jesus refused to do so). Elijah parted the Jordan (2 Kg 2:8), and then Elijah had a glorious ascent to heaven "And as they (Elisha was with Elijah) continued to walk and talk, from no where a chariot appeared, it and the horses that pulled it were made of fire and came between the two of them and Elijah went up to heaven in a whirlwind." (2 Kg 2:9-11)

c) It was then Elisha's turn as the anointed one (messias or christus) of Yahweh. He promptly parts the Jordan (2 Kg 2:14), and cleanses drinking water for the people (2 Kg 2:19-22). One of Elisha's not so nice miracles occurred when he was insulted when some boys called him "baldhead"; so Elisha cursed them and immediately two she-bears appeared and tore apart the 42 boys (2 Kg 2:23-25). Then with Elisha's blessing a widow's jar provides oil for her entire neighborhood (2 Kg 4:1-7). He, as did Elijah, brings a dead boy back to life (2 Kg 4:18-37). He fed a multitude of 100 men with one man's bread (2 Kg 4:42-44). He cures Naaman's leprosy (2 Kg 5:1-14). But, again, that mean streak of Elisha's showed itself as he makes a healthy man a leper (2 Kg 5:27). But then he steps up in power for a greater display, for Elisha prayed to Yahweh to strike the Syrian army with blindness, and Yahweh did (2 Kg 6:18). And even after death Elisha's power showed itself, for when a dead man's body touches the bones of Elisha the dead man is brought back to life. Not only did he raise the dead, his bones could do it after his death (2 Kg 3:20-21). When one considers all these miracles and the similarity of them to those credited to Jesus, it seems odd that Jesus should say in the Gospel of John "If you do not believe my words, then believe my works" if Jesus was claiming to be anything more than a Jewish prophet. The words of the Gospel of John (14:8-11) read thus:

> **d)** Philip said to him, "Lord, show us the Father, and we shall be satisfied." Jesus said to him, "Have I been with you so long, and yet you do not know me, Philip? He who has seen me has seen the Father; how can you ask, "Show us the Father'? Do you not believe that I am in the Father and the Father is in me? The words that I speak to you, I do not do so on my own authority; but the Father who lives in me does his works. Believe me when I say I am in the Father and the Father is in me; but if not, trust because of the works themselves.

Both cultures, the one of Elijah and Elisha as well as that of rest of the history of Israel and the culture of the land of Palestine at the time of Jesus believed that those anointed by God had the power to do such things, but today there are no "miracles" from above through specially appointed people. They are myths to the modern mind, and to be used as proofs of any kind is to take a step back deep into the past and make oneself irrelevant to the modern world. Asa, although condemned by the Tanak was wise to go to the physicians for a cure and not leave it to prayer alone.

IX. MISCELLANEOUS SHORTFALLS FOR MODERN MAN

19a) There are several other laws and statutes that, while perhaps understood in the age in which they were given, are certainly barriers to 21st Century morality or just plain irrelevant for one's spiritual well being today.

Psalm 14 attacks all mankind as being so corrupt and vile that Yahweh looks down in disappointment for "All have turned aside, all alike are tainted; there is not one good man left, not a single one" states verse three. If that were the case in any other industry, one would tend to blame the creator and designer of the the product. Just the idea that the Creator does not like any of us is not a comforting thought nor does it say much about the Creator's "love" and "kindness" to the little creatures he has made. Psalm 53 is a doublet of Psalm 14. The atheist is called a fool and this is completely out of date for us today, for it is not because a man is evil that he is an atheist, it is because his mind simply can not image a god existing.

b) Jeremiah has no love for those who do not acknowledge Yahweh, although they may have concepts of god that are otherwise and worship their god or gods in their own way. Jeremiah feels that Yahweh would be, as well as the world, better off without them. "Pour out your anger on the pagans, who do not acknowledge you, and on those races that do not call upon your name"(10:25). When one considers the amount of people in the world who either do not believe in a supreme being or worship some other god than Yahweh, the Psalmist and Jeremiah are asking the Creator to hate, punish, and even destroy the vast majority of mankind. Such teaching does not go over well with either atheists or people of different religions. To believe differently is each person's privilege, but to judge others for their beliefs and to ask one's God to hate, punish, and destroy all who have such differing ideas about the Eternal is truly a real abomination to a loving and caring God who has all humanity "in his hand".

c) It is likewise understandable among a small tribe such as Israel, whose thought covenant with God is to result in a vast nation whose children will number with the stars and the sands of the sea to oppose all forms of birth control and all sexual activities that can not create human life. But today, especially with an over crowded world being polluted by the minute, such an attitude is dangerous to all humanity, and is cruel to those who are have a homosexual inclination by the nature of the way the chemistry has evolved in their bodies or by the form of the body itself. There is also a matter of free choice that people must have to live the way they want to without the state or some religion cursing and imprisoning them. Let people be what they are and let them choose what they prefer to be.

d) It is also ridiculous for men and woman who have sex with animals to be put to death. Most of such happens at an early age and is probably playful in nature.

20a) While this has been referred to before, the idea of every other day having a chosen one talking, walking, and eating with God, seeing him face to face and deciding how to solve not only the individual's problems but also whom to kill, starve, invade, and boycott is hardly a claim that any normal sane person would make today. This is not to attack those who honestly feel an occasional deep and mystical experience of an ultimate spiritual power in their lives. But in the Tanak there are so many visitations by angels, visions, and appearances of God that are considered to be totally authentic that it falls into the category of the miraculous, and, frankly, unbelievable. The prophets claim they did not want to deliver their message, but God pushed them hard so that they could not resist: and they never proclaim their own views it is always "Thus says the Lord....".

b) Likewise outdated are the dietary laws. Ancient Israel realized that they were not too scientific in husbandry or botany or other agricultural tendencies. But they were disciplined and when something killed someone or made them sick, they spoke of it and similar animals as unclean. Since they didn't know for sure about an animal's safe preparation for preserving and eating, to play it safe and follow the knowledge they had was, of course, a wise decision. But today, edible things, both plant and animals, are much better understood. But the ancient wisdom of the dietary laws are with us yet today: e.g. If the last person died from eating a cow with mad cow disease, do not eat any more cows with the same or similar diseases. There was wisdom there, but its age is past for their classification of clean and unclean animals.

Cosmological knowledge has greatly improved thanks to ancient Egyptians and Babylonians, and most of all to the Greeks, whose Aristarchus taught that the planets, including the earth, circle the sun, not the earth. There is no blame for the world view of the cosmos among the Hebrews of antiquity. But the Tanak is not scientifically an "eternal truth".

c) Finally, one serious problem most modern believers have with the Tanak is that the individual has no hope of a life after death, despite the fact that in all cultures life was preferred to death, and many ancient cultures, especially in India held great hope for an eternal existence of one's person, one's "self". Israelites were thought to be blessed if they lived long, were wealthy and had many children and then buried with their fathers (Gen 25:8). This sad view weighed heavy upon the hearts of the ancient Israelites. Psalm 49 speaks of this:

> V.10ff "Yes, man sees even the wise ones die, and the fool and the stupid alike must perish; and their wealth, it is left to others. Their future homes are their graves--forever...man can not be pompous, he, like the beasts, will die...he will go to the generations of his fathers before him, who will never see the light of life again. Man can not be proud for, like the beast, he will die."

And it seems that the writer of Psalm 90 sees Yahweh's anger involved in man's misery and mortality: "For our entire life passes away under Your (Yahweh's) wrath, our years come to an end with the last breath......Our life ends at seventy years, or, at best, eighty during which **d**) is a time of toil and trouble, soon gone, and we disappear." (vs 5-10). The author of the book of Ecclesiastes is obsessed with man's mortality without the hope of life after death--to him it makes all things empty, without any meaning at all. All actions, thoughts, hopes and deeds are vain. All is vanity. There is no profit in working under the sun as each generation comes and goes. It is a very unhappy activity of living that God has given to the sons of men (1:13). "I searched my mind to find a reason for living and tried to cheer myself with wine hoping to find meaning for the few days of man's life"(2:3). But all his works and thoughts were empty of meaning: "All was vanity and a grasping at wind" (2:11). Even if a man has a fulness of eating and drinking, and, in addition, enjoy his work...it is still vanity, a chasing after the wind (2:24-26). God had make all so beautiful, and even puts the idea of eternity into man's mind...but man remains a beast. For the end of the beasts and the end of the sons of man is the same: they both end up dying. They have the same breath and give it up the same way, man has no advantage over the beasts: everything is vanity (3:10-19). "I thought the dead who are already dead more fortunate than the living who are still **21a**) alive; even the unborn are better off than those who have tasted life and seen all the evils that confront the living man"(4:3). "For who knows what is good for man while he lives the few days of his vain life, that passes like a shadow?"(6:12). There are six more chapters to the book of Ecclesiastes but it never gets better: man is brief and death is forever, why bother, it is all vanity? This lack of hope for another existence is too heavy for man to bear, and today many of the Jewish faith do believe in a life afterwards as Judaism as been influenced by other religions that have proclaimed such a hope to the people of their faith. But for the Tanak itself, there is no hope given to men by which they can entertain the prospect of a heavenly and eternal life.

CONCLUSION

b) While there are certainly many precepts and laws of ethics in the Tanah that at that time lifted man's concept of morality, it seems foolish to proclaim it as the Word of God, especially if that "Word" is supposed to be a container for all historical, moral, and scientific truth as well as eternal guides to morals and cultural developments for the 21st Century experience of modern man. Likewise the Tanak can not think of the historical element without myths, adorned legends, inconsistencies and contradictions, and post-facto prophecies. Most of all, it does not present a God that is forever loving and never swayed by the passions men have so often succumbed to at times of disappointment and displeasure. It does not guard against the anthropomorphic expressions that label God with such brutal anger and violence when his "covenant" is broken by his own beloved people, and even unleashes greater destruction on those who do not have any idea of his covenantal statutes. Those of Judaism and of the Judeo-Christian faiths are well aware of these defects of the Tanak, yet they cling to it as such a holy book that it is often considered evil not to follow it or believe it is an accurate picture of the Deity, and in the course of history, both before and after the Common Era, many have been disciplined, persecuted, stoned and killed by fire or by sword for not accepting it as the One God's Eternal Word. The Platonic Tradition offers an alternative and it will be proclaimed and explained later in the following chapters.

BETA

B

CHAPTER TWO THE CHRISTIAN CANON

22a) The Christian Scriptures are likewise presenters of ideas and concepts of God and the relationship of God and man that are in many ways objectionable to moral and spiritual people of the year 2000. It speaks of God's wrath, tries to prove doctrines on the basis of miracles, exhibits God's partiality while claiming that God is impartial, condemns without any mercy the "unbelievers" to a suffering and everlasting hell of fire, confuses the reader as to what it is that is the cause of justification before and angry God, predicted an early return of Jesus--which, of course, did not happen, and bases all such doctrines upon the "inerrant Holy Scriptures inspired by God himself". These canonized scriptures often are agents of fear and threats to the unbeliever; are filled with myths and legends; have historical errors and contradictions; presents visions and dreams as reliable ways to hear God's voice and directions; constantly misquotes the prophets of the Jewish Tanak; is filled with non sequiturs and inconsistencies; many of the books are pseudonymous writings claiming to be written by one who actually knew Jesus or by Paul; has many instances in which the church created stories post-facto for the purpose of empowering itself, and exaggerates many events to make them unworthy of belief. Paul himself, as well as letters falsely attributed to him display an enormous egoism, judgmentalism, and a person of many conflicts and inconsistent teachings and proclamations. Finally, the views related to the cosmos, slaves and women are hardly worthy of being proclaimed the "Eternal Word of Truth".

I. THE WRATH OF GOD

b) The Four Gospels use the phrase "the wrath of God" only once; "He who believes in the Son has eternal life; he who does not obey the Son shall not see life, but the wrath of God rests upon him"(Jn 3:36). Yet the anger of God is evident in the Four Gospels in numerous ways, and such will be discussed in section three as a presentation of Jesus. However, the rest of the Christian Canon makes it very clear that all men are under God's wrath because they are either evil by nature or because of the sin of disobedience of which all men are guilty. From the Book of Acts straight through to the Book of Revelation 22 one thing is certain, God is a God of Wrath and does not accept humanity unless some type of satisfaction is made to soothe his wrath, otherwise man suffers eternally in agony and pain in hell. The early church through such teachings presented their apology for the new faith with a two-edged sword: God's love is available for you if you believe our message and let it form your life or, if you refuse such a generous offer, then you deserve to suffer forever for insulting God's reprieve, and you then will suffer in the worst pain imaginable forever. Added to this was the comfort or fear, depending upon your choice, that Jesus was going to return before the end of the present generation and he will come, unsuspecting, as a thief in the night. Lure and frighten the masses to believe, hardly a concept of "good news" for everyone.

c) It starts with the fiery sermons and proclamations of John the Baptist, threatening doom and destruction upon those who do not repent and get right with God. "When John saw many of the Pharisees and Sadducees coming for baptism, he questioned them: 'You bunch of snakes! Who warned you to avoid the wrath that is coming?' Bear fruit....all trees that do not will be cut down and burned" (Mt 3:7-10). Luke had a different group to whom he spoke the same words: for he threatened, not the Pharisees and Sadducees, but the entire multitude (Lk 3:7-14).

Anything short of full commitment could be fatal. With the church in Jerusalem in need of finances from both their charity work and their irresponsibility (perhaps relying too much on the quick return of Jesus), it required a heavy price to avoid the wrath to come. Membership game with a donation of one's goods to the church. A certain couple, Ananias and Sapphira, sold a piece of property and gave a portion of it to the church, but evidently Peter pressed them for more money. They countered with a lie, for they obviously wanted some money to rely upon if Jesus didn't come back soon, and for that lie both Ananias and Sapphira were smitten and fell dead. "A great fear came upon the whole church, and upon all who heard of these things" (Acts 5: 1-11). **d**)Obviously, God was quite touchy about such matters. This story is suspicious in nature and probably never happened, but was created by the church to warn others not to hold back with "money committed to God". Nor is it too wise to take exaggerated praise. "And the people proclaimed 'The voice of a god, not merely a man.' Immediately an angel of the Lord struck him, because he did not shift the glory from himself to God. He was then eaten by worms that caused his death" (Acts 12:21-23). A "Jewish false prophet", that is one who doubted that Jesus was the Messiah, was opposed by Paul and called by him the son of the devil and called down the power of the Lord who caused temporary blindness in the man (Act 13:4-11). Paul, in preaching fear to his listeners, referred to the Tanak's story in which Yahweh bore with people in the desert despite their complaining and destroyed seven nations for them and gave them the land of the destroyed. This is the God you are dealing with my dear audience (who happened to be the people of Israel). (Acts 13:16ff) In his letter to the Romans, Paul defends God's impartiality by asking them who disagree with Paul's logic by stating: "But who are you, a mortal, to answer back to God?....What if God, wanting to display his wrath....has endured with much patience the objects of his wrath who were made to be destroyed in the first place" (Rm 9:19ff). Early in the Letter to the Romans, he had declared that the heavens had always declared God's wrath to wrong doers (1:18). God was upset with his own chosen people, whom He had hardened with a spirit of stupor, since they were not of the elect ones anyway (Rm 11:7-10). In the First Letter to the Corinthians Paul again goes to the Tanak to remind the people of God's wrath: for they had "grumbled" because the snakes were killing several **23a)** of them. Think about it, they grumbled in the desert where they were stuck for about 40 years and snakes were killing them. Now transfer that to humanity: what kind of father would kill his children, his special ones, if they grumbled during difficult times? What an image of God Paul passes on to his readers! (I Cor 10:6-12). Yes, Paul continues and warns his readers not to provoke the Lord to jealousy. Paul closes his letter with the warning that if anyone doesn't love this god, let him be cursed (I Cor 16: 21). But the Four Gospels and Paul's letters are only part of the teaching in the Christian Canon that God is wrathful and doesn't tolerate "sin", even to the point that he will demand a ransom, the death of Jesus before he is satisfied. For those seeking more of the wrath of God in the Christian Scriptures read: Ephesians 2:3, 5:5-6--Colosians 1:28, 2:14, and 3:5-6--1 Thessalonians 1:10, 2:16--Hebrews 3:7-11, 4:3, 10:26-31 and 39, 12:16-17, 25, 29--1 Peter 28, 4:17--2 Peter 2:4-9m 2L20-22 --Jude 6-7--Revelation 2:19, 26; 9:3-6, 15; 14:9, 16ff (the seven bowls of God's wrath). All this because men, declared Paul, are evil and there is not one, not one solitary person, who is good (Rm 7:18-20, 7:24-25, 8:3, 8). And to think that as children one often is taught that Berta, the Teutonic Goddess, was scary because she gave lying children a stomach ache.

II. MIRACLES USED TO PROVE STATUS OF JESUS

b) The Four Gospels are filled to the brim with recorded miracles that are then used to prove the status of Jesus as Christ and Son of God. The Gospel of Mark is not so much about the person Jesus as it is about Jesus The Miracle Man who has proved himself to be the Mighty Son of God. Many of the miracles are seen to be split second happenings to prove that the power in Jesus is immediate and overwhelming. The Greek word ευθυς (euthus) means "straightway" "immediately" or "instantly". It is used by Matthew 7 times, Luke once, John 3 times, and Acts once: a total of 12 times in the entire rest of the Christian Canon. But in Mark alone, the shortest Gospel, it is used 42 times; 11 times alone in the first chapter--so the reader "immediately" gets the message. The disciples (Peter, Andrew, James and John) immediately leave their nets and follow Jesus, the lame, blind, and diseased are immediately healed, and the paralytic instantly picks up his pallet and walks away cured. In Jesus' presence the power of God is instantly enforced upon any situation or problem. The book brings to the reader only a few sayings of Jesus, but miracles without end. Before the end of Mark's first chapter it is stated that because of his miracles Jesus' fame spread instantly throughout all the regions that surrounded Galilee (Mk 1:28). Jesus even had difficulties entering a town, because as he approached many had gathered before it to receiving healings. The people came from every quarter of the country. If this were so throughout all the land of Palestine, how could it possibly be that people turned against him and the **c)** Scribes and Pharisees did not believe in his power to heal? It really doesn't make sense at all, even if the Scribes and Pharisees were opposed to his teaching (although he did very little of it in Mark's Gospel), it would not make any sense, for they too had sick people among their families and friends, and surely, no one would be so evil to try to kill a man who could heal those suffering among his own loved ones. Mark's case for people rejecting Jesus simply does not hold up, if he were, indeed, the healer of every city and all who came throughout the land of Palestine. Yet Mark proclaims that the Pharisees came together with the Herodians and made a plan to kill him (3:6). Yet, over and over something similar to 6:56 is stated: "Wherever he went, into villages or country sides, people brought their sick ones to the area's market place and asked him if they could "touch even the fringes of his clothing; and as many as touched it were healed". Faith healers today have great difficulties in presenting even one authenticated miracle, even though they have proclaimed and "staged" many of them for audiences and even on television shows. The actors do well, but the diseased are not cured. It is a new age and the old age of the time of Jesus has been discarded and it is declared obsolete for the modern man. Miracle workers were also claimed by others in ancient times, but this hardly makes claims of miracles more honorable: myths at best, and, sadly, perverse lies at worst. Even if all Judeo-Christian testimony to miracles were real, that still would not affirm Mark's claim that they prove Jesus to be the Son of God, for, as shown in the previous chapter, Elijah and Elisha did all the same genres of miracles that Jesus did.

d) Mark is certainly not alone in proclaiming the good news that Jesus goes from town to town curing every one, He even sent thousands of demons into a local herd of swine in the Decapolis, an area of 10 Greek based cities. That would hardly make for good evangelism, to destroy the people's livestock instead of just conquering those demons as Jesus was according to legend so capable of doing. Matthew does not shy away from miracles, in fact he enlarged the area of Jesus fame due to his miraculous healings:

> "Then Jesus toured all of Galilee, teaching in their synagogues, proclaiming the good news of the kingdom, and healing every disease and every illness among the people. And the report of him went into the entire area of Syria; and they brought to him all of those who were ill, having various diseases and suffering from such tortures, and he also healed all the demon possessed, lunatics, and the paralyzed. And the crowds followed him from Galilee, from the Decapolis, from Jerusalem, from Judea, and even beyond the Jordan." (Mt 4:23-25).

d) The "entire area of Syria" is interesting because Syria was the Roman province of Syria that included today's Syria, Jordan, Lebanon and Israel. Considering that travel was by foot, and the length of Jesus' ministry according to Matthew is only a year or slightly more, it seems a near impossibility that Jesus could have traveled so far and ministered to such a vast amount of people. To add to that the fact that the educated of the Jews in Jerusalem and Judea rejected such reports and no secular writers in Syria, Lebanon (Tyre and Sidon area) and the Decapolis ever mentioned such healings or even the name of Jesus, is more than hard to understand. These many miracles of Matthew, like those of Mark could not have happened. Miracles are also mentioned by Luke and John, and the Book of Acts proclaims many miracles by the apostles and Paul. If such miracles happened, they were proclaimed in the Tanak and other religions also, so they would not prove that Jesus was divine or God's Son either--even if they existed. But today it is simply impossible to believe such, and if God foreknew that the 21st Century would reject miracles why would he use them as a proof for people of the future to believe. Why not some universal sign, if such were to be used, that every educated person on earth could have recorded for the entire world to be able to believe something big was happening? Especially if such a faith would be required for eternal salvation, without which all will be damned forever. Matthew as well as Mark and the rest of the Christian Canon are not books that can authenticate the doctrines that the church seeks to proclaim as the good news of God.

III. HOW IS MAN JUSTIFIED BEFORE GOD?

24a) The reformation of the 16th Century led by Martin Luther raised this question so forcefully that the Western Church of Christianity split into several pieces and led to mutual condemnations and wars between the groups in conflict. Perhaps an open minded and open ended Socratic discussion would have served the Church better than such internal and mutual slaughter of each other, thereby showing how far they had strayed from what the Gospel of John presents as the only commandment that Jesus gave his disciples: "love one another". The conflict was, in a sense, made inevitable. Since the Church had made the Christian Canon the ultimate source of doctrines, and the Christian Canon itself was, not only not clear on the subject, but presented several different answers to the question of how man is saved. Each segment of the Church grabbed one of the answers and demanded that that was the only valid one. More of this in the following chapter. Here it is only necessary to look at the Christian Scriptures to see the many ways the question of salvation was answered in the first place. All views seem to conflict with each other.

A. SALVATION BY GOD'S PREORDINATION

b) It is with the ministry of Paul that the idea of God's preordination of salvation upon some, the elect, flourished. It Acts 13 during the evangelistic preaching of Barnabas and Paul that a serious conflict broke out between the Jews and those who accepted the new doctrines presented to them. The statement is made, 13:48, "When the Gentiles heard this (Barnabas' and Paul's message), they were glad and glorified the word of God; and as many as were ordained to eternal life believed." The concept of God's predestinating or preordaining people to eternal life continues in Paul's ministry. Romans 11:5-7 reads: "So too at the present time there is a remnant, chosen by grace. But if it is by grace, it is no longer on the basis of works...What then? Israel failed to obtain what it sought. The elect obtained it, but the rest were hardened." In First Corinthians (2:6-7) Paul stated "...the rulers of this age, who are doomed to pass away. But we impart a secret and hidden wisdom of God, which God declared before the ages for our glorification." Some were given the secret wisdom of God that they might be glorified, but the others were doomed to pass away. God selects, even before the ages of mankind, to whom he is going to give his secret wisdom and whom he will doom. The pseudo-Pauline epistle of Ephesians follows the same pattern of reasoning.

c)

> Blessed be the God and Father of our Lord Jesus Christ, who has blessed us in Christ with every spiritual blessing in the heavenly places, even as he chose us in him before the foundation of the world (Gk "cosmos"), that we should be holy and blameless before him. He destined us in love to be his children in Jesus Christ, and this was in keeping with his plans and desire, ...We ...have been elected and predestined according to his purpose (Eph 1:1-5, 11-12).

"This...according to the purpose of the ages which he made for us..." (Eph 3:10-11).

B. SALVATION BY GRACE

d) While salvation by grace does not directly conflict with that of preordination, there is a difference between a mental choice of God and one of heart-felt love. Grace contains a sense of mercy and kindness despite what a person might be. Again, maybe because it is close to salvation by preordination, this concept flourishes in Paul's ministry but does not appear before Paul. After Paul and Barnabas returned to Jerusalem after their first missionary journey, and after a report to the church at Jerusalem, a conflict broke out concerning the question about what was necessary for salvation, and centered on circumcision. Peter took the side of Paul and Barnabas and declared: "We believe that we shall be saved by means of the grace of our Lord Jesus Christ" (Acts 15:11). That was a major cornerstone for Paul's future authority to proclaim salvation by grace, and not by works. But within Paul's grace there was a string attached which shows itself in one of his phrased declarations such as "...they are justified by his grace as a gift, by means of the redemption which is in Jesus Christ." (Rm 3:23). "By means of redemption" is another category that will be discussed shortly. Normally a gift freely given is not attached to a need of redemption or ransom paid. Therefore, this teaching of Paul has an innate inconsistency. Again in the

Fifth Chapter of Romans, Paul speaks much of the free gift, using the term "free gift" (χαρισμα – charisma, related to χαρις - grace) four times in four verses, but it is still attached to the redemptive work and sacrifice of Jesus, which would be a stiff payment for ransoming sinners, and that would hardly be a "free gift". Again, Romans 6:23 he unites the two conflicting concepts "For the wages of sin is death, but the free gift of God is eternal life, in Christ Jesus our Lord." Ephesians 2:8 again links this free gift to an attached string - you must believe: "For by grace you have been saved through faith". Colossians 1:12 does reflect a total act of God on our behalf by which he then transfers "us" who have this gift of life to the kingdom of his beloved Son (Jesus): "...giving thanks to the Father who has qualified us to share in the inheritance of the holy ones in light. He has delivered us from the domination of darkness and transferred us to the kingdom of his beloved Son". This statement reflects the grace of God alone without any strings attached. This conquering of evil and darkness for man's salvation by God himself was rather popular at various times in church history and is reflected in the so called classical view of redemption. It is in this statement that the idea of grace alone and salvation as a free gift is reflected in its purity, unlike the strings attached to the free gift in Paul's theology.

C. SALVATION BY BEING RANSOMED FROM GOD'S WRATH

25a) One of the strongest arguments against the grace alone as a free gift from God as man's way of salvation is the ransom doctrine that proposes that Jesus' innocent death was paid as a ransom to shelter man from God's wrath towards the sinner. Jesus had to die to buy God's grace for mankind. God's mercy basically had to be bought and paid for; it was not a gift. Mt 20:28 states: "the Son of man came not to be served but to serve, and to give his life as a ransom for many." However, where the ransom theory flourishes is in the Paul and pseudo-Pauline works. "It will be counted to us who believe in him who raised from the dead Jesus our Lord, who was put to death for our trespasses (against God) and raised for our justification"(Rm 4:24-25). "Therefore, since we are now justified by his blood, much more shall we be saved by him from the wrath of God. For, while being enemies of God, we were reconciled to

God by means of the death of his Son"(Rm 5:8-10). Paul reminds the Corinthian church that they were bought with a price, the vicarious death of Jesus. "You are not your own; you were purchased with a price" (1 Cor 6:20). How in the world can these passages be in harmony with the **b)** free gift of grace passages? Most of them also are by Paul. In the pseudo-Pauline works the same views are expressed. "...so making peace, and reconcile us both to God...and bringing hostility to an end" (Eph 2:15-16). In 1 Timothy one finds the same means of justification: "For there is one God, and there is one mediator between God and men, the man Christ Jesus, who gave himself as a ransom for all"(2:5-6). Speaking of Jesus, the Book of Hebrews states: "It was proper according to all things that he should become like us in order that he might be a merciful and faithful high priest so that he could make propitiation for the sins of people"(Heb 2::16-17). In Hebrews 9 Jesus even appears before the heavenly throne through the Eternal Spirit to offer himself to God to create a new covenant... "since a death has occurred that redeems them from the transgressions of the first covenant" (14-15). "Christ is the propitiation for our sins, and not only for ours but for the sins of the entire world" (1 Jn 2:1-2). This is the one mode of salvation that has been used most by the church, and why, is difficult to know. But with the history of the church being what it is, it is not improbable that it was to create sorrow for Jesus, guilt for ourselves, and a motive to "give back to the church" for bringing us this salvation, sometimes connected with the availability of the sacrament in which the body of Jesus is again presented to God; and also in this a way controlling the forgiveness of sins by excommunicating the individual and even putting kings and nations under the power of an interdict by which entire nations were cut off from the sacraments of forgiveness. Through many centuries the Church in the west used this to control all of society.

c) The opposite abuse came from the Protestants in claiming that Jesus died for all our sins and therefore we can live joyfully, but also irresponsibly, avoiding the disciple of strong morality. This, of course, made matters even worse leading to the reaction of "fire and brimstone" preachers who used hell as a threat as did the puritans. The vicarious atonement was born after Paul's influence on Christian theology and, even in Paul, is filled with inconsistencies.

D. JUSTIFIED BY FAITH

d) One of the paradoxes of the Lutheran faith is the phrase: by grace alone, faith alone, and scripture alone. For it ties grace and faith together, but each alone without need of the other. It simply can not be grace alone if faith also is needed: the statement is an oxymoron. Yet it does have a Biblical basis. Again this became a popular doctrine in the church after the influence of Paul. The concept does not appear in the Christian Scriptures until the book of Acts. Even though the words are put into Peter's mouth, they are put there by the companion of Paul, Luke, who wrote the book of Acts. "He is the one ordained by God to be judge of the living and the dead. To him all the prophets bear witness that everyone who believes in him receives forgiveness of sins through his name" (Acts 10:42-43). Any who believe in Jesus will receive forgiveness of sins, so say all the prophets. Of course the prophets of Israel said no such thing but this will be handled later. But here the emphasis is on faith, for it proclaims the forgiveness of sins is granted when man has faith in Jesus. Then later in Acts the true author of the "faith" doctrine appears. Paul is preaching in Antioch, and Luke has his saying "...that through this man forgiveness of sins is proclaimed to you, and by him all who believe are freed from the 'sins' from which the law of Moses could not set man free"(Acts 13:38-40).

26a) Next is the great book of liberation by faith, the Book of Romans, a letter written by Paul to the church at Rome. Rm 3:22 "...the righteousness of God through faith in Jesus Christ for all who believe"; Rm 3:26 "...it was to prove at the present time that he himself is righteous and that he justifies him who has faith in Jesus." Rm 4:3 "Abraham believed God, and it was counted for him as righteousness." And Rm 10:9-10 "Because if you confess with your lips that Jesus is Lord, and believe in your heart that God raised him from the dead, you will be saved." As one can see, this passage also has a string attached to believing, one must confess with his lips that Jesus is Lord. The confession section will soon follow. Lastly 1 Jn 5:1,5 "Every one who believes that Jesus is the Christ is a child of God...Who is it that overcomes the world but he who believes that Jesus is the Son of God?"

E. JUSTIFICATION BY WORKS

b) The Christian canon, especially the Gospels, stress works also as the way to salvation. In fact works are so emphasized in the Gospels and the vicarious atonement completely absent in those same Gospels leads one to believe that the Gospels were written as a correction to Paul's teaching about the justification of the individual. Over and over again the Gospels put into the mouth of Jesus the idea that man will be judged by his works on judgment day. Mt 7:21 "Not every one who says to me , 'Lord, Lord', shall enter the kingdom of heaven, but he who does the will of my Father who is in heaven." And again, Jesus declared "For whoever does the will of my Father in heaven is my brother and sister and mother."(Mt 12:50) "Then the King will say to those at his right hand, 'Come, O blessed of my Father, inherit the kingdom prepared for you...for I was hungry and you gave me food, I was thirsty and you gave me drink, I was a stranger...I was naked and you clothed me..etc. Then the righteous will say, 'Lord when did we see you hungry and feed you, or thirsty...or a stranger...or naked and clothe you?...And the King will answer them. 'This is true, I say to you, when you did it to one of the least of these my brothers, you did it to me.'"(Mt 25:31-46), The passage makes it clear that the King will judge men on what they did to the least of Jesus' human brothers. Luke 20:35 "For those accounted worthy to **c)**attain to that age and to the resurrection of the dead." Many will be invited to the banquet, but those not having on the proper garments (that is clothed in virtue) will be dismissed from the banquet. "Do not marvel at this; for the hour is coming when all who are in the tombs will hear his voice and come forth, those who have done good, to the resurrection of life, and those who have done evil, to the resurrection of judgment" (J:28 -29). "I very seriously tell you, if one obeys my word, he will never see death"(J 8:51). "We must work the works of him (God) who sent me, while it is day; night comes, when no one can work"(J 9:4). In this passage Jesus includes himself "we must" and later the Book of Hebrews declared that Jesus fulfilled his task, his obedience to God, and in that he perfected the way to salvation, and those who obey him and his words, will also come to eternal salvation. "Although he was a Son, he learned obedience (Mt 26:39) by means of what he suffered, and, when he was made perfect, he became the source of eternal salvation to all who obey him (Hb 5:8-9).

d) If one reads the Sermon on the Mount in Matthew then one will have a good idea of what it means to obey him. In the Parable of the Sower Jesus declared that the seed that prospered by falling on good soil represented those who have a beautiful and good heart and upon hearing the word, grasp it and hold it fast to themselves, and with endurance bear good fruit. They are the good soil who have a beautiful and good heart (εν χαρδια καλη και αγαθη) and received the word (λογον) and clutched it like "the pearl of great price", and in endurance bore good fruit, the works of virtue. One must notice that the heart of the persons were already beautiful and good. They were not ugly and sinful before the message of the Gospel arrived. If the Gospel writers disagreed with Paul's doctrine of justification, which seems obvious, then either they had sources of the sayings of Jesus that could be used to counter Paul's ideas or else they created them and put them back into the mouth of Jesus, but the former seems much more likely. There seems little doubt that Jesus stressed good works and forgiveness of others as the way to God, and he himself exemplified such and his own life became the incarnation of "the Way". Follow me was his command.

27a) The teaching of a moral life as the pleasing life to God could not be hidden and even surfaced in some of Paul's own writings, which further added to Paul's list of inconsistencies. "For he who sows to his own flesh will from the flesh reap corruption; but he who sows to the Spirit will from the Spirit reap eternal life. And let us not grow weary in well-doing, for in due season we shall reap." (Gal 6:8-9) Put into the mouth of Peter by Luke, this is the statement that was made to Cornelius: "Truly I realize that God shows no partiality, but in every nation any one who fears him and does what is right is acceptable to him."(Acts 10:34-35). That certainly puts virtue and ethics above all other doctrines of exclusivity within Christendom, for any one of any nation that reverences God and does good is acceptable to God. But that thought would, of course, take away much of the power of the church and as a result no church ever confessed this statement.

F. JUSTIFICATION BY WORDS

b) The spoken word, as either conversation or confession was also presented as the means of salvation. Mt 12:36-37 reads: "I say to you, every injurious word of men must be accounted for on the day of judgment; for from your words you will be justified and from your words you will be condemned." Words of confession are one half of the saving formula for Paul when he says to the church in Rome: "...if you confess with your mouth the Lord Jesus, and believe in your heart that God raised him from the dead, you will be saved. For believing with the heart results in righteousness, and confessing with the mouth results in salvation" (Rm 10:9-10). The First Epistle of John (4:15) states: "Whoever confesses that Jesus is the Son of God, God abides in him, and he in God."

G. JUSTIFICATION IS BY FORGIVING OTHERS

c) "Forgive us our debts, according to the way we have forgiven our debtors" (Mt 6:12). This is from the prayer that Matthew and Luke say that Jesus taught his disciples, when they had asked him to teach them how to pray. There are only seven simple petitions in this prayer, according to Matthew and only five in Luke, and this is one of them. Therefore, it is an essential doctrine of Jesus. Mark also records the concept: "And when you stand praying, if you have anything against anyone, forgive all, so that your Father in the heavens also may forgive you your trespasses"(Mk 11:25-26). Jesus also told a parable in which a man who was greatly in debt to his king but begged for mercy and forgiveness of the debt, which was for forgiven by the king out of mercy. Yet, that same man was owed a very small sum by another. He took him by the throat and demanded payment and had him thrown into prison. This was reported to the king and the king (master) was furious with him and handed him over to be tortured and held until he paid his enormous debt to the king. Jesus then said: "My heavenly Father will do the same to you, unless you each forgive your brother, and do it from the heart" (Mt 18:21-35). This justification by forgiving others was taught, evidently, only by Jesus, but after all, he is the central figure of Christianity and the Gospels.

H. JUSTIFICATION BY LOVING GOD

d) This teaching is from James only, but it makes sense that love can forgive a multitude of sins among not only men, but God also. "Hear me, my beloved brothers. Is it not true that God has chosen those poor in the world to be rich in faith and heirs of the kingdom which he has promised to those who love him?"(James 2:5).

I. JUSTIFICATION BY SUFFERING

28a) Paul puts forth another idea that plays into one's justification before God: "When we cry, 'Abba! Father!' It is the Spirit himself bearing witness with our spirit that we are children of God, and if children, then heirs, heirs of God and fellow heirs with Christ, provided we suffer with him in order that we may also be glorified with him."(Rm 8:16-17). In First Peter there is a similar, though not exact, statement. Suffering is required and Jesus gave us an example to follow. "But if when you do right and suffer for it you take it patiently, you have God's approval. For this you have been called, because Christ also suffered for you, leaving you an example, that you should follow in his steps"(1 Pet 2:20-21). To win God's approval, one must suffer as did Jesus, and it is to that that one has been called.

J. JUSTIFICATION BY RITUAL

b) While this may be a fringe doctrine, yet, given the history of the church on the importance of baptism, the two statements made by Paul, one to the Romans and one to the Corinthians seem to indicate that sacramental acts are a means of grace to some. To the Romans he wrote: "Do you not know that all of us who have been baptized into his death" (Rm 6:3). Baptism then connects the person with the death of Jesus by which all were redeemed. It seems more clear in his words to the Corinthians: "Otherwise, what do people mean by being baptized on behalf of the dead? If the wholly dead persons are not raised at all, why are people baptized on their behalf (υπερ αυτων)?" (1 Cor 15:29). The final commission given at the end of Matthew, which were, according to

Matthew's Gospel, the last words Jesus spoke to his disciples: "Go then and make disciples of all nations, baptizing them in the name of the Father and the Son and the Holy Spirit"(Mt 28:19). One is made a disciple first by baptism and then he is to be taught all things.

c) In conclusion to this section one can see why the churches through the ages have fought with each other as to what really saves a person. If Jesus died for the sins of the entire world and salvation was to have been given by free grace to all, then none of the other "strings" or "qualifications" or "sacraments" would have been needed. Thus one can see a number of problems and one overriding inconsistency, if not even a series of contradictions. But if Jesus did not, in fact, take away all the sins of the world so that all could be guaranteed eternal life without so many strings attached, then there stands the major problem of God's character, his partiality towards those who cling to or reject some of the attached strings. This was evident in the first part of this section: the question of God's electing some to be saved and not others. The two highly positioned contrary views then are displayed: the universal validity of Jesus' vicarious atonement and the election of God of some and his rejection of others for the eternal kingdom. To the question of God's partiality in the next section.

IV. GOD'S PARTIALITY: ETERNAL LIFE BY JESUS ONLY

d) The partiality mostly includes the demand of God that people must know and believe the name of Jesus and the story surrounding his mission. If this is rejected, then so-called salvation of all men won at the cross by Christ, this vicarious atonement Jesus performed for the whole world, and given freely by God to all, is all thrown out. The great string attached is that if you do not put Jesus' name into the computer of God's salvation, you will not get in. What good are all the benefits of a computer for all people, if only some know the password? In contrast to what it seems Jesus himself taught, that man will be judged by the beauty of his heart and the actions and fruits which flow from the good tree of man's inner being, the other scriptures and the church want to make the qualification that one must know the password. Perhaps, just perhaps, the church decided to empower itself using Jesus' name and preaching it along with the other attachments so that the church would be able to exert control of the people by fear of hell and hopes of heaven. This, instead of just proclaiming the "good news" that God loves everyone and all is forgiven. Now to the passages of God's partiality.

29a) In the "words of Jesus" as Matthew presents them: "So all people who acknowledge me before men, I also will acknowledge before my heavenly Father; but any who denies me before men, I also will deny before my heavenly Father." So the God of the universe needs Jesus to testify who is worthy or not? This is a grand assault upon the dignity of God as seen by those of the Platonic Tradition. It turns over to Jesus knowledge that God himself did not have, and makes God submit to the stipulations that Jesus wants to implement. It also attacks the humility of the actual historical Jesus who constantly prayed to learn what to do, especially in the Garden of Gethsemane "not my will, but yours Father'. This passages is an assault on a good man and a blasphemy towards the God "who so loved the world" and "who wants all men to be saved". Yet throughout the Christian Canon this same thought is presented: God is partial to those who know Jesus and wrathful to those who do not.

b)Matthew on three other occasions says similar things. One of them is Matthew 11:27 "All things have been delivered to me by my Father; and no one really knows the Son except the Father, and no one fully knows the Father except the Son and anyone to whom the Son chooses to reveal him." This passage is even worse. The author is trying to make Jesus the only person who can reveal the Father, and he only will do it when he chooses to. So God is evidently hidden, and only the Son, at his own choosing can reveal him. God can not reveal himself in some way without going through Jesus? This is simply making God inferior and subordinate to the man Jesus. Both the Jews and Muslims see the problem here, why can not the Judeo-Christians see it? Or is their claim on this "truth" too profitable to give up? In the next chapter the selfishness and brutality of the Christian Church through the ages will be discussed. But so much of its authority is based on this idea of God's partiality in working only through Jesus, and subsequently "his body", the church, that it is highly unlikely the church will give up the idea of God's working in partiality. Matthew has two more passages which proclaim the same message.

c) Acts 4:12 states "There is no salvation in anyone else, for there is no other name under heaven given among men by which men must be saved". And then this same Peter who spoke the above, says "I perceive that God shows no partiality"(Acts 10:34). But in the same speech Peter reverts to the exclusivity of the believers in Jesus: "He (Jesus) is the one ordained by God to be judge of the living and the dead. To him all the prophets bear witness that every one who believes in him receives forgiveness of sins through his name"(Acts 10:42-43). God turns over the judgment of the human race to Jesus? All the prophets bear witness to this? The passages of the Hebrew Scriptures quoted by the Christian Scriptures are simply mangled and twisted and allegorized and bent completely away from their original setting and meaning. This will be addressed later. Forgiveness of sin's through his name. One wonders what there is left for God to do, and one can also see why the church eventually declared Jesus to be God. The point is well made that God **d)**now can, or has chosen, to function as God towards man only through Jesus. If you are not connected to Jesus, you are under God's wrath for eternal condemnation. The entire Christian Scriptures are saturated with this "by Jesus' only" doctrine. In case one is interested it is declared also in: Rm 12:3, 14:8, 16:25-27: I Cor 1:18, 30; 6:11, 8:6; 2 Cor 2:15, 3:14-16, 4:3, 6:14-18, 7:1: Eph 2:12, 4:17-19; Philipians 3:18-19, Col 3:4; 1 Thess 1:10, 5:9; 1 Thess 2:10; 1 Tim 1:3-7, 1:16; 2:5-6, 4:7,10; Heb 7:25, 1 Jn 4:2-3; 2 Jn 7-11. It is in these John passages that one runs across the "anti-Christ" because he does not believe that the Eternal Word was made flesh in Jesus. Of course, all of this was on behalf of the early church to promote itself as the only keepers of the knowledge of eternal life, for they had the message and no one else did. Added to the fact that they also preached that if you did not believe in Jesus you would suffer eternally in hell, they could present a two edged sword by which they could control the spiritual emotions of the less educated people of antiquity. Paul even admitted they were not the wise ones of the world.

V. THE UNBELIEVERS

30a) Just what would a God of love do to someone who does not believe one of the many myths or legends that is developed by mankind? The Christian Canon has an answer: he will send them to a miserable place of tortuous pain where they will continue to suffer for eternity. God will say to them on judgment day: "Depart from me, you cursed, into the eternal fire prepared for the devil and his angels"...and they will go away into eternal punishment."(Mt 25:41, 46). Or "...it is better to enter life maimed than with two hands to go to Gehenna, the unquenchable fire" (Mk 9:44). Also, "...the rich man also died and was buried; and in Hades in torment, he lifted up his eyes"(Lk 16:23). Again, "...when the Lord Jesus is revealed from heaven with his mighty angels in flaming fire, inflicting vengeance upon those who do not know God and upon those who do not obey the gospel of our Lord Jesus. They shall suffer the punishment of eternal destruction and exclusion from the presence of the Lord and from the glory of his strength"(1 Thess 1:6-9). Hebrews 6:3 refers to the "eternal punishment" and even the very short Book of Jude weights in with "...the angels...just as Sodom and Gomorrah and the surrounding cities, all which were immoral and indulged in unnatural lust, serve as an example by undergoing a punishment of eternal fire" (6-7).

VI. THE RETURN OF CHRIST (PAROUSIA AND AFTERLIFE)

b) The reason for including the parousia is to show how wrong the early prophets and writers of the Gospels were in predicting the return of Jesus and the resurrection of the dead and judgment day. This also could have served as a fear tactic in their preaching: "Christ is coming soon, make your decision now or be forever lost!" was their proclamation to their listeners. Attributed to Jesus in Mark's Gospel are the words: "Really, I am telling you, there are some standing here who will not taste death before they see the coming of the Kingdom of God in power"(9:1). Of course, it did not happen, all of those people of that generation died, and the parousia did not come. Again Mark puts forth the warning: "Really, I am telling you, this generation will not pass away before all these things take place...But of that day or that hour no one knows, not even the angels in heaven, nor the Son, but only the Father. Be ready in watchful prayer, for you have no idea when the time will come"(Mk 13: 30-33). "For whoever is ashamed of me and of my words, of him will the Son of man be ashamed when he comes in his glory and the glory of the Father and of the holy angels. But I am telling you truthfully, some of you standing right here will not taste death before they see the kingdom **c)** of God"(Lk 9:26-27). Paul said in his letter to the Romans: "For salvation is nearer to us now than when we first believed. The night is long gone and the day is near"(Rm 13:11-12). Paul tells the Corinthians not to trouble themselves with marriage and family concerns because "the appointed time has become very short...For the form of this world is passing away"(1 Cor 7:25-31). To the Philipians he reminds them that "The Lord is at hand" (Philipians 4:5). The church at Thessalonica seemed to be so anticipatory for the return of Jesus that normal functions seemed to come to an end. Paul must have preached the parousia heavily when he was there. He had to comfort them that Jesus would be coming with all his holy ones, and they were not to worry about those who had died in the mean time. For those still alive, they will not precede those who have died in meeting the Lord (1 Thess 4). Evidently people even quit working and in idleness waited for the Lord, and Paul said that if they do not work they ought not eat (2 Thess 3;10-11). The books of Hebrews, the two books of Peter, First John and the book of Revelation **d)** all speak of Jesus' return with some urgency. Of course, it never happened, yet it was repeated for the next 70 years after Jesus' death. Why? Was it still profitable as a fear tactic to gain converts? It is only in 2 Peter that some doubting was admitted, for "Peter" (year about 130 to 150 CE) had to answer those who were ridiculing the Christians for their waiting for the parousia. 2 Peter 3:3 "First, above everything else, you must understand that scoffers will come in the last days, scoffing from their own passions, and saying 'Where is his promised coming? For ever since the fathers have died, everything has continued as it has from the beginning of creation."

VII. THE BASIS OF DOCTRINE: THE "HOLY INERRANT SCRIPTURES"

A. THE INSPIRATION OF THE BIBLE

31a) The Christian Church has always claimed that the Christian Canon was not a mere work of human beings who were believers in the doctrines they recorded. The early church had many discussions, disputes, and compromises over what books qualified for this honor of being inspired and inerrant before they settled somewhat by the middle of the third century after Jesus ministry, about 350 CE. The question was raised again during the Reformation in the Western Church and a dispute arose over the Deuto-canonical intertestamental works accepted by the Roman Catholic Church. Nevertheless, especially in the Protestant Churches, the canon which each church accepted was claimed to be the Word of God and therefore inerrant in all its proclamations, even in science, history, and, of course, the nature of God and the way of salvation. Paul, speaking of the Tanak and its prophecies that "Christ died for our sins accordance with the scriptures, that he was buried, that he was raised on the third day in accordance with the scriptures" (1 Cor **b)** 15:3-4). Of course, the Tanak made no such claims. It had to have referred to the Tanak or intertestamental literature because the Christian Bible did not exist at the time and it would be another twenty years before the first extant gospel, Mark, was written. Paul also took the Tanak literally when he referred to the myth of Adam and Eve, and even made that myth the basis of comparison with Jesus. As in Adam all fell into sin, one man, so in the one man, Jesus all had been redeemed from sin: 1 Cor 15:20-22. And the pseudo-Pauline epistle called Second Timothy presented the ultimate·in such doctrine: "Every scripture is God inspired and profitable for teaching, for testing, for correction, for instruction in righteousness, that the man of God may be fit and furnished for every good work"(2 Tim 3:16). Yet it was still the Protestant Orthodoxy that put the Christian Scriptures on the highest level, but the Roman Catholic Church still held them infallible enough to condemn Galileo. Therefore, it is well that one looks with a historical-critical mind and see how they were used in the church and how reliable in all things the Christian Scriptures are.

B. BIBLE USED TO PREACH DEATH AND FEAR

c) It is without doubt, and has been mentioned enough above, that the preaching of the evangelists used death, punishment, and fear of God's wrath as a psychological instrument to gain converts. The Bible in recording these events established for the church a record of events in which it too at a later time could use to instill fear and trembling in their audiences. One only has to think of the story of Ananias and Sapphira and the threats and descriptions of hell to see how the Christian Scriptures could be and were used for this purpose.

d) One of the biggest players for a role by which people could be frightened into faith was the constant preaching and teaching that evil was personified in a powerful force that was desirous of bringing the worst diseases, accidents, violent acts, and the deceptions needed to keep you from "the faith" so that you would suffer in his kingdom of hell forever. Listeners, they proclaimed, meet Satan and his evil angels, he is roaming about the earth eager to destroy you forever. "Be awake, be watchful, for your adversary the devil prowls around like a roaring lion, seeking someone to devour"(1 Peter 5:8). That devil attacked Jesus the Lord himself in the desert with temptations during his forty day of preparation for his ministry. Jesus himself recognized Satan (Mt 12:26). Paul refers to Satan in Rm 16:20 and in 1 Cor 2:11 he explains some of his actions were for the purpose of "keeping Satan from gaining advantage over us, for we are not ignorant of his designs". In 1 Thess 2:18 Paul complains that he didn't get some things done because "Satan hindered us". Paul definitely used Satan as a fearsome one to promote his own doctrines in 2 Thess 2:9-10: "The coming of the lawless one by the activity of Satan will be with all power and with pretended sign and wonders, and by total wicked deception against those who are to perish, because they refused to love the truth (Paul's Gospel) and be saved." The Second Epistle to the Thessalonians is filled with the tactics of fear. Pseudo-Pauline epistles also use Satan to preach fear. Eph 4:27 "...give no opportunity to the devil". Again in 6:11-12:
32a)

> Put on the entire armor of God that you may defend yourself against the clever acts of the devil, because our conflict is not against blood and flesh, but against the rulers, the authorities and the world rulers of this present darkness and even against the spiritual ones of evil who dwell in the heavens. Therefore, take up and put on the entire armor of God in order that you might be able to resist that evil day.

The entire universe is geared against you, so you better hold on to the Gospel of Jesus and his good doctrines, or you will have no chance. How different is Plato's cosmos, beautiful and pleasing to the good Father and Creator of all things, where harmony is throughout and all rejoice without jealousy of another: "there is no envy in the heavenly choir" declared Plato. There are, unfortunately, other passages in 1 Peter and

Revelation that are used to create fear that people might seek the shelter of the church. Today, of course, the modern man does not believe in Satan and therefore such teachings look rather childish and foolish. But for 18 centuries the church used this fear to control people.

C. MYTHS AND LEGENDS

b) Miracles were discussed earlier, but there are many other myths and legends in the Christian Scriptures that have been taken, taught, preached, and declared dogma as actual historical happenings. The myth of the miraculous birth of Jesus and all the circumstances that are presented about it by both Matthew and Luke have been taught as doctrine and declared as dogma by the Christian churches throughout the ages. In Matthew everything seems to be presented to those involved by an angel who appears only in dreams. Dreams today are not considered reality or messages from God as they were 2000 years ago. Then the so called prophecy of Jesus' birth in Isaiah is presented: "Behold, a virgin shall conceive and bear a son, and his name shall be called Emmanuel" (Mt 1:23). This was handled in the first chapter, but to quickly resummerize: Syria and the Northern Kingdom were plotting to overthrow Judah and the message was simply that a young woman (even in the Greek parthenos does not mean exclusively a virgin) would bear a son and his name would be "God is with us" because before the child **c)**reaches the age of 3 both Syria and the Northern Kingdom will be rendered helpless and defenseless and the people of Judah would be spared for "God was with them". Even this was a post-facto "prophecy" credited to Isaiah. How it could have applied to Jesus is literally impossible. But to bend and manipulate statements of the Tanak for the benefit of the Christian community was a regular habit of the early apologists for the new faith. The next fantasy myth in Matthew was the coming of the Magi from the Fertile Crescent, probably in Southern Iraq **d)** today. A star appeared and led these astrologers up the Euphrates and then down towards Jerusalem where they stopped and asked where Jesus was to be born, which seems odd and needless, since the star came and stood over the very house where Jesus was in Bethlehem. Imagine a star of the heavens considered directly over a single house: it must have been very close to earth and a true wanderer if it led the magi all the way from

Iraq. That none of the astronomers of Babylon or of those among the Greeks ever mention such an event would be very odd indeed. For they were constant star gazers, as well as the priests of the Roman Empire who saw any heavenly irregularity as an omen from the gods. Not even among the Jews is there any indication of such a happening. All this even without the scientific problem of the pull of gravity, for a star so close to earth would pull it in and consume it. Of course most people of that day had no idea of how large stars actually are. But today the story has absolutely no credibility at all. It is a pure myth. Yet its story is read at Christmas time in all the churches and believed by the faithful. Next is the slaughter of all the children by Herod the Great. There is no other source referring to such a thing. The story based on four of Joseph's dreams (by the way, how would the author of the Gospel of Matthew know what Joseph was dreaming?), an impossible cosmic star appearance, an unauthenticated slaughter of the children by Herod, and a distorted and manipulated "prophecy", and a pregnancy without male semen simply could not have happened.

33a) Luke's account does not help. Luke admits in his first few verses of his Gospel Story that he gathered information from the people of Jerusalem and put them together as an orderly account for "Theophilus" that he might know more about the Christian beginnings. Even if Luke is totally accurate in his replication of what he heard, what he heard was at least second hand and most probably third or fourth hand information. In addition to this, he repeats the virgin birth myth, and adds another unbelievable event,: the Roman census. There was a census when Quirinius was governor of Syria, but it was limited to Syria, and it was in 6 or 7 CE, and all other indications are that Jesus was born about 6 BCE, because in Matthew's story Herod was alive yet and he died in 4 BCE. The two stories based on this are not incompatible. But the claim by Luke that the entire Roman Empire was to be enrolled to be taxed is nowhere recorded in secular history and this added to the totally crazy idea that all would have to return to their city of origin in order to enroll **b)** in the census which would have caused total havoc within the vast Roman Empire that even the thought of it is incomprehensible. Of course, there were never any such enrollments decreed by Caesar Augustus or any other emperor. The virgin birth of Jesus and the accompanying stories are mythical, and probably are based more on Virgil's Fourth Eclogue than Isaiah's Seventh Chapter.

c) The story of the transfiguration of Jesus, although recorded by all three synoptic gospels (Matthew, Mark, and Luke), is also mythical. One would have to wonder how the three authors knew about this since none of them even knew Jesus. Also the problem exists for those who believe that the apostle John was the author of the Gospel of John. The synoptics all record the story of the transfiguration, yet John who was said to be there (Peter, James and John) did not record it. But scholars realize the apostle John did not write the gospel attached to his name. This was a story that Mark wrote in his gospel and the author of the Gospel of Matthew and Luke simply copied it from Mark. Yet, remember that Mark never knew Jesus and he certainly wasn't there. This was propaganda handed down to Mark for the sake of enhancing the status of Jesus: both to encourage the believers of the early church and serve as proof of Jesus' status as the Son of God to the non-believers.

d) The Book of Hebrews refers to many of the myths of the Tanak as a basis for his apology for the Christian Faith. He presents the myth of Melchizedek as an actual historical event and says more about this mythical figure than the entire rest of the Judeo-Christian Scriptures. But his historicity is important for his theological argument; a pattern that often occurs in the "Holy Scriptures", theology first and then create and mold "historical" events to prove the theology or how it is to be allegorized for the present need. Related to this is the Eleventh Chapter where all the important mythical and legendary figures of the Tanak form his source to present heroic faith figures to encourage those whose faith has weakened under stress or persecution. He also has the same problem that Paul had: how can a changeless and eternal God of perfection and all wisdom make his law to his favorite and chosen people so inadequate that he must now make a new covenant; the old becoming both inadequate and obsolete. So myths and allegories are to be remolded to meet the present time. The so called Second Epistle of Peter also uses the stories of Noah, Sodom and Gomorrah, and Lot to warn his readers of God's wrath for the purpose of using fear to keep them from questioning the faith they have been believing. Matthew's account of Jesus' baptism **34a)** presents an opening of the heavens (?) And a dove descending and landing on Jesus and a voice from heaven declaring Jesus to be the Son of the heavenly Voice. This too is a story created to promote Jesus' status to the hearers.

D. HISTORICAL ERRORS AND CONTRADICTIONS

b) In Matthew's genealogy of Jesus he has 4 less generations than the book of Chronicles. Matthew states that Joram was the father of Uzziah, and Uzziah the father of Jotham. So Joram was grandfather to Jotham. But 1 Chronicles 3:11-12 separates the two, not by one, but four generations: Joram was the father of Ahaziah (1), Ahaziah of Joash (2), Joash of Amaziah (3), Amaziah the father of Azariah(4), and Azariah of Jotham. Whether the Tanak is correct or the Christian Canon is correct, it is sure that the both of them are not correct. Matthew is wrong later in the chronology when he makes Josiah the father of Jechoniah, whereas Josiah was the grandfather of Jechoniah, and Jechoniah the son of Jehoiakim. So his conclusion is also incorrect when he states that from **c)**Abraham to David was 14 generations, from David to the Babylonian Captivity 14 generations, and from the captivity to Jesus 14 generations. In Chronicles it is 14, 17, 13 generations between the events described. Matthew was trying a little symbolic numerology in making all three events separated by 14: first to give a rhythm to God's actions in history and secondly to show that Jesus and David were the central figures, for the three consonants of David's name in Hebrew numerology were valued at 4 + 6 + 4 = 14. Therefore, it was time for the Son of David to come and reestablish the Kingdom of Israel. A third problem for Matthew's genealogy is that of Luke's genealogy which is completely different, and the numbers of people involved from Abraham vastly different. In Luke the genealogy there are 56 generations (56 names) and in Matthew there are only 42 generations separating Abraham from Jesus. Obviously the Christian Scriptures have both errors and contradictions in them.

d) Above it was shown that the prediction of the return of Jesus within the time of Jesus' own generation was wrong and all subsequent declarations of an early return in the rest of the Christian Scriptures also were wrong. Matthew's account of the fate of Judas was disputed by Luke who gave a different ending to the life of Judas: in Luke he did not return the 30 pieces of silver and hang himself, but he went and bought some land and later died horribly upon it. Who was right? if either. But certainly there is at least one historical inaccuracy and one contradiction.

35a) Mark wrote that Jesus said that the end times, which were to appear shortly but never did, would see the stars falling from heaven to earth. Again a complete lack of cosmological knowledge. He also declares the earth to have sides from which the four winds will come (Mk 13:24-27). Mark says all the disciples forsook Jesus and fled at his trial and crucifixion, but the Fourth Gospel declares that John stayed at the foot of the cross and Jesus told him to take care of his mother (Jn 19: 26). There also are many contradictions within the Four Gospels as to the events of the resurrection, which will be presented later.

b) Paul's vision of Jesus on the road to Damascus also presents itself in contradictory terms: Acts 9:1-9, 22:9, 26:12-18. They all disagree as to what happened and to what extend Jesus communicated with Paul. In Acts 9 a light flashed about Paul and he heard Jesus and talked to him. The men were confused and speechless for they heard the voice, but saw no one. In Acts 22 the men saw the light, but heard no voice. In Acts 26 the light flashed around Paul and the men with him and Jesus spoke more words than in the other two accounts. In Acts 9 Paul falls to the ground and in Acts 26 the men with him fell to the ground. Certainly, since Luke wrote all three accounts, one would think they would sound more alike to each other. But enough said.

E. DREAMS AND VISIONS

c) In addition to those previously mentioned, it must be acknowledged that through out the Christian Canon God seems to hide himself and let the people try to decided which dream and which vision to follow or believe. Dreams come, not from the outside of man, but from within and are not credible for any decisions concerning the important actions of life. Visions seem to be more complex, but unless they are for personal spiritual growth as many mystics claim to have had, they are probably self-generated and have little to do with reality of the happenings of the world. Any world leader that would start a war based on a dream or a vision, ought not to be followed and if he claimed that the both of them came from God that would qualify him for impeachment. How much more ought scientific minds mistrust the "dreams" and "visions" of the ancients for their spiritual welfare and "eternal fate" today. Also most all of the dreams and visions of the Bible are reported second hand, as Luke reported Paul's. Exceptions are even more suspicious about the Hebrew prophets' declaring "Thus says

Yahweh" and the author of "Revelation" that closes out the Christian Scriptures.

F. NON SEQUITURS AND INCONSISTENCIES

d) There is a consensus among the writers of the Christian Scriptures that there were 12 disciples. Matthew, Mark, Luke, and Acts name the twelve:

Mark (3:13) Peter, James and John, Andrew, Philip, Bartholomew, Matthew, Thomas, James (s of Alphaeus), Thaddaeus, Simon, and Judas.

Matthew (10:2). The same as Mark, may be copied from Mark.

Luke (6:13-16). Judas the son of James is listed instead of Thaddeus.

Acts (1:12-14). Judas the son of James is listed instead of Thaddeus.

John (21:1-2). John does not list the 12, but he refers to the disciples and listed Peter, Thomas, Nathanael, the sons of Zebedee (James and John) and two other disciples. Even though this chapter (21) is a later addition to John, it does show even another grouping of the 12.

Matthew and Mark agree and Luke is consistent listing Judas the son of James in place of Thaddeus in both of his books. John with no list of 12, but included Nathanael. So who were the "12" disciples?

36a) Matthew 4:11, if Jesus is the mighty Son of God, why did he need angels to minister to him after his 40 days in the wilderness and confrontation with the devil? He had no trouble with the devil in other confrontations.

Matthew 4:20-22. It seems rather rude that Peter, Andrew, James, and John would leave their nets and instantly follow Jesus. We know

Peter was married, and would not have Jesus granted them sometime to help prepare their families before they left them to travel the land?

b) Matthew 11:15-16. Jesus had been for some time healing the masses about every where he went and all knew him, so why in the world would "...many followed him, and he healed them all, and ordered them not to make him known", this after his fame had gone out into the entire region? Also it is a non sequitur that after healing all these people and all knew of him, why would the scribes and Pharisees ask for a sign? Were they hidden in a closet all this time? After many more miracles of healing the scribes and Pharisees again ask him for a sign (Mt 16:1). Mark 1:21-28 claims that he even healed people in the synagogue. Lk 5:17 states that Pharisees and scribes witnessed Jesus heal the paralytic. Not only that he healed an entire city of all the sick people and the people possessed with demon over whom he had complete control. Under the section on miracles all this was covered, but the non sequitur is, why then were so many yet unbelieving and as previously stated, why would they want to do him harm? Not only scientifically, but also logically it can not be believed that he did such miraculous things.

c) Also if Jesus was seeking to spread his good news and blessings to all people in hopes that they would believe in him, then why would he go into the Decapolis, the ten Greek cities, and destroy their livestock? as claimed by the story of the 2000 swine that he destroyed by sending the demons into them? (Mk 5:1-13). .

d) Mark 9:40 has Jesus saying, "He that is not against us, is for us". But Matthew 12:30 has Jesus saying, "He who is not with me is against me, and he who does not gather with me scatters". In fact, how does Mark know any of the statements he attributed to Jesus, he never knew him? The First Epistle of John seems to contradict himself as 1:8-10 does not harmonize with 3:6-10. "If we say we have no sin, we deceive ourselves and the truth is not in us...if we say we have not sinned, we make him a liar, and his word is not in us": basically saying that all are sinners and we need his forgiveness. But then the latter passage: "No one who abides in him sins; no one who sins has either seen him or known him...no one born of God commits sin; for God's nature abides in him, and he cannot sin because he is born of God."

37a) The non sequiturs, inconsistencies, and contradictions are endless in the Christian Canon. For one to say that it is the inerrant word of God and can not lead astray or deceive in matters of teaching, morals, history, cosmology, logic and science is really incomprehensible.

G. THE PSEUDONYMOUS WRITINGS

b) The Christian Canon is made up of books by Paul, who never knew Jesus, four designated "Gospels" by four people who never knew Jesus, and several pseudonymous books credited to Paul and Peter, and a man exiled on the island Patmos who had a "revelation" while there of better things to come for the believers and a brutal vengeance to come for the unbelievers. Also included is a book addressed to the Hebrews by a totally unknown person, and a certain Jude who has little to say. The only possible person who might have known Jesus is the author of the Book of James, and since the time of Origen until the 19th Century it was commonly thought that it was the brother of Jesus that wrote it, although today that is doubted by most scholars.

c) However, James, even if not written by Jesus' brother, might more correctly represent the true historical Jesus far better than any other book in the Canon. It is written in excellent Greek. It has no direct antagonisms towards Paul but definitely corrects any views that man is justified by faith alone. Works are the basis of verification of justification, much like the apparent teachings of Jesus in the Gospels. The author of James has no creedal statements, works being more important than spoken creeds. He has no virgin birth, no miracles of Jesus, no reference to a resurrection of Jesus, no deification of Jesus as well as no indications that there could possibly be a "Holy Trinity". God alone is to be served and worshipped. There are not prayers or any other acts "in the name of Jesus". There is no vicarious atonement overtures: salvation comes from loving God, loving the neighbor, and good works. There are teachers, but no bishops or deacons mentioned. Finally man himself is to take the initiative towards God: "Draw near to God and he will draw near to you"(4:8), even though man lives from the grace of God and the spirit that God has given within us to draw us back to him. "He yearns jealously over the spirit which he has made to dwell in **d)**us"(4:5). In the book there are no "prophecies" fulfilled by the misquoting of the Tanak. In fact one can say that this Book of James fits perfectly the Platonic tradition while, at the same time, does not profess the doctrines proclaimed by the growing church, led by Paul's teachings. **38a)** As to the rest of the Christian Canon, the mixture of second, third and fourth hand myths and legends, many created to empower the church itself, there are some worthy teachings, not unlike those of the Platonic Tradition, but they along with the rest of the Judeo-Christian Bible are excluded from this Bible, for the Platonic Tradition is rich enough in itself and actually is the source of the vast majority of those worthy sayings in the Christian Canon, but unacknowledged by the ungrateful Christian Church.

H. OTHER DISTORTIONS OF ACTUAL HISTORY

b) The resurrection story will be handled in the next chapter of the book, but also within the Christian Canon many post-facto prophecies attributed to Jesus in order to "prove" happenings that took place after his death. These and other created stories by the Church to empower itself in the minds of the readers, e.g. "Whosesoever's sins you forgive are forgiven, etc", are created to empower the bishops of the church to hold the salvation of the believer in their hands. Such a declaration also is in conflict with the many other stories of Jesus' return when he, not the church, would judge the living and the dead. The exaggeration of the events also, especially the miracles, which seem to come by truck-load to every village that Jesus visited all the way to Tyre and Sidon, and one has to ask why ancient Phoenician culture and literature never made any mention of these massive gatherings of healing that the Christian Scriptures claim took place in their two largest cities and regions, Tyre and Sidon.

c) Since the Christian Faith is based on its Holy Scriptures and they are filled with unbelievable miracles, God's eternal wrath and punishment, God's partiality, a confusing of how God can be pacified and man justified in his sight, the many myths and legends that are presented as actual history, the false prophecy of the immanent return of Jesus, doctrines created from reported dreams and visions, historical errors and contradictions, logical inconsistencies and non sequiturs, the false stories and prophecies written back into the life of Jesus in order to empower the church, teachings and threats of fear of hell--with the devil waiting to devour you, and the gross exaggeration of many other events, how can one possibly build one's life, hopes, morals, and relationship to God upon these very same "Holy Scriptures"? Certainly the need of a new book of worship, philosophy of life, guide to ethics, and a decent and kind view of the God one seeks to worship is obvious. In the West the Platonic Tradition is the core of the best and most beautiful and transcendental philosophic religion available to us.

ΓΑΜΜΑ

Γ

CHAPTER THREE
CHURCH TAKES CONTROL OF THE EMPIRE

40a) I. JESUS, WHO WAS HE?

The quest for the historical Jesus started immediately after his death and by his own disciples. "Just who was this man whom we have known for just over one year?" they must have asked. Some answers seemed simple: he was a Galilean, a carpenter, and someone who was strongly God-centered in his thinking. He had a mission to proclaim the nearness of God and the necessity for man to repent and confront God now and not tomorrow. He saw each person in a state of confrontation with his destiny; a destiny that was forcing the issue of one's existence. He has been seen as an existential and eschatological preacher, and teacher of high personal ethics. He disliked those who hid behind traditional teachings that seem to clog up the true spiritual longing that all had for the blessed life. Lying and hypocrisy grated mightily against his open purity of thought and deed, and he accused many of the religious leaders of his day as being almost satanic for their lack of love, concern, and mercy for the downtrodden. His confrontation with them led to his execution on a cross.

b) Much more than this can not be known about him. The extant four Gospels written about him by people who did not know him and were written from 40 to 90 years after his life time, simply can not be relied upon because of the quick growth of glorified stories about him. He was made, in a very short period of time, to be a special Son of God, prophesied by the ancient Jewish Scriptures, verified by many many miracles, delivered from the punishment of death by being resurrected from the dead, and, after seeing his disciples and others, was taken up into heaven, promising to return soon to establish the Kingdom of God. This mode of hero glorification and deification was a common practice in the ancient world, and the followers of Jesus used it greatly, adding certain features such as eternal salvation for all his followers and forgiveness of all their sins by choosing him as their spiritual teacher and savior, and this to further enhance his glory and his appeal to others.

c) It should be noticed that two early writings of the early church, the Letter of James and the later Gospel of Thomas, either came before much of the glorification process developed or else chose to reject such stories. The Epistle of James is written in excellent Greek, states no antagonism towards Paul, but strongly rejects faith as the vessel of salvation, was thought by Origen to be written by James the Brother of Jesus and Eusebius agreed with that suggestion. Modern scholars remain mixed on the epistle's authorship. However, in the Epistle itself, it certainly appears to be very early. It has no creedal statements -- just the encouragement to follow the teachings of Jesus. It has no virgin birth, no miracles by Jesus, no reference to a resurrection of Jesus, no deification of Jesus, God alone is to be worshipped and called upon, no vicarious atonement (forgiveness by the acts of Jesus), teachers referred to but no bishops or deacons are mentioned, and, finally man himself must take the initiative towards God which he can do because of the implanted spirit within him (4:8). Also there are many Platonic thoughts present in the Epistle. The spiritual life must be focused upon God and the Eternal (1:28 & 4:5). The love of God is the driving force to spiritual fulfillment **d)** (1:12 -- makarios) and love is also the basis of salvation (2:5), not faith. Desires and passions must be controlled (1:14 epithymia) and (4:1-4 hedone and epithymia). God, the Father, does not change (1:17). Mankind is the first fruit of God's creation (1:18). God implants the spirit (1:12 -- agape, 1:21 & 4:5 -- logos) that is able to save one's soul (Psyche). Actualized virtues (doers of the word) are the basis of happiness and salvation. The moral law is a unit (2:10-11) as are Plato's four cardinal virtues. God's given statutes are open to reason (3:17), and no swearing and no oaths (5:12). Because the author has such excellent Greek and he has so many allusions to Platonic philosophy, he probably was, if not a teacher, one who was quite at home with Hellenistic culture. Since Jesus himself was also much acquainted with Platonic thought, it is possible that it could have been his brother who was the author of this book, for they both grew up in Galilee of the Gentiles. The fact that the

Epistle had no indications of the more advanced christology, church structure, and a lack of creedal statements, it does seem that it is a very early witness to Jesus of Nazareth.

41a) The second work is the Gospel of Thomas, an acknowledged Platonic-Gnostic influenced work. In it there are no references to: the virgin birth, no prophecies fulfilled, no miracles attributed to Jesus, no account of the resurrection or ascension, no vicarious atonement, no sacraments, no deification of Jesus. All this despite Jesus asking the question "Who am I?" (L 13). The Platonic themes are obvious in Logia 3, 24, 29, 67, 83, 84, and 111.

A third work is the DIDACHE (the Teachings or Instructions) attributed to the 12 disciples, but was written sometime about the middle of the Second Century CE. This teaching manual was reliant upon the Gospel of Matthew (written about 80 CE) and two other early works: Barnabas (written in the very late First Century CE) and Hermas (written about the middle of the Second Century CE). It is a type of halfway house that is in a transitional period of the development of Church doctrine concerning the person of Jesus and the way to salvation. Basically it presents immediately the life of virtue as the way of life and salvation: love of God, love of fellow man, and the Golden Rule. The work starts thus:

b) The Lord's Teaching to the Heathen by the Twelve Apostles: There are two ways, one of life and one of death; and between the two ways there is a great difference. Now, this is the way of life: "First, you must love God who made you, and second, your neighbor as yourself." And whatever you want people to refrain from doing to you, you must not do to them."

The Didache presents no prophecies fulfilled, no miracles of Jesus and no virgin birth of Jesus (despite having Matthew available). There is no reference to an apotheosis of Jesus to the Godhead, and no miracles among themselves. On the other hand the rite of baptism has taken on a magical mystical order of ritual, Jesus is called "The Christ", even though the anointing of Jesus seems to be only for the purpose of teaching the way of salvation, and there is no vicarious atonement stated. The great commission of Matthew is borrowed that all should be baptized with the formula "In the Name of the Father, the Son, and the

Holy Spirit." Lastly there is a reference to the appointment of bishops **c)**and deacons which implies a growing church order.

What the Didache shows is a movement of legend, sacraments, and church hierarchy that is growing along with the status of Jesus into a Savior, and eventually into the Holy Trinity Godhead as an equal to God the Father. But the transition takes three centuries and many councils in which there were many dissenters who were then classified as heretics, and by 451 at the Council of Chalcedon the Church had frozen its well developed doctrines, and from henceforth those doctrines if not believed whole and undefiled could inflict a curse of heresy and even death upon the one who chose not to believe all those doctrines. The Greek word used for the term heresy is αιρεσις, which means "choice". Those who chose to believe something different than the councils. Constantine was the first to impose an empire-wide punishment and even death for those "choosers" (heretics) who did not accept the teachings of the Council of Nicea in 325 CE. In the future the claim of "heresy" by the church was a powerful weapon of controlling the people of Europe: fear was the main power of the church, not love or "good news".

d) The frank condemnation of this development and glorification of Jesus by myth, legend, and fear has come under criticism of the modern skeptic, both those of Christian background and those outside the Christian faith. The story of the resurrection of Jesus in bodily form was proclaimed by the church in such an inconsistent way by people who were at the mercy of third and fourth hand propaganda that it is no wonder why there is so much disagreement in the four canonized gospels themselves.

Gospel of Mark proclaims:

1. Mary Magdalene, Mary the Mother of James, and Salome went to the tomb.
2. No earthquake.
3. There was no angel, but a young man.
4. Man says: go tell his disciples and Peter
5. Jesus will meet them in Galilee.
6. Women were afraid and said nothing to disciples.

42a) Gospel of Matthew proclaims:
1. Mary Magdalene and the "other Mary" went to the tomb.
2. There was an earthquake.
3. There was one angel.
4. The angel says Jesus is risen: go tell his disciples
5. Jesus will meet the disciples in Galilee.
6. Jesus meets the women, and they worship him.
7. Jesus tells women that he will meet the disciples in Galilee.

Gospel of Luke proclaims:
1. The women who had come with Jesus from Galilee went to the tomb.
2. There were two men at the tomb.
3. Two men remind women that Jesus had told them he would die and rise again on the third day.
4 The women told the 11 disciples and to all the rest of the people.
6. The women were: Mary Magdalene, Joanna, Mary the mother of James, and the other women with them.
7. The disciples refuse to believe the women.

b) Gospel of John proclaims:
1 Mary (Magdalene) alone was at the tomb.
2. The stone had been rolled away from the tomb.
3. She ran to Peter and "the other disciple" telling them that someone had taken away the body of Jesus.
4. Peter and the other disciple ran to the tomb.
5. Peter enters the tomb and finds nothing but the empty clothing.
6. The other disciple believed.
7. The two, Peter and the other disciple, returned to their homes.
8. Mary stays weeping at the tomb.
9. Two angels in white appeared and declared the resurrection of Jesus.
10 Jesus himself appears to Mary, who has trouble recognizing him.
11. Jesus and Mary speak briefly as she, recognizing him, calls him teacher (Rabboni).
12. Jesus ends the conversation asking Mary to release her grip on him,

And tells her: "I am ascending to my Father and your Father, to my God and your God."

13. Mary Magdalene went and told the disciples the story.

c) One can easily see the growth of the story from Mark, the first Gospel to record it, and John, the last to record it. Virtually every detail in the accounts are different. The time elapsed between the two stories is about 30 or 40 years (Mark about 70 CE and John about 100 to 110 CE). Yet, even in John, Jesus makes a firm distinction between himself and God: "I am ascending to my Father and to your Father, to my God and to your God."

The appearances of Jesus after the resurrection come from accounts that are just as contradictory as the accounts of the resurrection itself. Paul lists only appearances, no places or sayings or any kind of details. He throws out big numbers as a substitute, that Jesus appeared to 500 brethren. According to the book of Matthew, Jesus appears to the disciples in Galilee, but according to Luke and John in or around Jerusalem. In Mark he does not appear at all. In Matthew Jesus appears only once to the disciples, but in John three times.

d) A few comments by modern Christian theologians are:

Guenther Bornkamm:

"The 'event' of Christ's resurrection from the dead, his life and his eternal reign, are things removed from historical scholarship ...There is an undeniable tension between the singleness of the Easter message and the ambiguity and historical problems of the Easter narratives." (*Jesus of Nazareth*).3.1

Ernst Kaesemann:

One can "postulate with certainty that none of the Evangelists himself knew the historical Jesus". (*Essays on New Testament Times)* 3.2

"The message of Jesus presented by the synoptic Gospels is for the most part not authentic, but is stamped by the faith of the primitive Christian in its various stages....is received only as

> embedded in the preaching of primitive Christianity and superimposed by it (*Exegetische Versuche und Besinungen)*3.3

> Only a few words of the Sermon on the Mount and of the conflict with the Pharisees, a number of parables and some scattered material of various kinds go back with any real degree of probability to the Jesus of history himself. (*Essays on New Testament Themes).*3.4

43a) Martin Niemoeller:

> I am personally convinced that in religious instruction we ought to teach nothing which we ourselves cannot consider to be "authentic".(*Eine Welt oder keine Welt*).3.5

Klaus Wegenast:

> The miracle stories in the Bible are now buried in legends and sometimes misunderstood as reports to be taken as true. ("*Wundergeschichten der Bibel in der Grundschule" from Evangelische Unterweisung*) February 1966.

Walter Hartmann:

> (That one must have the) the courage to set the situations of Jesus constantly in parallel to present day situations, and the deeds of Jesus in parallel to the deeds of present-day men. That presupposes that we finally begin to grasp Jesus as a real man, and no longer consider him to be a god, who was changed into a man...We must say openly and clearly that Jesus was a man and nothing other than a man...Everything which men are basically not capable of, Jesus also could not have done, for he was a man. (ibid).3.6

b) Jesus was a man like any other man, even the Book of Hebrews declared that he was like us in every way and had to learn by obedience to become what he became, a pioneer of faith for us. He bowed his head to the heavenly Father and said "not my will but yours be done". In that he was our supreme pioneer leading us to bow down before the Father of the cosmos and gain harmony and unity with Him who gave life to all. He, Jesus, was such a man, but the process of one-upmanship that the church resorted to in order to claim his way, as well as himself, as the only way to the Father resulted in constant "adornment" of his virtue until the final step was taken and he was proclaimed God. This was the Christian Church at it most hypocritical level, simply to be able to claim **c)** the rights to preach to and in some cases withhold from men the salvation of God. Who was Jesus? A man like all of us who long for God, for His love, and to enjoy Him eternally. His authentic mission was pointing us away from himself and towards God. Why do we dishonor his own directions and in the process dishonor God's nobility and love, which is sufficient for our forgiveness without a human sacrifice being offered to him? God's love does not need to be paid off, nor do men need redemption from His wrath. There is no hell, no wrath, no separation from God in the first place for His love in itself covers a multitude of sins. Let us be in honor of Jesus, but to pray to him and think of him as God, for Heaven's sake, no!

II. THE CHURCH TAKES CONTROL OF THE ROMAN EMPIRE

d) A. The Church Under Fire

As the primitive Christian Church expanded it did not find a welcome mat put out for it. Yet Rome protected the Christians from the Jewish persecution of them, thinking that it was a squabble between two Jewish groups. But Nero knew the difference, that the younger religion was a completely new religion with a new leader, Jesus. When Rome accidentally caught fire and devastated a good portion of the City of Rome, killing tens of thousands of people, the people accused Nero of starting the fire, probably because many did not like him and more particularly because he had constructed a model of a new Rome, a grand urban renewal project. They figured he would easily gain support if something happened to the old Rome. That is why they suspected Nero of setting the fire to the old part of the City to make way for his new pet project. Since the fire was so devastating, the people were furious against Nero, who actually had nothing to do with the fire. But knowing that

Christianity was a new and forbidden religion, he blamed the Christians for the fire. Rome had a policy that when they conquered a people and **44a**) established a new Roman Provence, the people could retain their traditional religion. But if after Rome had conquered a new territory the people started a new religion, it was considered a front for a patriotic rebellion against Rome. Therefore, since Christianity was established a full century after Rome had conquered Palestine, Christianity became an illicitum collegium -- an illicit collection of people disguised as a religion. Since they were, in the eyes of the Romans very turned inward and acted as a special people who alone were God's favorites because their leader was the Christ (anointed one) of the only God they worshipped, Rome came to distrust them after Nero pointed the finger of guilt at them. Under Nero they were unjustly rounded up, impaled, and burned to death at night, being used as lanterns. Subsequently Christians were seen as superstitious and self-centered disrespecters of the Empire's **b**) gods, dishonoring the Emperor, refusing military service, condescending towards much of Rome's social activities, and doing evil things in secrecy such as sexual orgies and the eating of a young baby (holy communion's words "take and eat, this is the body..."). The persecutions were for the most part quite mild and sporadic, but in time of national insecurity Christians were always suspected of causing the anger of the gods upon the Empire. Under Domitian, Decius, and Diocletian they suffered, but not in large numbers. In fact, the first years of the Christian Empire, 325-451 CE, the Christians killed more of each other because of heresy disputes and competition between the Arian Christians and the Athanasian Christians than Rome killed in the previous 275 years. But Christians have played up and greatly exaggerated their years of persecution under the Romans who were actually much kinder to them than the Christians were to their own "heretics" and to the pagans after Constantine's legalization of Christianity.

c) Constantine won a decisive battle at the Milvian Bridge outside of Rome for the struggle for the emperorship of the Roman Empire, and in 312 he marched into Rome to claim his prize and establish himself as the new Roman Emperor. He claimed to have seen a Chi with a Rho superimposed upon it in the sky. Since the Chi and the Rho are the first two letters in the spelling of the word Christ, and since he also thought he saw a cloud formation declaring that in this sign you will conquer (in

hoc signo vinces), he, after his victory, took up faith in the Christian religion. He was still in the process of unifying the Roman empire under his power when in 325 CE he called a council to unify the Christian Church as a means to helping him unify the Empire. He certainly was not a theologian, and had no interest in learning the distinctions of Greek metaphysics, but he was intent that all Christians believe in and subscribe to the same creed. The Church had long been in disputes over doctrines, even from the time of Paul of Tarsus, and had smaller groups of bishops gathering in various sites to discuss and condemn various views. But local decisions were often in conflict with other local decisions, and it should be remembered that there was as of yet no such thing as an accepted canon of the Christian Scriptures (no Christian Bible), even though there was a general consensus on the Four Gospels and some of the Pauline epistles. A General council was called to make a unity of the Christian doctrines and to develop a creed to which all "Christians" would have to agree, and the Council of 325 CE was held in Nicea, east
d) of Greece. The attendance was larger than the previous local synods, but was in no wise representative of all of Christianity--travel was still a major problem. Only two or three west of Rome attended. Things did not go as Constantine had hoped and a large segment of the group left early or would not sign the final creed, and for many more years, till the Council of Chalcedon in 451 CE the Church was in a virtual state of civil war, the two great opponents being the Athanasians, i.e. The Homoousians and later called the Catholics and the Homoiousians, called Arians. This happened despite the severe penalties that Constantine established for the dissenters: punishment, exile, and death. Likewise, Constantius II, Constantine's son, when he took over the empire after his father's death, sided with the group condemned by his father. These Christians were more cruel and devastating to each other than the Roman Empire had been to them.

45a) The dissenters were called by Constantine "enemies of the truth, foes of life and counsellors of destruction" and they were called a spiritual disease and led others to eternal death, and their places of worship (remember, these were also Christians) were confiscated and they were prohibited from meeting together even in private homes. Resentment of Constantine boiled under the surface. How could it be that one vote of a small group of bishops, even though there was a large group against the creed, determine for all of Christianity the absolute truth that all must follow. Constantine did not care, he wanted unity and the dessenters would feel his wrath. In the next generation the dissenters, led by the Arians, were the favorites of the Emperor and all was reversed. Oh Christians, how they love one another! When Julian, the Platonists, became emperor he scornfully replied to the Christians that they, both sides, were safer now than when one of them was in control. Yes, it took a Platonic Pagan Emperor to bring peace to them. However, Julian died in battle after only three years after taking office, and after 363 CE the Christians continued to battle, kill, and burn the books of each other until the Council of Chalcedon in 451 CE.

b) During this time the Christians began the brutalization of the pagans of which the most pious and philosophical were the Platonists. All their temples and altars were eventually destroyed, beginning with Constantine himself, who carried off the beautiful objects and bronze doors that he used to adorn the churches, he took the gold and put it into his treasury. Constantine then became the first Caesaropapist, controlling both Empire and Church. He gave a consent to all the Church wanted destroyed of the pagans and, exclusive of the army and the court, he empowered the church to do as it pleased in order to stop all dissent and heresy. Yet even there he mingled ethics by means of the control of the court. He encouraged the rich to stay in business and had the church ruled by the poorer (most uneducated) of the people, for that would limit intellectual dissent. He used the court system to limit divorce, at the expense of women of course. A woman was no longer allowed to argue for a divorce because of her husband's drunkeness, his family destroying gambling, and his adulterous affairs. She could only ask for a divorce because her husband murdered someone. Even unmarried women were put to death if they had sex with a household slave (many of the slaves in the Roman Empire were Greeks, Syrians, Jews and Egyptians), and the slave was burned alive. He also solidified the serf status of poor, but free, Roman citizens, forbidding them to change landlords and seek better conditions for working. He wrote in 332 CE: "It will be appropriate that those who are planning escape should be in chains like slaves, that they may be forced in virtue of a servile condemnation to fulfill those duties which are fitted for free men."3.7

c) Constantine was not a saint, despite the honors given him by the Eastern Church, and his political murders and the execution of his wife and one of his children did not go well with many of the more pious

Christians. But he started the New Age of Christian Power and Dominance in Europe, a power which it used to control completely the lives of men and women for almost 1200 years before the Reformation of the 16th Century. Jacob Burckhardt saw Constantine as the personification of the demonic and declared of him "such a man is essentially unreligious" and as "a murderous egotist" full of "fearful malignancy."3.8

d) B. Doctrines, Creeds, and Dogma

When the Church committed itself to an unbendable creed by which to judge the faith of others it was stepping into an area that the Greeks called "hybris", that is, arrogance or excessive pride before the gods. It always led to disaster. Human words can not accurately describe any portion of the metaphysical world, let alone describe God. Quoted below is such an arrogant statement of a church father by the name of Vincent of Lerins (written between 431 and 450 CE) in a work called "Against Heresy". It could be called "The Holy Trinity Made Simple".

46a) "In God there is one substance, but three persons; in Christ two substances, but one Person. In the Trinity, another and another person, not another and another substance (distinct persons, not distinct substances); in the Savior another and another substance, not another and another person, (distinct substances, not distinct persons). How in the Trinity another and another person (distinct persons) not another and another substance (distinct substances)? Because there is one person of the Father, another of the Son, another of the Holy Ghost; but yet there is not another and another nature (distinct natures) but one and the same nature. How in the Savior another and another substance, not another and another person (two distinct substances, not two distinct persons)? Because there is one substance of the Godhead, another of the manhood. But yet the Godhead and the manhood are not another and another Person (two distinct persons), but one and the same Christ, one and the same Son of God, and one and the same person of one and the same Christ and Son of God."3.9

b) And if you did not believe this whole and undefiled, you were a heretic and subject to death. Are these not some type of magical rites and formulas that one can memorize and thus be "saved", saved at least from burning at the stake? Jesus himself would surely have been burned at the stake because if this was so simple and necessary for salvation, why would he not have taught it? This is dogma at it's worse and most horrible form. It is obvious that they did not even read their own holy book. The book of Ephesians stated that Christ abolished dogma (δογμα) that he might bring unity and reconciliation to God (Eph. 2:15). Again it is stated that Christ canceled the bonds of the legal dogmasin (δογμασιν); he set it aside and nailed it to the cross. Let man never be tied to such dogma again, for Christ has destroyed it, says the author of Colossians (2:14), and again he declares "Let no one pass judgment on you...food and drink...festival...new moon, they are only shadows of Christ (2:16). Words likewise are only symbols or shadows of spiritual truth. They, if put into creedal statements, can never be used to judge others.

c) Aldous Huxley in his "*The Perennial Philosophy*" warns his readers that creedal statements and formulas have been "taken too seriously and are treated with the reverence that is due only to the FACT they are intended to describe". He further warns that they, the statements, are not at all part of the religious experience. "To suppose that people can be saved by studying and giving ascent to formulae is like supposing that one can get to Timbuctoo by poring over a map of Africa. Maps are symbols, and even the best of them are imperfect symbols."3.10 Maps and creeds are only symbols of reality, and poor ones at best, and they never can be substituted for the experience itself, either in travel or religious.

d) The book *The Joy of Embracing God* states:

"This step towards unification of the believing community by creedal expression can be a most dangerous step in many ways. ...Representation, even in stories and prayers, can be difficult in terms of expressing the nature of God, and at very best can only be symbolic on a rather low level. And, of course, they can be, not only poor representations of the Deity, but misleading also. Any teaching about God must be clothed in deepest humility, and then with the Hindu's view of the Supreme Brahman and Plato's view of the Good Beyond Being considered, one must constantly be aware that he is dealing, not so much with God's ultimate nature, but with man's desperate attempt to declare it. The danger of Creeds is that they usually take on an absolute and unbending character, claiming ultimate spiritual truth, and forsaking the original intent of being only symbols. How many "heretics" have been burned at the stake for such arrogance of shallow religious fanatics? How many wars have been fought to kill the "infidels", the "pagans" and the "heathen"? While it is understandable that a community of believers wants to represent what it believes in simple words, it must certainly know that they are, at very best, an inferior and human view of the Divine, and if taken to be Truth Itself, that is absolute hybris before God and the appearance of utter foolishness before men. Justification for an act of violence or discrimination ought not to be "It is in our Scriptures" or "It is in our Creeds". Maybe that is fine to designate who should be or not be in that particular group of believers, but to use such statements seriously as representations of Truth Itself is spiritual arrogance, which is a far greater evil than any "misunderstanding" of an "attribute" of God. As to such religious expressions, "yes!" to creeds and scriptures, they are necessary for our communicating our faith and its implications for living a good and holy life, but for unbending declarations about the very nature of God Himself, then "no!" to them."3.11

47a) C. "Pagans" and "Heretics"

After Constantine's Christianizing of the Roman Empire, there were three divisions established for Europeans and surrounding Mediterranean countries: Orthodox Christians, Unorthodox (heretical) Christians--but usually treated like insiders trying to destroy the Christian Faith, and Pagans. Only one was favored by the Empire and only one had full legal status to represent his religious beliefs completely. At times there was some thin tolerance towards the two non-Orthodox groups, but in large the were pushed down, robbed, persecuted and often executed, especially if a political crisis was at hand and the two oppressed groups supported a non-Orthodox politician, especially if such sought to be the next emperor.

A *paganus* in Latin simply meant a rural villager or a person who lived in the country side. Christianity in its earliest years spread from city to city and usually those outside the city were not converted for many years, and, thus, the unconverted were called pagani, country folk who had not heard of Christianity yet. A pagani was not a negative term at all, that is, until they were classified as such by the young and expanding church, and forever afterwards the church referred to the unconverted as pagans. They were those who also held for the longest period of time to their pre-Christian religions, not because they were less intelligent but simply because they lived in a rural area. Actually, the most enlighted of the ancient world were the longest surviving non-Christians in the Roman Empire, usually philosophically oriented--most of them Platonists--who saw Christianity as a foolish and superstitious religion relying on myths, rituals, fear, exclusiveness and hopelessness. The Empire certainly did not lack personal, state, mystery oriented or philosophical religions. In fact, Rome prided itself for it democratic acceptance of so many different religions coming together within its domain. True, sometimes they were agitated at the Jews for being exclusive, the philosophers who questioned too much the Roman order or rule, the sexual oriented religions (Kybele), and the Druids because they practiced human sacrifice (as if the Roman games were not human sacrifices), and occasionally such religions were banned in certain regions within the Empire.

b) There was the state religion with its tradition and political need to unify all people under Jupiter, Juno, Minerva, and Apollo and several others: the pantheon was made up of twelve gods and goddesses. The twelve of the Romans are very similar to the twelve of the Greeks from whom they borrowed them, at least for the most part. The Greek name is first and the Roman counterpart follows:

Zeus - Jupiter (chief god, and made the only god by philosophers)
Hera - Juno (wife of chief god)
Ares - Mars (god of war)
Athena - Minerva (goddess of wisdom and defensive war)
Artemis - Diana (goddess of nature and the hunt)
Aphrodite - Venus (god of beauty and love)
Poseidon - Neptunus (god of water and ocean)
Hephaestus -Volcanus (god of fire and volcanos)
Hermes - Mercurius (messenger of Zeus - Jupiter)
Apollo - Apollo (god of culture, art, music, and medicine)
Kronos - Saturn (god of time)

Dionysus - Bacchus (Fertility mystery cult, sometimes replaced with
Eros - Cupid, in popular view a god of romantic love)

c) Roman Household Gods

Every house had an altar, within or on the property, in order to serve the family's personal gods: Penates, Vesta, & Lares

Every farm had a shrine or temple (templum meant a sacred place even if there were no building there)

The family Genius (a guardian of a man's ancestors and posterity, Not too unlike "The God of Abraham, Isaac, & Jacob)

The Mysteries

Osiris (Serapis: union of Osiris and Apis) - Isis

Kybele (Cybele) - a sensual goddess from Phrygia

Mithras - who came from the east and represented the Sun

The Sun God

Sometimes worshipped directly, but the sun usually symbolized the Creator and Preserver God.

The Philosophical Faiths (the intellectual quest for God)

Platonism - middle Platonism - new (neo) Platonism

Epicureanism

Aristotelianism

Stoicism

Pythagoreanism

d) The Outside or Unincorporated Religions

Judaism

Druidism

Zoroastrianism

The German gods (Woden, Thor, Tiu, & Frei - after whom are named Wednesday, Thursday, Tuesday, & Friday)

There were many other gods and goddess, especially the numina - the spirits and demons (demons were not necessarily evil: Plato's were all good, but the Christian Canon's demons are all bad). There were also some who believed they could reach the metaphysical world by means of magic, oracles, astrology, haruspicy, omen, and witchcraft. All of the above gods, in all categories, were available The Greco-Roman Empire had a rich culture and a rich diversity of religions available for the spiritual quests of its people. Those who were too self-centered, did not borrow from others or accept them as also being honest in their quest for God and eternity, and claimed an exclusive and the only path to God, were generally out of step with the culture and often criticized and even persecuted sometimes as being, if not a danger, a nuisance: Judaism and Christianity fell into that category.

48a) As to the "Christian Heretics" they were about as numerous as the pagan religions, and initially after Constantine they suffered even more than the pagans, for they were "betrayers of Christ", at least according to the majority vote of certain councils. Socrates Scholasticus, a church historian who lived from 380-450 CE, started his history of the church with Constantine's reign and limits his history to the eastern part of the Empire, yet he had plenty of "heresies" with which to deal. There were, first and foremost, the Arians, but also many others who "disturbed" the Church by using their own minds and choosing to believe what they thought was the best way to God and the best teachings for a moral and happy life. Constantine tried to abolish, in addition to his effort against the "pagans", all Christian heresies starting with the Novatians, then the Manicheans, the rejection of local groups and their elected officials of their local region. His sons carried on the prosecution of the unorthodox, the problem was, however, that the sons took opposite sides: Constans in the West was a homoousian (Athanasian-Catholic-Orthodox) and his other son who ruled the East, Constantius, was a homoiousian (Arian and non-Orthodox) Again homoousian believes that Jesus was equal to God in substance, but a homoiousian believes that Jesus was like God, but not of the same substance of the Father, who was superior to the Son. Same substance or similar substance to the Father was the questions and the cause of Christians hating each other, judging and killing each other. The Augustus (Emperor) of the West, Constans was a "same substance" believer and the Augustus of the East, Constantius was a "similar substance" believer. In the name of one whose only command to his disciples, according to the Gospel of John, was love one another, they judged, murdered and executed each other. This particular battle went on **b)** for more than two hundred years. Socrates gives this account of

George of Alexandria, an Arian. Although Socrates' account was undoubtedly colored by his being an Athanasian, such happening did occur on both sides:

"Having kindled a fire, he set the virgin women (possibly nuns) near to it, in order to compel them to say that they accepted the Arian faith: but seeing they stood their ground and despised the fire, he then stripped them, and so beat them on the face, that they could scarcely be recognized. Seizing also about forty men, he flogged them in an extraordinary manner that many, unable to bear the agony, died under its affliction. All the survivors they banished to the Great Oasis (a nearly isolated place far up the Nile towards central Africa)." (Bk 2 Chapter 28)

c) These kinds of violence happened often on both sides of the conflict. But there were other "heretics" and other conflicts also. Macedonius and his followers were heretics. The Apollinarians were heretics. The religious situation was total havoc, fear and terror over which creed to believe and what creed the new Emperor had. In one short succession of Emperors it was crazy. Athanasius went into exile five times. Julian was a Platonist and called a halt to the lunacy of the Christians, but his reign was only three years. He was followed by Jovian, a homoousian, and he was followed by Valentinian, a strict Athanasian homoousian, and he was followed by Valens who was an Arian. One had to constantly change his position to stay alive. No wonder the Platonists were furious with the Christians and longed for the old democratic Rome of paganism. Constantine's desire to unify the Empire by forced indoctrination did not work, and the church could not figure it out that forced belief is concession, not faith. Everything, due to Christian zealotry, was in turmoil. Another passage from Socrates reads: "The bishops of Egypt, Arabia and Cyprus, combined against Flavian, bishop of Constantinople, and insisted on his expulsion from Antioch: but those bishops of Palestine, Phoenicia and Syria, contended with equal zeal in his favor. (Bk 5 Chapter 10). Heresy trials with death attached to it continued in Christian Europe until about 1800 CE.

d) D. The Church's Destruction of Spiritual Competitors

Many groups within the Church were striving to understand as best as possible the meaning of Jesus and his teachings of goodness and his implied way of salvation, and many of these conclusions were not satisfying to the Church which then condemned them. These were sincere people who chose to express their views, but they were labeled as heretics: docetists, those who objected to calling Mary the Mother of God, Sabellianism, Lucian and his followers, Anomoeans, Eunomeans, Nestorians, and the monophysite Eutychians. The creeds were stiffly frozen by 451 CE and any objection or unapproved interpretation of them were condemned. The Church now controlled all reasonable discussions and conclusions. Even in science the Bible and Church councils were the judges of what was heretical or not. What was left of free thought was killed off in 529 CE by Justinian, who closed all the schools of philosophy (Plato's Academy, the Stoa was closed, the Garden of Epicurus, and whatever was left of the Lyceum of Aristotle), their buildings were burned as well as their libraries, and all artifacts of value **49a)** were confiscated by the Emperor. In the late fourth century anything left to the pagan priests by will of a dying person was confiscated by the Christian emperors. Bury stated of Justinian: "Justinian surpassed them (preceding emperors) all in religious bigotry."3.12 Libanius asked for protection from the Emperor Theodosius in 386 against the monks who were destroying and robbing all the traditional temple sites in the East. In 389 Theodosius burned the Alexandrian library at the Sarapeion to destroy as much classical literature as possible. By 391 all access to pagan temples were forbidden. Eugenius, a liberal Christian, restored some of the pagan temples, and in 393 Theodosius defeated his guard and had him beheaded. Gibbon stated: "It must be acknowledged that the Christians, in the course of their intestine dissensions, have inflicted far greater severities on each other, than they had experienced from the zeal of the "infidels".3.13 In 380 CE Theodosius I issued his famous Edict that all in the Empire should be Christians. The following was said about the treatment of non-Christians during he reign of Valens by Sozomen, a Christian historian: "Therefore all were arrested; Theodore and the constructors of the tripod were commanded to be put to death, some with fire and some with the sword. Likewise...the most brilliant philosophers of the empire were slain; since the wrath of the emperor

was unchecked, the death penalty advanced even to those who were not philosophers, but who wore garments similar to theirs." (Bk 6 Chapter 35).
b) Concerning Justinian, the pagan historian Procopius, in his *The Secret History*, painted this picture of him:

"In fact he never even gave a hint of anger or irritation to show how he felt towards those who had offended him; but with a friendly expression on his face and without raising an eyebrow, in a gentle voice he would order tens of thousands of quite innocent persons to be put to death, cities to be razed to the ground, and all their possessions to be confiscated for the Treasury...to achieve his aim he engineered an incalculable number of murders. His ambition being to force everybody into one form of Christian belief he wantonly destroyed everyone who would not conform, and that while keeping a pretence of piety. For he did not regard it as murder, so long as those who died did not happen to share his beliefs. Thus he had completely set his heart on the continual slaughter of his fellow-men, and together with his wife he was constantly engaged in fabricating charges in order to satisfy this ambition."(13.3 ff).

c) The brutal murder of Hypatia shocked even some of the more pious Christians. Hypatia was probably in her 60s, was well known, highly honored and respected throughout the world, considered a type of noble who was adored by her many students in Alexandria. She was a devout Platonist and that is what she taught. Synesius was one of her students and wrote many letters to her, all in high praise of what she had done for him, as she was a type of Mother Philosophy to them all. She was the most respected Platonist of her age. Christian monks shamed and killed her and mutilated her body. Even Socrates Scholasticus who was a strong apologist for Christianity was so shamed that he had to report the disgrace of the act in his *Ecclesiastical History*. His sad account is as follows:

d) "There was a woman at Alexandria named Hypatia, daughter of the philosopher Theon, who made such attainments in literature and science, as to far surpass all the philosophers of her own time. Having succeeded to the school of Plato and Plotinus, she explained the principles of philosophy to her auditors, many of whom came from a distance to receive her instructions. On account of the self-possession and ease of manner, which she had acquired in consequence of the cultivation of her mind, she not unfrequently appeared in public in presence of the magistrates. Neither did she feel abashed in coming to an assembly of men. For all men on account of her extraordinary dignity and virtue admired her the more. Yet even she fell a victim to the political jealousy which at that time prevailed. For as she had frequent interviews with Orestes, it was calumniously reported among the Christian populace, that it was she who prevented Orestes from being reconciled to the bishop. Some of them therefore, hurried away by a fierce and bigoted zeal, whose ringleader was a reader named Peter, waylaid her returning home, and dragging her from her carriage, they took her to the church called Caesareum, where they completely stripped her, and then murdered her with tiles. After tearing her body in pieces, they took her mangled limbs to a place called Cinaron, and there burnt them. This affair brought not the least opprobrium, not only upon Cyril, but also upon the whole Alexandrian church."(Bk 7 Chapter 15)

50a) While this seems to be a straight forward account, more secular views attach Cyril to the entire plot to get rid of Hypatia. The church, of course, made Cyril of Alexandria a saint, and is referred to as St. Cyril of Alexandria. It is difficult to become a saint indeed, and murdering a noble and brilliant and beloved Platonist must have helped immensely. The fact that the mob took her to the church called Caesareum showed how proud they were of this act that they had to do it before the presence of their God. The glories of killing a heretic must surely please God was their thinking. Hypatia had stopped writing to one of her favorite students, Synesius, because he became a bishop in Ptolemais in Cyrene. Even though he told the people he was a Platonist and would preach Platonism, the people still wanted him as their bishop -- they were obviously afraid of an actual Christian being their bishop. But Hypatia, probably long attacked by Christians, never forgave him, if not answering many letters begging her to do so is so interpreted. Synesius was spared the terrible murder as he died the year (414 CE) before Hypatia was murdered (415 CE).

b) Once the Church won a favored position within the Empire it pushed the emperors towards the destruction of the pagan religions and philosophies. In all the political battles the Church was deeply involved in who was favored and who was not. Listen to the push that the church father Firmicus Maternus gave to the two Augusti, Constantius and Constans, one an Arian Christian and the other an Athanasian Christian. He sought to bring them together, not for peace itself, but for a united force against the Platonists and traditional religionists of the Roman Empire.

"To you, O Constantius and Constans, most sacred Emperors, must I now appeal--to you and to the might of your revered faith, which rises above our human level, withdraws from earthly frailty and joins the company of heaven, which, in its every act, serves to the best of its powers the will of God. Only a little remains to do ere the devil lies in utter ruin before your laws, ere the deadly contagion of the dead idolatry ceases to be. The venom of the poison has grown weak; day by day the reality of its profane desires declines. Raise high the standard of the Faith. Blessed are ye whom God has chosen to be sharers of His glory and His will, blessed ye for whose hands Christ in His favour has reserved the destruction of idolatry, the overthrow of the heathen temples." (*De Errore Profanarum Religionus*, 350 CE, Chapter 21)

c) And again from Maternus:

"Most sacred Emperors, strip the temples of their ornaments, strip and fear not. Let those vain gods be melted down by the fire of the mint or the blaze of the metal-worker's flame. Transfer all the temple gifts to the use of yourselves and of the Lord. Since you destroyed the temples, you have advanced mightily by the strong help of God...It only remains to destroy the forbidden idols." (Chapter 29)

The Church expanded by means of proclaiming myths, promising eternal life to believers, claiming they were chosen favorites of God -- the Elect (which carried with it a certain snob appeal to those of the poorer and less educated classes), destroying and confiscating the buildings of other religions and other believers, and also by fear in threatening their hearers with eternal hell of suffering if they did not believe. On top of that, after they took over the Empire, their very own lives were threatened if they did not conform to the "accepted" Christian Faith. This could hardly have been the desires of Jesus of Nazareth, who is attributed with saying, "blessed are the meek, pray for those who persecute you, turn the other cheek, love your enemies, give to those who are too poor to pay you back, and be perfect as your Heavenly Father is perfect."

d) III. THE DISSENTERS

Already early in the Second Century CE the Christians were to be seen as a pollution to society and dangerous to society by the Roman people. Tacitus, although sympathetic to their sufferings under Nero, still sees them as a negative development within the Empire. He calls them, "hated for their abominations, whose leader was put to death under Pontius Pilate, a people whose belief was a horrible superstition that was breaking out all over the Empire and by and large they had a hatred for the human race (Tacitus' *Annals*, 15, 44). Pliny the Younger was serving in the East under the Emperor Trajan and was confused as to how to handle the Christians. He was uneasy about punishing them, although he had ordered some "obstinate" ones to death after refusing to disown their Christianity. This action bothered him, nevertheless he saw the spread of Christianity to have severe evil effects upon the morality of the Empire. He was afraid that they would contaminate others with their superstitious way and bring them to moral harm. He stated about his judgment of them:

51a) "All I could discover was an evil and extreme superstition. I therefore postponed the trial and have resorted to asking your counsel. The chief reason why I have thought it proper to consult you is the number of the persons in jeopardy (of being corrupted by Christians). Many of all ages, of all ranks, of both sexes, are being brought into danger, and will continue to be brought. The blight of this superstition has not been confined to towns and villages; it has even spread to the country." (Epistle 96, Pliny to the Emperor Trajan)

b) A generation after Pliny, a Platonists scholar by the name of Celsus made a comprehensive and critical study of Christianity. It is no surprise that it did not survive. But the foremost Christian scholar of the time, Origen, who himself was sympathetic to Platonism, tried to answer Celsus' criticisms. In his work we have much of Celsus' complaints against the Christians because Origen addressed them. But it would be only natural that Origen would address those criticisms that he was capable of, for no one brings up a difficulty of an opponent's argument that he can not answer, but only those he feels he has a good answer against. In Origen's work *Contra Celsum* one finds the following arguments of Celsus against Christianity.

c)

1 Christianity is a *collegium illicitum*. "The Christians entered into secret associations with each other contrary to law".

2 They come out of Judaism which is barbarous in origin.

3. They teach and practice their doctrines in secrecy.

4 They try to identify with our philosophers, saying they are not a new branch of instruction.

5. They believe a myth that God wrote their commandments.

6. They claim their kind of monotheism is a common teaching.

7. They use the name of Jesus as a magical name by which they can overcome others. Magical incantations like theirs is superstition.

8. They claim that Jesus worked miracles like a sorcerer. For by his name alone the magical is performed.

9. Christians hold many irrational opinions.

10. Christians are upset when a logical investigation of their doctrines show inconsistencies and difficulties. They simply can not think critically.

d)

11. They despise philosophy and logic, and claim that their holy scriptures lead them to ultimate truth.

12. Christians realize that Moses is incorrect, but hide it by means of allegorical interpretations.

13. Christians believe that the world is not even 10,000 years old because they rely, not on science and logic, but Moses' books.

14. They believe Moses was ascended above all created things and made known the Creator and was far superior to Plato and other wise men of the Greeks and Romans.

15. The God they present is a case of emotional insecurity.

16. Yahweh's emotions run wild, proving he has little wisdom.

17 Jews claim to have initiated circumcision, when the Egyptians did.

18. The name of God is irrelevant, but Christians insist on Yahweh and Jesus as the only names to God.

19. Christians believe that because they know the proper name of
52a) God they have the power to expel evils of all kinds.
20. Jesus is presented as a wonder worker and his fame was spread throughout the entire world, but no one in the Empire has heard of it.
21, Their claim of the virgin birth of Jesus is even disputed by the Jews.
22. They claim Jesus was fully dead but then rose from death to life again.
23. They mangle and allegorize the Jewish prophecies to their own liking, and destroy the original meaning of them.
24. Both the Jewish Scriptures and the Christian teachings are full of myths. The myth among us that Plato had a virgin birth was rejected by us, realizing that some overly ambitious followers who did not know him created the myth.
25. God, as a Holy Spirit, appeared as a dove they declare: another foolish myth.
26. Their entire scriptures both of the law, the prophets, and about Jesus are full of myths.
27. Christians accuse Jews of corrupting their own Hebrew Scriptures when in reality it is the Christians who are corrupting them.
28. Against all history and reason, the Christians are determined to believe such stories.
29. They practice fantasy astronomy declaring an unknown star to have shown where Jesus was born.
30. If Jesus was God, or even a god, how could the magi honor him with such simple earthly gifts?
31. Herod's slaughter of the children of Bethlehem is likewise a myth and is not even, if it actually took place, a thing to be wondered
b) about.
32. Again they declare Jesus' divine origin.
33. Greeks do not believe Greek fables, but Jews and Christians believe theirs to be actual history.
34. Jesus, the God, is said to have hungered and thirsted and eaten food. Gods have no need of food.
35. It is obvious that his followers invented statements of Jesus after the fact.
36. God shows partiality if he loves only those whom Jesus knows.

37. Christians talk of God in a manner that is neither holy nor pious.
38. It is beneath the dignity of God to think that because of one blunder God would destroy with fire an entire area of people in both Sodom and Gemorrah.
39. Neither Jew nor Christian has ever invented anything in science.
40. Jewish and Christian genealogies are myths.
41. Creation of woman a myth: a rib from Adam is ridiculous.
42. The speaking serpent is a fairy tale.
43. The story of Noah's ark does not make any sense.
44. That nations and their future characteristics could be effected by Jacob's blessings is foolish.
45. The entire story of Lot, his wife turning to stone, and his daughters getting him drunk to have intercourse with him is far

c) beyond reason.

46. Many of the stories are so ridiculous that they take refuge in allegories.
47. All wise men know that the allegory game is an admission of a rather stupid story.
48. Concerning the resurrection of the body to eternal life, Celsus declared that no product of matter is immortal.
49. The nature of God and his sense of justice are insulted by stories like the flood, the famines, and Sodom and Gommorah.
50. God is not the creator of natural disasters, they happen because of the laws of nature.
51. Jews and Christians put too much, almost magical, emphasis on what they call the Supreme Being. No name can properly symbolize God.
52. Christians believe they have special favor with God and to them alone he sends messengers (angels). God is not partial.
53. Plato does not claim any special revelation. He is given reason as are all humans.
54. The marvels and myths the Gospels' writers claim of Jesus are fictitious.
55. In Plato God is beyond words.
56. The venerable character of the Christian Scriptures is contrary to human reason.

57. Special revelations by souls being lifted to the heavens are
d) mythical.
58. There is no Satan or Devil as Christians claim.
59. Mosaic cosmology is contrary to science.
60. Evil, in itself, has no real existence.
61. The creation periods of "days" before days existed shows as lack of both logic and science.
62. That God forgets, awakes from slumber, and limits his activity to Palestine is irrational.
63. Prophetic sayings are post facto and created falsely to prove their God has the power over time and the future.
64. All these ludicrous legends and myths are allegorized to save face and the embarrassment they give when taken literally.

53a) One can see, despite not have the writing of Celsus himself, simply by Origen's long defense, that Celsus pointed to many of the beliefs of the Christians that would be unacceptable to a Platonist philosopher, which Celsus was. But there were many others who dissented against both early Christian evangelism, and to the forced conversions after Constantine's Nicene Creed of 325 CE.

Galen who was born 129 CE was a contemporary of Celsus and a religious man who studied both science and philosophy. He is best known for his medical works. Working with the mangled bodies of the Gladiators, both the living and the dead, he came to study human anatomy and how the body functions. He did experiments and cures for the cuts and infections and figured that science and religion could be harmonious with each other. But he rejected all religions that refused scientific research for repairs of the body and depended only on faith. It was in this sense that he thought Christianity was a second rate and even dangerous religion. Physicians and philosophers were wise, but to the followers of Moses and Christ one is just as well off teaching them novelties. For all they talked about were undemonstrated and unverified laws. They were simply, with their mindset, incapable of scientific thought. Yet, Galen admitted, some of them live ethically a life worthy of a philosopher. But they were certainly a hindrance to science. This was, of course, 150 years before Constantine, and after Constantine science and human anatomy and other such studies were forbidden. Yes, Christians were dangerous in the sense that they stopped research for the cures of the body well as all scientific study about life, "leave it to God in faith" was their way of healing. After all, if God wanted a man to be cured he would send a saint and a miracle would be performed, and to reject the concept of miracles and saints was heresy. Christians were not yet a threat to Galen and he thought more of their primitive and childish thoughts than their danger to his own day. Lucian also saw Christians as

b) believing things "without any definite evidence". The Stoic Marcus Aurelius saw Stoics as being controlled by reasoned and dignified actions but Christians by thoughtless obstinacy and opposition to logic. Aristides, the teacher of Marcus Aurelius, despised the Christians, not so much for their own thoughts, but for their missionary tactics of scaring people with hell and Satan so that many Roman families were torn apart by their different reactions to Christian evangelism. Lucian mocked Christians as people who would follow any self proclaimed prophet who was really a con artist, and he created one such Cynic to Christian priest named Peregrinus Proteus, who very quickly had the Christians he too was a god, for, in Lucian's mind, Christians had no common sense or logic to their choice of leaders.

c) There was a man by the name of Apollonius called the wise man of Tyana. Julia Domna, the wife of the Emperor Septimius Severus who ruled from 193-211 CE., wanted to know more of this proclaimed wonder worker and wise man. She commissioned the historian Philostratus to write a history of Apollonius, and Philostratus accepted (it was both wise and profitable to say yes to the Emperor's wife). The motives of Philostratus remain unclear because he did not finish the work until 220 CE, three years after Julia Domna died. He presented a very fictional life of this wonder worker despite her death. Being a good historian it is doubtful that Philostatus actually believed the account he gave. So why give it? Some have suggested that he paralleled the life of Jesus as found in the Gospels who was also proclaimed as a wonder worker, and he did it to spoof the beliefs of Christianity. No one, of course, knows, and Philostratus never told. But since most of the pagan scholars felt that Christians believed such illogical things it is possible that he did a spoof of them. The Church historians Zosomen, Socrates Scholasticus and Eusebius all recorded the "miracles" of the followers of Christ throughout the first centuries of Christianity. And there is no doubt that the vast majority of Christians believed in miracles.

d) A more serious and philosophical attack on Christianity came about 55 years later, about 275 CE by the Platonic Philosopher Porphyry. It was welcomed by the general pagan public and was popular until Galerius' act in 311 CE, who felt his sickness was due to his anti-Christian exploits and then begged the Christian God for forgiveness and this brought down the popularity of Porphyry's work. But it remained a force among the Platonists until the Caesar-papist church demanded (by decree of Theodosius II) that all copies be burned to bring its existence to an end in 448 CE. As with Origin's *Contra Celsus*, some of the attacks of Porphyry were preserved by Macarius' replies to his works. Macarius was a Christian apologist and thankfully his replies give posterity some of the fragments of Porphyry's work. From Macarius Magnetis' *Apocriticus* it can be determined that Porphyry claimed that:

54a) Christ was merely a human being, and declared so himself with the question "Why do you call me good, no one is good except God?" (This is from Mark 10:18).

Christ contradicts himself when he says "If I bear witness to myself, then my witness is not true", and then he goes on and declares himself to be the light of the world.

The Gospels themselves are fictions and often contradict one another.

That Satan exists.

Why would Jesus pray so fervently to avoid death if he knew he was going to be raised within a couple of days?

Why does Jesus refer to the writings of Moses when all those writings were by Ezra and his contemporaries?

b) It is a totally unbelievable story that Christ would cure two demoniacs by slaughtering 2000 swine.

Jesus told the disciples that the anointing of his feet with precious ointment was justified because he was not always going to be with them, and then later telling them "I shall be with you to the end of the world".

It is totally unreasonable that one would be able to move a mountain if one had faith no bigger than a mustard seed.

The story of Ananias and Sapphira is fiction, and if true portrays a vicious god.

Paul creates an entire new theology than Christ taught.

c) Porphyry had many more complaints to which Macarius Magnes gives replies, but these are sufficient to show that the dissent against the Christian claims continued while it was possible.

Julian, Emperor from 361-363 CE, tried to restore liberties, benefits, temples and altars, and prestige to Platonist and other philosophers. He took back many of the temples that were confiscated by the Christian emperors before him, restored the traditions benefits to run them that they had enjoyed in the pre-Christian years, and neglected the Christians except to make them quit killing each other. He even mocked them that they were safer now than there were during the civil strife between Arians and Athanasians--and, in fact the Christians were safer under his rule, their mutual slaughtering of each other was harnesed the three short years he ruled before being killed in battle against the Persians. He also, being a well educated Platonic philosopher himself, he wrote extensively; one of his works critical of Christianity called *Against the Galileans*, in which he spoke much the same way as did Celsus and Porphyry before him. He declared the Christians to be basically troublemakers because of their constant battles with each that seemed to turn everything upside down. He wrote a letter to one Hecebolius condemning the Arian Christians for attacking the less popular Valentinian Gnostic Christians in Edessa for it was destroying the city. He was angry with another group of Christians who set fire to the temple of Apollo at Daphne, a beautiful suburb of Antioch. Even Sozomen, the church historian, calls Julian's "persecution" a wise shifting of political benefits instead of an attack on the structure or leaders of the Church. With other religions he seemed very open, but he **d)** disliked those who practiced castration to avoid the evil of sexual pleasure--sex was never an evil among Platonists. Julian was also a somewhat ecclectic and thought those who claimed to "own" God as their personal possession as being ridiculous. Unfortunately he died very young, no older than 31 years. Libanius (314-395 CE), another Platonist, kept a rather low profile despite his near adoration of Julian, whose death grieved him greatly.

55a) Eunapius, 346-414CE, was a Platonist and historian of philosophers who lived during this terrible age for philosophers and lived a life of hatred and fear of the growing power of Christianity. His period saw the final decline of classical studies of the ancient Greeks and Romans, a sadness felt also by Libanius of Antioch. Sacrifices to the gods was proscribed during his lifetime and the official abolition of paganism under Theodosius I in 391 CE. His *Universal History* did not survive the Christian burnings of books. He talks of the time of fear for pagans for "Constantine was pulling down the most celebrated temples and building Christian churches". He tells of the terror that Theophilus, the bishop of Alexandria, exercised against the Platonists and philosophers of the pagans. He and Evagrius "girding themselves in their wrath against our sacred places as though against stones and stone-masons, made a raid on the temples, and though they could not allege even a rumour of war to justify them, they demolished the temple of Serapis and made war against the temple offerings, whereby they won a victory without meeting a foe or fighting a battle...next, into the sacred places (that had been taken away from the pagans) they imparted monks, as they called them, who were men in appearance but led the lives of swine, and openly did and allowed countless unspeakable crimes."(472).

b) This chapter will be closed by statements from William Ralph Inge (1860-1954 CE) who was Lady Margaret Professor of Divinity at Cambridge (1907-11) and Dean of St.Paul's Cathedral in London (1911-1934 CE). He makes the following statements in his *Platonic Tradition in English Religious Thought* about the horror of Christian rule in Europe.

"After Constantine, there is not much that is not humiliating--the long period of dogmatic squabbling while the Empire was falling to pieces; the destruction or loss of most of the irreplaceable treasures of antiquity; the progressive barbarisation of Europe; we need not follow the melancholy record. It is the story of a corporation [the Christian Church] growing rich and powerful, not of a spiritual leaven gradually leavening the whole lumb...The record of Christian institutionalism is one of the darkest chapters in history...An ecclesiastical institution...lives partly exploiting the credulity of the vulgar, and partly by making unholy alliances...The few moral and humanitarian reforms which may be justly be set to the credit of organised religion have been, I think, mainly the work of sectarians. It seems to me equally plain that ecclesiasticism has been, from the highest point of view, a dismal failure...we want a faith which need not be afraid of scientific progess...the disciples of Plato have perhaps given us an outline of the solution."

ΔΕΛΤΑ

Δ

CHAPTER FOUR
CHRISTIAN EUROPE

I. THE CHURCH SOLIDIFIES ITS POWER AND GREED

56a) Justinian who solidified the power of the Church also laid down a solid foundation for the Church's control of all aspects of man's life in Europe. There were several law codes extant when Justinian decided update and change them into a more unified power, which he did in his Corpus Iuris Civilis, The Corpus of the Civil Law. It will be adequate to quote just a couple of sections for the reader to identify the lust for power that was desired for the Church by Justinian. First he claims an obligation to empower the religion of the Holy Trinity because by the Majesty of God the state is maintained and it is successful at war.

"With the aid of God governing our Empire which was delivered to us by His Celestial Majesty. We carry on war successfully. We adorn peace and maintain the Constitution of the State, and have such confidence in the protection of Almighty God that we do not depend upon our arms, or upon our soldiers, or upon those who conduct our wars, or upon our own genius, but we solely place our reliance upon the providence of the Holy Trinity, from which we are derived the elements of the entire world and their disposition throughout the globe."

b) Now notice, since they feel they run the entire globe, how they silence dissent and the free choice of both Christians and non-Christians:

"The holy patriarchs of every diocese, the metropolitans and the remaining reverend bishops and clergy, shall observe inviolate and in conformity with the sacred canons the rules which we have above established, and shall, for the future, observe the worship of God and the discipline of the Church unimpaired, under the penalty of being rejected by God, and excluded from the sacred order of the priesthood as being unworthy of it...and in accordance with the sacred apostolic canons of the Church, may inflict the proper penalty upon those who are guilty...If this was done, ...all would themselves master the sacred liturgies, and live temperately through fear of being rendered liable to condemnation under the divine canons."

c) Whenever the Church had problems in controlling everyone it found ways to justify its control. In the middle of the Eighth Century, 750 CE, it created a document claiming that Constantine himself gave over to the Church all authority on earth, including authority over the Emperor and all those who succeeded him in power including all future emperors and kings. It was used to empower the Church, especially in conflicts between the emerging European states and the Church of Rome, and did so successfully for 700 years until Lorenzo Valla during the Renaissance proved it was a forgery. The Church lamented, but never repented. Below are some of the phony claims made by the Church that Constantine gave it power over the Roman Empire and its successors.

"We (Constantine's court) decreed that his (Papacy's) sacrosanct Roman church should be honored with veneration to the extent of our power, and that the most sacred seat of St. Peter's is gloriously exalted above our empire and earthly throne. We gave it imperial power, the dignity of glory, strength, and honor...We ordain and decree that he should have dominion over the four principal dioceses of Antioch, Alexandria, Constantinople, and Jerusalem, as well as over all the churches of the world....If anyone, which we do not believe possible, scorns or despises this decree, he shall be bound by eternal damnation. He shall know that the holy chiefs of the apostles of God, Peter and Paul, will oppose him in the present and future life, and that having been burned in deepest Hell, he shall perish with the devil and all impious men."

Yes, the Church was doing its job and proclaiming the Good News of God's love and forgiveness and the hope of everlasting life. The Church used fear probably more than any other institution in the course of human history and used it for the longest time, and it even clothed it in hypocrisy. The amount of spiritual harm and destroyed minds the Church caused to those under it domain is truly staggering.

d) But there was even more to come. As developing areas of Europe became conscious of their identities there was a movement towards primitive nationalism, and their kings wanted out from some of this control that the Papacy had over them and their people. Henry the Fourth of France was headed in that direction and this caused a serious conflict with the Pope, Gregory VII (1073 -- 1085). Popes, of course, used things like excommunication (if you died while under its judgment, you went to hell forever) and interdict, which forbad the clergy of a certain land from performing the sacraments and other services thereby withhold the forgiveness of sins for all those of a region, especially those who supported their own king against the Papacy. But Gregory wanted even more power and brought forth his own Dictatus Papae: a Statement of the Pope. Listed below are some of his claims.

e)

1 That the Roman Church was founded by God alone.

2. That the Roman Pontiff (Pope) alone is rightly to be called universal.

3. That he alone can depose or reinstate bishops.

4. That his legate, even if of lower grade, takes precedence, in a council, of bishops and may render a sentence of deposition against them.

5. That the Pope may depose the absent.

6. That for him alone it is lawful to enact new laws according to the needs of the time, to assemble together new congregations, to make an abbey of a canonry; and, on the other hand, to divide a rich bishopric and unite the poor ones.

7 He alone may use the imperial insignia.

8. That the Pope is the only one whose feet are to be kissed by all princes.

9. That his title is unique in the world.

10. That he may depose Emperors.

11. That no synod may be called a general one without his order.
12. That no chapter or book may be regarded as canonical without
57a) his authority.
13. That he himself may be judged by no one.
14. The Roman Church has never erred, nor ever, by the witness of scripture, shall err to all eternity.

Those are only some of the claims that Gregory VII made for himself. They were uncontested. The church, and its leader, took control over all of Europe in every way: who had the keys to salvation, who had the only doctrines all must believe, who could control schools and dictate and close monasteries, who can interpret the Scriptures, the previous synods and laws, whether any chapter or book of the Bible could be translated from the Latin. He had the total power over sacraments and the priests, the bishops and the princes, the kings and the emperors. And he could never be wrong, or challenged. Women and "witches", Jews and Moors, heretics and priests with wives, teachers and medics, monasteries and nunneries, and every other part of Europe suffered under his control. Those who wrote novels always had to conclude in last pages of the book **b)** that if a person described within the novel, especially if he had a couple of lovers, did not repent before he died, he would be damned forever. So writers went ahead and wrote some rather raunchy stuff, but always tacked on the finishing pages an admonition that if anyone lives that way he will surely burn in hell. In general this was not too much of a problem, because during the Middle Ages the clerics were the only ones who, generally speaking, could read and write. Those outside the clergy, unless from royalty, had little chance of reading. Even as late as Martin Luther (1483 -- 1546), after 200 years of the Renaissance and 50 after Gutenberg's printing press, still, it is estimated, only 4% of all Germans could read. The "Dark Ages" were brought on more by the Church who destroyed classical culture, their libraries, their temples, and burned private collections of books than by all the Vandals, Huns, and Goths combined. In fact, the Goths, because they were Arian Christians, had all their books burned by edict by the council of Toledo in 589 by King Reccared who formally renounced the Arian creed, and the works of Ulphilas were also destroyed.

c) Our period of 529 CE to 1300 CE ends with another extravagant claim by the Bishop of Rome, Boniface VIII who issued, in 1302 CE, the *Unam Sanctam* declaring that there was only One Holy and Apostolic Church, the one in Rome of which he was the leader. It did not really proclaim anything new, but for a new age of learning and the growing desire of nations for their own rule, it was a firm reminder that everything is under the authority of the Papacy in Rome. It emphasized that the Pontif Maximus was the God-appointed ruler of the world; exerting power over both the spiritual and temporal realm on earth. Kings were justified only if they accepted their inferiority to the Pope, and acknowledged that they were only in their position of authority because the Pope appointed them to their position. It claimed very clearly that outside the Roman governed Church there was no salvation for any person on earth.

d) This lust for total control of human activity was seen in the Church even before Constantine, it simply did not have the power to exert itself fully until after Constantine. Gibbon declared that Christianity even during the reign of Diocletian was a race of political hungry priests seeking higher appointments so that they could exert more authority. He said:

"Prosperity had relaxed the nerves of discipline. Fraud, envy, and malice prevailed in every congregation. The presbyters aspired to the episcopal office, which every day became an object more worthy of their ambition. The bishops, who contended with each other for ecclesiastical pre-eminence, appeared by their conduct to claim a secular and tyrannical power of the church; and the lively faith which still distinguished the Christians from Gentiles was shown much less in their lives than in their controversial writings." (*Decline and Fall of the Roman Empire*: Chapter XVI).

II. ALL KNOWLEDGE AND RELIGIOUS MORALS ARE SUBJECTED TO THE CHURCH

58a) The most intimate human act, that of physical love and intercourse, was invaded by the arrogance of the Church which declared what acts can be done without sin, when they can be done, when the woman or the man was in a state of defilement or uncleanness, what penalties related to what sins, and whether or not they were permitted in church or could partake of the sacraments (this was particularly hard on women), and with whom acts of intimacy can take place. The Church had come into the bedroom and haunted, like a flock of evil demons, those who shared the human embrace.

It did not help much when a monk became Pope Gregory I "The Great" (590 CE to 604 CE) and issued his letters to the missionary Augustine, a monk whom he had sent to England with forty other monks to convert the Anglo-Saxons and who became known as Augustine of Canterbury. Naturally when Augustine found a vibrant race of Saxons there he wanted to know what to tell them about sex, at least "approved sex" so that they would not fall into grave sin and make themselves liable for hell. After hearing what Augustine had to tell him about Christianity and its restrictions on human intimacy, King Ethelbert was hospitable, but not converted. First Augustine is told that those marriages already functioning among the English, if they do not conform to Papal law, then they must be broken up. How arrogant of these missionaries to come into a new country, be received politely and hospitably, and then to tell their hosts that they must destroy their marriages lest they suffer the punishment of such grave sins! Pope Gregory writes Augustine:

b) "But since there are many among the English who, while they were still heathen, seem to have contracted these unlawful marriages, when they accept the Faith they are to be instructed that this is a grave offence, and that they must abstain from it. Warn them of the terrible judgement of God lest their bodily desires incur the pains of eternal punishment."(I.27)
[All quotations are taken from Bede's *A History of the English Church and People]*.

During the menstrual period women were also considered unclean, and even after having a child she would remain untouchable until the child was weaned. "Until the child is weaned, a man should not approach his wife...for even apart from childbirth, women are forbidden to do so (have sexual intercourse) during their monthly courses, and the Old Law prescribed death for any man who approached a woman at this time." (I.27). Sexual relations could make a man defiled as well as a woman. "It

c) is not fitting that a man who has approached his wife should enter church before he has washed, nor is he to enter it at once, though washed. A married man and woman both risk being polluted merely by the fact of being married, for the natural lust of sexual relations was always there. "In making this observation, we do not condemn marriage itself, but since lawful intercourse must be accompanied by bodily pleasure, it is fitting to refrain from entering a holy place, since desire itself is not blameless." (I.27)...."In saying this, he does not term the union of married people iniquity, but the pleasures of such union. For there are many things that are lawful and legitimate, and yet in the doing of them we are to some extent contaminated." (I.27) And again:

"Lawful intercourse should be for the procreation of offspring, and not for mere pleasure; to obtain children, and not to satisfy lust. But if any man is not moved by a desire for pleasure, but only by a desire for children, he is to be left to his own judgement either as the entering church, or to receiving the Communion of the Body and Blood of our Lord; for we have no right to debar one who does not yield to the fires of temptation. But when lust takes place of desire for Children, the pair have cause for regret." (I.27)

d) Unfortunately this set the standard judgmental opinion against the joy of human intimacy and held captive the consciences of Christians for centuries plaguing them with feelings of guilt and frustrating the one who desired the sheer pleasure of intimacy while the other succumbed to church doctrine for the sake of conscience. How many marriages were ruined by the Church because of this: how controlling and how condescending! In 1215 the papal decree Omnis Utruisque Sexus was issued by the Fourth Lateran Council. Annual confessions were to related the exact circumstances of all sins, with whom, when, and all the particulars. It is almost like asking the confessors to portray and adult mental video for the sex hungry priests. And sexual sins were rated as to how evil they were, and according to one manual there were 16 degrees or levels of sexual sins. Remember, sex was only for procreation, and even innocent touching and caressing were sinful. An "unchaste" kiss was a sin, even between the married, for it gave pleasure without the ability of producing children. Also, the following, although hard to believe, believe it: that the act of a father having forbidden sex with his daughter (most likely against her will) was a lesser sin than masturbation. For, at least, incest between the sexes could produce a child, but masturbation was simply for pleasure--and to the Church that seemed to be the root of all evil, even from Augustine of Hippo and ever thereafter. A book published in 1955 edited by Heribert Jone and Urban Adelman, high officials of the Roman Catholic in Germany published Moral Theology. It was used by many Catholics and had total consent **59a)** from the Roman Church: the Nihil Obstat and the Imprimi Postest by four different Catholic authorities and was translated from the German, not only in English, but also in French, Italian, Polish, Dutch, Portuguese and Spanish and, at that time, 1955, had 16 reprints (editions). Of course, it had a lengthy section on the sins of impurity. Since all sexual pleasure was forbidden even to the married, how much more was it sinful for those not married. Any type of sexual stimulation was forbidden, any sexually romantic kiss was sinful, all petting was sinful. "Fornication" "is voluntary sexual intercourse between unmarried persons." Concubinage and prostitution "do not differ specifically from fornication." Of course, and it seems that all religions would agree, that all adultery, rape, and abduction is gravely sinful. The "unnatural sins of impurity" are: any self-stimulation is gravely sinful; a nocturnal "pollution" is sinful if you are half awake; sodomy even by the married is sinful--because it can not produce children; any sexual commotion--bodily movements that might produce some sexual stimulation is sinful; ardent, prolonged and repeated kissing is sinful, even among the married and likewise tongue-kissing. It is also sinful to look at one's genitalia for curiosity or levity. But this is far and enough to show the great powers that the Church exerted, or at least tried to exert, over all the people of Europe from Justinian to the Renaissance and Reformation when a rebellion took place that it could not totally destroy. All of this while the hierarchy of the Church had concubines and swam abundantly in the deepest waters of sexual pleasure themselves. Therefore, they added to their arrogance of power to control the sin of hypocrisy. Nigel Cawthorne has written a book called *Sex Lives of the Popes* and it was published in 1996 by Prion in London. For those interested it is comprehensively thorough and carries the reader back to the time of Justinian.

b) Because human intimacy is so vital to human happiness I have handled it somewhat in length, but it is only one way during this time of

"Babylonian Captivity", to use a phrase of Luther, in which the Church crushed individual freedom, mental thought, medical care, and the pursuit of happiness. Another, most important aspect of human happiness is health, which Plato called the greatest of earthly virtues. The Platonists themselves, including Galen and many others, especially Aretaios who in many ways was said to have surpassed Galen, but his writings did not survive well. Julian, the Platonist Emperor from 361-363 CE, sponsored Oribasius (325 to 403 CE) who then compiled a medical encyclopedia and was personal physician to Julian. In the Greek East medical treatment was less hindered than in the Roman West. But even after Paul of Aegina (607 to 690 CE), the last of the Byzantine encylopedists, nothing new was developed for the next thousand years. Basically, the Church froze medicine to immobility by accepting the uses of Galen, for he was not permitted at his time to do autopsies, and because the Church **c)** froze Galen into the accepted views, nothing could develop further until Harvey's discovery of the circulation of the blood in 1628 CE. Yet, the dissent was alive, and under very limited conditions the West was seeking medical help to improve the life of the sick, and it was in Salerno as early as the ninth century that a school of medicine was coming alive to initiate some type of medical progress. The French also slowly awakened to the need of surgery and medical treatment, and Guido Lanfranc (died 1315 CE) conservatively made some progress in freeing breathing with a silver tube and trying to understand concussions and the brain. He had a humanistic education but his academic career fell short when excluded from University of Paris, because the professors there were obligated to live in celibacy. But it was not until the Renaissance that humanistic, most of it Platonic and Aristotelian, endeavors begin to break out into the open and challenge the Church.

d) In Astronomy it is enough to mention the names of Copernicus and Galileo to show the stubbornness of the Church towards anything it could not understand itself. If forbid the teaching of Copernicus' ideas and forced Galileo to recant. How shameless!

III. THE CHURCH'S SOLUTIONS TO HAPPINESS AND HEALTH: SUPERSTITIONS, RELICS, THE HEALING MAGIC OF THE SACRAMENTS, MIRACLES, OILS, LAYING ON OF HANDS, PRAYERS, RITUALS AND EXORCISMS..

60a) It will not be necessary to see the anti-scientific, anti-logical, and fear of facing the fact that the Church simply did not have all the answers to human health and happiness. So it came up with rituals or sacraments, or long prayers often purchased with money, relics that could be seen for a fee, exorcisms that could be received for a fee, and miracles that just seemed to happen to those faithful to the Church. Of course, it is amazing how the number of miracles diminished with the discoveries of science. In all these things, the "first modern men" of the 1300s, building upon the progress of the High Middle Ages, and starting, as some believe, with Petrarch who discovered and purchased so many ancient manuscripts so that a rebirth (renaissance) of the ancient Greeks and Romans could instill the spirit of the quest for knowledge, science, and personal freedoms.

ΕΨΛΟΝ

Ψ

CHAPTER FIVE
RENAISSANCE - REFORMATION - DISSENT

I. CHURCH. LOSING CONTROL, TRIES AN INQUISITION

61a) When the Cathedral Schools gave way to secular universities the Church began to lose some control over men's minds and souls. Peter Lombard listed some Sentences that required thinking in order to discuss them but Peter Abelard went further and presented many contradictory statements by the church fathers and asked for a yes or no (Sic et Non). Learning to think again, men's minds became more selective in reaching conclusions. Even Thomas Aquinas posited many apparently contradictory statements but he gave more orthodox answers and was in less conflict with the church than Abelard. But Abelard became popular and soon the old Cathedral schools lost out to but were a foundation for the coming of the universities, the first of which was the University of Paris, founded in 1200 CE. Shortly thereafter, because of the many recovered manuscripts from antiquity that was accomplished first by Petrarch, the "Rebirth" ("Renaissance" in French) of ancient culture was born. For the first time in almost a thousand years, the wisdom of the ancients was able, by the courage of a few intellectuals, to offer a competing view to man's dignity and value, and the Church fought back with a vengeance. Yet in the long run it would lose the conflict, for within another century the Greeks fleeing the onslaught of the Turks brought their books to Italy and the great Greek humanism and philosophy, with Plato the soul and Aristotle the structure, men had something else to look to for the beauty of life, and man again found his personal dignity. Led by Cosimo and Lorenzo de Medici a "Platonic Academy" was founded in Florence, and men like Ficino, Pico della Mirandola, Patrizi, Bruno and others led the way with the rebirth of Platonic Thought from the writings of Plato himself. Platonic thought was always there but in Neo-platonic form: from Augustine, Plotinus, and the Pseudo-Dionysius. But now they had the entire corpus of Plato's writings, not just the Timaeus, but some twenty more dialogues.

b) The Church responded with the Inquisition. Added to fear of hell, excommunications, interdicts, persecutions, slaughters of groups and executions of individuals, was torture. The inquisition had its beginning with the heavy handed Emperor Frederick II in 1232 when he issued an edict for the entire empire that the heretics and distrusted officials were to be found out. But Pope Gregory IX quickly took over the idea-- he did not want the political order to have so much authority-- and he appointed Papal inquisitors: but instead of theologians and bishops he sent Dominicans and Franciscans who wandered the country to find heretics. The Dominicans justified their name (hounds of the Lord) by smelling out as many offenders as possible. After Boniface VIII, the stress was more on punishment than an honest judgment, and after Innocent the IV, 1252 CE, the guilty and unrepentant were handed over to the secular authorities to be burned at the stake. Torture made its way into the process under Innocent IV, and it gained efficiency under Ferdinand V and Isabella of Spain starting in 1479 CE. All suffered: doctors of medicine, chemists-alchemists, teachers, astronomers, theologians, printers, general dissenters, and those who suffered most brutally were those accused of being witches, of whom probably 90% were women. Joseph Bonaparte abolished it in 1808 CE, but it started up again in 1814 CE and came to a final end in 1820 CE. For only a dozen years short of 600 years the Roman Catholic Church's Inquisition brutalized, tortured, and executed innocent people simply because they would not bend to and live in accordance with the tyrannical demands of the Papacy.

c) Because those accused of being witches were so brutally treated, and there were so many of them, it is necessary for a few pages to show how ugly the Church became. First of all, it must be understood that every advantage possible was taken of these frightened and tortured women of all ages. The idea that there were witches was not a well accepted view during the "dark ages", and, in fact, in Eighth Century CE Boniface, the English apostle of Germany taught that it was unchristian to believe that witches and werewolves existed. Likewise Charlemagne decreed the death penalty for the just conquered Saxons if any of them accused a person of being a witch and burning them. He considered it a heathenish custom. But the Church changed slowly until 1490 CE it was clearly taught that there were witches and they were satanic and dangerous for all Christians, and they were to be found out and punished. Every woman was in fear of being accused of being a witch. Rumors magnified their relationship to Satan and their numbers were said to be enormous: supposedly there were 800 meeting places in Lorraine alone where thousands of witches would meet to do honor to Satan their personal lover, in which many would have intercourse with him. When he appeared as a goat, the superstitious rumor was that they all kissed him under his tale. The inquisitors lacked no sense of the imagination in describing how corrupted and evil these witches were. It was said that at a French resort by the name of La Hendaye in South-West France, as many as 12,000 witches would meet for a gathering called the Aqularre. At some other meetings, known as Sabbats, the meetings were frequent, and the women were corrupted, loved by, and encouraged by Satan to destroy believers. Christians were led to believe much worse things about witches than the Romans ever believed about Christians. The Church leaders were perfectionists in propagandizing by their most evil accusations.

d) Pierre de Lancre (d. 1630 CE) was appointed by the parliament of Bordeaux to find out the witches of the territory, and, being a great admirer of the Spanish Inquisition, he desired to improve on its efficiency. In his sadistic reports he stated that a "witch" named Detsail, refused to receive a "kiss of pardon" from a handsome young man simply because she was tied to a stake and was about to be burned to death. Lancre could not understand why she would reject his kind jesture, after all, he declared, "she had kissed the 'back' of the devil many times before." However, Lancre was more encouraged by the fact that he could report a "witch" of fifteen was saved by repenting and after a session of brutal torture, with her "confession" proceeded to find other witches and detect other witches by an examination of their bodies for marks of the devil. Lancre honored her, for by detecting these marks of the devil she brought many others to be burned at the stake. That was the modus operandi, mode of operation, of the inquisitors. Torture the young and weak ones so brutally that they would "repent" and accuse any one they could of being fellow witches just to stop the torturing.

62a) The bishopric of Wuerzburg had a list of its people that they had burned, listed by each burning. Three examples follow:

The Sixth Burning, six persons:
The steward of the senate, named Gering
Old Mrs Canzler
The tailor's fat wife
The woman cook of Mr Mengerdorf
A stranger
A stranger, a woman.

The Thirteenth Burning, four persons:
The old smith of the court
An old woman
A little girl, nine or ten years old
A younger girl, her little sister.

The Twenty-Eighth Burning,
The wife of Knertz, the butcher
The infant daughter of Dr Schultz
A blind girl
Schwartz, canon at Hach
Ehling, a vicar
Bernhard Mark, vicar in the Cathedral. (5:1)

b) These people were executed for no other reason except someone accused them of being witches. Man or woman, cleric or artisan, adult or child, it made no difference to the Church As Kurt Seligmann pointed out, there were so many executions in every village and city that there developed a "witch industry" employing judges, jailers, tortures, exorcists, wood-choppers, scribes and experts. For the industry to continue, like a modern military industry needs wars, witches were needed. There was little hope of escaping death once one had been accused of being a witch, the industry must go on.

c) There were many "experts" on witch detection in all different areas of Europe. No person was safe. Johann von Schoeneburg, notorious heresy hunter in the area of Trier, who began his reign in 1581, destroyed first all Protestants, then all the Jews, and then he went after the witches. In the 22 villages of the area 368 "witches" were burned and in two of the villages only one woman was left alive. The industry was so wide spread that the Church needed an official "bible" by which to find out and "justly" kill the witches discovered. The papacy turned over that project to two theologians who held positions high up in the Church hierarchy. Pope Innocent VIII in December 1484 "aghast" of all the witches in Germany and their constant growth recruited two of his **d)**"beloved sons in the Lord", the Dominican inquisitors Heinrich Kraemer and Jacob Sprenger to exterminate Germany of its many thousands of witches. The two of them wrote the "bible" or "encyclopaedia" of demonology called the *Malleus Maleficarum*, the Hammer of Those Evil Ones, that is, the witches. And was it ever popular, for everyone wanted to find out the witches and have them killed. Between 1487 CE and 1520 CE there were 14 editions printed, and, again, between 1574 CE and 1669 CE there were 16 editions printed.

The very first word of the Malleus Maleficarum are:

63a) "Whether the belief that there are witches is so essential a part of the Catholic faith that obstinately to maintain the opposite opinion manifestly savours of heresy."

And again shortly later:

"Because the authority of the Holy Scriptures says that devils have power over the bodies and minds of men...Therefore those err who say that there is no such thing as witchcraft, but that it is purely imaginary."

Later again, but still in Part I. Question I. it is stated.

"Let it be known that all those who are commonly called sorcerers, and those too who are skilled in the art of divination, incur the penalty of death."

b) And why do women become witches and have sex with the devils? It is because women are so wicked. Part I. Question 6 it declares:

"What else is a woman but a foe to friendship, an unescapable punishment, a necessary evil, a natural temptation, a desirable calamity, a domestic danger, a delectable detriment, an evil of nature, painted with fair colors. Therefore if it be a sin to divorce her when she ought to be kept, it is indeed a necessary torture."

Of course this view of women was not unusual in the Catholic Church and seemed to prevail among the monks, especially the hounds of the Lord, Dominicans. Now, try to absorb this biblical interpretation:

c) "But the natural reason is that she is more carnal than a man, as is clear from her many carnal abominations. And it should be noted that there was a defect in the formation of the first woman (God messed up), since she was formed from a bent rib, that is, a rib of the breast, which is bent as it were in a contrary direction to man. And since through this defect she is an imperfect animal, she always deceives."

"All witchcraft comes from carnal lust, which is in women insatiable....... Wherefore for the sake of fulfilling their lusts they consort even with devils."

These two high ranking theologians at the right hand of Pope Innocent VIII continue at length about the evil, lustful, deceptive and carnal nature of women. Now on to torture. These two sons of the Church recommend in Part III. Question 14 the following for witches when they do not confess "the truth", that is, that they are witches with the above characteristics:

d) "The next step of the Judge should be that, if after being fittingly tortured she refuses to confess the truth, he should have other engines of torture brought before her, and tell her that she will have to endure these if she does not confess. If then she is not induced by terror to confess, the torture must be continued."

Of course the devil is a tough adversary and the inquisitors themselves are in great danger, but they must show courage to do the Church's work. But each first must, to take all precautions, "cross himself and approach her with courage, and with God's help the power of that old Serpent will be broken."

64a) The witches while being investigated were to be stripped of all their clothing, all bodily hair must be shaved off, and even "the most secret parts of her body" wherein she might hide some object that the devil gave her must be searched so that she would not have this devilish power to inflict harm on the inquisitor or others. Throughout the entire process the nakedness of the woman or her personal dignity is never considered, because she is a front for Satan (Part III. Question 15). It seems all too likely this was an excuse to molest or rape the woman by stripping her, shaving off all her hair and searching out the cavities of her body. It really seems that these churchmen were sadistic and filthy old men using these poor women for carnal gratification before they executed them. Often too the ordeal of the red hot iron, usually carried in the hands for some distance, was used. Likewise she is to be given false promises that if she tells of other witches who have slept with the devil she will be forgiven. But after she points to others and gives more names for the industry of the witch hunters, she is still executed. In Cologne (Koeln) one third of all the women who were executed were midwives, who made childbirth safer for all other women; this during the period between 1627 CE to 1630 CE. It has been estimated that during the 16th and 17th centuries alone there were about 200,000 women burned at the stake for practicing witchcraft. The numbers are staggering, especially when one considers the smallness of the population at that time: in Germany the largest city at the beginning of the 16th Century was Augsburg and it had only 35,000 people.

b) In the United States witchcraft had a short but ugly history. Most famous, of course, are the trials and executions in Salem. Founded by "puritans", it was one of the most intolerant groups of people ever to live on earth. They wanted a Puritan theocracy, all power to God, their God, and their views of God. And their views of God were that he was totally intolerant and hateful of those who did not worship him in the way that the Puritans thought he ought to be worshipped, the way they interpreted the Judeo-Christian Scriptures. They were intolerant to any deviation of opinion or thought or action that did not fit their theological straight-jacket. Roger Williams was among them, but with a truly pure heart and love for people: he made friends with the Indians, he understood those who were of a different mind, he believed in a separation of the power of the church and the power of the state. But he was virtually alone in his opinions and he was banished. He fled in 1636 CE with the help of his Indian friends and founded Providence, Rhode Island, and there he put his theories into practice. Non conformists had been persecuted since 1629 CE when Bishop Laud instigated the persecutions. Among those of these Puritans were John Winthrop and the Rev. John Harvard who founded the first university in America, although it was founded for the training of clergy for the Puritan Faith. In 1639 CE the General Court passed a law that none of a woman's arms be exposed by short sleeves. Schools were founded, but they were for the sole purpose of the indoctrination into Puritanism. In 1647 CE an act was passed that would punish any Catholic priests who were found in the colony. Later a similar act was passed against the Quakers. In 1648 CE Margaret Jones was executed in Boston for being a "witch". In 1651 CE **c)** legislation against all forms of "immorality" is enhanced. Blasphemy and worship of any but the "true God" are listed as capital crimes. There are also by this time legislation against drunkenness, games, dancing, and showy apparel. It has been said in jest that the Puritans were at least consistent, they never permitted any one else to have any joyful fun and they never had any themselves. A horrible condition of living was imposed by these Protestant Puritans who themselves came to America for "religious freedom". Why America still celebrates their coming is beyond this writer, unless it is a historical colored celebration of jingoistic patriotic inebriation. In 1656 CE another witch by the name of Ann Hibbins is hanged. The following year there is a growing fear of those "dangerous" Quakers. After all, how is this Christian Puritan group going to tolerate a group of people who refuse to hurt any one? This Quaker threat to their Theocracy called for tough punishment:

"A Quaker, if male, for the first offense shall have one of his ears cut off; for the second offense have his other ear cut off; a woman shall be severely whipped; Also for the first offense, he or she shall have their tongues bored through with a hot iron."

d) In 1692 CE the witchcraft war came to a head and during that summer 14 women and 5 men were hanged and one pressed to death. This is what happens when radical true believers of any religion will do if the frenzy of self righteousness takes over their minds. The Salem hysteria began in the home of a clergyman; how deadly an evil, in the house of a "spiritual" leader of the community. And to defend these horrible actions, Governor Phipps summoned Boston's leading clergyman, Cotton Mather, for moral and theological support to justify the hangings. Mather complied. His work on witchcraft was called *TheWonders of the Invisible World.* Mather wrote such a superstitious book that one can only wonder **65a)** at the intelligence of his readers in believing what he had to say. He reported witches flying, cursing 14 cows and only one survived, and for everything that went wrong, a witch was found to blame: a man loses his money -- blame it on a witch; a wagon loses a wheel and crashes -- blame it on a witch; if one has a nightmare -- a witch had visited him while he was sleeping; diseases, tragedies, accidents all happened because a witch was near. They were working Satan's hatred of mankind and had to be stopped and thoroughly rooted out. At the trial of Susanna Martin she was accused of throwing to the ground (without touching them) women who approached her, she flew over a bridge. She cursed and killed 13 or 14 oxen, and she became a big cat and attacked a man at night while he was in bed and nearly killed him. These were all "verified" as proof that she was a witch.

b) But Mather gave hope with his advice that it had been proven that by saying the name of Jesus Christ, the witch devil will vanish at once. Also there was judicial help, the ghosts of those murdered would show up and identify the witch that had killed them. There was even a case where a witch made the cattle jump up high and talk, and then falling dead. Often before the trials a counselor, like our psychologists, would talk to the witch and would inevitably declare that she could never be cured, and death was the only solution. That is enough for the witch hunts. Mather was also terribly afraid of the evil that the Quakers would bring upon the colony. This is his letter to John Higginson in 1682.

c) "There be now at sea a ship called *Welcome*, which has on board 100 or more of the heretics and malignants called Quakers, with W. Penn, who is the chief scamp, at the head of them....(he requests that the ship *Porpoise* intercept the *Welcome*)...and make captive the said Penn and his ungodly crew, so that the Lord may be glorified and not mocked on the soil of this new country with the heathen worship of these people. Much spoil can be made of selling the whole lot to Barbadoes, where slaves fetch good prices in rum and sugar and we shall not only do the Lord great good by punishing the wicked, but we shall make good for His minister and people.

Yours in the bowels of Christ,
Cotton Mather"

d) Yes, they were just doing their duty glorifying the Lord and making a little profit on the side. Truly they were giving in the name of Jesus a nice Christian welcoming to the ship *Welcome.* Fortunately William Penn and his Quakers eventually settled southwest of Boston, and had a state named for them (Pennsylvania = Penn's Woods; and Pennsylvania is known at the "Quaker State") -- at least some justice that history gave these persecuted people. Today, except among the Christian Fundamentalists, Cotton Mather's name stands for the bigotry that was truly his own.

Literature of all kinds also came under the investigation of the Church, and if found not acceptable, it was destroyed and both the writer and, later, the printer were warned and made to repent or give some type of retraction. The great Fourteenth Century CE English writer, Chaucer, not wanting to risk further the anger of the Church wrote the following retraction:

66a) "Now praye I to hem alle that herkne this litel tretis or rede, that if ther be any thing in it that liketh hem, that therof they thanken oure Lord Jesu Crist, of whom proceedeth al wit and al goodness. And if ther be any thing that displese him, I praye hem also that they arrette it to the defaute of myn unconning, and nat to my wil, that wolde ful fain have said bettre if I hadde had conning. For oure book saith, 'Al that is writen is writen for oure doctrine,' and that is myn entente. Wherfore I biseeke you mekely, for the mercy of God, that ye praye for me that Crist have mercy on me and foryive me my giltes, and namely of my translacions and editinges of worldly vanitees, the whiche I revoke in my retraccions: as is the *Book of Troilus*; the *Book also of Fame*; the *Book of the Five and Twenty Ladies*; the *Book of the Duchesse*; the *Book of Saint Valentines Day of the Parlement of Briddes*; the *Tales of Canterbury,* thilke that sounen into sinne; the *Book of the Leon*; and many another book, if they were in my remembrance, and many a song and many a leccherous lay: that Crist for his grete mercy foryive me the sinne. But of the translacion of Boece De Consolatione, and othere bookes of legendes **b)** of saintes, and omelies, and moralitee, and devocion, that I thanke I oure Lord Jesu Crist and his blisful Moder and alle the saintes of hevene, biseeking hem that they from hennes forth unto my lives ende sends me grace to biwaile my gilts and to studye to the salvacion of my soule, and graunte me grace of verray penitence, confession, and satisfaccion to doon in this present lif, thurgh the benigne grace of him that is king of kinges and preest over alle preestes, that boughte us with the precious blood of his herte, so that I may been oon of hem at the day of doom that shalle be saved. Qui cum patre et Spiritu Sancto vivis et regnas Deus per omnia saecula. Amen." (1386-1400)

c) The Latin is "Who with the Father and Holy Spirit lives and reigns, God throughout all ages."

Such necessary retractions are very sad indeed, and only encourage hypocrisy. Galileo had to recant, which he did hypocritically. It was common among many who failed in the courage to face the Church, but one must remember, the Church would kill you and damn you to hell forever. That was extremely scary to the people of that era. The Church had control of their minds and consciences and knew it, and used it to the limit lest there be any cracks in the dam, and the people seep through the armored wall of the Church's imprisonment of the human psyche.

d) Andreas Capellanus, at the end of his rather risque *The Art of Courtly Love*, adds on a final chapter called the *Rejection of Love* to avoid condemnation. One must remember that marriages were arranged for financial and political reasons in those days, and love came only romantically when one was attracted to another than one's married partner. This book, basically tells the reader how a sexual affair outside of marriage can be pulled off without detection: It is the *ART of Courtly Love*. It is addressed to his friend Walter, and the *Rejection of Love* reads in part:

"...You should know that we did not do this (write this book for you) because we consider it advisable for you or any other man to fall in love, but for fear lest you might think us stupid; we believe, though, that any man who devotes his efforts to love loses all his usefulness. Read this little book, then, not as one seeking to take up the life of a lover, but that, invigorated by the theory and trained to excite the minds of women to love, you may, by refraining from so doing, win an eternal recompense and thereby deserve a greater reward from God. For God is more pleased with a man who is able to sin and does not, than with a man who has no opportunity to sin. Now for many reasons any wise man is bound to avoid all the deeds of love and to oppose all its mandates. The first of these reason is one which it is not right for anyone to oppose, for no man, so long as he devotes himself to the service of love, can please God by any other works, even if they are good ones. For God hates, and in both testaments commands the punishment of, those whom he sees engaged in the works of Venus outside the bonds of wedlock or caught in the toils of any sort of passion...."

67a) This warning goes on for several pages and makes it sound almost sincere, but it was a necessary part of the book that he might be spared the inspectors of the inquisition.

Theologically all are aware of the condemnations of Hus, Luther, Calvin and their followers by the Roman Catholic Church, and, in turn, the condemnations of the Baptists and Quakers by the Protestant Churches. Such is generally common knowledge. It was sporadic for about 100 years and then all Europe broke loose in "Holy War" with Christians killing each other for both religious and political reasons. The 30 Year war, 1618 CE-1648 CE, devastated Europe, but the Germans suffered the most because it was in Germany where the main fighting took place. Some German historians claim that during the war four out of five Germans died, 80% of the population. All contestants were trying to show who the "true Christians" were.

b) All the scientists, astronomers, poets, surgeons, moralists, and philosophers were under the radar of the inquisitors. There were many dissenters in every field. Roger Bacon, John Wyclif, Marsilius of Padua, Martin Luther, Servetus, Castellio, R. Williams, Locke, Paracelsus, Erasmus, Calvin, Copernicus, Galileo, Bruno, Scot, the mystics who hid their displeasure in words of mysticism, those who sailed America (unfortunately where they set up their own dictatorships), Henry IV, and many more, especially the Platonists of England in the Tenth Century, at Chartre in the Twelth Century, Italian Florentines in the Fourteenth and Fifthteenth Centuries: among the Germans, English and Dutch - Lessing, Erasmus, Frank, and Colet and friends in the Sixteenth Century, the

Cambridge Platonists in the Seventeenth Century, and the many humanists and transcendentalists of the "Age of Reason" who had a love of Plato, into the modern age of Paine, Leibnitz, Kant, Schleiermacher, Jowett, A.N. Whitehead, Inge and many more that shall appear in the coming chapters.

c) The Church also either established or supported the suppression of women, colonization, sexual repression, and the slave trade. All will be taken up in due course in the rest of the book. And much of this opression was excused and even justified on the basis of the Judeo-Christian Scriptures. There are basically two major idols that must be destroyed before the Judeo-Christian Church can become relevant again in the future: their "Holy Scriptures" and the "Dogmatic Doctrines, Creeds, and Decrees". They both have been used to justify the horrible historical acts of the Church. Yet it persists in defending both.

II. THE FUTILE EFFORTS OF THE CHURCH IN TRYING TO SALVAGE THE JUDEO-CHRISTIAN SCRIPTURES

A. The Scriptures as Typology or Allegory

d) Philo(n) Judeus, of Alexandria, used allegory by which to reinterpret the Hebrew Scriptures by which he was able to Platonize them to make them more appealing to his fellow Jews who lived in Alexandria and were all well Hellenized in their culture, language, and even in their religion, as their "Hebrew Scriptures", the Tanak, had been translated into Greek a few generations before Philo, who was an older contemporary of Jesus. The God of Philo is the God of Plato, although "Moses taught the same thing", <u>if</u> he is properly allegorized. To take Moses literally was the sign of ignorance and of misunderstanding. Moses really did not mean that God became angry, disappointed, repents for his anger. Yahweh even says he gave bad laws to mankind (Ez 20:25), and was jealous. Philo then, using Plato's view that God is ever good and unchanging, claims that Moses simply can not be taken literally, but through a process of allegory the God of Moses becomes clothed in Platonism. In *Plato's Gift to Christianity* it is stated (p.188):

68a) "Of course it is not only the nature of God that is Platonized, but the entire framework of the creation itself. For, like Plato, Philo teaches that

God used a preexistent Pattern (the world of forms) by which to make the Cosmos (*De Opificio Mundi* 16). In a further commentary of the Pattern, the Transcendental and Eternal World, he states its relationship to the Word of God (HE THEOU LOGOS) through which all the visible world is made (*On The Creation* 24-25). Once creation is effected, then its physical elements are then also allegorized that Plato may be taught in the "clothing" of Moses. The four rivers of Genesis Two become the four cardinal virtues of Plato's Republic: prudence (PHRONESIS), selfcontrol (SOPHROSUNE), courage (ANDREIA), and justice (DIKAISUNE) (*On The Creation* 63). Platonic providence is also available for our human race, for God loves virtue, all that is good and beautiful, and He loves also man and provides for his beloved (*On The Creation* 81). Also the wives of the patriarchs are really Platonic virtues: **b)** Hagar is only the lower education, but Sarah is philosophy and incorporates the four cardinal Platonic virtues of the Republic: temperance, courage, justice and wisdom (*On The Cherubim* 5-6).

After Philo all the Christian theologians of Alexandria used the same method for dealing with the inconsistencies, horrors, and incompatibilities of the ancient Hebrew Scriptures: Clement and Origen use allegory incessantly. Instead of admitting to the incompatibility of many of the stories of the Tanak, they " baptized" them into Platonism and made them acceptable to the cultured people of Alexandria. The Christians added typological interpretations also by which they were able to find many pre-Christ figures in the Tanak and the fulfillment of many prophecies. All of this to cover up the fictional and sometimes ugly stories of the Tanak, which they felt needed an upgrade in morality.

B. Finding the Moral and Spiritual Truths

c) Another exegetical game was to take terrible story and find the moral or spiritual truths involved. After a brutal slaughter of innocent people who happened to be uncircumcised, one could teach that those who were not moral, according the Tanak, and did not obey the Sabbath or circumcise their children would be punished, and tragedy would be their end. No mention would be made of the invaders who slaughtered the innocent. Philo, Origen, and a host of others used this method of interpretation also. As mentioned earlier, the pagan Platonists saw the smoke screen and saw such justification of those stories as an insult to human intelligence and the dignity of God.

C. Liberal Approaches -- Half-Way Houses to Honesty

d) It is often taught that there is an evolutionary development of spiritual morality, and one must see the progress that is being made in this "Salvation History" of "God's People", for even sacred history is evolutionary. One can find "interim" ethics, things of "secondary value", an early "dispensation" that was just a primer for the subsequent coating of paint that would color the finished religious product; also hyperbole and symbolism played roles in finding something good in those very difficult passages. Yet, the entire Bible is Sacred. How and why should it be so? Where is the honesty and courage just to say that the book has so many faults in so many ways that it simply is not worthy of modern man's spiritual needs? That is, if it ever was worthy to any thinking or philosophical person. There is, in reality, no difference from the basic thinking of the Liberal and the Fundamentalist, because they are both trying in some way to hold on to the Judeo-Christian Bible, the difference of attitude is only in the degrees and ways in which they hold on to it. Liberation from it seems to be unthinkable for both parties: it is, frankly, an idol to both. Instead of acknowledging the gross weaknesses within it, and eliminating it, they argue with each other about the way they should interpret it. One of the most common statements made when they are in conflict is "It's all in the way you interpret it."

D. Demythologizing and Coming to Symbolic "Truths"

69a) One of those ways used to interpret the Judeo-Christian Bible that appeals to some on the liberal side is the method of demythologizing the obvious myths contained in it. By doing this, they claim, they will find the basic truths of man's being and his necessary confrontation with God. But one must ask, why hold on to a book that one has to demythologize in order to find something of spiritual value, especially when one has to put up with superstitions, vicarious atonements, myths, damnations, hell and the devil, and fairy tales (Balaam's donkey speaks as does the serpent in the garden)? How can one demythologize the slaughter by Yahweh of the first born of all Egyptians, a flood unleashed by an angry god, the invasion in order to slaughter innocent people to take over their land, and lastly, in climax of ugliness, that God would be so bitter and self-centered that he would, in wrath, send people to hell to suffer grievously forever, and ever, and ever? It depends how you look at it? It depends on how you demythologize it? Hardly!

E. Selective Reading: Avoiding The Whole

b) The idea of selective readings of the Bible justifies its entire existence is as foolish as saying a man is good because he only steals once a week and kills only monthly. If you select any of the other days, he is wonderful and a great aid to one's character, virtue, and spirituality. Would you want your children to hang around with him? Then why have your children read the Bible, saying that some sections are really quite spiritual? Those sections like Psalm 23, I Corinthians 13, and sections of the Sermon on the Mount are, indeed, delightful, but can they justify the whole of the Bible? No! Who can find fault with the Epistle of James (well, maybe Luther, but he had his own faith-only concept to grind) and the lovely story of Jonah that presents a God that has much more mercy than the main character of the obviously fictional story? But let them come out of the whole and be liberated, and then freed to teach and lead others. There are pearls in unseemly places, but they should not be cast there forever. A good soldier or two can not justify and evil war. Let them be freed of the action.

F. "Believe it Because it is Absurd." Syndrome

c) For Tertullian "Credo quia absurdum est." was enough. But more rational and less radically passioned people do not believe things because they are totally absurd. Kierkegaard's reasoning of a desperate leap of faith is not much different. One wonders about both of them, especially Kierkegaard who seemed to be so anti-Hegel that he would mock him in his own life, being engaged but never married or just the opposite by, without, and even against, rational knowledge he would take a leap of faith. This is not an honest agnostic deciding to believe. It is a leap of spiritual desperation. It is more like Tertullian's "I believe because it is absurd." Tertullian seemed to have a problem as to what to believe and probably ended up, after being a Montanist, an Encratite as a possible follower of Tatian. Nevertheless, despite the irrationality of both of them, at least they were deeply honest in their spiritual struggles, and for that there must be some admiration. But to believe, simply because it is absurd or because one is spiritually desperate, can not appeal to many as a faith that gives joy, peace, and understanding.

G. Developing Irrational Doctrines for an Irrational Faith

d) Not too different from the above is the device of confronting an irrational spiritual teaching by then developing an irrational doctrine to fit the needs of it. Irenaeus ridiculed the Gnostics for believing in the idea that there were two natures of Jesus, the Christ. This Church Father could not believe anything more irrational. Yet, within two hundred years when the Church was confronted with the arguments between Eutychus and Nestorius, the former believing that Jesus was only in reality divine, while the latter believed he was in reality only human, it made a doctrine that he was both divine and human. Two totally different views by reason, became an irrational doctrine of the unification of the two different natures of Jesus, and it proved very helpful to the absurd teachings of the Church about Jesus. When he suffered and hungered and died, that was his human nature, but when he healed, taught, and rose from the dead, that was his divine nature. When he did not know something or accepted the validity of the medical practices of his day, that was his human nature. But, when he knew all things, which Peter protested, then that was his divine nature. This likewise led to the three in one God, a mathematical oxymoron, yet had to be believed for more than a thousand years or one was burned at the stake.

70a)

H. Neo-Orthodoxy

The Neo-Orthodox movement, given great life by Barth, was not too different from the Absurd argument. The immediate center of all thought was "Christ-centered", and all theology must grow out of and conform to the Incarnational View, that taught that God became man and that initial premise set the stage for everything else. "Forget reason and history, and let mythology and the glorified legends that grew up in the Church for the purpose of Church doctrine rule, that the utter reliability of the Bible and the Incarnation of God in Christ may be established forever. There can be no other avenue of spiritual doctrine than from Jesus Christ himself." Such is the quite popular thinking among the Christian fundamentalists, who believe a priori that all of God's revelation, grace, love comes through Jesus, as the appointed one (the Christ) and without him there is absolutely no knowledge of the "One True God". It is a position that is so narrow that it has no room for any type of discussion. You simply believe in the Bible and in the Incarnation of God in Jesus or you are damned. That is their preaching of "The Good News".

I. The "Sitz im Leben"

b) A German created doctrine that all must be understood by the "setting in life" of the person being discussed. Of course this is true when you are talking about a man and his era and the culture in which he was raised, but not when you are talking about the Eternal and the Absolute Truth from eternity to eternity. When teachings are "time and culture adjusted" it just proves that they are relative, which is fine, but when they are declared to be eternal and absolute, then how can they be time and culture adjusted? There is a natural failure to any absolute doctrine or standard of confidence if it every few years must be time adjusted. The Christians used this argument from the beginning, for Paul, the Gospel writers, and the author of book of Hebrews all saw the teachings of Jesus as absolute, yet admitted that that meant that the teachings of the Tanak had to be time adjusted because they were now obsolete. Now after two thousand more years, that would mean that much of the Christian Scriptures are obsolete also. But that is logic and opposes the very claims that their teachings that, although given in a much different historical setting, are still absolute and eternal. How can the "Eternal Christ" assume that there is a hell and a devil, and then a theologian 2000 years later declare that Jesus' teachings must be time and setting adjusted? The rational person does not accept it, and even the Platonists of Jesus own time rejected such ideas.

J. Other Futile Ways of Trying to Salvage the Judeo-Christian Scriptures.

c) These have not been overly popular, but shows that people of the Christian Faith simply can not let go of the Bible, regardless of what history, reason, or science may say. The Bible "decoders" are the most illogical yet, for why would one preach the eternal good news, die for it, and then code it so that no one could get the message. Those who bend all scriptures to justify their own eschatological views, popularized as the "voices of prophecy", likewise show an immense historical ignorance, yet they use religion for tons of financial profit. Sure, some are sincere, yet this does not validate their mutilation of the historical setting and teachings of the Christian Canon. Finally, there are some who justify the teachings of Jesus' miracles, resurrection, and visions of heaven as simply adorned legends that were also popular in Jewish Midrash. At least there is the honesty here to admit that those very well adorned legends were not in reality historical facts. But then why hold on to these legends as those stories in human history by which all spiritual, scientific and historical truths are to be judged? It can help one to understand how the Christian Scriptures developed their stories, but it can not justify those stories being used as ultimate truth, much less to execute people for not believing they were historical records to begin with.

d) All of these "intellectual interpretations" that are used to justify the position of the "Holy Scriptures" as the ultimate measure of all spiritual, moral, scientific, and historical truth are simply futile efforts to salvage that which is not salvageable. Now it is time to move on to a beautiful, rational and philosophical faith, the foundation of which was laid by the teaching of Plato and his followers.

ZETA

Z

CHAPTER SIX
PLATO: HIS PERSON AND PHILOSOPHICAL FAITH

I. HIS PERSON AND LIFE

71a) Plato lived from 427 - 347 BCE, being born of two prominent citizens of Athens, Ariston was the name of his father and Perictione was the name of his mother. The were both distinguished people who lived during the Hellenic glory years of Periclean Athens. Perictione was the sister of Charmides and the cousin of Critias, both of whom are mentioned by Plato in his dialogues. He was one of four children from the marriage of his parents: his two brothers Adimantus and Glaucon and a sister Potone, whose son Speusippus took leadership of the Academy after Plato died; he also had a half brother, Antiphon.

The influences upon Plato's life and way of thinking are manifold: the philosophies of Pythagoras, Heracleitus, and (Father) Parmenides are certainly prominent. Being raised in Athens, of course, exerted a tremendously strong influence upon him, both good and bad. He loved Athens, but not its political structure, a so-called democracy. Nor did he overly care for Pericles who managed to get Athens into a losing war with Sparta. And the fact that its democracy executed his favorite teacher, Socrates, whom Plato called the most righteous man of his age, caused a deep animosity towards such a form of government. Needless to say that Socrates himself, had a profound influence upon him and for many, especially of his earlier dialogues, Socrates became the spokesman for his own ideas. He also was influenced by Orphism, a mystery cult that was quite popular. The common doctrines of the mysteries, some of which had produced in Plato certain thoughts, were:

1. Grace was needed from the spiritual realm
2. Man was seen to be potentially immortal
3. Some Soter (Savior) was present and gave to his followers a divine experience
4. There were rites and precepts that were seen as means of grace and assimilation
5. Ethics, being good and moral, helped to merit grace
6. They were egalitarian
7. They were open and universal

b)

It was thought that Plato himself was an initiate of Orphism.

When he was 40, about a dozen years after Socrates' death, he decided to establish a scientific and philosophical school that could offer more than the simple yet fundamental generally taught courses within the scope of the traditional set of disciplines, often called the Greek Paideia. One may consider the traditional education to be similar to high school in the United States, and Plato wanted to start the university level of teaching. He expected a solid background of education to be had before one was acceptable to enter his Academy, called so because it was dedicated to Academos, a lesser Greek deity. Above the entrance to his Academy were the words: "If you do not know mathematics, do not enter". He recognized the value of a good faculty and lured to the Academy Eudoxus of Cnidus, the best mathematician of that time, and his fellow scholars to the Academy He taught: that which made men good, political science, and most of all, pure mathematics as the basis of all true and lasting knowledge. A.E. Taylor says it very well: "The founding of the Academy is the turning point in Plato's life, and in some **c)** ways the most memorable event in the history of Western European science...The novel thing about the Platonic Academy was that it was an institution for the prosecution of *scientific* study.6.1 Even though they were followers of Plato, those we call Platonists, they were for centuries referred to as Academics, and if one reads Cicero or Epictetus one can expect some references to Academics, and they were the ones who studied the Platonic Tradition at the Academy. Diogenes Laertius makes the following statement about Plato's teachings.

d) "He was the first to introduce argument by means of question and answer, says Favorinus in the eighth book of his Miscellaneous History; he was the first to explain ...the method of solving problems by analysis; and the first who in philosophical discussion employed the terms antipodes, element, dialectic, quality oblong number, and among boundaries, the plane superficies"(Diogenes Laertius III. 23-25). He had many students, some of whom studied many years under him (Aristotle was his student for 20 years). Below some are named according to Diogenes Laertius (III. 44-46):

72a) "His disciples were Speusippus of Athens, Xenocrates of Chalcedon, Aristotle of Stagira, Philippus of Opus, Hestiaeus of Perinthus, Dion of Syracuse, Amyclus of Heraclea, Erastus and Coriscus Scepsus, Timolaus of Cyzicus, Euaeon of Lampsacus, Python and Heracides of Aenus, Hippothales and Callippus of Athens, Demetrius of Amphipolis, Heraclides of Ponus, and many others, among them two women, Lastheneia of Mantinea and Axiothea of Phlius, who is reported by Dicaearchus to have worn men's clothes."

Other possible students included Theophrastus, Hyperides, Lycurgus, and even Demosthenes. It should be noted that there were two women named. Plato's only requirement was that they know their mathematics, there were no other barriers to those who sought to study with him. Likewise it is to be noticed how most came from other places to Athens to study under Plato. Axiothea, who wore men's clothes may have been one of the first truly liberated women in the world: her name means "The Goddess is Worthy".

b) The next section will present the basic Platonic Theology; the many other teachings of Plato will appear in the following chapters according the topics being discussed.

II PLATO'S HUMBLE THEOLOGICAL QUEST TO KNOW GOD

When a person reads Plato he soon becomes aware that the purpose of each dialogue is to direct the reader to an absolute concept of an abstract virtue, and that within the entire corpus of Plato's writings, those absolute virtues are unified, and in some way that unification of absolute virtues points to God, whether He is Absolute Beauty, Absolute Goodness, or the absolute of mental capacity itself, Reason or Mind, which draws all other virtues into Itself. Every virtue, law, and concept find their final reality and meaning in God, the Father and Creator of all, the Good beyond being, and the First Cause of all. The reader will also soon realize how devotionally and humbly such subjects are approached; Plato is constantly reminding his readers that only God is wise and men can only discuss Him in reverence without dogmatism, hoping for God's guidance so that at least their conclusions will present a rational and probable witness to His goodness and beauty, because, in fact, He is past finding out by the minds of men. Plato puts into Socrates' mouth these words.

d) And I thought that I had better have recourse to the world of mind and seek there the truth of existence. I dare say that the simile is not perfect--for I am very far from admitting that he who contemplates existences through the medium of thought, sees them only 'through a glass darkly,' any more that he who considers them in action and operation (Phaedo 99e-100a)

His lack of dogmatism is especially evident in the Timaeus in which he talks about God and the creation. He, first of all, refers to this dialogue as a Mythos, a myth (also a word used for a story or an account), not a presentation of knowledge. However, he insists on using reason, logic, and mathematics in order that this "account" of God and creation would be the most probable based on the scientific knowledge of his day. "Wherefore, using the language of probability, we may say that the world became a living creature truly endowed with soul and intelligence by the providence of God"(30b). Again he states by the mouth of Timaeus:

73a)

I will not now speak of the first principle or principles of all things, or by whatever name they are to be called, for this reason--because it is difficult to set forth my opinion according to the method of discussion which we are at present employing. Do not imagine, any more that I can bring myself to imagine, that I should be right in understanding so great and difficult a task. Remembering what

> I said at first about probability, I will do my best to give as probable an explanation as any other, --or rather, more probable; and I will first go back to the beginning and try to speak of each thing and of all. Once more, then, at the commencement of my discourse, I call upon God, and beg him to be our Saviour out of a strange and unwonted enquiry, and to bring us to the haven of probability (48d-e).

b)
Again Plato declares,

> Concerning the soul, as to which part is mortal and which is divine, and how and why they are separated, and where located, if God acknowledges that we have spoken the truth, then, and then only, can we be confident; still, we may venture to assert that what has been said by us is probable, and will be rendered more probable by investigation (Timaeus 72d).

Plato, even though in his humility admitting the sacredness of the task of thinking about God, who is far beyond our wisdom, firmly believes that God himself has planted in each of us the intellectual desire to reach up to Him.

c) We declare that God has given to each of us, as his daimon, that kind of soul which is housed in the top of our body and which raises us--seeing that we are not an earthly but a heavenly plant --up from earth towards our kindred in heaven (Timaeus 90a).6.2

This Plato, greatest of all philosophers in both thought and influence, was a man of great intellect, humble heart, and a deeply devotional spirit, who sought above all that which is eternal, good and beautiful, God.

III. THE NATURE OF GOD

This section on the nature of God will be divided into six parts: God as First Cause, Plato's monotheism, the absolute perfection of God, God beyond human understanding, God as intellelect or mind "nous" (νους), and the personality (personhood) of God.

A. God as First Cause

d) Plato was the first to try to prove the existence of God, and this he sought to do by combining science and reason to form a conclusion which then could not be refuted by either, and this is generally known as natural theology or the natural proofs of God. He did not resort to imaginative "inspiration", unexplained events, or weird dreams. The astronomical sciences of the day declared the absolute precision with which the heavenly bodies moved, giving the heavens a rhythm and harmony which was, to Plato, impossible to explain by chance. Such movement logically predicated a rational source which had an orderly mind and the power within to activate movement; this one source was the essence of soul, and therefore worked with one thought-out pattern. It is in the Timaeus that Plato most elaborates on the creation process.

> The Cosmos...it has come into existence...And that which has come into existence must necessarily, as we say, have come into existence by reason of some cause. Now to discover the Maker and Father of this universe were a task indeed; and having discovered Him, to declare Him unto all men were a thing impossible...Now if so be that this Cosmos is beautiful and its Constructor good, it is plain that He fixed his gaze on the Eternal ...for the Cosmos is the fairest of all that has come into existence, and He is the best of all Causes (28c).6.3

74a)
In the Tenth Chapter of the Laws, Plato also presents the source of all to the Soul which has self movement (896a), and by it all things are stirred into motion (896e). In the Cratylus, Socrates explains the name of Zeus as a combination of *zena* and *dia* which mean together that Zeus is the author of life to us and to all, the lord and king of all...the God through whom all creatures always have life (396a).

B. The Monotheism of Plato

There are, of course, numerous references to the gods and particular gods throughout Plato's works, and this may lead the person not well acquainted with Plato to think that he is a traditional polytheist, which is certainly not the case. A.E. Taylor was correct in his statement professing Plato's monotheism.

> That Plato was personally a monotheist, however, seems plain from the fact that when he is speaking with most moral fervour and earnestness, he so regularly says not "gods" but God, just as Socrates in the Apology always speaks of his mission to the souls of his fellow-Athenians as laid on him not by Apollo, nor by "the gods," but by God. Also note that God is definitely said to be "the best soul."6.4

b)
But we can add much more to Taylor's statement. The entire theme of the creation account of the Timaeus is monotheistic and even names the other gods, the lower gods, as created by the Father and Maker of the Cosmos. In the creation account the Creator is called by many names: the Maker, the Architect, the Constructor, the Father, the Framer, the Saviour, and simply God, and all the names and their corresponding verbs are in the singular. *Theos* (God) is by far the most used name, and it is used only in the singular from sections 29e to 53e of the Timaeus. When the plural is used, *Theoi* (the gods) it always signifies those creatures made by the Father for the purpose of administrating the Cosmos with the same care and love for it that He had in creating them; they were to imitate their Father's goodness. They would be like the Christian's view of guardian angels, who also have particular names like Gabriel, Raphael, Uriel, Michael and many others, who are eternal caretakers of mankind, but in no way like the Father: they are simply His messengers and caretakers of mankind. Both Xenophanes and Anaxagoras before Plato had taught monotheism, calling God the *arche* (Beginning) and *nous* (Mind, Reason, or Intellect) who started and ordered the universe. Monotheism was quite common among the Greek philosophers, but after Plato's natural "proof" of One Creator, one pattern, and one Cosmos, no serious Greek philosopher ever returned to polytheism, except perhaps Epicurus who really did not care about any theological questions as to whether or not the gods exist.

C. God as Absolute Perfection

c) In the Republic Plato forcefully and consistently condemns the poets for the way that they present God as well as the lower deities; they constantly tell tales of jealousy, hatred, lust, arrogance, self-centeredness as being normal activities of the divine beings, and he feels that such literature should be banned from his perfect city, the Republic.

> First of all, I said, there was that greatest of all lies, in high places, which the poet told about Uranus, and which was a bad lie too,--I mean what Hesiod says that Uranus did, and how Cronus retaliated on him. The doings of Cronus, and the sufferings which in turn his son inflicted upon him, even if they were true, ought certainly not to be lightly told to young and thoughtless persons; if possible, they had better be buried in silence.....

d)

> Something of this kind, I replied:--God is always to be represented as he truly is, whatever be the sort of poetry, epic, lyric or tragic, in which the representation is given....
>
> Then God, if he be good, is not the author of all things, as the many assert, but he is the cause of a few things only, and not of most things that occur to men. For few are the goods of human life, and many are the evils, and the good is to be attributed to God alone; of the evils the causes are to be sought elsewhere, and not in him. (Republic 378-379)

This discussion continues to the end of Book Two of the Republic which ends with the following:

> Then God is perfectly simple and true both in word and deed; he changes not; he deceives not, either by sign or word, by dream or waking vision (382e).

75a)

Upon careful reading of this part of the dialogue, one can see that it is characteristic for Plato, who uses Socrates as his spokesman, to reply to any questions about the gods by using the singular, God; for as all virtue is ultimately one for Plato, so is his God ultimately good, perfect, and singular. The problem of evil for Plato is a simple one: man has a free choice in all matters, but when the lower part of the soul is tempted by the desires of necessity, and he then yields to such emotive impulses, evil results are created. However, in all things God remains blameless: "The responsibility is with the chooser--God is justified" (617e).

Because God's goodness is so often mentioned in Plato, some passages seem to imply that God is the Good, and while it has often been debated, there is no doubt that God is the absolute in all the virtues and qualities of perfection: God is Absolute Good(ness), Absolute Beauty, Absolute Harmony and Simplicity, and Absolute Intellect. According to Aristoxenes, a student of Plato, in his Elements of Harmony, Plato taught that the One was the Good.6.5 This is further fortified by the following passage from the Republic:

b)

> In like manner the Good may be said to be not only the Author of knowledge to all things known, but of their being and essence, and yet the Good is not essence, for He himself is not generated (509b).

God is good and He is beyond Being, in fact, He is the cause of being. This will be referred to again in the next section, but it was necessary to mention it here while discussing God's absolute goodness and perfection. While I do not agree with Wilamowitz-Moellendorff's general depersonalization of Plato's God, I do agree with his statement that "his God remained to the end the Good, True, Beautiful, who penetrates, moves, and vitalizes all, a Godhood which we love."6.6

c) Because God is absolute perfection, He then becomes the measure of all that is good or beautiful in both concept of laws and the function of living. And he who would be dear to God must, as far as possible, be like Him and such as He is. Wherefore the temperate man is the friend of God, for he is like Him; and the intemperate man is unlike Him, and different from Him, and unjust. It is the good man whose prayers and sacrifices have a true communion with heaven, and that the evil man is not pleasing to God regardless of his prayers and sacrifices, for God desires virtue, not sacrifices. Indeed, God is the standard of perfection and the man who imitates God's perfection in his life is truly pleasing to God. For man's goal, even in this life is a perfected virtue. For Plato, this generous God, who made creation to share existence with us, is always good and constantly perfect; there being no change or fluctuation of his beautiful nature. Plato states in his Timaeus:

d) Let me tell you then why the creator made this world of generation. He was good, and the good can never have any jealousy of anything. And being free from jealousy, he desired that all things should be as much like himself as they could be. This is in the truest sense the origin of creation and the world, as we shall do well in believing on the testimony of wise men: God desired that all things should be good and nothing bad, so far as this was attainable (Timaeus 29e-30a).

76a)

The last words "so far as this was attainable" are often repeated in the Timaeus. For God, to Plato, was not all powerful, but rather limited by αναγκη (*ananke*), which is usually translated "necessity" or sometimes, perhaps more accurately, "laws of nature". There was a basic substance of the material world with which God had to deal, and He was not able to change the basic laws of nature as to how the material world would be shaped and respond to his ideal world. The pattern was perfect, but the ordering of the matter had its own laws and this world of becoming or evolving would follow its own nature. Thus, God copied in material form the pattern of his ideal as closely as possible. Giving the eternal spiritual souls a chance to experience life in the body was a gracious enough gift and experience so wonderful that God did not withhold the experience from man simply because the material world would not be perfect like his eternal pattern. If there were some bad experiences for man, that would be the result of the weakness of the bodily form man was to take. But the real person, in Plato, is the soul which is eternal and can suffer no harm except when man chooses to depreciate the value of his own soul.

b)

D. God is Beyond Human Understanding

Plato was well aware of man's limited knowledge and even his lack of potential to discuss with proven knowledge the ultimate questions which men confronted with their own existence and the invisible powers beyond themselves. As mentioned above, he approached such questions with great humility and asked God for guidance and leadership in the dialectical process. He also professed that in this world men will live by correct opinion (*ortho-doxa*) and probability rather than live with the assurances of proven knowledge of that which is unseen and not of the beings and things that are beyond human understanding. When it came to God, Plato lived by faith. He was on sacred ground when speaking about God and was fearful that even he in all his caution would say something about God that was really inferior to God's perfect nature. As mentioned above in the Republic passage (509b), God is that which is beyond being, beyond essence, both in dignity and power. Ultimate principles of reality are known by God only, unless He reveals them to a favorite. "But the principles which are still higher than these are known only to God and the man who is dear to God" (Timaeus 53d). For all practicality man must accept that he can love wisdom, but can not himself be wise. "Wise, I may not call them; for that is a great name which belongs to God alone,--lovers of wisdom or philosophers is their modest and befitting title" (Phaedrus 278d). For, in reality, God is beyond our mental abilities.

c)

> Now that which is created must, as we affirm, of necessity be created by a cause. But the Father and Maker of all this universe is past finding out; and even if we found him, to tell of him to all men would be impossible (Timaeus 28c).

In that sense of scientific knowledge, man can not know God, but he can rationalize and come to have a firm faith in him. Socrates admitted that he did not know of the future life (indeed, he never professed to know anything--and that was his mark of being the wisest among men, for others thought that they knew when they did not--he was at least aware of his ignorance), but his conviction and faith were very strong, stronger than all those who accused him of unbelief: "For I do believe that there are gods, and in a sense higher than that in which any of my accusers believe in them. And to you and to God I commit my cause" (Apology 35d). But given all these human limitations, a man of faith can be guided by God himself to knowledge of things divine. Where there is faith, prayer, and God's guidance, knowledge may come, if God wills it:

d)

> Clinias: With all my heart. Make your prayer, my dear sir, in faith, and then go on with such fair discourse of gods and goddesses as your are moved to utter.

> Athenian: And so I will, if God himself will vouchsafe us his guidance. Only you must join in the prayer (Epinomis 980c--A.E.Taylor's translation).

In the Epinomis, the Athenian is Plato's mouthpiece, replacing Socrates who does not appear in this dialogue. For men to grow in goodness and things divine, especially of the divine virtues, is a joyful thing to the lower deities for they are not envious of their Father and Creator, but rather joyful when God himself helps men grow in goodness: "a joy pure of all envy at seeing him (man) growing in goodness by God's aid" (Epinomis 988b--A.E. Taylor's translation). There is joy in heaven when men grow in goodness.

E. God as NOUS

77a) God's utter transcendence compelled the philosophers to use terms which often seem void of personality, and this chapter will build upon the terms used already, such as first Cause (*Arche*), Maker (*Poietes*), Artificer (*Demiougos*), and to look at God as Reason, Mind, or Intellect (*Nous*).

Wisdom, reason and thought were the cardinal features of God in the creation of the Cosmos; He was, in fact, the Mind behind it all. Plato states:

> But it is clear to everyone that his gaze was on the Eternal; for the Cosmos is the fairest of all that has come into existence, and He the best of all the Causes. So having in this wise come into existence, it has been constructed after the pattern of that which is apprehensible by reason and thought and is self-identical (Timaeus 29a).6.7

Again, the Artificer's mind is far beyond the mind of men.

> But should any inquirer make an experimental test of these facts, he would evince his ignorance of the difference between man's nature and God's--how that, whereas God is sufficiently wise and powerful to blend the many into one and to dissolve again the one into many,

> there exists not now, nor ever will exist hereafter, a child of man sufficient for either of these tasks (Timaeus 68d).6.8

b) Diogenes Laertius says of Plato "he set forth two universal principles, God and matter, and he calls God mind and cause (*noun kai aition*)"(Diogenes Laertius III 69).

Stephen Menn has written Plato on God as Nous stating his main argument thus:

> I will argue that the demiurge of the Timaeus and Statesman is, as he seems to be, a single substantial unity, identical with the NOUS of the Philebus (and Phaedo and Laws) distinct from the world soul and from all other souls, superior to souls as he is to bodies.6.9

Menn continues:

c)

> The main point to note is that all the attributes and functions that the Philebus, Phaedo, and Laws assign to *nous* recur in the Timaeus and Statesman. The Philebus speaks interchangeably of the class of the cause (*aitia aition*) in general or the *poioun*(26e) or *demiourgoun*(27b); both Timaeus and Statesman describe their gods as *demiourgos* (Statesman 273b, Timaeus 28a and following, also Republic 530a and Sophist 265c), the Timaeus also as *aition* (28a) and *poietes* (28c).The Philebus describes *nous* in particular as *basileus* (cf. 274e-275a) and as *kubernetes* (272e, 273c).6.10

Menn adds many other connections between passages which designate *nous* as God, that Plato uses the word *nous* more than 350 times and never once in the plural, and the several difficulties in separating *nous* from both soul and cause. Menn's study is thorough and should be consulted if the reader has further interest in this transcendent designation by Plato that God is *Nous*. The purpose of this section, God as *Nous*, is to show that Plato protected the transcendence of God; that He was far above our thinking, and therefore incomprehensible by the mind of man. Man is a rational animal, but God is pure and absolute intellect, and His depth is so great that even for the wisest of men, He is passed finding out.

d)

F. The Person of God

Plato also recognized that despite man's inability to mentally reach out and touch the incomprehensible majesty of God, he still had to express man's need to know God's will, His love for His creation, and His providence for mankind. Therefore, as much as the necessity for human communication about God was obviously for the good of man, Plato used anthropomorphic pictures of God's goodness and nearness to His creation, and mankind in particular. God, of course, had personality or personhood, but to use human terms necessitated absolute care that God himself was not spoken of in a way that was beneath his absolute Majesty, not because God was a jealous divinity who would be offended by man's sincere but misdirected descriptions, but because it was proper to show absolute love and respect for the Good Creator in whom all absolute beauty and virtue existed. The One Highest God, the Maker and Father of all that is, most certainly is not just an abstract idea, but one that cares for, loves and rejoices in His creation.

79a) In the Timaeus there are several names and attributes given to God's nature that present Him as a God that loves, and one that may be loved. Since Plato's God has been so unfairly attacked by both Jewish and Christian theologians as an abstract and cold God, it might be well to remember that it was not Genesis One that told us that the Creator was good or that he was not jealous, or that he rejoiced over his creation, it was Plato who told men such. In the Timaeus we find such words as: "He was good, and the good can never have any jealousy of anything. And being free from jealousy, he desired that all things should be as like himself as they could be...God desired that all things should be good and nothing bad, so far as this was attainable...Now the deeds of the best could never be or have been other than the fairest...For which reason, when he was framing the universe, he put intelligence in soul, and soul in body, that he might be the creator of a work which was by nature fairest and best. Wherefore, using the language of probability, we may say that the world became a living creature truly endowed with soul and intelligence by the providence of God" (Timaeus 29e-30c). "Such was the whole plan of the eternal God"(Timaeus 34a). "Having these purposes, he created the world (*kosmos*) a blessed god"(Timaeus 34b)....When the father and creator saw the creature (i.e. the Cosmos) which he had made moving and living, the created image of the eternal gods, he rejoiced, and in his joy determined to make the copy still more like the original; and as this was eternal, he sought to make the universe eternal, so far as it might be"(Timaeus 37c-d). "The Father and Maker of all this universe" (Timaeus 28c)..."God lighted a fire, which we now call the sun,...that it might give light to the whole of heaven, and that the animals, as many as nature intended, might participate in number"(Timaeus 39b-c). "Once more, then, at the commencement of my discourse, I call upon God, and beg him to be our saviour out of a strange and unwonted enquiry, and to bring us to the haven of probability. So now let us begin again"(Timaeus 48d). "...but himself contriving the good in all his creations"(Timaeus 68e). "...to be a remedy for this, God combined with it the liver" (Timaeus 71a). God made our whole body upright (Timaeus 90a). In the Timaeus we see a God who loves his creation, makes it as good as possible, and as much like himself as possible (in his own image--for He is the Father), who even cares about the details of how man's material body operates, and implants in man the vision and reason to see the Creator in His very works of creation that man might be drawn back to Himself. In the Statesman God is called the Divine Shepherd(275a). God's qualities and attributes are also often personified in the lower gods which He himself made in his own image, which we shall fully discuss in the next section, but for now let us see him as the God of love and beauty which is expressed in Plato's Symposium. "Love is the oldest and noblest and mightiest of the gods, and the chiefest author and giver of virtue in life, and of happiness after death"(180b). Agathon declares "The previous speakers, instead of **b)** praising the god Love, or unfolding his nature, appear to have congratulated mankind on the benefits which he confers upon them. But I would rather praise the god first, and then speak of his gifts; this is always the right way of praising everything" (Symposium 195a). Moses Hadas was correct when he declared that the Greeks taught us that God loves mankind 6.11 In fact, the Greek word *Theophiles* (usually translated in one of three different ways: one dear to God, a friend of God, and a beloved of God, i.e. One whom God loves) is used by Plato 20 times, and all 20 are used in his more mature works written in the middle or later period.

God also rejoices in the goodness of men, for men who are good are dear to him, and men who honor their parents and grandparents give God a special delight: "a father or grandfather, or of a mother stricken in year?

whom when a man honors, the heart of the God rejoices, and He is ready to answer their prayers" (Laws XI 931d).6.12

c) Plato's God is without doubt a personal God with a personhood or personality of His own. He rejoices at his beautiful creation which he made for the benefit that man might enjoy life and goodness and His very own beauty. He cares for and wills the best for men, and men are dear to him, not by favoritism, by race, by power, or by gender, but by the way they are like unto him, i.e. by their goodness. He wills, He feels, and He hears prayers and "enjoys perfection with a sense of pleasure" to use the words of Constantin Ritter, who continues:

> The animated cosmos, an image of the creator, according to the Timaeus is a "blessed god," and--this seems to have more proof--good people are supposed to be "loved by God." Plato likes to use this expression frequently. But if we may speak of God as a loving Being, then it can no longer be questioned whether God feels. We are told so frequently that God wills, that he always wills the good for the whole world and for every feeling being, and that this understanding orders everything.6.13

d)

IV. THE ORDERING OF THE COSMOS

Plato's Timaeus is his final word concerning the creation of the universe; it is both late in his life and a work that is intent on answering previously unanswered questions about his philosophy, especially those in the Parmenides. It is also the work which left the most influence on his followers in the Academy, the Stoics, the Jewish Platonist-Philo of Alexandria, the translation of the Genesis One account into the LXX, Christian theologians well through the Middle Ages, as well as the Gnostics and even Aristotle (who made more references to the Timaeus than to any other work of Plato). Benjamin Jowett called the Timaeus "the greatest effort of the human mind to conceive the world as a whole which the genius of antiquity has bequeathed to us."6.14 Francis Cornford stated that it was in the Timaeus that "introduced, for the first time in Greek philosophy, the alternative scheme of creation by a divine artificer, according to which the world is like a work of art designed with a purpose."6.15

80a) Plato purposes the Timaeus as a likely account of creation based upon science, logic, and probability. He is humble but serious in his presentation that this is truly the most likely account of the reality of the creation of the universe. He approaches the subject with prayer, declaring that "All men, Socrates, who have any degree of right feeling, at the beginning of every enterprise, whether small or great, always call upon God"(Timaeus 27c). When he concludes the account and wants to review it, again he states, "Once more, then, at the commencement of my discourse, I call upon God, and beg him to be our saviour out of a strange and unwonted enquiry, and to bring us to the haven of probability"(Timaeus 48d-e). If the reader has an open minded approach to the Timaeus, he will find it a delightful way of presenting God's love and care in giving life to the universe, making it as lovely as possible for all creatures, and blessing man with a higher soul implanted with a rational desire to be like God himself.

b) The Maker and Father of the universe was good, and not envious in any way, and decided to share existence by creating a beautiful universe in the empty space and fill it with movement and life of all kinds. He wanted it to be as perfect as possible and therefore worked from a pattern of eternal perfection (whether or not this pattern of forms was separate from God's own thinking is a disputed question which will not be addressed at length here; many scholars feel they were eternal and separate entities, but subsequent generations of Platonists felt that if they were apprehended only by thought, then God's gaze upon them was simply His thinking process and the patterns were simply a blueprint of ideas in God's mind). God used this model of eternal perfection by which to construct a material universe, which Plato calls the cosmos (kosmos), which means the beautifully ordered one (hence our beautifying word "cosmetics"). God gave this beautifully ordered universe movement and life (soul), and directed its movements in harmony that all might see His own beauty in the beauty of the cosmos. He made the parts of the cosmos alive with soul, and thus was the creation of the lower gods, the stars, and planets, whom God called his children, who were to imitate His goodness, love, and orderly harmony in all that they did. He was not jealous and gave to them the most perfect material beings that were possible, and when it moved in its beautiful and harmonious way, He was delighted and rejoiced. He then had these lower gods imitate His actions; as He had made them, now they were to make the birds of the air, the creatures of the waters, and the land animals, of which man would receive the greatest portion of God's reasoning powers. They were to make the bodies only, but with the same love, generosity, and care with which He had made them; and as He would continually care and render what they needed to remain eternal, He desired that they should render the same providence upon the earthly beings. God himself would **c)** supply mankind with the eternal portion of his being, his soul, a soul which was implanted with reason, memory, and longing for the eternal existence and for God himself. The lower gods were to help man in his earthly efforts: to be virtuous on earth and establish justice among all in imitation of the lower gods and to long for the ultimate friendship with absolute goodness and beauty itself, God. The Creator God, not being jealous, did not envy the prayers and honors which mankind were to give to the lower gods, for that was in His eternal plan. This is much like Christianity, where the Creator himself appoints angels and archangels to be the guardians of mankind on His behalf, and to serve as His messengers to us humans, imitating and bringing God's love and care to us as Plato's lower gods imitated their Father and Maker in bringing His love and care to humanity. In fact, as we shall see later, the Christian heavenly hierarchy was probably born out of Platonism's transcendental hierarchy.

d) The creation, then, was a loving and generous gift of a good and non-envious God, who delighted in sharing life with all His creation. Man was implanted with a soul that sought to enjoy the beauties of the creation and with a longing for the Eternal Beauty, God Himself, the true Father and Maker of all, who rejoiced in man's longing for Him.

Also it must be mentioned that God cares for every living creature that exists in his loved universe, whether great or small--it was loved and cared for by God and to be watched over and helped by the lower gods upon God's appointment. He made them to be eternal beings and to be "indissoluble" but reserved the right to dissolve them (if they could not be refined and brought to virtue by God's constant and powerful loving care). God the Creator spoke thus to his lower gods:

81a)

> "Gods, children of gods, who are my works, and of whom I am the artificer and father, my creations are indissoluble, if I so will. All that is bound may be undone, but only an evil being would wish to undo that which is harmonious and happy. Wherefore,

since ye are but creatures, ye are not altogether immortal and indissoluble, but ye shall certainly not be dissolved, nor be liable to the fate of death, having in my will a greater and mightier bond than those with which ye see bound at the time of your birth" (Timaeus 41a-b).

b) ...how that the first birth should be one and the same ordained for all, in order than none might be slighted by Him; and how it was needful that they, when sown each into his own proper organ of time [as each soul is put into a material body], should grow into the most god-fearing of living creatures (Timaeus 41e).

And man was given the inner drive and desire for the eternal and divine so that he might feel and hope for that blessed and eternal life, for this too was evidence of God's goodness (Timaeus 68e).

The Timaeus is, of course, the definitive work of Plato concerning the creation, however, there are several other passages from earlier dialogues which refer to the One who creates and gives life to men, although He may be called by several different names. In the Cratylus, which is a dialogue about the origin of names, the name Zeus is considered a combination of two words *Zena* and *Dia:* which to Plato implied that God was the King of all and the giver of all life (Cratylus 396a).

c) In the Statesman the creation of the One is again referred to and the Creator's giving of his blessings to men as his gifts to his beloved creatures (269d-e).

In the Epinomis we can see Plato's great astronomical perception, well before its time, despite remaining geocentric, when he states:

> The [the stars] are not really the tiny things they look to be; the bulk of any star is enormous; that we must believe, for the proofs are convincing...and every one of the moving stars, is, in fact, of amazing magnitude. (Epinomis 983a--A.E. Taylor translation).

Plato uses the enormity of the universe to logically argue the existence of God, because such a thing in its great vastness must have a coordinator who is the mental force behind it all. However, even the things of the earth indicate a divine cause to their existence:

d)

Stranger. Looking, now, at the world and all the animals and plants, at things which grow upon the earth from seeds and roots, as well as at inanimate substances which are formed with the earth, fusile or non-fusile, shall we say that they come into existence--not having existed previously--by the creation of God, or shall we agree with vulgar opinion about them?

Theaetetus. What is that?

Stranger. The opinion that nature brings them into being from some spontaneous and unintelligent cause. Or shall we say that they are created by a divine reason and a knowledge which comes from God?

Theaetetus. I dare say that, owing to my youth, I may often waver in my view, but now when I look at you and see that you incline to refer them to God, I defer to your authority (Sophist 265c-d).

82a) Diogenes Laertius, a historian of philosophy who lived in the early third century after Christ, gives us these words that Plato taught that the Creator created the universe in His own image; and it thereby became the first-born of creation and the whole of it called His children:

And the creation as a whole is caused by God, because it is the nature of the good to be beneficent, and the creation of the universe has the highest good for its cause. For the most beautiful of created things is due to the best of intelligible causes; so that, as God is of this nature, and the universe resembles the best in its perfect beauty, it will not be in the likeness of anything created, but only of God (Laertius 72).6.16

Constantin Ritter summed up Plato's creation with these words:

b) The Idea of the world can be conceived only as God's purpose and as being grounded in His spiritual nature. If the Timaeus informs us that God in his goodness "desired that everything be as much as possible like himself," He himself evidently was the prototype after which He patterned the world, and looking at himself He took from the fulness of His own Being that which He imparted to the world. 6.17

> According to their logical content the Ideas are divine thoughts, a part of the content of God's way of doing things. Only by abstraction can we separate and distinguish the two...in short, the world stands before us as "the visible image of God whom we can conceive in thought alone." From this statement we can see that God's will to give to this world the best possible form was completely realized. We may, therefore, say that God's power is adequate for the realization of all His thoughts.6.18

Friedrich Solmsen draws attention to Plato's constant references to the goodness of God and the goodness of all that He does while creating the good, orderly and beautiful cosmos, and then concludes:

c)

> Needless to say, he [Plato] knew infinitely more about the Good and about Perfection than anyone before him--we have seen how rich and diversified the connotations of *To Agathon* (The Good) have become with Plato. This superior knowledge alone would account for his great advance over all his predecessors. 3.18

The good God, sharing and generous, with whom there could be no jealousy, created a universe as beautiful and good as himself--as much as possible--, despite its natural laws of constant change, and endowed its members with soul, and called them his children, being delighted in them when He saw them become a unified harmony. This material world, ordered and arraigned by God, because it, by the laws of nature, is always changing, Plato referred to it as the world of becoming, that is, it is constantly evolving, decaying, dying, and being reborn. It is Hearcleitus' world of panta rei (παντα ρει), everything flux, all is constantly changing. But God was helping it, in its changing, to become as good as possible. But it is not the real world, the world of being that has an eternal nature, and that is mankind's true and ultimate goal, for it is the Fatherland of the eternal soul.

HTA

H

CHAPTER SEVEN
PLATO'S WORKS
AND
THE EULOGIES PAID HIM THROUGHOUT HISTORY

I. THE BEAUTY OF HIS WRITINGS

83a) Even in translation one of the things a person comes to appreciate is the absolute beauty of his writings, and therefore it comes as no surprise to learn that he initially was a poet before he became a philosopher. Unfortunately, he himself destroyed his own poetry after meeting Socrates, and in seeking truth, was happy to discard what he might call poetic rhetoric. To him, philosophy was a serious quest for truth and could not afford to think in terms of the rhythm or the meters by which it was expressed. Likewise he despised the moral teaching of the poets, especially Homer. Yet, he retained the ability to say things in the most sublime way. Perhaps a term like prosetic would be proper: the lovely union of the prosaic and the poetic. An entire work called *On the Sublime Writing* attributed to Longinus, a Platonist himself who uses Platonic writings as the ultimate standard of beautiful writing, should also be read by writers to appreciate Plato's works. But the more important features of Plato's writings were about God, man's need to imitate his goodness, the definitions of the virtues, the importance of one's ultimate being -- his immortal soul, personal happiness, the joy and the scientific value of mathematics and one's function in human society.

b) While there are seldom any difficulties in understanding the arguments that his characters make throughout the dialogues, much of the spice, humor and even parody and sarcasm are missed because the reader is not acquainted with the setting or the character of the people alluded to. On the other hand, that is one of the rewards of extending learning of the Athenian setting and the knowledge one can attain about the people about which certain statements are made. The Menexenus is one giant satire while the Laws appears to be an exaggerated spoof of the Athenian in which he gives so many laws that the basic freedom and flexibility of thinking that most Athenians had would find it repulsive, the exact reaction for which Plato was hoping. Socrates jokes about his beauty, that of a satyr (he did have a pug nose but not perhaps the pointed ears), until he then talks about the internal beauty of his soul, for that is **c)** the real person, not the fleshly clothing that it is wearing. He was beautiful, despite the appearance of the fleshly body in which he was living for the temporal period. He alludes to himself as a midwife, then explains that he is giving birth to the quest for knowledge and virtue to those whom he taught or at least dialogued with. Only then are they truly born. He tells everyone that the Oracle of Delphi revealed that he was the wisest of all men, and then claims wisdom for the fact that he knows that he does not know anything definite about ultimate reality and that makes him much wiser than those who do not know but think they do. He has knowledge of his ignorance, but they are living in a fantasy thinking that they have wisdom when they do not.

d) The dialogues themselves are masterpieces in flowing and excellent Greek pointing the readers to every serious question man can ask about his existence. He does not address superficial things like making money, having large estates, the physical beauty of ones companion and fame. To strive after such shows a childish and unworthy attitude towards philosophy, the love of wisdom. Below are some of the subjects that he discusses in his dialogues:

The control and subjection of lustful and negative emotions (Charmides)
The meaning and power of friendship (Lysis)
The question of courage and duty (Laches)
Virtue's unity and absoluteness (Protagoras)
The immortality and salvation of the soul, and its greater importance than
84a) the body (Phaedo)
Holiness and purity (Euthyphro)
Suffering wrong does not hurt the soul, but doing wrong does great

damage to it (Gorgias)
Love (Phaedrus and Symposium)
Justice within the community and within one's soul (Republic)
Wisdom and knowledge (Theaetetus)
The harm to the soul when one repays evil with evil (Crito)
Seeking the greatest good (Gorgias)
The value of virtue (Meno)
Wisdom of the Divine is greater than earthly pleasures (Philebus)
The question of ultimate reality (Parmenides and Sophist)
The ordering of the cosmos by God the Father's goodness (Timaeus)

b) Everything that is important to man is discussed, including health and music and humor and many other elements of man's existence. His stress on mathematics and science were also the foundation of modern scientific thinking, and his open mindedness to most all of those answers given is balanced with a critical assessment of their values. Dialogue is the best way to exchange ideas and balance their relative values, even if no definite answer can be given to the questions. To be aporetic, that is, open ended with no conclusion, is preferable than concluding one's opinions with insufficient data. For there will always be another day to discuss the subject further.

II. Humanity's Unceasing Appreciation and Praise of Plato

c) Those Academics or Platonists who closely followed Plato were not reluctant to referring to him as the "Divine Plato"; Plutarch, Ficino, and Erasmus did so, feeling that they had to express a feeling they had that in some way they sensed a godlikeness in his character, in moral purity and spiritual beauty, and brought his followers closer to God. Because so much of the general public is not aware of Plato's tremendous influence upon everyone in the West in many different ways, the many different comments that follow will help in some way to bring attention to the one who laid the solid foundation to all Western Spirituality as well as his tremendous influence in ethics, politics, logic, science and mathematics.

Friedrich Solmsen stated in his *Plato's Theology*:

d) "It would be difficult to name a later theological system that is not in some way or other, directly or indirectly, indebted to Plato...By presenting the nature of the divine principle in a new light Plato transformed 'physics' and created a new hierarchy of values. Nor is this all. A history of the influence of Plato's theology would have to include the relation between religion and the State in the post-Platonic eras; all ideas concerning the function of Reason in the Cosmos, the place of Soul in the world, all systems of Nature, especially those that recognize a spiritual principle, and finally -- though we have by no means exhausted the subjects -- all speculations about the nature of evil, true and apparent, would have to form a part of this history." 10:84 PG

And from Constantin Ritter's work *The Essence of Plato's Philosophy*:
85a)
"I bring this presentation to a close with the same statement with which I closed my larger work on Plato. In this I tried briefly to characterize Plato's meaning for all time. To me, he is a philosopher second to none; an artist of first rank; a man favoured by God as few others have been; unforgettable for all time; releasing spiritual powers which have been a blessing to many and which will continue to be a blessing for all time." 10.85 PG

Paul Elmer More declared:

"Without it (the Platonic Tradition), so far as I can see, we should have remained barbarians; and, losing it, so far as I can see, we are in peril of sinking back into barbarism." P.E. More, *The Religion of Plato*, pp. VI-VII.

Alfred Edward Taylor stated:

b)

"If we sometimes underestimate our debt in these matters to Plato, it is only because Platonic ideas have become so completely part and parcel of our best tradition in morals and religion. His influence, like the pressure of the atmosphere, goes undetected because we never really get free from it." Alfred Edward Taylor, *Platonism and its Influence*, p.57.

G.. F. W. Hegel put forth these words:

"For what is peculiar in the philosophy of Plato is its application to the intellectual and supersensuous world, and its elevation of consciousness into the spiritual realm of spirit." 7.1

George Santayana in his *Interpretations of Poetry and Religion*, p.120 stated:

"We are often Platonists without knowing it. In some form or other Platonic ideas occur in all poetry of passion when it is seasoned with reflection. They are particularly characteristic of some Italians poets, scattered from the thirteenth to the sixteenth centuries. These poets had souls naturally Platonic."

c)

Desiderius Erasmus stated:

"For it was not ill-advised that the Divine Plato wrote that the only way for a state to attain happiness was for the supreme command to be given to philosophers, or else, inversely, that those who govern should themselves follow philosophy." *Erasmus On His Times*, MM Philips, p39.

"The divinely inspired Plato wrote of all these things in his Timaeus". Section 4 of his *Enchiridion Militis Christiani*.

Gottfried Wilhelm Leibniz in comparing the merits of Aristotle and Plato said in 27th Section of his *Theory of Knowledge and Metaphysics*:

"This position is in accord with the popular conception, as Aristotle's approach usually is. Plato thinks more profoundly."

d)
Giovanni Pico Della Mirandola in his *Oration on the Dignity of Man* makes 1 reference to Seneca, 1 to Cicero, 1 to Aristotle, 2 to Augustine, 4 to the New Testament, and 10 (ten) to Plato. In other words, if you want to know something about the dignity of man, Plato, in Pico's mind, says more about it than The New Testament, Augustine, Aristotle, Cicero, and Seneca combined.

Marsilio Ficino in his great work *Platonic Theology*, his dedication page to Lorrenzo de Medici starts with the following few words:

"Noble-souled Lorenzo! Plato, the father of philosophers, realizing that our minds...".

And he then continues:
86a)
"Nor does our beloved Plato only urge this pious duty on others, but he himself takes the lead. And that is why he has been considered indisputably divine and his teachings called "theology" among all peoples. For whatever subject he deals with, be it ethics, dialectic, mathematics of physics, he quickly brings it round, in a spirit of utmost piety, to the contemplation and worship of God"

And:

"Once they (those who become aquainted with Plato) are impressed by the arguments of Plato, will contemplate the higher objects which transcend the senses, and find happiness in putting things themselves before their shadows...This is what immortal Plato, with God's favor, accomplished without difficulty for the people of his own day. And this is what I, in imitation of Plato, but wholly dependent of God's help, have labored to achieve for the men of my own day in this present work."

b)
In a letter to Angelo Poliziano, Ficino declared:

"As everyone knows, I have followed the Divine Plato from my youth.. ...in my letters...if occasionally there is anything in them in some way relating to love, it is certainly Platonic and honorable". (In this and other works Ficino coined the phrase "Platonic Love".)

Aristotles' own words to the memory of Plato are:

"Of that unique man
Whose name is not to come from the lips of the wicked.
Theirs is not the right to praise him --
Him who first revealed clearly
By word and deed
That he who is virtuous is happy.
Alas, not one of us can equal him. 7.2

From Diogenes Laertius the following epitaphs upon Plato's tomb are taken: (One must remember that Plato actually was his nickname and his given name was Aristocles)
c)
"Here lies the god-like man Aristocles,
Eminent among men for his temperance and
the justice of his character.
And he, if ever anyone, had the fullest meed
of praise for wisdom, and he was too great for envy."

A second epitaph:

"Earth in her bosom here hides Plato's body,
but his soul has its immortal station with the blest,
Ariston's son, whom every good man,

even if he dwell afar off,
honors because he discerned the divine life.

d)

A third epitaph reads:

"Phoebus gave to mortals Asclepius and Plato,
the one to save their souls, the other to save their bodies.
From a wedding banquet he has passed to that city
which he had founded for himself and planted in the sky."

A fourth epitaph given by Diogenes Laertius himself:

"If Phoebus did not cause Plato to be born in Greece,
how came it that he healed the minds of men by letters?
As the god's son Asclepius is a healer of the body,
so is Plato of the immortal soul."

87a)

Walter Burkert in his great book *Greek Religion* states:

"Whoever reads Plato is fascinated by the encounter with an inexhaustibly rich mind who at the same time is one of the most refined masters of Greek language. Plato...established forever the measure for what is to be called philosophy...Since Plato there has been no theology which has not stood in his shadow...Since Plato and through him, religion has been essentially different from what it had been before...Then again there was the crucial progress in mathematics and astronomy from which Plato took method and model in order to reach a new level of discussion." (pp 321-322)

Ralph Waldo Emerson in his *Representative Men* made the following comments about Plato:

b)

"Without Plato we should almost lose our faith in the possibility of a reasonable book."

"These sentences (the works of Plato) contain the culture of nations; these are the corner-stone of schools; these are the fountain-head of literatures. A discipline it is in logic, arithmetic, taste, symmetry, poetry, language, rhetoric, ontology, morals or practical wisdom. There was never such range of speculation. Out of Plato come all things that are still written and debated among men of thought. Great havoc makes he among our originalities. We have reached the mountain from which all these drift boulders were detached. The Bible (Plato's works) of the learned for twenty-two hundred years, every brisk young man who says in succession fine things to each reluctant generation, --Boethius, Rabelais, Erasmus, Bruno, Locke, Rousseau, Alfieri, Coleridge, -- is some reader of Plato, translating into the vernacular, wittily, his good things. Even the men of grander proportion suffer some deduction from the misfortune (shall I say?) of coming after this exhausting generalizer. St. Augustine, Copernicus, Newton, Behmen, Swedenborg, Goethe, are likewise his debtors and must say after him. For it is fair to credit the broadest generalizer with all the particulars deducible from his thesis.

c) Plato is philosophy, and philosophy, Plato -- at once the glory and the shame of mankind, since neither Saxon nor Roman have availed to add any idea to his categories. No wife, no children had he, and the thinkers of all civilized nations are his posterity and are tinged with his mind. How many great men Nature is incessantly sending up out of night, to be his men, -- Platonists! the Alexandrians, a constellation of genius; the Elizabethans, not less; Sir Thomas More, Henry More, John Hales, John Smith, Lord Bacon, Jeremy Taylor, Ralph Cudworth, Sydenham, Thomas Taylor, Marcilius Ficinus and Picus Mirandola. Calvinism is in his Phaedo: Christianity is in it. Mahometanism draws all its philosophy, in its hand-book of morals, the Akhlak-y-Jalaly, from him. Mysticism finds in Plato all its texts. This citizen of a town in Greece is no villager nor patriot. An Englishman reads and says, 'how English!' A German, -- 'how Teutonic!' An Italian, -- 'how Roman and how Greek!' As they say that Helen of Argos had that universal beauty that every body felt related to her, so Plato seems to a reader in New England an American genius. His broad humanity transcends all sectional lines."

d)

Giambattista Vico declared about his two favorite men:

"For with an incomparable metaphysical mind Tacitus contemplates man as he is, Plato as he should be." 7.3

From Plutarch's *The Lives of the Noble Grecians and Romans*:

> Demosthenes: "Demosthenes was a scholar to Plato."
>
> Cicero: concerning the words of Cicero; "...and said of Plato's dialogues, that if Jupiter were to speak, it would be in language like theirs."
>
> Demetrius: "However, he (Demetrius) did but justify the saying of Plato, that the only certain way to be truly rich is not to have more property, but fewer desires."

88a)
Erigena said of Plato:

"The greatest of those who philosophized about the world." 7.4

W.R. Inge from his *Platonic Tradition in English Religious Thought*:

"Plato is for ever unintelligible till we read him as a prophet and prose-poet, and cease to hunt for a system in his writings."

Plotinus from *The Enneads* 4.8.1:

"The Divine Plato had so much to say that is beautiful to say of the soul."

Karl Jaspers from his *Socrates Buddha Confucius Jesus*, p.15:

"The *Phaedo* along with the *Apology* and the *Crito* is among the few irreplaceable documents of mankind. All through antiquity men of philosophical mind read it and learned how to die at peace by accepting their lot, however cruel and unjust."

Karl Jaspers also in his *Way to Wisdom* stated:

"In the study of Plato, as of Kant, we obtain no fixed knowledge but learn to philosophize for ourselves. All subsequent thinkers reveal themselves in their manner of understanding Plato." p.177

b)

"In Plato we find balanced form, supreme lucidity, the keenest knowledge of method, artistic expression of philosophical truth, without sacrifice of clarity and force." p. 192

And to close this section the popular saying of Alfred North Whitehead in his *Process and Reality*:

"The safest general characterization of the European philosophical tradition is that it consists of a series of footnotes to Plato." Chapter 1 Section 1.

c) From these men are only a few of the laudatory praises of Plato in the history of mankind. For it is in Plato that the foundation for all Western Spirituality is laid. But that is not all: every endeavor of human intellectual quest for truth and knowledge in every field of scientific exploration lives under the shadow and influence of Plato. His greatest desire, however, was to help men and women to be as much like God as possible for that would bring true happiness into their souls and also give the power of the ascent of the eternal soul to God, initiating the process now and fulfilling it in eternity.

Θ

ΘETA

CHAPTER EIGHT
THE EVER PRESENT PLATONIC TRADITION

ARISTOCLES (PLATO) SON OF ARISTON AND PERICTIONE (427-347 BCE)

89a) Plato was Aristocles' nickname for he was broad (platon) indeed in knowledge and maybe also in physique, since he had been a wrestler and was said to have broad shoulders. In any case, he was not narrow in either thought or knowledge or interest, and his inquiries were about everything that had value for human life. He was a lover of wisdom (philosopher) and sought to have knowledge about both the material and the abstract, the visible and the invisible, the heavenly things and the earthly things, the temporal and the eternal, the mathematical and the harmonious, the real and the imitation, the orderly and the beautiful, the pure and the mixed, the full and the empty. He sought to know of life's meaning and fulfillment both in the worldly and heavenly realms. He sought to know God, the Good beyond Being, the One who could not be found nor expressed but who gave life, beauty, harmony to both the material realm, as much as possible, and to the spiritual realm--and that forever. He wanted to know what was, how it was, why it was, and that it could not be otherwise, at least, as much as possible. He envisioned an eternal realm of perfection and sought to imitate it in human society, in a perfect republic and also in each man's soul: that that which is truly divine might be experienced both in human community and in the souls of each individual. Such was his quest and that is the quest of those who follow him and call themselves Platonists. Below are listed some of those who sought to follow his way for the goodness of human society and the blessedness of each individual soul.

b)

EUDOXUS OF CNIDUS (408 -355 BCE) Pupil and colleague of Plato at the Academy: was a celebrated mathematician and astronomer. Other members of Plato's Faculty at the Academy were:
MENAECHMUS, THEAETETUS, PHILIPPUS OF OPUS, HESTIAEUS, HERACLIDES, AND HERMODORUS (who wrote down some of Plato's lectures which were unwritten by Plato, the 'agrapha': Simplicius spoke of them in his writings).

SPEUSIPPUS (407-339 BCE) nephew of Plato and head of Academy after Plato's death.

XENOCRATES (396-314 BCE) head of the Academy after Speusippus

POLEMON (?-270 BCE) first head of the Academy that did not know Plato: during his tenure, Zeno of Citium studied at the Academy and later founded Stoicism, which accounts for the Platonic base of Stoicism.

PHILO(N) OF LARISSA (160-80 BCE) After years of Skepticism at the Academy, Philo restored the "Old Academy" again.

ANTIOCHUS OF ASCALON (130-68) was influential in the Roman Scipio's Circle of friends which included Cicero, who had also studied in Athens.

c)

ZENO OF CITIUM (in Cyprus)(335-263 BCE) studied under Polemon for ten years at the Academy before founding the Stoic school of philosophy and that accounts for the strong Platonic flavor found in most Stoics, including much use of Plato's four cardinal virtues: wisdom, courage, justice, and temperance.

ARATUS (315-240 BCE) astronomer, who wrote the beautiful astronomical poem *Phaenomena.*

CLITOMACHUS (187-109 BCE) wrote over 400 works but none survive.

<u>THE GREEK MATHEMATICIANS AND ASTRONOMERS</u>:

ARISTARCHUS OF SAMOS (Third Century BCE) who taught the solar system,

HIPPARCHUS (190-126 BCE) measured year to 365 ¼ - one three hundreds of a day, and invented trigonometry

d) ERATOSTHENES (275-194 BCE) calculated the circumference of the earth at 252,000 stades, that is 24,662 miles, within 195 miles of the correct figure of 24,857 miles)
POSIDONIUS (135 - 50 BCE) recognized the enormous size of the sun and measured its distance from the earth with amazing accuracy for his time
PANAETIUS (185-109 BCE) a Platonic/Stoic eclectic
THEODOSIUS OF BITHYNIA (150-70 BCE) mathematician and astronomer who developed astronomical tables for different geographical locations, sundials that could be used anywhere
MARCUS TULLIUS CICERO (106-43 BCE)
VIRGIL (PUBLIUS VERGILIUS MARO) (70-19 BCE)
EUDORUS OF ALEXANDRIA (fl c 25 BCE)
MANDEANS --- Jewish Gnostics (from First Century BCE)
PHILO(N) JUDAEUS OF ALEXANDRIA (30BCE-45 CE)
LONGINUS (First Century CE)
MODERATUS OF GADES (c.50-100 CE)
NICOMACHUS OF GERASA (between 50-150 CE)
PLUTARCH (50-120 CE) He was alive during the period in which the
90a) Christian Canon (New Testament) was being written.
ALBINUS (fl during mid Second Century CE)
VALENTINUS (middle of the Second Century CE)
APOLLONIUS OF TYANA (d. 98CE) a Pythagorean-Platonist about whom many myths and legends were recorded by Philostratus.
THEON OF SMYRNA (fl.115-140 CE) mathematics, music, astronomy
LUCIUS APULEIUS (123-170 CE)
MAXIMUS OF TYRE (fl late Second Century CE)
ATTICUS(c.150 -200 CE)
HERMETIC LITERATURE OF EGYPT
CHRISTIAN GNOSTICISM
CELSUS A Platonic critic of Christianity (writing about 177-180 CE)
GALEN OF PERGAMUM (129-199 CE) A physician and critical of Christianity
GAIUS (Second Century CE) Roman jurist: Justinian thought highly of
b) his works and called him “our Gaius”
CLEMENT OF ALEXANDRIA (150-215 CE) a Christian Platonist
AMMONIUS SACCAS OF ALEXANDRIA (first half of Third Century CE) teacher of both Origen and Plotinus.

ORIGENES ADAMANTIUS (185-254 CE) a Christian Platonist. Eusebius Pamphilus' *Ecclesiatical History*, Book 6 Chapter 19, he states of Origen: "He was always in company with Plato, and had the works also of Numenius and Cranius, of Apollophanes and Longinus, of Moderatus and Nicomachus, and others in his hands." Origen was indeed a Platonist and surrounded himself with the thoughts of other Platonists as well, but also a Christian and he let the Christian element corrupt the pure Platonic doctrines and used allegory to reframe the horror stories of the Tanak so that they would appear more rational, kind, and

c) Platonic.

AMELIUS GENTILIANUS (Third Century CE) pupil of Plotinus

EUNAPIUS (345-420 CE) a strong opponent of Christianity

NUMENIUS OF APAMEA (Second Century CE) influenced both Plotinus and Porphyry: Plotinus was accused of copying from him.

IAMBLICHUS (c 250-325 CE) pupil of Porphyry

PLOTINUS (205-270 CE) greatest and most influential of the early "Neoplatonists", after whom virtually every philosopher of Western Antiquity was a Platonist in one form or another: Stoicism and Epicureanism were now irrelevant and even Aristotelian thought was taught only as an attachment in understanding Plato.

PORPHYRY (232-305) Neoplatonist and editor of Plotinus' lectures

CALCIDIUS (Fourth Century CE) a Christian Platonist: wrote a commentary of the Timaeus

LIBANIUS OF ANTIOCH (314-393 CE) Platonic teacher in Antioch

d) and friend of both Basil and Julian

JULIANUS (332-363 CE) Platonist and Emperor of Rome 361-363

SALLUSTIUS (Fourth Century CE) a friend of Emperor Julian

MACROBIUS (? Late Fourth Century CE) Neoplatonist

SYNESIUS OF CYRENE (370-413 CE) a pupil of Hypatia and bishop of Ptolemais in Lybia who preached Neoplatonism

HYPATIA OF ALEXANDRIA (d. 415 CE) noble and renowned Platonist who taught philosophy, mathematics and astronomy, killed by Christian monks.

OLYMPIODORUS (before 380 - 425 CE) Neoplatonist

MARTIANUS CAPELLA (fl 410-439 CE) allegories of the heavenly
91a) ascent of the soul
TIMAEUS (probably Fourth Century CE) compiled an accurate lexicon of Plato
AUGUSTINE OF HIPPO (354-430 CE) a Christian Platonist early on; but later more of a heresy hunting bishop: he listed 88 heresies
NEMESIUS OF EDESSA (fl 400 CE) a very Platonist Christian
PROCLUS (410-472 CE) a Neoplatonist who wrote a commentary on Plato's Timaeus and other writings.
JOHN PHILOPONUS (490-570 CE) Christian Platonist
AUTHOR OF PSEUDO-DIONYSIUS (c 500 CE)
BOETHIUS (480-524 CE) wrote Consolation of Philosophy
JOHN SCOTUS ERIUGENA (810-877 CE)
MICHAEL PSELLUS (1018-1078 CE)
THIERRY OF CHARTRES---(middle of Twelfth Century CE) the
b) Platonic School of Chartres
BERNARD OF CHARTRES (d. 1130 CE)-- of the School of Chartres
WILLIAM OF CONCHES(1080-1154 CE) -- of the School of Chartres
GILBERT OF POITIERS (1076-1154) -- of the School of Chartres
ANSELM OF CANTERBURY (1033-1109 CE)
PETER ABAILARD (1070-1142 CE) -- wrote a commentary on Porphyry and *Sic et Non*
PETER LOMBARD (1100-1160 CE) wrote the *Sentences*
ALAIN OF LILLE (1128-1203 CE)
ROBERT GROSSETESTE - (1175-1253 CE) often quoted Augustine and Anslem and had many references to Plato himself.
MOSES MAIMONIDES (1135-1204 CE) a Jewish Platonist
ROGER BACON (1214-1292 CE) a "Renaissance Man" before the Renaissance, including Greek.
BONAVENTURA (1221-1274 CE) A Christian Platonist
DANTE (1265-1321 CE) fitted his entire works into the framework of Platonic thought.
PETRARCH (1304-1374 CE) whose Triumphs and his hopes of heaven are based mainly on Cicero's Dream of Scipio and Plato's
c) Phaedo
MEISTER ECKHART (1260-1327 CE) he as well as all "Christian mystics" was greatly influenced by Platonism. Jacob Burckhardt closes his work *The Civilization of the Renaissamce in Italy* with

these words: "Echoes of medieval mysticism here flow into one current with Platonic doctrines, and with a characteristically modern spirit. One of the most precious fruits of the knowledge of the world and of man here comes to maturity, on whose account alone the Italian Renaissance must be called the leader of the modern ages."

MANUEL CHRYSOLORAS (d. 1415 CE) the first true teacher of classical Greek in the West; taught in Florence

GEORGE GEMISTUS PLETHON (d. 1464 CE) encouraged Cosimo de Medici to establish the Florentine Academy.

NICHOLAS OF CUSA (CUSANUS)(1401-1464 CE) brought back Greek manuscripts from the east, including the *Platonic Theology* of Proclus and thereafter eagerly studied; Meister Eckhart, Pseudo-Dionysius, Augustine, Bonaventure, and Thierry of Chartres all of whom were deeply seasoned with Platonic

d) doctrines.

PARACELSUS (THEOPHRASTUS BOMBASTUS VON HOHENHEIM) (1493-1541 CE) philosopher of nature

BESSARION (c.1400 -1472 CE) became a councilman in Florence, later a cardinal in the Church.

JOHN PICO DELLA MIRANDOLA 1463-1494 CE) wrote *The Dignity of Man.*

MARSILIO FICINO (1433-1499 CE) numerous great works on Platonism.

COSIMO DE MEDICI (1389-1464 CE) sponsored the establishment of the Florintine Academy.

PIETRO BEMBO (1470-1547 CE) the most famous representative of the spiritualization of love in the Italian Renaissance which found its support in Plato's doctrine of the soul.

JOHANNES ARGYROPULOS (d. 1486 CE) head of Greek studies in

92a) Florence and later in Rome. Reuchlin was one of his pupils.

LORENZO DE MEDICI (1449-1492 CE)

MICHAELANGELO BUONARROTI (1475-1564 CE)

TELESIO (Middle of Sixteenth Century CE)

JOHN COLET (1467-1519 CE) English Humanist

HEINRICH CORNELIUS AGRIPPA VON NETTESHEIM (1486-1535 CE)

DESIDERIUS ERASMUS (1466-1536 CE)

JOHANNES REUCHLIN (1455-1522 CE)
WILLIBALD PIRCKHEIMER (1470-1539 CE)
SEBASTIAN FRANK (1499-1542 CE)
MARTIN BUCER (1491-1551 CE)
THOMAS MORE 1478-1535 CE)
NICHOLAS COPERNICUS (1473-1543 CE) AND GALILEO GALILEI
b) (1564-1642 CE) revived the solar system first taught by Aristarchus of Samos (3rd Century BCE), mathematician and astronomer.
FRANCESCO PATRIZZI (1529-1597 CE)
GIORDANO BRUNO (1548-1600 CE) humanist, burned at the stake
TOMMASO CAMPANELLA (1568-1639 CE)
JACOB BOEHME (1575-1624 CE)
BENJAMIN WHICHCOTE (1609-1683 CE)Cambridge Platonist
HENRY MORE (1614-1687 CE) Cambridge Platonist
RALPH CUDWORTH (1617-1688 CE) Cambridge Platonist
JEREMY TAYLOR (1613-1667) Cambridge Platonist
JOHN SMITH--(1618-1652 CE) Cambridge Platonist
PETER STERRY -- (1613-1672 CE)Cambridge Platonist
NATHANIEL CULVERWEL (1618-1651 CE) Cambridge Platonist
THOMAS BROWNE (1605-1682 CE) his Platonic influence made him kind and tolerant in an age lacking in it - similar to the Cambridge Platonists.
SPENSER (1552-1599 CE)
WILLIAM LAW (1686-1761 CE)
ISAAC. NEWTON (1642-1727 CE)
JOHANNES KEPLER (1571-1630 CE)
FRANCIS BACON (1561- 1626 CE) who believed, following Plato, that
c) philosophy and mathematics were central in science, yet he did not embrace the solar system of Copernicus and Galileo.
GOTTFRIED WILHELM LEIBNIZ (1646-1716 CE)
JEAN JACQUE ROUSSEAU (1712-1778 CE)
IMMANUEL KANT (1724-1804 CE)
JOHANN CHRISTOPH FRIEDRICH von SCHILLER (1759-1805 CE)
GEORG WILHELM FRIEDRICH HEGEL (1770-1831 CE)
JOHANN WOLFGANG von GOETHE (1749-1832 CE) in his Faust he presents the rational quest and the inner longing of one for the ultimate knowledge and the ineffable at the top of all existence.

Santayana stated in his *Three Philosophical Poets* (p 130) about Goethe's work the following: "Now Faust is the foam on the top of two great waves of human aspiration, merging and heaping themselves up together, -- the wave of romanticism rising from the depths of northern traditions and genius, and the wave of the new paganism (Platonism) coming from Greece over Italy"

d)

FRIEDRICH ERNST DANIEL SCHLEIERMACHER (1768-1834 CE)
WILLIAM WORDSWORTH (1770-1850 CE)
SAMUEL TAYLOR COLERIDGE (1772-1834 CE)
FRANZ XAVIER von BAADER (1765-1841 CE)
MARY SHELLEY (1797-1851 CE)
FRIEDRICH WILHELM JOSEPH von SCHELLING (1775-1854 CE)
DAVID FRIEDRICH STRAUSS (1808-1874 CE) taught Plato
RALPH WALDO EMERSON (1803-1882 CE)
BENJAMIN JOWETT (1817-1893 CE) comprehensive translater of all genuine works of Plato into English
JOHN RUSKIN (1819-1900 CE)
CHARLES BIGG OF OXFORD (published 1870 CE)
CONSTANTIN RITTER (died 1936 CE)
PAUL ELMER MORE (1864-1937 CE)
ALFRED EDWARD TAYLOR (1869-1945)
WILLIAM RALPH INGE (1860-1954 CE)

93a)

One must remember that all education before Plato stopped in antiquity at our high school level. It is true that some learned from traveling Sophists in Greece and Gurus in the East and in Ancient Israel, the religious spirit of a prophet was often passed on by certain followers sometimes referred to as a school of prophets. But only beginning with Plato's Academy was there a fixed school on the university level in which students from all parts of the ancient world could come to and meet with others scholars and teachers (not only Plato taught at his academy but others, such as Eudoxus, taught there likewise as a type of primitive faculty). There were many subjects taught at the Academy, and it is a mistake to consider a person a Platonist only if he believed in a metaphysical world or an immortal soul or any other spirit or religious teaching as such. For the Academy was a true university where not only all the metaphysical questions were asked and discussed but also ethics, politics, logic, mathematics, science, psychology, nature, cosmology, education and the principles of it, the arts -- even the mechanical arts based on mathematics, history, writing -- even poetry, music, gymnastics and human conditioning and health, and the nature of man, All advances in all such subjects in subsequent years are in the shadow of Plato and his Academy. His brightest student, Aristotle (if it were not Eudoxus), after studying under Plato for 20 years, then in imitation of Plato, also started **b)** a school that emphasized zoology, botany and biology -- Aristotles' father was a physician. Zeno of Citium, also a student at the Academy for several years, started the school of the Stoics. Higher education spread throughout the Hellenized world like wildfire with schools of university level "academics" were planted in Alexandria in Egypt -- between 400,000 (Koester) and 700,000 (Tarn) volumes of no less than 1100 different Greek authors, on the island of Rhodes, in Pergamum which was second in volumes at 200,000 to Alexandria, in Antioch, Smyrna, and Cos. There were also many smaller schools at Tarsus, Syracuse, Apamea, Miletus and many others that had libraries, museums, and a gymnasia.

c) Wherever there was a school, it had a Platonic flavor whether in science or mathematics, or the arts, or philosophy and theology. No learning on that level was without a flavoring of Platonic teaching, tradition and spirit. Platonism while it did not become a big organized religion, became the salt of the earth for those seeking truth in every human endeavor so that their function in life would be most proficient and reflect the beauty and power of the human mind. Let man's mind ascend to the highest and let his soul ascend to the Eternal and Good. No serious thinker in the Western World after Plato can disown him, whether he wants to or not. As A E Taylor so well spoke that Plato is like the air of the atmosphere, we need it and we breathe it without even being aware that it is there. So let not the unlearned ask, "If Plato is so important why do we not hear more about him? I have never met one of his followers?" Let that man look into the mirror, for without realizing it, he, at least in one way or another, is a follower of Plato. And if he is not, let him feel pity for himself.

I

IOTA

CHAPTER NINE
THE NATURE OF GOD IN PLATONIC TRADITION

I. THE KNOWLEDGE OF GOD IS BEYOND HUMAN CAPACITY

94a) Plato makes it very clear that God is far above man in every respect, for even to know him directly is beyond human capacity. He stated in the Timaeus:

"The Father and Maker of all this universe is past finding out; and even if we found him, to tell of him to all men would be impossible" (Timaeus 28c)

Nevertheless, Plato believed without a doubt ever expressed that God existed, that he was good, beautiful, compassionate, and eternal. He pointed to logic and the indirect "evidence" of the nature and being of God. He saw him, according to the best science and logic of his day, as the cause of the form of material existence and the well orderedness of the universe. Likewise he believed God necessary for the eternal forms of absolute values upon which all ethics could be based as an eternal standard. Thirdly, he based it upon the "wonder" of the universe and the thought of the unending eternity beyond time and the vast deepness of space. Fourthly, he gives indications that he felt the awe-inspiring idea of the Holy, the One, beyond being. And lastly, he believed that God had placed a daimon within each person that caused the longing all have to participate in ultimate beauty and eternity itself. He believed man was

made for eternity and death was only for the material part of man's nature. People believe in God for various reasons, as did Plato, without claiming knowledge or scientific proof. Albert Einstein believed in God
b) because it was through such faith that man had a desire to know and delight in science: "I maintain that cosmic religious feeling is the strongest and noblest incitement to scientific research." His Last Will and Testament began with these words: "In the Name of God". Otto Hahn, the father of nuclear fission, never questioned the existence of God. Likewise men like A. N. Whitehead, philosopher; Werner von Braun, father of space travel, Dag Hammarskjoeld, Secretariat General of the United Nations; and many others from all fields, in their own minds, without scientific proof, found enough about life and the universe to confirm in themselves a solid faith in God. They too, as did Plato, realized that God is simply past finding out, in terms of mathematics or science; but the soul's logic, longing, idea of the holy, the infinities of time and space, and the desire of an ethical standard, all combined to convince them that God is there in his goodness, his eternity, his absolute virtue, and in his beauty. Plato and his colleagues in teaching and dialogue often referred to the need and propriety of praying to God before undertaking a task, even if small, and especially when it was a difficult one.

c) In general terms about God, Plato agreed with and developed the idea about God from his elder contemporary, Euripides, who had declared that "If the gods do anything shameful, they are not gods." Plato continued this thought into his monotheistic view adding that anything evil in either nature or among men is not from God. Nature has its own laws, and God does not interfere, even if He could, with them. And among men and their disharmony among themselves, only men themselves are to blame. Leibniz in his Discourse on Metaphysics (1686 CE) (part one), defines God with these words:

"The conception of God which is the most common and the most full of meaning is expressed well enough in the words: 'God is an absolutely perfect being.' The implications, however, of these words fail to receive sufficient consideration. For instance, there are many different kinds of perfection, all of which God possesses, and each one of them pertains to him in the highest degree."

This is pure Plaontic thought, as Plato believed that God is the absolute Unity of All Virtues, for He alone is the One (`ο ϖν), the Good Beyond Existence (or Being).

Plutarch, the Greatest Platonist of Middle Platonism, puts the Platonic thinking in these words:

d)

"Socrates and Plato agree that God is that which is One, has its original from its own self, is of a singular subsistence, is only One Being who is perfectly good: all these various names signifying goodness do all centre in mind; hence God is to be understood as that mind and intellect, which is separate idea, that is to say, pure and unmixed of all matter, and not mingled with anything subject to passions."9.1

Many times Plato referred to God as nous (νουs) which is generally translated as either mind or intellect. The Hermetic literature in most cases is simply restated Plato and when it is not corrupted with other thoughts it can be very clear and devotional. Excerpt 1 of the Stobaeus restates Plato in a full way declaring:

95a)

"To conceive is difficult; and to describe Him is impossible (a direct quotation from Plato), even if one is able to conceive Him. For it is not easy for that which is imperfect to apprehend that which is perfect, and it is hard for that which is of short duration to have dealings with that which is everlasting. The one ever is, the other passes; the one is real, the other is but shadowed forth by sense-picturing. So widely is that which is mortal separated from that which is divine. And the wide interval between them dims men's vision of the Beautiful. With our eyes we can see bodies; but that which is incorporeal and invisible and without shape, and is not composed of matter, cannot be apprehended by senses as ours."

Also from the Egyptian Gnostic Platonized thought is a similar statement in The Tripartite Tractate (I.5):

b)

"Not only is he the One called 'without a beginning' and 'without an end,' because he is unbegotten and immortal. But just as he has no beginning and no end, so he is unattainable in his greatness, inscrutable in his wisdom, incomprehensible in his power, and unfathomable in his sweetness. In the proper sense He alone is the Good, ..the Complete Perfect One. He is the One filled with all his offspring and with every virtue and with everything of value."

One can here see Plato's unity of all virtues, the incomprehensible nature, the goodness, the measure of all morality, and the eternal nature of God. The Egyptian Gnostics were at time more Platonic than some of those who called themselves Platonists.

c)

Plotinus who absorbed Plato's religious writings completely made them very personal and even mystical. He, as most mystics, stressed the feeling of awe of in the presence of God but in softer but intimate terms. He stated:

"The chief difficulty (in knowing God) is this: awareness of The One comes to us as neither by knowing nor by the pure thought that discovers the other intelligible things, but by a presence transcending knowledge ...therefore we must go beyond knowledge and hold to unity...That is why Plato says of The One, 'It can neither be spoken nor written about.' If nevertheless we speak of it and write about it, we do so only to give direction, to urge towards that vision beyond discourse, to point out the road to one desirous of seeing."9.2

d)

This feeling of The Presence is likened to the Awe of the Holy One that Plato felt in a state of wonder when viewing the universe, and was well developed by Rudolf Otto in his book *The Idea of the Holy*. Otto refers to a recorded conversation between Eckermann and Goethe in which Goethe replied:

"Dear Boy, what do we know of the idea of the divine, and what can our narrow conceptions presume to tell of the Supreme Being? If I called Him by a hundred names, like the Turk, I should yet fall short and have said nothing in comparison to the boundlessness of His attributes."9.3

96a)

Goethe often called himself "the pagan", for his views about the Deity certainly were closer to Plato's than were the views of Christianity. John

Colet the English Renaissance Platonist quotes approvingly of such Platonic doctrine of the God beyond knowledge with these words:

"Even more important, Dionysius had, with Plotinus, declared the One-Good-Beauty to be 'above being' and 'super-essentially Essence."9.4

The Christian mystics, as well as the Sufis (Islamic mystics) are much closer to the humility of Plato than the Christian Dogmatists who write creeds like the Athansasian Creed that tries to tell humanity exactly what God is like and if you do not believe it you will be damned forever. One such mystic of the Eastern Church, Maximus the Confessor, put it this way in trying to express God's unknowableness:

b)

"If God is essential knowledge, then God is subordinate to the intellect, for clearly the intellect is prior to all knowledge that it embraces. Therefore God is beyond knowledge because He is infinitely beyond every intellect, whatever the knowledge it embraces."9.5

Iamblichus, in his Life of Pythagoras, believed that if one looked to the heavens and saw its orderly beauty, one, with the help of God himself, could detect the Intellect that so arranged such beauty out of mere loose preexistent formless matter. This followed Plato's doctrine of natural argument for the First Cause's existence. He stated:

"For that which is capable of being fashioned by reason, which has an intellectual perception of things beautiful and base, can erectly extend itself from earth, and look to heaven, and can perceive with the eye of intellect the Highest...with the assistance from above."9.6

c)

Even here, however, the natural argument needs to be supplemented by Divine help, that probably means some type of enlightenment or inspiration from above.

In the Pseudo-Dionysius, written about the year 500 CE, there are many statements both positive and negative about trying to express the nature of God. For he distrusts any human conception of God as well as any of the words we use in trying to describe Him. He stated: "The all-perfect and unique Cause of all things transcends all affirmation, and the simple preeminence of His absolute nature is outside of every negation--free from every limitation and beyond them all."9.7

d) Paul Tillich also cautions his readers about claims of knowing or experiencing God:

"Thomas (Aquinas) was right in denying that the vision of God is a human possibility, in so far as men in time and space are concerned. Neither should the word 'experience' be used, because it ordinarily describes the observed presence of one reality to another reality, and because the Unconditioned is not a matter of experiential observation."9.8

Martin Buber in his *Eclipse of God* speaks of the living and true faith of a believer, even though he knows nothing and can not know anything about God or His nature. He presented these thoughts:

"It is not necessary to know something about God in order really to believe in Him: many true believers know how to talk *to* God but not *about* Him. If one dares to turn toward the unknown God, to go to meet Him, to call to Him, Reality is present....In Aeschylus' ..Agamemnon the chorus says:

97a) Zeus, whoever He is,
If it pleases Him so to be called,
With this name I invoke him.

(Then Buber refers to Plato's Cratylus: "We know neither the nature nor the true name of the gods." In addition Buber refers to a passage in Euripides' Trojan Women:)

O Foundation of the earth and above it throned,
Whoever thou art, beyond our mind's poor grasp,
Whether Zeus or Fate or spirit of men,
I implore thee.

Thus runs the teaching of Buber: even though God is "eclipsed" beyond our being able to know anything about Him, our faith comes alive when we adore Him, seek Him, and pray to Him.

b) In conclusion to this section it must be stated clearly again: man does not know God nor His nature, but he can love Him, adore Him, speak well of Him, and pray to Him. This will put the electricity into one's spiritual life and lift his soul to the Eternal and the Good that surpasses all human comprehension. And that is the nature of religion, the spark of an electric spirit that is shared between the believer and God. To claim more than that purity of spirit and presuppose that one has knowledge that no one else has is an illusion and the type of arrogance among mortals with which God is certainly not impressed. Those who have claimed more and taught more and tried to impose their view upon others have done tremendous harm to humanity and made the term "religion" ugly and hateful to many, especially those who have been harmed by such "true believers" who hunt out the "heretics" and "infidels" for persecution. Julian Huxley put it very powerfully in his book *Religion Without Revelation*. These are his words:

c)

"The insufferable arrogance of those who claim to be in sole possession of religious truth would happily disappear, together with the consequences which arise when such people are in a position to enforce their views--consequences such as bigotry, religious war, religious persecution, the horror of the Inquisition, attempts to suppress knowledge and learning, hostility to social or moral change. The appeal to absolute authority (a product of the race's intellectual childhood) could no longer be admitted, whether an appeal to a sacred book, a divine founder, a revealed code, or a sacred church. All such appeals would continue to carry some weight, but could not be considered a court of absolute appeal, beyond the bar of reason or change. No longer could the legitimate affairs of this world be neglected on the pretext of attending to those of the next, nor unscrupulous medicine-men, priests, or religious organizations feather their nests out of the pretended supernatural power which they wield. No longer would the hideous terror of everlasting hell torment innocent children or distort the lives of men and women, nor the true comfort of religious worship and contemplation be turned out of its course, as the result of fear of a personal, omnipotent, and exacting God, and forced into the channel of propitiatory sacrifice, the meaningless mumbo-jumbo of certain types of ritual and what I can only describe as the 'begging-letter' type of prayer."

II. SYMBOLS -- MYTHS -- WORDS

d) Because man can not know God or His Nature, he must use symbols, myths, and words to express himself to others, and they act as media of communication giving concessions to man's lack of the possibility of true knowledge. It must, however, be understood that they can not present themselves as actual knowledge of God nor can they be used to establish any dogma by which one can judge another. That would be exactly the type of arrogance so described and detested above by Julian Huxley, and, as a matter of fact, by all people of humble faith and some intellectual wisdom.

98a) As mentioned above, Plato himself expressed the fact that we do not know either the nature or the true name of God. Yet, we must speak of Him in order to honor Him and try to express His true nature, for if we believe that He is indeed the perfect unity of all virtues, and man's goal is to imitate God as much as possible, then it is necessary for the sake of the standard of ethical beauty and moral health that we be able in some way to relate God's nature as much as possible. Of course one can never be dogmatic about such teachings because we all approach God with a different mindset in trying to frame a perfect picture of Him. That is why in many of Plato's dialogues there is no closure or agreement on what the particular virtue they have been discussing actually is. While such dialogues are frustrating to certain people who want a simple answer, Plato reminds us that when discussing that which is abstract and ultimate it is in the last word, past finding out. But the dialogues teach us how to think, and that is the great value of philosophy in its quest for truth. Pythagoras was once called a wise man, and he rejected the accolade, saying that only God is wise, he, being only a man, was a lover of wisdom, Philo-sophia, a philosopher. In this he is said to have coined the word philosopher. Plato followed that concept: only God is wise, the rest **b)** of us are seekers of wisdom. This applies to our knowledge of God and of all things abstract and eternal, we are mere seekers of the knowledge of such things. Thus all our words, our expressions and thoughts, our icons and our myths are only symbols: but symbols that do indeed try to symbolize the Good, the Pure, the Beautiful and the Eternal. All people of all philosophies and religions need to be baptized into this mental framework so that they can be delightfully honest, open, and accepting of others who are also seekers of wisdom, and not be judgmental towards them who are trying in their own way to find and love that which is Good and Eternal.

Walter Burkert, after referring to Plato's defense of Socrates states that, in Plato, and in most thinking Greeks, "a creed or confession of faith is as foreign to Greeks as the Spanish inquisition." He then continues with the following words:

c)

"It is Plato who brings about a revolution in religious language and in piety at one and the same time. Thereafter we find faith supported by philosophy, love transcending the world, and hope for an afterlife; there is humility, service to the gods, and at the same time the goal of assimilation to God."9.10

Sextus the Pythagorean stated: "Do not investigate the name of God, because you will not find it."9.11 Sextus then goes on to say that for an inferior like man to put a name on the greatly superior being, God, is quite haughty and is best left undone.

The work called the Pseudo-Dionysius, before discussing the many names of God that have been passed down in sacred scriptures, makes this "beware" statement: "This is why we must not dare to resort to words or conceptions concerning that hidden divinity which transcends being...the unknowing of what is beyond being is something above and beyond speech, mind, or being itself."(*The Divine Names*: Chapter One)

d) Clement of Alexandria, a Christian Platonist before the Church's arrogant take over of Western Society and the implementation of creeds to be believed, was not concerned about his openly Platonic teachings and stated the following:

"Human teachers, speaking of God, are not reliable, as men. For he that is man cannot speak worthily the truth concerning God: the feeble and mortal cannot speak worthily of the Unoriginated and Incorruptible--the work, of the Workman. He who is incapable of speaking what is true respecting himself, is he not much less reliable in what concerns God? For just as far as man is inferior to God in power, so much feebler is man's speech than Him...For human speech is by nature feeble, and incapable of uttering God. I do not say His name. For to name it is common, not to philosophers only, but also to poets. Nor do I say His essence; for this is impossible, but I speak of the power and works of God." (*Stromata or "Miscellanies":* Book VI, Chapter 18).

Yet, for the sake of human communication, men use names anthropomorphically so that they can express what they consider the beautiful and delightful nature and qualities which they believe God has, even if human expressions fall short.

III. ANTHROPOLOGICAL EXPRESSIONS OF HONOR TO GOD

99a) A. THE FATHERHOOD OF GOD

One of the earliest and most endearing anthropomorphisms is referring to God as a Father. Father Zeus was common among the Greeks and Plato in his creation myth often used the word "Father" and the two words "Father and Maker" and called his creation his "children" in whom He was delighted. In *The Epic Cycle*, the fifth verse, it is stated: Eumelus somewhere introduces Zeus dancing: he says--'In the midst of them danced the Father of men and gods." God was the Good Father and the total embodiment of Happiness which showed in his delight that he had for the beauty of the creation. To say that God danced as a Happy Father is certainly putting human concepts forth in the description of God and can not be taken literally, but spiritually. Yet, it says so much to us who understand it spiritually, for it gives intimacy to the entire universe which would normally seem impossible. It is the electricity that brings forth the energy of spiritual life among men and makes them feel at home in the vast cosmos. In the *Hermetic Corpus,* Libellus 14, words of such gentleness are spoken:

b)

"Thus is it meet for us to think, and thus thinking, to marvel, and marveling, to deem ourselves blest, in that we have come to recognize our Father; for what is dearer to a child than his true father? Who is he then, and how are we to recognize him? Are we to say that it is right that the name of God alone should be assigned to him, or that of Maker, or that of Father? Nay, all three names are his; he is rightly named God by reason of his power, and Maker by reason of his works, and Father by reason of his goodness."

c) In this 21st Century CE it is more proper to think of God as our Parent, for Father seems overly directed to the male being, but one must again remember Plato's concept that God is the Good Beyond Being, thus making God beyond male or female. Plato backed such lack of discrimination toward women by his works, especially in his Republic where he proposed that both the decision-making leaders and the priesthood be divided equally in numbers between men and women. It was not a simple platitude to him. But in antiquity Father was used as the term for the One, and its use too became a concession to anthropomorphical ways of speaking about the Deity. One of the dangers of taking the spiritual concept of God as a "father" or "parent" is that people somewhat automatically switch back to the normal human meaning of the word and then try to "personalize" God and even act as if God owes them something as a human father owes an upbringing to his **d)** children. An upbringing, yes, but only spiritually, for our transient bodily existence is subject to the laws of the physical nature of which our bodies are made, and this has no eternal relevance for our souls. This will be discussed later, but here is just a caution for those who want to demand from God certain things that perhaps they were able to demand from their earthly parents. Anthropomorphisms are always subjected to material or earthly interpretations and can mislead those not attached spiritually to the Eternal Father.

B. GOD IS NOT ALL KNOWING OR ALL POWERFUL

100a) Nothing could be more explicit in the Timaeus, Plato's creation myth, than that God is not all powerful or all knowing. He worked from a pattern, probably a blueprint he had in his mind, and after ordering the preexistent matter as best he could, he rejoiced, and then tried to improve on it. Constantly during the workings of God in the ordering of the material realm Plato uses the expression "as much as possible", for the material physical substance with which God worked had its own laws of nature, and God could not overcome that. He worked against αναγκη usually translated "necessity" or "laws of nature", and he could only do what αναγκη (ananke) was capable of within its own innate laws. Creation out of nothing (creatio ex nihilo), taught by Christianity, would not make any sense to Plato at all: for why would God create a material over which he could not have total control? For everything material changes and all life in bodily form is mortal. More will be presented later about these concepts. Here it is just necessary to present Plato's idea that God is not all knowing and all powerful.

C. GOD'S LOVE AND GRACE

b) What is much more important for Plato is that God is loving and gracious, and that is all loving and all gracious. One of the things God did in Platonic tradition was to give man an inner daimon that longed for the good, the beautiful, and the eternal, for God knew that only with such mind can man ever be truly and deeply happy. God himself was the embodiment of happiness and he wished his creatures to be as much like himself spiritually as possible. The ancient pagan festivals were given to men as a break from their tedious work so that they could celebrate, dance, and feast in joy. While earthly fun is good to have, Plutarch reminds us that "ten thousand times more and greater is the good hope, the true joy, that attend it" i.e. the special holidays set aside to celebrate life and the gods, i.e. the lower gods that the Father God has given to be guardians to men. Religious festivals were for the body, the joy of human fellowship, and the spiritual uplifting it gave to those who celebrated the **c)** presence of the gods. Plutarch also reminds his readers of the indiscriminate love of God by pointing out that all workers, even the lowest, old men and women, all together with all others "are strangely elevated and transported with mirth and joviality. Rich men and princes are used at certain times to make public entertainments and to keep open houses for all... (concerning God's over seeing presence, he continues)...for what recreates and cheers us at the festivals is not the store of good wine and roast meat, but the good hope and persuasion that God is there present and propitious to us, and kindly accepts of what we do."9.12 Of those lower gods, Pindar said "Phoebus was by mighty Zeus designed of all the gods to be to man most kind."

d) Against older Greek traditions, such as Homer, Plato rebels, for he will not permit in his *Republic* Homer to be read for he defiles the dignity of God. Plato's God has no passions, such as jealousy and anger, and he does mankind no evil or harm. Homer was the most read of all the Greek poets and Plato was simply aghast at the devotion given to him. He made no bones about it though, Homer was condemned reading for the people of his utopian city, the *Republic*. Looking at Homer one can easily understand Plato's reaction. It was a book of war, a warrior's epic with a warrior's ethical standards; and even more so, the squabbling, jealous, and self-centered gods joined in the conflict. It was an assault upon the dignity of all the gods. Below is a glance at those things in Homer's *Iliad* that were abhorred by Plato:

101a)

1 Upon victory the warriors confiscated the town, raped and claimed ownership of the women and girls, for the women were considered no more than "prizes" to be taken--I 133-135, II 506-510

2. Honor is given to troops who were declared "heroes and servants of Mars" II 110

3. Men are taken from the defeated Trojans to be made slaves, as "each desired to have a Trojan householder to pour out their wine" II 110-141

4. Rape was considered a side-benefit: "Therefore, let none make haste to go till he has first lain with the wife of some Trojan" II 333-368

5. The honoring of the warring and jealous gods for their favors Athena II 448-458

6. Jealousy and pride among the gods spark their involvement in the war (Mars egged on Menelaus to get him killed V 561ff, and Athena mounts a chariot with Dromed V 835ff)

7. Adrestus asks for mercy from Menelaus, but Agamemnon demanded total annihilation of the Trojans "Let us not spare a single one of them --not even-- let all in Ilius perish" Homer's

b) editorial addition was "His words were just." VI 30-66

8. Kill all and get booty afterwards VI, VIII 288-291

9. Zeus, above all, demands the gods stay out of the war, but gives in to Athena's plea VIII 1-15, 38-52 (Even Father Zeus is polluted.)

10. Concerning booty and war rewards. When Achilles was pouting, Agamemnon offers him a reward to rejoin the battle: 7 excellent workwomen, all of surpassing beauty from Lesbos (which he could raid after the war with Troy), 20 of the loveliest of the Trojan women, make him a son in law by giving him one of his three daughters and a large dowry, the daughter of Brisius, 7 cities that he could tax and all of them fertile and near the sea.

Achilles rejected the offer. IX 115-162 ((good grief! how they treated women))

11. They used prayers, sacrifices, frankincense, and drink offerings as a means to atonement with the gods they had offended. IX

c) 285ff, 500-511. (Plato taught that sacrifices were an attempt by scroundels to bribe the gods to overlook their crimes. For Plato only the good man who attempts virtue is aided by grace, and to try to bribe God with sacrifices and plea with dirty hands a prayer is only to insult the dignity of God, as if God in some way would accept them and their actions with open arms). Plato, indeed believed in the love of God and God's grace and forgiveness, but he believed that they were aids to help men to become good in their attempts to imitate his goodness.

12. Neptune gets involved because his human grandchild, Amphimachus, had fallen in battle XIII 206

13. Hera bathed in Ambrosia and perfume and seduces Zeus. XIV 166ff and distracts him because he favors the Trojans whom Hera hates and then perjures herself before him later XV 34ff

14. The gods even use force among themselves to decide issues XV 119ff, XX 1-85

15. Death's only reward was an honorable burial. Homer did not believe in the eternal soul, that Plato held so precious and the divinity in man.

16. The gods again are quarreling with each other XXI 383ff

17. Captured women were prizes to the winners of the games held by Achilles after Patroclus' funeral XXIII 262ff, 700 ff.

d)

Such things Plato totally rejected. For to him there was Zeus, God, the One and Holy, Beautiful and Pure, who never inflicted harm but gave only good to mankind. Also, to Plato the lower gods were a heavenly choir of harmony among which there was no envy and who as a group rejoiced to see men doing righteous acts and anticipated their reception among the eternal ones. Aggressive war, the brutalization of women, the acquiring of slaves, shallow acts of religiosity without ethics, the heroes made to be self-centered, moody, and greedy much like the Homeric gods themselves; all these things were repulsive to Plato, and Homer's works were banned from the *Republic*. John M Rist sees Plato's love in the gracious act of giving that Plato declares of God. "Plato, whose Demiourgos, as we recall, though not said to have "Eros" for the created world, accomplishes his function of bringing order into the universe as a kind of goodness, which, like the highest Eros of the *Symposium* and the *Phaedrus*, desires to make others as good as possible."9.13 Yet this can be taken further: Eros is a type of attraction to the beautiful in both the *Symposium* and the *Phaedrus*, and Plato named that very universe that God created "cosmos" the beautifully ordered one, and that explains His delight in it when it was finished. He delighted or loved it because it was beautiful. That God loves that that He has created is beyond doubt. The word θεοφιληs (beloved of God) occurs 22 times in Plato's later works, the word is sometimes translated as the "friend of God", but the Greek literally means "God-loved". At any rate it declares a love relationship between God and man. Constantin Ritter referring to the use of theophiles so often made the following statement:"Good people are supposed to be "loved by God". Plato likes to use this expression frequently. But if we may speak of God as a loving being, then it can no longer be questioned whether God feels."9.14 God even helps those who try to be good but fail. *The Pseudo-Dyonysius* speaks thus:

102a)

"This is why theologians call it 'redemption,' because it does not permit the truly real to fall to nothingness and because it redeems from the passions, from the impotence and deficiency anything which has gone astray toward error or disorder or has suffered a failure to reach the proper virtues. Redemption is like a loving father making up for what is missing and overlooking any slack. It raises a thing up from an evil condition and sets it firmly where it ought to be, adding on lost virtue, bringing back order and arrangement where there was disorder and derangement, making it perfect and liberating it from defects."9.15

God can be patient in his love, for he made the soul of man eternal and for the purpose of enjoying Him forever. In due time, God will redeem him by making him good and acceptable by His own grace and love. God will not permit what he has made in love to be lost and fall into nothingness.

b) Maximus the Confessor displays his Platonism with the following words:

"Just as evil is a privation of good, and ignorance a privation of knowledge, so non-being is a privation of being...The first two privations mentioned depend on the will of creatures; the third lies in the will of the Maker, who in His goodness wills beings always to exist and always to receive His Blessings." 9.16

Maximus the Confessor again says: "God, who yearns for the salvation of all men hungers after their deification."9.17

c)

It is very note worthy that Platonism has no devil and no eternal hell of suffering. He does have places between heaven and earth, at least in his myths--which must be taken as myths, and he also refers to reincarnation as a possible way of making men good so that fully clothed in virtue they may enter into their eternal abode with God forever. No one is ever totally lost because God made his soul to be eternal and to enjoy existence forever. Maximus, above, refers to man's deification and that must be understood that anyone who is eternalized, as man's eternal soul, is "deified". The basic definition among the Greeks of a god was an immortal. That is why Plato often refers to man's soul as the divine element in man. God also made things as much like himself, absolute and eternal Beauty, and therefore man, in himself, is made into a being with eternity as an proper element of his very nature. To do this, God has shown his love. He was not jealous but wanted to share existence with others, and that was the motive of his creative works in the first place.

d) Ficino ties God's work of creation with his love for it, even, using Plato's doctrine of the implanted daimon of love, giving to man that desire of the good by which happiness comes.

"If He does everything for His own ends and He Himself is the highest good, then He disposes everything for the good, as Plato says in the *Timaeus*, with the result that individual things receive the divine goodness each according to its nature. Furthermore, since all things desire the good and the desire for the good is good (and therefore comes from the prime good which is the source of all goods), it follows that things seek the divine goodness attracted by the divine goodness. How can one deny that God is at the helm when He steers everything towards the good?"9.18

103a)

Jacob Boehme states it similarly, "If a man desires God and groans for Him, it does not come from the man. It is the pull of the Father." The man who lets his "divinity within", that is, the daimon of Eros that God has planted in him, follow its nature to seek out the beautiful and eternal, then such a man will automatically be drawn towards God, Who is Beauty, Goodness, and Eternity itself.

Gabriel Marcel hits the nail on the head when he says that in man's relationship with God, man treats himself as a problem to be solved by God. But man as man is not a problem to his Creator, rather he is a delight to God: from the very beginning God rejoiced in his creation and delighted in it. Man must feel this warmth from above in order to understand the true goodness, love and grace of his Heavenly Father. In Platonism such things as the wrath of God, the enmity between God and man, the incarnation and the vicarious atonement are not needed. God is Love and his kind charity is always there for the spiritual nourishment that gives power to the soul to ascend to the highest virtues, happiness, and even to God himself, and if such a journey is not completed here then it will be in the next life.

b) Proclus in his massive *Commentary on Plato's Timaeus* tells of the Maker of the cosmos as the One by whom all creatures are cast into a friendship with both each other and the gods by means of the love which is divine and of which He himself is the source. It is a "bond of love heavy with fire" indeed for it seeks to bind all things together for an "infinite time, woven together intellectually in all the light of the Father." "For on account of this love, all things are adapted to each other, that the elements of the world might remain running in love." Bound together in love the elements of the creation remain in friendship with one another. For the Demiourge (Maker) produced Love as a goddess in order that "she might beautifully illuminate all mundane natures with order, harmony, and communion...For He is the first generator and He himself the much pleasing Love." (Book III)

c) God is Love and he distributes it to his creation graciously, and those who prepare themselves for it can enjoy it and let it freely bear fruits of goodness and friendship. Nicholas of Cusa prayed:

"Lord, You have given me my being of such a nature that it can continually make itself more able to receive your goodness and grace. And this power, which I have from You, wherein I have a living image of

Your almighty power, is free will. By this I can either enlarge or restrict my capacity for Your Grace."9.19

In Plato's *Symposium* (sometimes called the *Banquet)* Agathon is presented with making the following statements concerning the God of Love.

"For to my way of thinking the speakers we have heard so far have been at such pains to congratulate mankind upon the blessings of Love that they have quite forgotten to extol the God himself, and have thrown no light at all upon the nature of our Divine Benefactor...Our duty is first to praise him for what He is, and secondly, for what he gives."

d)

Plato often referred to God as the Unity of all virtues and in Him all virtues become One. Thus Agathon's speach continues:

"Of His courage and justice and temperance I have spoken, but I have yet to speak of his wisdom; and according to the measure of my ability I must try to do my best."

Here are Plato's four cardinal virtues upon which his entire moral philosophy is built, and therefore, if a man is to become good by imitating God as much as possible, then God naturally would incorporate all virtues, but with special attention paid to the four cardinal virtues themselves, which Plato uses for the harmony of an individual's soul as well as the basis for community living, the very foundation of a city: self-control (temperance), justice, wisdom, and courage. Neither soul nor city can have a harmony of being without the four of them. God, of course, has this internal harmony and peace. This is, by Agathon, all within the God of Love.

D. GOD IS THE GOOD BEYOND BEING, BEAUTY ITSELF, THE ETERNAL ONE

104a)

In the *Republic* (509b) Plato refers to God as the "Good Beyond Being" or as another translation as "the Good Itself is not essence but still transcends essence in dignity and surpassing power". Those things that are eternal are considered of the world of Being, and those things that change, that is, the entire material realm, is the world of Becoming and constantly evolving and changing. To Plato, God is above all including those that are eternal, and even the eternal in some way has its existence due to that which is beyond it and more dignified than it, that is, God. Likewise, God is Beauty Itself, so beautifully expressed in the *Symposium* which will be presented in a later chapter. God is One, Eternal, Good, and Beautiful.

b) Iamblichus stated:

"God therefore is neither good through learning virtue from anyone, nor is he happy through being attended by good fortune. For he is good by nature, and happy by nature, and always was and will be, and will never cease to be such; since he is incorruptible, and naturally good."9.20

This sounds simple, but it is important. While other religions often present their gods as moody, self-centered, angry and wrathful, disappointed and repenting that they ever made man, Platonism has always maintained that God is far beyond those negative passions that men themselves have, and that if a being is angry or moody or violent and destructive, then that being is not a god.

Epictetus declared:

"God is beneficial. The good also is beneficial. It is consistent then that where the nature of God is, there also the nature of the good should be. What is the nature of God? Flesh? Certainly not. An estate in land? By no means. Fame? No. Is His nature intellect, knowledge, and right reason (nous, gnosis, logos)? Yes, and it is therein that one can seek the nature of the good." (Discourses II, 8)

c) The *Corpus Hermeticum*, Libellus VI professes:

"Good belongs to none save God alone. There is nothing that God lacks, so that he should desire to gain it, and should thereby become evil. There is nothing that God can lose, and at the loss of which he might be grieved. There is nothing stronger than God, to do him wrong, and so provoke him to quarrel. God has no consort, to excite in him the passion of possessive love; no (object or subject) to arouse anger in him; there is none wiser than God to make him jealous. And since his being admits none of these passions, what remains, save only the good?"

d) Boethius, a Christian who was accused of being in the wrong political party, although both parties were "Christian", and sentenced to prison where he was held before his execution at age 44. He lived from 480-524 CE, and deserved a much better fate. While he was waiting his execution he naturally asked the "why me?" Question. He was a good man, a Christian, with clean hands, yet he will soon be executed by the Christian powers that were in control at that time. He asked himself, "if God is good and He has any providence over us at all, then why is this happening to me?" At this point in his meditation, he gives up on the Christian answers and listens to the Platonic philosophy that he had also learned, and behold! Lady Philosophy comes to his mind and communicates with him. He does not listen to the Judeo-Christian Scriptures or the early church fathers, he listens to Plato and the Neoplatonists, and they give him a consoling answer. Not once in the work is there any reference to or mentioning of Christianity or any Christian doctrine. This is his account of the approach of Lady Philosophy to him in his distress:

105a)

"I recognized my nurse, Philosophy...'Should I', she said, 'desert you, my nursling, nor share and bear my part of the burden which has been laid upon you from spite against my name? Surely Philosophy never allowed herself to let the innocent go upon their journey unbefriended. Should I, terrified, fear calumnies, as though they were a novel misfortune? Do you think this the first time that wisdom has been harassed by danger among men of shameless ways? Have I not even in ancient days, before the time of my child, Plato, fought many a mighty battle against the recklessness of folly? And, though Plato did survive, did not his master Socrates win his victory of an unjust death with me present at his side?...But if you have not heard of the exile of Anaxagoras, nor of the poison given to Socrates, nor of the tortures suffered by Zeno--for these things, after all, did not happen in Rome--yet you may know of Canius, Seneca, and Soranus, whose memory is still fresh and famous. For nothing else brought all these men to ruin but that, being instructed in my ways, they appeared at variance with the desire of unscrupulous men. Therefore you need not wonder if in this sea of life we are tossed about by storms from all sides, for we fulfill our calling best when we displease the worst." (*The Consolation of Philosophy*, Book One Prose III).

b)

Lady Philosopher goes on to let him know that he has exiled himself from the true fatherland in eternity and judged everything by his earthly existence. He must keep his eyes on the eternal and not let the temporal destroy his spirit. She continued:

"When I saw you in sorrow and tears, I knew immediately that you were unhappy and in exile, but I knew not how distant was that exile until your speech betrayed it. Yet you have not indeed been driven but have wandered this far from your native land (that is, the eternal Fatherland); or if you prefer that you be considered driven then you have been driven by yourself rather than by another, for no one else could have done this to you. If you call to your mind what, really, is your fatherland, you know that it is not governed, as was Athens of old, by the multitude, but 'there is one Lord, one King,' who rejoices in his citizens' great number, not in their banishment."(Book One Prose V)

c)

The dialogue is long, but gradually Boethius is lifted up step by step to be consoled fully by relying upon the wisdom and goodness of God, whose wisdom and goodness are eternal and not limited to the temporal. He then finds that he has returned to his true Fatherland and puts himself in the hands of the Eternal One. And visualizing himself before God, he sees that God is both goodness and happiness, and His presence is rest from his deceitful passions, and also the tranquil peace he has been seeking. The book is short, and a must read for one ascending to spiritual fulfillment.

d) Ficino made this reference of the soul's vision of the goodness of God with these words: "So, according to Plato, the soul saw justice itself, wisdom, harmony, and the marvelous beauty of the divine nature."9.21 In fact Plato, in his *Symposium*, refers to God as Beauty Itself and those who ascend in mind to see that Beauty face to face knows that he has become a friend of God, who was raised up in spirit and mind by the Same, and can then see and anticipate his immortality.

Ralph Waldo Emerson speaks of the ascent of simple thoughts to those eternal with the idea of longevity of one's being in mind:

106a)

"Some thoughts always find us young, and keep us so. Such a thought is the love of the universal and eternal Beauty. Every man parts from that contemplation with the feeling that it rather belongs to ages than to mortal life. The least activity of the intellectual powers redeems us in a degree from the conditions of time. In sickness, in languor, give us a strain of poetry or a profound sentence, and we are refreshed; or produce a volume of Plato...or remind us of his name, and instantly we come into a feeling of longevity. See how the deep divine thought reduces centuries, and millenniums, and makes itself present through all ages." 9.22

b) The *Theologia Germanica*, so beloved by Martin Luther, is the product of an unknown Platonic German Mystic, and was a great influence upon the reformer and many others that did not have direct access or knowledge of Plato. "Behold! even as God is the One Good, and Light and Reason, so is He also Will and Love and Justice and Truth, and in short all virtues."(Chapter 32) Later it refers to the Unity of all virtues in the One, for all (aforementioned) virtues "belong to God in the true Good and His own, is loved and praised; and all that is without this Good, and contrary to it, is a sorrow and a pain."(Chapter 43)

The emphasis upon God being One is strong throughout the Platonic Tradition, because he is basically unified and simple and unmixed. He has only one personhood, one being, one Absolute and eternal Good. This thought is one that William Ellery Channing presented in his "Baltimore Sermon". God is One in all unity and is not mixed with the person of Jesus of Nazareth, who is human and inferior to God. Likewise Channing rejected the idea that Jesus saved us from God's wrath, rather he was sent by God to help effect a moral and spiritual redemption of man by his teachings and the morality of his life. He rejected the Christian standard doctrine of the Trinity as well as the concept of the vicarious atonement: "We conceive that Christians have generally leaned towards a very injurious view of the Supreme Being", and then goes on to say the following words which are part of the general **c)** Platonic Tradition: "We believe that God is infinitely good, kind, benevolent, in the proper sense of these words: good in disposition, as well as in act; good not to a few, but to all; good to every individual, as well as to the general system." He condemns the idea that all are wholly depraved and that God "selects from the "corrupt mass of men" a number to be saved, and that they are plucked, by an irresistible agency...for God's grace." Channing rejected these ideas of man's total corruption and the partiality of a God who would select only a few to be saved, and he rejects such insulting-to-God concepts just as any good Platonist would. God is One, and is good and gracious to all humans in whom he delights when they live ethically, and the heavenly choir also rejoices to see lives of virtue imitating God's nature, as mirrors reflecting the Sun to give joy, warmth and light to others.

K

ΚΑΠΠΑ

CHAPTER TEN
THE NATURE OF MAN

I. MAN AS A MATERIAL BODY

107a) Platonic thought divided man into two parts, body and soul, and the soul into three parts, and to speak of only one part at a time is quite difficult because of the natural overlapping when one speaks of the nature of man. Yet, for the sake of some order, a division will be made in this presentation. As a physical man, man was a wonder among the animals, yet, in many ways quite inferior in speed, strength, difficulty in swimming and the impossibility to fly. It is without doubt that it was the one section in the soul, the mental part--that which could reason (the Logos), in which man found his great gift to not only compete with the stronger and faster animals but to surpass them and even gain control of them. This knowledge of man's logos was that in which man most prided himself, and by it felt an element of the divine within him. He was a logos made flesh. Not that other animals did not have reasoning power, but man's seemed to be so much more pronounced that he saw his reasoning power as that which separated him for all other creatures. That being said, how did the philosophical Greeks, especially in the Platonic Tradition, feel about the body?

b) First of all, the body was good and blessed with many wonderful senses, especially the sense of sight which could take him deep into the space of the cosmos. He also experienced several material pleasures, such as eating tasty food, the rest after work or exercise, physical contests at the games, and the sexual pleasures of touch and sexual activity. All these were considered to be blessings from the Father and Maker who designed the body. The following are passages from Plato's Timaeus, his creation myth, and they pertain to the body of man. He, the Father and the Maker of the universe, makes the eternal souls, but he turns over the making of man's body to the lower gods and he gives them the following instructions:

c)

"Interweave the mortal with the immortal and make and beget living creatures (mankind), and give them food and make them to grow, and receive them again in death." (*Timaeus* 41d)

"Then in the first place, it would be necessary that they should all have in them one and the same faculty or sensation...in the second place, they must have love (sexual), in which pleasure and pain mingle." (42a)

"...the body which was in a state of perpetual influx and efflux." (43a - which means that the body is constantly changing, for, unlike the soul, it is temporal and meant for only a short period of time)

d)

"...the head, being the most divine part" (because it contains the intellect and reason -- the highest part of the soul, and in Platonic philosophy, even though the body is good, its function, other than physical pleasures, is mainly to house the eternal soul with its intellect and reason)

"And of the organs they first contrived the eyes to give light...God invented and gave us sight to the end that we might behold the courses of intelligence in the heaven, and apply them to the courses of our own intelligence which are like theirs...that we might from them learn the natural truth of reason " (47c) From the harmony of the heavens then man was to learn harmony, rhythm and music.

108a)

Plato goes on and speaks of all the parts of the human body and the wonder of their functions that give and sustain the material life. There is no reference to its being evil, although the soul is to regulate it so that it does not become immoderate in its desires for excess pleasures. The soul is also to remind the person that the body is temporal and is not the essence of the real person. If that happens man's priorities are mixed and he falls into error and if continued for a period of time, he becomes "imprisoned" by the bodily needs. It is an error of reason to become overly attached to the body, for it is by nature constantly changing, decaying and in the end it is mortal.

Pliny the Elder in his *Natural History* warns man not to be so arrogant around other animals, but rather to remember how he started life, so humble and so very helpless. The first paragraph of his book stated:

b)

"Man alone, at the very moment of his birth cast naked upon the naked earth, which abandons it to cries, to lamentations, and, a thing that is the case which no other animal whatever, to tears: this, too, from the very moment that he enters upon existence. But as for laughter, why by Hercules!--to laugh, if but for an instant only, has never been granted to man before the fortieth day from his birth, and then it is looked upon as a miracle of precocity."

Man when he is born does not come up running in a few hours as most of the other animals do. He is crying, he is helpless, and he is naked and quickly put into some garments of warmth. Crying he is good at, but laughter must come later. Yet, from this humble birth, man becomes the ruler of the earth. But the struggle was not easy and came about only because of man's logical mind (logikos).

c) Proclus, in his *Commentary on Plato's Timaeus*, relates that the soul is better than the body and is the best of all because it is belongs in the eternal realm whereas the body to the temporal realm. Yet the body is not only not evil, but it is good and even beautiful. His words are:

"And again you see, the difference of the soul with reference to body. For Plato had before called body the most beautiful of generated natures; but now he calls the soul the best of things generated. But it is common to both to have been generated by the most excellent cause. The soul however, as being nearer to its Maker, is the best; but body, as being more remote from him, is indeed most beautiful, yet not the best. For the most beautiful, is secondary to the best."(Book III)

Nowhere among those who followed Plato closely is there any proclamations of the evil body. Life in the flesh is good, yes, even beautiful, but due to its material nature it will change, decay and die. In that sense it must be put secondary to the soul, the eternal nature of man, **d)** in every respect. At Plato's gatherings and discussed gatherings wine, laughter and food were there; so were the young women entertainers there to sing and dance; so was humor and music--even singing by individuals there, but they were all secondary to mental exercises that took place in the form of philosophical dialogue which was often begun with a prayer. Plato discussed the role of the arts in human life and he himself participated in the games as a wrestler. The joys and pleasures of the body never provoked any concept of guilt, shame or repentance. This beautifully made body was indeed to be enjoyed. In the Philebus (61-62), after the pleasure of the sciences and the arts came the question of the pleasure's of the body. It was agreed that they too are to be mingled with the total life, especially those that procured a healthy life, but there was a caution also that some pleasures must be controlled by temperance. Drink the wine, yes, but too much causes a man to lose his wisdom and also harms his body. Self-control or Temperance is that virtue that regulates pleasures and keeps them from becoming destructive to both the body and the soul, which it can harm by distracting it from the higher pleasures of science and the arts. Know yourself (γνωθι σαυτον) and nothing too much (μηδεν αγαν) were the two great oracles of Delphi. It **109a)** must be remembered that after the four cardinal virtues of Plato, called the heavenly virtues, he also taught about the four "earthly" virtues: health, comeliness, strength, and wealth--in that order. Of the eight total virtues: the heavenly being temperance, courage, justice and wisdom; the earthly being health, comeliness, strength, and wealth. All four of the earthly values were subordinate to the heavenly virtues, and all the other earthly virtues were subordinate to health. For example, if a man had wealth, but was disfigured, unattractive, and sick it would be of little value--and added to this if he were afraid to live (lack of courage) or lacked wisdom (whereby he would soon lose his wealth) what good would wealth do? Plato's philosophy is not only spiritual to lead one to the embrace of God, but also very humanly practical for human earthly happiness. Even a sick, ugly, weak, and poverty stricken man can be beautiful within and be happy if he is just, self-controlled, courageous, and wise. But, of course, the earthly virtues are beneficial and can greatly adorn the beauty of life: still however, they are secondary. If they remain secondary they are a great blessing, but when they become the primary goal of man, they are destructive to his happiness.

II. MAN AS AN ETERNAL SOUL

b) To Plato and his followers the real and only true person of man was his soul, for it alone was his ultimate reality and his eternal element. All that was material about man would come to an end in a very brief time in comparison with the eternity of the world of being. Material man, like the material universe, was fashioned with substance that had its own laws; that of birth, growth, change, decay and death. And, in that sense, only the eternal is real and the temporal is but of short lived copy of the true essence of any being. The soul was that true essence of man. The soul was seen to have three basic functions while in the body: the rational part that learned and executed knowledge properly and its fruit was wisdom--both in the spiritual and material realms; the spirited element of the soul was that of will and courage; and the other part was the function of moderation so that the needs and pleasures of the body would not be in excess and a threat to health and happiness Here one can see Plato's four cardinal virtues: wisdom, courage, temperance (self-control or moderation), and if they all functioned properly, the man's soul was in a just state, and experienced spiritual, intellectual and physical harmony and that was called justice. We often see a person who has difficulties with life because these virtues are missing and we often say "you have to get yourself together" or "put it together". For we know that there is disharmony within the man himself, and that can not lead to happiness.

c) The chief of these four was wisdom or the rational element in man, and that is actually the only element even of the soul that is eternal. It is called both the neus (νευς) and the logos (λογος), The neus is the mind or the intellect--the substance of that eternal element and the logos is the function of the neus, reasonable thought or logic. When the intellect functions, man become a logical animal, and it is this great logic, or use of reason, that separates man from the other animals and from his body and from his mortality. It is his true and eternal being. It makes man the "homo sapiens" the wise creature, the thinking man.

Sallustius the Platonist friend of the Platonist Emperor of Rome, Julian, followed Plato's idea of the soul most completely, and expressed it this way:

c)

"The entire soul consists of three parts, reason, spirit, and desire. The excellence of reason is wisdom (αρετη δε λογου μεν φρονησις); of spirit, courage; of desire, temperance; of the whole soul, justice. Reason must make a right judgment, spirit must in obedience to reason, despise seeming dangers, and desire must pursue not seeming pleasure but reasonable pleasure. When these conditions are fulfilled life becomes just. For this reason in the educated all virtues may be seen, while among the uneducated one is brave but unjust, one temperate but imprudent, one prudent but intemperate," (*Sallustius* X)

Theages in his treatise *On The Virtues* also follows Plato closely.

"It is necessary, however, that virtue should have these three things: reason, power, and deliberate choice. The virtue, therefore, of the reasoning power of the soul is prudence (φρονησις); for it is a habit of judging and contemplating. But the virtue of the irascible part, is fortitude; for it is a habit of resisting, and enduring things of dreadful nature. And the virtue of the epithymetic or appetitive part is temperance; for it is a moderation and detention of the pleasures which arise through the body. But the virtue of the whole soul is justice."10.1

d)

Seneca put it this way in a letter:

"The wise man and devotee of philosophy is, needless to say, inseparable from his body, and yet he is detached from it so far as the best part of his personality is concerned, directing his thoughts towards things far above. He looks on this present life of his, much like the man who has signed on as a soldier, as the term he has to serve out. And he is so made that he neither loves life nor hates it. He endures the lot of mortality for he knows there is a finer life in store for him."10.2

If one feels that there is a negativity to these thoughts about the present life, that is unfortunate, but remember two things: Seneca was an

eclectic, not a total Platonist, and also he held office under Nero who made life hell for many people and did ultimately call for Seneca's suicide. Yet, the thought is truly Platonic: the temporal world is only a prelude to something better to come.
110a) Epictetus in his *Discourses* (II.10) stated: "Consider then from what things you have been separated by reason (logos). You have been separated from wild beasts: you have been separated from domestic animals. Further, you are a citizen of the cosmos." It is reason by which we have union with the eternal cosmos and likewise separation from the material bodies of other animals. In the *Corpus Hermeticum* (Libellus X) are the lovely words: "And human souls, when they have attained to a beginning of immortal life, change into daimons, and thereafter pass on into the choral dance of the gods; that is the crowning glory of the soul." In Judeo-Christian thinking "the gods" should be thought of as angels and the daimons are to be thought of as the good eternal spirits that would be slightly less than the angels, but they, daimons and angels, dance together in heaven. They have joined Plato's "heavenly choir". R.W. Emerson in his *Self Reliance* gave us this short simple lovely thought: "The relations of the soul to the Divine Spirit are so pure, that it is profane to seek to interpose help." Emerson also quotes "Socrates'" words to Callicles,:
b)
"I, therefore, Callicles, am persuaded by these accounts, and consider how I may exhibit my soul before the judge in a healthy condition. Wherefore, disregarding the honors that most men value, and looking to the truth, I shall endeavor in reality to live as virtuously as I can; and when I die, to die so. And I invite all other men, to the utmost of my power; and you too I in turn invite to this contest, which I affirm, surpasses all contests here."(*Plato* from his *Representative Men*)

When Benjamin Franklin's brother, John, died, he wrote in a letter these words of comfort to John's second wife, who had survived him:
c)
"I condole with you. We have lost a most dear and valuable relation. But it is the will of God and nature, that these mortal bodies be laid aside, when the soul is to enter in the real life. This is rather an embryo state, a preparation for living. A man is not completely born until he is dead.

Why then should we grieve, that a new child is born among the immortals, a new member added to their happy society? We are spirits. That bodies should be lent us, while they can afford us pleasure, assist us in acquiring knowledge, or in doing good to our fellow creatures, is a kind and benevolent act of God. When they become unfit for these purposes, and afford us pain instead of pleasure, instead of an aid become an encumbrance, and answer none of the intentions for which they were given, it is equally kind and benevolent, that a way is provided by which we may get rid of them. Death is that way. We ourselves, in some cases, prudently choose a partial death. A mangled painful limb, which cannot be restored, we willingly cut off. He who plucks out a tooth, parts with it freely, since the pain goes with it; and he, who quits the whole body, parts at once with all pains and possibilities of pains and diseases which it was liable to, or capable of making him suffer. Our friend and we were invited abroad on a party of pleasure, which is to last for ever. His chair was ready first, and he is gone before us. We could not all conveniently start together; and why should you and I be grieved at this, since we are soon to follow, and know where to find him?

Adieu,

B. Franklin"

d)

While one does not generally think of Benjamin Franklin as a Platonic philosopher, it is quite evident that he was deeply nourished in the Platonic Tradition.

Man, as a unit, body and soul, is wonderfully made and is truly a wonderful creature, born of earth inspired by heaven and given a rational soul. How wonderful! Let each man and each woman rejoice in what they are as rational animals. This life is good, a gift, an absolute wonder--humanly speaking, miraculous. Sophocles, honoring man, puts these words into the mouth of his chorus in the *Antigone*:

"Wonders are many, and none is more wonderful than man;
the power that crosses the white sea,
driven by the stormy south-wind,
making a path under surges that threaten to engulf him;
and Earth, the eldest of the gods, the immortal, the unwearied,
does he wear, turning the soil with the offspring of horses,
as the ploughs go to and fro from year to year.

And the light-hearted race of birds, and the tribes of savage beasts,
and the sea-brood of the deep,
he snares in the meshes of his woven toils,
he leads captive, man excellent in wit. And he masters by his arts
the beasts whose lair is in the wilds, who roams the hills;
he tames the horse of shaggy mane, he puts the yoke upon its neck,
he tames the tireless mountain bull.
And speech, and wind-swift thought,
and all the moods that mold a state, he has taught himself;
and how to flee the arrows of the frost,
when 'tis hard lodging under the clear sky,
and the arrows of the rushing rain; yea, he has resource for all;
without resource he meets nothing that must come;
only against death shall he call for aid in vain;
but from battling maladies he has devised escapes.
Cunning beyond fancy's dream is the fertile skill which brings
him, now to evil, now to good.
When he honors the laws of the land,
And that justice which he has sworn by the gods to uphold,
proudly stands his city; no city has he who, for his rashness,
dwells in sin."(Antigone 332-372)

111a)

Yes, indeed, man is a wonder and human life wonderful!

III. MAN'S PURPOSE AND GOAL: HAPPINESS AND THE PURIFICATION OF THE ETERNAL SOUL

Basically man's purpose and goal can be generally and simply be put into two categories: personal happiness and the purification of his eternal soul. All else, in one way or another, relate to one of those two categories. Not only that but, as in Plato all virtue is one, both of these two categories are very intimately related, yet they shall be discussed separately as much as possible. One of the concepts that bind together the two categories is the imitation of God (imitatio dei) as much as humanly possible, because in the final analysis God is the source of both happiness and eternal life that comes with the purification of the soul.

b) In just about all books of philosophy there seems to be a consensus that happiness is the goal that all people really pursue, or at least say that is their true desire in life. Plato's course of logic runs this way: only the good are happy, and only when one has knowledge of the good can he pursue it. Therefore, knowledge is the foundation that leads to goodness and goodness gives birth to happiness. A person ignorant of what is good has no way to imitate it or become good, and that negates knowledge and wisdom at the very start of the pursuit toward the blessed life of joy and happiness. In his *Republic* the entire community is to be geared by education and example to make people good, and in that way there will be harmony in the community because each person will have realized his goal of being happy. If one looks at the many dialogues of Plato one can see the topics are all focused on virtue and knowledge: on duty and conscience in the *Crito*, on temperance in the *Charmides,* on courage in the *Laches*, on friendship in the *Lysis,* on piety in the *Euthyphro*, on the knowledge of good art in the *Ion*, whether knowledge is teachable and goodness is worth suffering for in the *Gorgias*, virtue is one with wisdom in the *Protagoras*, knowing and teaching virtue in the **c)** *Meno*, the origin of words and how to communicate knowledge in the *Cratylus*, beauty and its power to attract love in the *Phaedrus* and *Symposium,* justice in the individual and the city in the *Republic*, epistemology (the study of knowledge) in the *Theaetetus,* what is truly real and eternal in the *Parmenides*, false teachers are a hindrance to knowledge in the *Sophist*, the knowledgeable art of statesmanship in the *Statesman*, wisdom of the intellect is more gratifying than the pleasure of the senses in the *Philebus,* and God made us to be as much as possible like Himself in the *Timaeus*. These dialogues do not come to dogmatic conclusions, but they teach the reader how to think and how to set his priorities correctly in life in his pursuit of personal happiness. These dialogues have never been equaled, and all philosophers stand in the shadow of these dialogues. Likewise, nothing can equal the actual reading of them by the one seeking happiness.

d) Sallustius, even though he mentions the final goal of eternal life with the heavenly chorus, also states that right here and now virtue gives the good life and happiness:

"Souls that have lived in accordance with virtue have as the crown of their happiness, that freed from the unreasonable element and purified from all body, they are in union with the gods and share with them the government of the whole universe. Yet, even if they attained none of these things, virtue itself and the pleasure and honor of virtue, and the life free from pain and from all other tyrants, would suffice to make happy those who had chosen to live in accordance with virtue and had proved able." (*Concerning the Gods and the Universe* XXI)

112a)

Epictetus links the nature of the soul of man with the desire of the good and the beautiful: (*Discourses* III, Chapter III)

"The business of the wise and good man is to use appearances conformably to nature: and as it is the nature of every soul to ascent to the truth, to dissent from the false, and to remain in suspense as to that which is uncertain; so it is its nature to be moved toward the desire of the good...For this reason the good is preferred to every intimate relationship. There is no intimate relationship between me and my father, but there is between me and the good. 'Are you so hard-hearted?' Yes, for such is my nature; and this is the coin which God has given me. For this reason, if the good is something different from the beautiful and the just, both father is gone, and brother and country, and everything."

b)

Yes, Epictetus, every value and every honorable relationship depend upon the good and the beautiful and the just! The entire life is to be nourished with the good, and it is absolutely necessary that it end with the good. Seneca in a letter stated:

"Every life without exception is a short one. Looked at in relation to the universe even the lives of Nestor and Sattia [who lived to 99] were short. ...As it is with a play, so it is with life--what matters is not how long the acting lasts, but how good it is. It is not important at what point you stop. Stop wherever you will--only make sure that you round it off with a good ending."10.3

c) In the works of Jacob Boehme we find this prayer which asks enlightenment for the path of virtue that leads ultimately to one's return to God.

"O Lord stay with us and in us, and teach us to consider that our external life, on which we trust so much, walks toward evening and its end, and that it is soon over for us. Teach us to travel the right way. Be with us on our pilgrim's path, and lead us home to You."10.4

In the last chapter the nature of God was discussed, that is because in Platonic philosophy the imitating of God was the way to happiness and even to God himself. Therefore, the nature of God had to be established before one could present the nature of man and his goals if he had not yet understood, in the most possible way for him, what God was like. That being established, Epictetus' words of encouragement make sense:
d)
"The philosophers say that we ought first to learn that there is a God and that he provides for all things; ...The next thing is to learn what is the nature of (God)...and as being then an imitator of God, he must do and say everything consistently with this fact." (*Discourses* II, 14).

Sallustius (XV) speaks of how natural imitation is in learning and becoming good, for when he wants a spiritualized setting man tries to imitate the beauty of heaven in his temples and altars on earth and in life he tries to imitate God himself. In this imitation man does no good to God, who does not need it, but he does good to himself, similar to the good man does to himself in prayer and praise, for God himself has no need of his prayers. To become spiritually fit, man imitates the virtues and God himself, even as a youth imitates the training of the athletes to perfect his physical body.
113a) The truly dedicated man will seek to be like God as much as possible, and some Platonists, especially the Neoplatonists use the phrase "become God", meaning to become of the same nature of God, or Godlike. Hear the words of Ficino:

"We have shown that our soul in all its acts is trying with all its power to attain the first gift of God, that is, the possession of all truth and goodness. Does it also seek His second attribute? Does not the soul try to become everything (good) just as God is everything? It does in a wonderful way; for the soul lives the life of a plant when it served the body in feeding it; the life of an animal, when it flatters the senses; the life of a man, when it deliberates through reason on human affairs; the life of the heroes, when it investigates natural things; the life of the daimons, when it speculates on mathematics, the life of the angels, when it inquires into the divine mysteries; the life of God when it does everything for God's sake. Every man's soul experiences all these things in itself in some way, although different souls do it in different ways, and thus the human species strives to become all things by living the lives of all things."10.5

b)

Ficino then later adds: "To conclude, our soul by means of the intellect and will, as by those twin Platonic wings, flies toward God."

In man's quest for true knowledge, Plato puts a tremendous stress on mathematics and geometry. He had at the entrance to his Academy the saying "If you do not know geometry, do not come in." This was the highest of educational facilities man had known at that time, and the one thing closest to knowledge and truth was mathematics. For mathematics trained the mind how to think objectively and abstractly, nothing known to man could match its discipline. By mathematics one could make a perfect calendar, follow the heavens, predict eclipses, measure weights and capacities of vases and receptacles, number livestock, make maps, and measure distances and weigh water and all things. Likewise, the truth of mathematics was always pure. If a man owed a debt of ten drachmas and made two payments of five each, he had paid his debt in full. Mathematics does not change, ever. It is truthful in every circumstance. In fact Plato seems to use mathematics as another name for rational thought, for in declaring man's uniqueness he sometimes points to man's reason and at other times declares that from God man had the "gift of numbers" that separated him from the animals. Leibniz, a late 17th early 18th Century Platonist, echoed Plato when he said:

c)

"But true reasoning depends upon necessary or eternal truths, such as those of logic, of numbers, of geometry, which establish an indubitable connection of ideas and unfailing inferences. The animals in whom these inferences are not noticed, are called brutes; but those which know these necessary truths are properly those which are called rational animals, and their souls are called spirits. These souls are capable of performing acts of reflection, and of considering that which is called the ego, substance, monad, soul, spirit, in a word, immaterial things and truths. And it is this which render us capable of the sciences and of demonstrative knowledge." 10.6

d)

In this life such balance and the joy of scientific discovery is a foretaste, in Leibniz's mind, of the future life. For therein one finds the love of God for us. God himself used mathematics to order the cosmos so that it would be beautifully balanced and dependable in terms of man's needs such as the sun's warmth and the rain of the clouds and various forms of plants and animals. This love of God for us gives us a present contentment and also assures us a future happiness. God's love, like mathematics, is always correct, always pure truth, and totally dependable. Leibniz continued:

"For the love of God fulfills also our hopes, and leads us in the road of supreme happiness, because by virtue of the perfect order established in the universe, everything is done in the best possible way, as much for the general good as for the greatest individual good of those who are convinced of this and are content with the divine government; this conviction cannot be wanting to those who know how to love the source of all good. It is true that supreme felicity, by whatever beatific vision or knowledge of God it be accompanied, can never be full; because, since God is infinite, he cannot be wholly known. Therefore our happiness will never, and ought not, consist in full joy, where there would be nothing farther to desire, rendering our mind stupid; but in a perpetual progress to new pleasure and to new perfections."10.7

114a)

"Never" seems to imply that Leibniz extended this concept to the eternal life; that man will never reach the point in eternity that he can feel that he knows God completely, for the beauty, goodness, and perfection of God has an endless depth. He is simply infinite, and man ceaselessly is increased in the joy of attaining infinite levels of the love and being of God.

b)

God also gives man free will, for he puts man's fate in man's own power, and man has personal responsibility for his own progress in developing

virtue, gaining knowledge, and following the natural desires for the ultimate Beauty. He may cast himself down to be on the level of a brute animal or he can raise himself to a virtuous and spiritual level of the angels. Pico della Mirandola declared it openly to his Renaissance brothers: "You shall be able to descend among the lower forms of being, which are brute beasts; you shall be able to be reborn out of the judgment of your own soul into the higher beings, which are divine." (*Oration on the Dignity of Man*). After a thousand years of man's being taught that he is sinful and ugly in the eyes of God, who but for the sacrifice of his own Son, would have sent us to hell, and even after that sacrifice, if man does not conform to all the dictates of the church, he will suffer forever. Yes, after all that, now comes the Platonic humanism of the Renaissance and tells man that God ever loved him, he is a good creation, and he has free will to rise up in virtue by his own will: no need of Jesus' suffering and no need to placate the wrath of God, for in Platonism God was never wrathful towards him. Man had regained his dignity and his mind and heart could rejoice in being human, made so by the love of God. Men went back to what Plato wanted them to be in the first place: Renaissance
c) Men. The Renaissance man sought in every part of life to be learned, adept, and fulfilled to the utmost of his ability. His life would be harmonized by culture, pleasure, music, athletic ability, philosophy, science and wonder. Plato said much about education that will be handled later, but the importance of it all was to make man a culturally and intellectually complete person in both qualities and abilities. He concludes his teaching of this in the *Protagoras* with these words: "For the life of man in every part has need of harmony and rhythm" (*Protagoras* 326b). His life experience in the body is to be as fulfilled and rewarding as possible. Life is simply good and every aspect of it shall be fully enjoyed, for that was the will of the Maker and Father of mankind in ordering the cosmos and giving man a body in the first place. What a difference of mindset for those born again in the Renaissance! No more threatening God, vicious Satan, an anti-pleasure Church and the ever present fear of hell. Redemption by Platonism!

d) One can see many Platonic elements in Alexander Pope's *An Essay on Man.* He speaks first of society's imitation of cosmic harmony, and then of the same harmony within man's own psyche, with reason as the controller and director of man's life. Then he encourages his readers to use their self-love to learn how to love all humans within one's society, and lastly he reminds man that happiness depends upon virtue. It is a poem well within the Platonic Tradition. Likewise in his *The Universal Prayer* he shows devotion to God, gratitude for life and providence and the opportunity to love others with the same mercy that God has shown him:

115a)

"Father of all! In every age,
 In every clime adored,
By saint, by savage, and by sage,
 Jehovah, Jove, or Lord!

Thou Great First Cause, least understood:
 Who all my sense confined
To know but this--that thou art good,
 And that myself am blind:

Yet gave me, in this dark estate,
 To see the good from ill;
And binding Nature fast in fate,
 Left free the human will.

What blessings thy free bounty gives,
 Let me not cast away;
For God is paid when man receives,
 To enjoy is to obey.

Yet not to earth's contracted span,
 Thy goodness let me bound,
Or think thee Lord alone of man,
 When thousand worlds are round.

Teach me to feel another's woe,
 To hide the fault I see;
That mercy I to others show,
 That mercy show to me.

To thee, whose temple is all space,
  Whose altar, earth, sea, skies!
One chorus let all being raise!
  All Nature's incense rise!"

b)

One liberating thought especially is expressed in the verse that encourages a man to take the blessings God has given and not cast them away. Rather enjoy them, for that is the way to repay God for that which He gives. "For God is paid when man receives--To enjoy is to obey." Those monks, celebrates, vowers of poverty are serving only themselves, not the blessings of God. The body of man and all that he can enjoy, is to be enjoyed--that is to obey. To despise God's gifts of life, body, senses and pleasures is to scorn God, not thank him.

c) Pierre Teilhard de Chardin in a letter to a friend by the name of Max Begouen encourages him with these words: "Because you are doing the best you can, you are forming your own self within the world, and you are helping the world to form itself around you. How, then, could you fail from time to time to feel overcome by the boundless joy of creation?"10.8

Yes, man looks to eternity to his "return" to his everlasting home in the universal and grand mansion of God, but let him not despise the interim and temporal gift of material life that God has given him so that he can experience the wonder of bodily life, the beauty of nature, the awesome substantial universe and human friendship and intimacy. To enjoy is to obey. That is virtue and that is happiness.

IV. THE DAIMON PLANTED WITHIN

d) Plato believed that God put a daimon (demon) into the soul of every man, that daimon he gave the name of love (εροϛ), eros. Eros was symbolic of the divine within, a god of sorts, called both god and daimon in the Platonic Tradition. The purpose of this daimon of love was to draw men to God, for it was an innate love of beauty within the mind of men. That love became a forceful longing for beauty in all its forms, but especially for Beauty Itself, that is, God. No where in any literature is it better expressed than in Plato's *Symposium*. In the *Symposium* there is a series of speeches made by those at the banquet, and finally it comes to Socrates, who pleads that he doesn't know what love is, but a wise woman by the name of Diotima (the honor of God or one who honors God), and she told him the essence and power of love and its ultimate goal. The longing element of the soul is the love of beauty that God has planted in the soul for the express purpose of driving man back to him, for God Himself is Absolute and Everlasting Beauty, and man will never be fully happy until he meets God face to face, and that beatific vision gives to man his ultimate fulfillment and happiness. But this ultimate vision is at the end of a long process in which beauty ascends up a divided line seeking beauty first in the material objects that can be seen with the eye and crossing the divided line and seeing the abstract beauties of the mind until at last he is able to "see" Beauty itself. Love seeks out beauty at the lowest level by beholding a beautiful body. But then moves to the beauty of all the bodies of humanity, as best one is capable of seeing all such beauties. Then to step up again, he, by reason, looks upon the soul or the mind (the thinking soul), the true man within, and sees the glory of a beautiful soul, and then again, the souls of all men point him even higher. The fifth step involves beauty in a different light, such as an institution that mends the suffering body so that it becomes well, and that which give light to the soul, and to harmony giving laws and the, yet higher, to sciences and mathematics, for they represent in thought a higher reality of beauty and harmony, balance, symmetry, as with mathematics the truth within its laws never changes or fades. Then Diotima brings to close her speech to Socrates with this lovely climatic statement:

116a)

"He who has been instructed thus far in the things of love, and who has learned to see the beautiful in due order and succession, when he comes toward the end will suddenly perceive a nature of wondrous beauty, and this Socrates, is the final cause of all our former toils--a nature which in the first place is everlasting, not growing and decaying, or waxing and waning; secondly, not beautiful in one point of view and foul in another, or at one time or in one relation or at one place beautiful, at another time or in another relation or another place foul, as if beautiful to some and foul to others, or in likeness of a face or hands or any other part of the bodily frame, or in any form of speech or knowledge, or existing in any other being, as for example, in an animal, or in heaven, or in earth, or in any other place; but beauty absolute, separate, simple and everlasting, which without diminution and without increase, or any change, is imparted to the ever-growing and perishing beauties of all other things. He who from these ascending under the influence of true love, begins to perceive that beauty, is not far from the end. And true order of going, or being led by another, to the things of love, is to begin from the beauties **b)** of earth and mount upwards for the sake of that Other Beauty, using these as steps only, and from one going on two, and from two to all beautiful forms, and from beautiful forms to beautiful practices, and from beautiful practices to beautiful ideas, until from the beautiful ideas he arrives at the idea of Absolute Beauty Itself, and at last knows what the essence of beauty is. This, my dear Socrates, said the stranger of Mantineia, is that life above all others which man should live, in the contemplation of Absolute Beauty; a Beauty which if you once beheld, you would seek not to be after the measure of gold, or garments, beautiful young people, whose presence now entrances you;...But what if man had eyes to see the True Beauty--the Divine Beauty, I mean, pure and clear and unmixed, not clogged with the pollutions of mortality and all the colors and vanities of human life--looking towards, and beholding converse with the True Beauty Simple and Divine? Remember how in that communion only, beholding Beauty with the eye of the mind, he will be enabled to bring forth, not images of beauty, but realities--for he has hold not of an image but of a Reality--and bringing forth and nourishing true virtue to become the Friend of God and be immortal." (*Symposium* 210-212)

c) That love implanted in the soul that drives man up this ladder of beauties until the soul reaches God Himself, that Absolute Beauty, was given and implanted by God himself, to draw, even drive, all men back to himself. For man could not find peace or rest, until he reached, with his mind, the beatific vision of God Himself. Plato describes the strong longing of this love in our soul in various places, especially in the *Phaedo, Phaedrus, Symposium*, and the *Timaeus.*

That implanted love of the Eternal Beauty is also called by some Platonists man's "personal deity" within. It is Plutarch's contention that in life it serves as a reminder of the Eternal Beauty but in other ways leaves man on his own in his struggles, that man may develop his own personal innate virtue in facing the ups and downs of living. However, when men approach the end of life and the vision of the eternal realm comes into his mind, his personal deity aids, encourages, and comforts him at that critical yet anticipated time. He likens the situation to a man struggling at sea swimming desperately to make shore and the people on shore are rather passive and silent as they watch him struggle using his own power and abilities, but when he gets close to shore they yell and scream to him to encourage him, now that he is close, not to give up but to be focused on his struggle in order to make it to shore.

d)

"...as we try to survive and reach a safe harbor by utilizing our innate virtue; but when a soul has endured challenge after challenge with grit and determination..and now that its tour is coming to an end draws near the inhabitants of the next higher realm, sweating profusely from the danger and the effort involved in its emergence, God does not forbid its personal deity from helping it, but allows any deity which sets out to help to do so. Each deity sets about saving the soul in its charge by encouragement, and when the soul gets near enough it listens to the deity and is saved."10.9

117a)

One can see here the obvious Platonic teaching that God's concern is with the eternal joy of our souls, but man's physical existence is left to the laws of the material nature in which man comes into temporal existence. God is not a personal physical cure-all; He leaves man to live within the normal laws of nature, and he does not break into those laws as an act of partiality towards any one person. God is not partial. People who are focused only on the earthly life in the physical body will not receive any help except for God's universal help to mankind in general. Many Christians who erroneously think the Deity is their personal servant, feel uncomfortable with such a "spiritual deity" who will not come in time of physical danger and offer them special help to save the body. For Christianity, despite all its protestations, is not a very "spiritual" religion, and thus insists upon the resurrection of the body, not being able to project mentally a spiritual, non material, existence. Thus many cry out that God is unfair when they are faced with a struggle and He does not help them if sick or with a chronic disease, for God leaves that to the material realm and its laws and does not intervene, for He is concerned about the eternal element of man. In the human life man must depend upon his own virtues, self-control, faith and courage when confronted with the normal decay of the material body. To ask for a special help and expect God to break into the laws of nature for one's own personal benefit is to consider oneself the center of the universe, and from such a one the cry is often heard, "Why me?" Boethius, referred to earlier, had fallen into that complaint, and had to be reminded by Lady Philosophy of his Platonic and philosophical heritage and that he had lost his spiritual focus and thus fallen into a type of slavery of the material realm. Lady Philosophy reprimands Boethius thus:

b)

"...You, made like God through reason, take from the basest things the adornment of your higher nature, and do not comprehend how greatly you thereby wrong your Creator. He intended the human race to be above all earthly things; you thrust down your dignity beneath the very lowest...For such is the condition of human nature that it surpasses other classes only when it knows itself (as an eternal being, not a temporal one), but is reduced to a rank lower than the beasts when it ceases to know itself. For in other animals ignorance of self is natural; in men it is a moral defect.." (Book II. Prose V)

Boethius, awaiting execution, was swimming close to the eternal shore, and Lady Philosophy was really his personal deity, reminding him to take courage and to ascend to the higher realm of existence. Plotinus puts it this way:

c)

"Further proof that our good is in the realm above is the love (Eros) innate in our souls; hence the coupling in picture and story of Eros and Psyche. The soul, different from the divinity but sprung from it, must needs love...As long as soul stays true to itself, it loves the divinity and desires to be at one with it, as a daughter loves with a noble love a noble father."(VI.9.9)

And the implanted Eros (love) and longing of man's psyche is expressed this way by the *Pseudo-Dionysius*:

d)

"Now when we apply dissimilar similarities to intelligent beings, we say of them that they experience desire, but this has to be interpreted as a divine yearning for that immaterial reality which is beyond all reason and all intelligence. It is a strong and sure desire for the clear and impassible contemplation of the Transcendent. It is a hunger for an unending, conceptual, and true communion with the spotless and sublime Light, or clear and splendid Beauty. Then there will be an unfailing and unturning power, seen in the pure and unchanging yearning for Divine Beauty, and in the total commitment of the real object of all desire."(144a-144b).

Longinus in his *On the Sublime* :

"...implanted at once into our souls an invincible love for all that is great and more divine than ourselves. That is why the whole universe gives insufficient scope to man's power of contemplation and reflection, but his thoughts often pass beyond the boundaries of the surrounding world. Anyone who looks at life in all its aspects will see how far the remarkable, the great, and the beautiful predominate in all things, and he will soon understand to what end we have been born."10.10

118a)

Posidonius declared:

"The cause of the passions--the cause, that is, of disharmony and of the unhappy life--is that men do not follow absolutely the daimon that is in them, which is akin to, and has a like nature with, the Power governing the whole cosmos, but turn aside after the lower animal principle, and let it run away with them. Those who fail to see this neither thereby set the cause of the passions in any better light, nor hold the right belief regarding happiness and concord. They do not perceive that the very first point in happiness is to be led in nothing by the irrational, unhappy, godless element in the soul."10.11

Crito wrote in his *On Prudence* the following lovely words:

b)

"God fashioned man in such a way as to render it manifest, that he is not through the want of power, or of deliberate choice, incapable of being impelled to what is beautiful in conduct. For He implanted in him a principle of such a kind as to comprehend at one and the same time the possible and the pre-eligible; so that man might be the cause of power, and the possession of good, but God of impulse and incitation according to right reason. On this account also, He made him tend to heaven, gave him an intellective power, and implanted in him a sight called intellect, which is capable of beholding God. For it is not possible without God to discover that which is best and most beautiful, nor without intellect to see God."10.12

c)

Epictetus also declared the joy and the comfort of the "daimon within":

"He (God) has placed by every man a guardian, every man's Daimon, to whom he has committed the care of the man, a guardian who never sleeps, is never deceived. For to what better and more careful guardian could He have intrusted each of us? When, then, you have shut the doors and made darkness within, remember never to say that you are alone, for you are not; but God is within, and your Daimon is within, and what need have they of light to see what you are doing? To this God you ought to swear an oath just as the soldiers do to Caesar."(*Discources* I.14)

d)

If one reads the Christian Fathers of the Church one will find an immense amount of Platonic thought in their teachings, unfortunately corrupted by the myths, legends, the Devil, and fear of hell. Yet, the Platonic element still shines brightly in those thoughts taken from the Platonic Tradition. Notice has closely Antony of Egypt (c mid Third Century to mid Fourth Century CE) follows Epictetus' statement above.

"When you close the doors of your dwelling and are alone, you should know that there is present with you the angel whom God has appointed for each man; the Greeks call him the personal daimon. This angel, who is sleepless and cannot be deceived, is always present with you; he sees all things and is not hindered by darkness. You should know, too, that with him is God, who is in every place."10.13

119a)

Plato's Gift to Christianity: The Gentile Preparation for and the Making of the Christian Faith presents a most comprehensive study of the Platonic influence upon both the Christian Canon and all the early Church Fathers.

Leibniz, in discussing whether or not something is planted within man that reflects a type of innate knowledge or inclination of thought, simply says "I believe, with Plato" and then speaks of such internal flashes or living fires of reason as indications of "something divine and eternal, which appears especially in necessary truths". 10.14 And again he said, "I have always favored, as I do still, the innate idea of God."10.15 Henry More, the Cambridge Platonist, wrote: "I grant that it is still the Light within us, that judges and concludes after the perusal of either the volumes of nature or divine revelation."10.16

b) In the longing for God and the eternal, which stand for the "religious element in man", Auguste Sabatier sees it in himself and in all men. "Why am I religious? Because I cannot help it: it is a moral necessity of my being...The necessity which I experience in my individual life I find to be still more invincible in the collective life of humanity. Humanity is not less incurably religious than I am."10.17 Pierre Teilhard de Chardin in his beautiful *Hymn of the Universe* stated: "Lord, it is you who, through the imperceptible goadings of sense of beauty, penetrated my heart in order to make its life flow out into yourself."10.18

c) Abraham H Maslow in his *Religions, Values, and Peak-Experiences* criticized the 19th Century scientists for throwing out the religious element in man's life because they did not like the answers that organized religions were giving to the questions. For despite the answers of organized religions, which, granted, no "self-respecting scientist could swallow" there is a religious nature that is inherent to being human: "...it is increasingly clear that the religious questions themselves--and religious quests, the religious yearnings, the religious needs themselves--are perfectly respectable scientifically, that they are rooted deep in human nature." 10.19

d) Mircea Eliade presents the idea that indeed even if we go back to the most primitive societies the innate longing for the Eternal, the Paradise, and the idea of immortality appears often. "We encounter the "paradise myth" all over the world in more or less complex forms." 10.20 To close this section and chapter of the nature of man, the words of Louis Pasteur seem appropriate:

"Happy the man who bears within him a divinity, an ideal of beauty and obeys it, an ideal of art, an ideal of science, an ideal of country, an ideal of the virtues."10.21

Λ

ΛΑΜΒΔΑ

CHAPTER ELEVEN
THE NATURE OF RELIGION IN THE PLATONIC TRADITION

I.. RELIGION, WHAT IS IT?

120a) The word itself, Religion, is from the Latin, but in the Latin the word religio or relligio is not that clearly precise. However, it probably does relate to a union of re and ligo which means to bind, bind together, or link. That would lead to a concept of a re-binding or re-linking to something. But to what? It was used in Latin for the rebinding of one to something sacred: a customary law, conscience, or the spiritual element of man to the supernatural, a deity or to the numina. But it was always considered a serious commitment in a person's life. Perhaps the thought was that somehow man became detached from generation to generation from the basic element of the spiritual and had to re-attach himself in some way to the holy or sacred. At any rate the word itself did not imply any set of teachings or doctrines or hierarchy of spiritual beings. It was a very general term. The following statements will show what men have believed religion to be.

b)

Epictetus stated:

"The business of the wise and good man is to use appearances conformably to nature: and as it is the nature of every soul to ascent to the truth, to descent from the false, and to remain in suspense as to that which is uncertain; so it is its nature to be moved toward the desire of the good....I possess decency, he possesses a tribuneship: he possesses a praetorship, I possess modesty. But I do not make acclamations where it is not becoming: I will not stand up where I ought not; for I am free, and a friend of God, and so I obey Him willingly."(Discourses III.3: IV.3)

c)

Benjamin Whichcote said:

"Besides this, it is the general direction of wisdom, to acknowledge God in all our ways; therefore in things remarkable, so much the more, and it is the effect of religion to do it, for what is religion but a participation, imitation, and resemblance of the divine goodness, both in the temper of the subject, and in its expressions of gratitude, ingenuity, acknowledgment, and the like? I know no other result of religion but this."11.1

Jeremy Taylor in his book Holy Living seeks to show that religion flavors a person's life and plants within him love and justice for all and in all interactions. He stated:

d)

"Religion, in its large meaning, signifies the whole duty of man. It includes justice, charity and sobriety. Because all these are commanded by God they become part of that honor and worship which we are bound to pay to Him. Thus it is used in St. James: 'Religion that is pure and undefiled before God and the Father is this: to visit orphans and widows in their affliction, and to keep oneself unstained from the world' (1:27) But in a more restricted sense, religion refers to our worship and adoration of God, in confessing His excellence, loving His person, admiring His goodness,...and doing all which may in a special and direct manner do Him honor."(p.109)

121a)

Hegel in his Lectures on the Philosophy of Religion said the following:

"The object is religion. This is the loftiest object that can occupy human beings; it is the absolute object. It is the region of eternal truth and eternal virtue, the region where all the riddles of thought, all contradictions, and all the sorrows of the heart should show themselves to be resolved, and the region of the eternal peace through which the human being is truly human."

And

"Religious consciousness has the conviction that God is really the midpoint, the absolutely true, that from which everything proceeds and into which everything returns, that upon which everything is dependent and apart from which nothing other than it has absolute, true independence."

b)

Hegel again said:

"Stated in a cursory way, religion is our relation to God." 11.2

Auguste Sabatier gave us these thoughts:

"Religion and Nature, the voice divine and the voice of conscience, the subject and the object of revelation, penetrate each other and become one. The supreme revelation of God shines forth in the highest of all consciousnesses and the loveliest of human lives." 11.3

William Ralph Inge said simply: "Religion is the introduction of the Divine life into the soul of man." 11.4

c)

Rudolf Bultmann showed his personal and passionate faith in his declaration of a an existential experience as the essence of religion:

"The understanding of God as creator is genuine only when I understand myself here and now as the creature of God...Belief in the almighty God is genuine only when it actually takes place in my very existence, as I surrender myself to the power of God who overwhelms me here and now"

And again, Bultmann declared: "We must, therefore, say that to live in faith is to live an eschatological existence, to live beyond the world, to have passed from death to life." 11.5

Martin Buber in *Eclipse of God* reminds us that religion is not knowledge of an object, but contact with a Person:

d)

"Religion, on the other hand, insofar as it speaks of knowledge at all, does not understand it as a noetic relation of thinking subject to a neutral object of thought, but rather as mutual contact, as the genuinely reciprocal meeting in the fullness of life between one active existence and another. Similarly, it understands faith as the entrance into this reciprocity, as binding oneself in relationship with an undemonstrable and unprovable, yet even so, in relationship, knowable Being, from whom all meaning comes."(pp 32-33)

Paul Tillich in his *Christianity and the Encounter of the World Religions* makes this statement:

122a)

"Religion is the state of being grasped by an ultimate concern, a concern which qualifies all other concerns as preliminary and which itself contains the answer to the question of the meaning of our life. Therefore this concern is unconditionally serious and shows a willingness to sacrifice any finite concern which is in conflict with it. The predominate religious name for the content of such concern is God."(pp 4-5)

Again Paul Tillich, this time in his *Theology of Culture* stated:

"Ultimate concern is manifest in the realm of knowledge as the passionate longing for ultimate reality...For Kierkegaard it is the immediate personal experience of the individual in the face of eternity, his personal faith--although interpreted by a most refined dialectical reasoning.(pp 8-9, 88)

b)

However simple or complex the concept is, religion always seemed to attach itself to examples or myths or teachings or rituals, and the more developed it became, the more attachments it had. It is this developed, yet confining and somewhat a stiffening of the heart, mind, and passion of religion, form of religion that seems to lose its truthful and spiritual vitality and becomes an organized burden to both those who belong to it and those who are often judged and oppressed by it. In the name of this form or organized religion the great tragedies mentioned in previous chapter takes place. It is this kind of organized religion that becomes empowered and then tries to convert and control others, even at the cost of personal freedoms and even extended to persecutions, slaughters and wars. From such a form of religion, every true person seeking the fellowship of the Sacred and the Holy must separate himself. For, in the long run, religion is the relationship between the mortal and the Immortal, between the human and the Divine, between time and Eternity, and that is of far greater value to the human soul that having temporal power and "acting" religious.

c)

II. RELIGION AS ETHICS AND PIETY

It is this form of religion, that of the ethical and pious nature, that may be what was originally meant by the word religion (re-ligo or re-binding). In primitive society one within the group, to be considered moral or ethical, would have to conform to the group's laws, customs and taboos. Each time he would conform to them he would re-bind himself to the group, verifying himself as one who would be reliable to "keep the faith" of the group. Likewise, such customs and taboos could be seen as the sacred element that bound the group together, so ethics itself would not lack the participation in that which the group considered holy or the metaphysical power that sustained them all for keeping the taboos or morality codes of the past. Of course, one group's ethical standard would be different than another's, and that would make for moral relativity and an inevitable conflict if one were to wed into another group than one's own. As humanity spread there was a philosophical quest for the absolute ethical standard, which was by pursued by no one more than Plato who sought the ultimate and eternal standard of the virtues, and, indeed, did believe they existed, but could be comprehended **d)** only by a dialectical form of philosophical and rational thought as climbing a staircase one step at a time. Even then he admitted such a difficulty of finding the absolute truth of any virtue such as courage or justice; and if found, like God, to communicate such to others would be impossible. Yet, it was necessary for the quest to take place if men would ever know what goodness really was. Many have spoken about morality, ethics and piety through out the years, and the following will present some of those views, for, to their thinking, ethics was the basic element of any religion.

123a) The ancient Greeks used the stem seb (σεβ) for many cognate words that speak of reverence or piety or righteousness or awe and even fear of the Holy. Sebastos was used for venerable, reverend, august (the Latin translation of Sebastos was Augustus); Sebema (σεβημα) was used for the acts of worship or honoring; sebomai (σεβομαι) was used to mean to fear, to reverence, and to feel awe before God, and sometimes even to feel shame or humiliation before God; eusebeia (ευσεβεια), literally "good sebia", was for the concept of loyalty, piety and reverence for God or for one's parents. The verb form eusebeo (ευσεβεω) meant to act or to live piously or ethically. Some of the Christian Church Fathers had the name of Eusebius. None of the ancient Greeks used the term "my God" for that lacked eusebia or the proper reverence; rather they would say something like Dear (philos - φιλος) Zeus or Dearest Theos. But to use a possessive term like "my" would be considered an attitude of hybris or arrogance, and that a wise man would never display before God. The following quotation from Walter Burkert's book, *Greek Religion*, reflects how Plato handled the concept of eusebeia:

b)

"It is Plato who brings about a revolution in religious language and in piety at one and the same time. Thereafter we find faith supported by philosophy, love transcending the world, and hope for the afterlife; there is humility, service of the gods, and at the same time the goal of assimilation [becoming like or similar to] to God."(p.275)

Many times, indeed, did Plato state that the goal of man was to become as much like God (`ομοιωσις – homoiosis) as possible in all virtues. Theophrastus' name meant (reflection of God), he was a student of Plato, who, after Plato's death, joined Aristotle in the Lyceum and it is to him that we owe the notes of Aristotle's lectures. To be like God or reflect God in one's life was to become, from Plato onwards, a mainstay of all **c)** philosophy and all religions influenced by him, including Christianity where the concept in the West was in Latin, imago dei, the image of God. For in Platonic thought, God was the unity of all virtues, and to imitate Him was to seek to be virtuous on the eternal and abstract level, leaving behind the weakness of relativism. Epictetus spoke of man having a mark by which he knows himself to be good. The mark is like an image, and if he bears the mark of a bad person, he needs to throw away or cast off that mark from his make-up. If he has the mark of a Nero, throw it away, but if the mark is of Trajan, then keep it. For Trajan's mark is suitable. What is your mark or stamp he asks his readers? If it is gentleness, a sociable disposition, a tolerant temper, a disposition to mutual affection, then keep it. The ultimate mark or stamp is to be one that resembles God as much as possible, and that coin can be held up with praise, and the coin that has Nero's image on it can be gladly thrown away.

d) Iamblichus taught that man was good and happy when his actions are performed while focussing on virtue; "just as the pilot looks to the motions of the stars. For thus, he who does this will not only follow God, but will also co-arrange human with divine good."11.9

Sextus "The Pythagorean" is strongly Platonic in his desires and teaching about the imitation of God as the way to be both ethical and happy. Some of his brief sentences read:

"You have in yourself something similar to God, and therefore use yourself as the temple of God, on account of that which in you resembles God."

124a)

"The greatest honor which can be paid to God, is to know and to imitate him."

"Before you do any thing think of God, that his light may precede your energies."

"The knowledge and imitation of divinity, are alone sufficient to beatitude."

Sextus also suggests as a measuring stick to morality the "Golden Rule": "Such as you wish your neighbour to be to you, such also be you to your neighbor" 11.10

b) Paul Tillich said it well: "It is the question of the intrinsic aim of existence--in Greek, the telos of all existing things...In the telos-formula of the Greek philosophers their whole vision of man and world was summed up, as when Plato called the telos of man ομοιωσις τω θεω κατα το δυνατον (becoming similar to the God as much as possible).

c) Plato gave a warning to those he taught that ethics can not be compromised by a person who then thinks he can appease God with those acts which Plato considered outside the realm or true religion or ethics such as sacrifices, rituals, and other acts or litanies that are both superficial and non spiritual. God is not bribed or bought off with such tactics. Sorrow, contrition and a spiritual and mental change in the entire mind set (μετανοια - used in the Christian Scriptures for "conversion" or "repentance") was necessary, and out of it works of reparation, satisfaction and purity were to flow. God will forgive and revive a compromised soul, but he will not be bribed with words or rituals.

d) The mystics of the middle ages sought this assimilation with God, peak experiences of the mind and soul, and, often overlooked, was the reborn attitude after the peak experience that would bring a high ethical standard of good works and charity to the community. Those who talked of having an experience with God had to prove the validity of such an experience by a pious and good life. All things were measured by one's ethics, one's honesty, and one's kindness and love for others. This was quite apparent in the lives the female mystics who "returned to their normal lives" by founding schools, charitable organizations, and even primitive hospitals. They were driven to live out the life of God's virtues in their own persons.

125a) No one understood Plato's drive for moral goodness better than Immanuel Kant. Some of Kant's words below from his Lectures on Ethics (Vorlesung ueber Ethik).

"We can also conceive a mystical ideal, in which the Supreme Good consists in this: that man sees himself in communion with the Highest Being. This is the Platonic ideal, a visionary ideal."

(Having experienced this "communion with the Highest Being), man then has a type of universal ethical standard to which he is obligated. "Moral goodness consists, therefore, in the submission of our will to rules whereby all our voluntary actions are brought into a harmony which is universally valid."

The rules are obligatory, but if a man trains himself into moral goodness, he will freely want to follow the universal moral obligations, and then the obligation to be ethical will not come from the outside, but will come from the inside, and thus man has been free in his choice, for his nature would be repulsed at doing anything less ethical than the universally valid standard of morality. "All obligation is either external or internal", and the man who has them instilled by habit to be part of his free will, will be the most free of all men: "he would be completely free". Kant continues:

b)

"God wants all men to be happy. He wants men to be made happy by men, and if only all men united to promote their own happiness we could make a paradise...God has set us on the stage where we can make each other happy. It rests with us, and us alone, to do so. Wretchedness and misery are our own fault. If a man be in distress, as so many of us are, it is not because God wills it so. God does not wish any one of us to be wretched; His purpose is that we should all unite in helping each other, and if a man is in distress, God leaves him in that state as a sign to his fellows who allow him to suffer though they could combine to help him."

c)

Yes, it is imperative for men to help men. How can men be immoral when another has need of his goodness? When that happens, mankind is destined to be unhappy. Kant goes on to say that the happiness is not only in the act of kindness, but also in the motive of the doer. The man who helps is helpful, but the man who wants to help and feels the joy and power he has when he helps, he is the happy man. Religion that is separated from that inner desire and joy of being ethical is empty, a vacuum pretending to be fulfillment. He also warns his readers that religion that is only concerned with mental concepts of theology, and does not live out the ethical and good life, is a religion that is for the indolent, impotent, and does not have the spiritual energy even to justify itself. "For moral worth is the worth of the person himself."

d)

Sarvepalli Radhakrishnan (1888-1975 CE), who taught at Oxford for almost two decades, followed the Platonic Kant very closely when he wrote:

"Only a philosophy which affirms that they are rooted in the universal nature of things can give depth and fervour to moral life, courage and confidence in moral difficulties. We need to be fortified by the conviction that the service of the ideals is what the cosmic scheme demands of us, that our loyalty or disloyalty to them is a matter of the deepest moment not only to ourselves or to society, or even to the human species, but to the nature of things. If ethical thought is profound, it will give a cosmic motive to morality. Moral consciousness must include a conviction of the reality of ideals. If the latter is religion, then ethical humanism is acted religion. When man realizes his essential unity with the whole of being, he expresses this unity in his life. Mysticism and ethics, other worldliness and worldly work go together."11.12

126a) One of the things that was warned against was a type of dogmatism that dictated that every action was either good or bad. From Plato on there was the teaching that some things were neither good nor bad, that they were insignificant in the quest for goodness, and basically they were indifferent to the entire process. The word for this was adiaphoria (αδιαφορια) indifference or lack of difference, that is, that it lacked enough significance to be classified as either good or bad. Both Aristotle and Zeno of Citium studied at the Academy and both incorporated the concept of adiaphoria into their teachings on ethics. That is very important as a warning to those who are prone to judge other people over petty things, protesting that the actions of those they are judging warrant a judgment against them, when in reality the actions of the accused are insignificant and have no "differencia" of their own. This teaching is screaming out to people not to be petty, for it is broadcasting their own judgmentalism and doing nothing for the distinction of good and evil. Plutarch in one of his moral essays stated that there is a difference between true and false in every situation, but in morality that is not so. "For I see a difference here: that which is not true must immediately be false; but that is not of necessity evil which is not **b)** good: because that between true and false there is not a medium, but between good and evil there is the indifferent (adiaphoria)."11.6

Opposite of the petty minded is the idea of being more judgmental towards oneself and less judgmental towards others. Pliny the Younger in a letter to Rosianus Geminus stated: "My own idea of the truly good and faultless man is one who forgives the faults of others as if he was daily committing them himself, and who keeps himself free of faults as if he could never forgive them."11.7 Seneca is upset with those whose words are gloriously moral, but whose actions are ingloriously immoral. "Let them put their preaching into practice." is his suggestion to those "acting" like philosophers.11.8

c) The importance of the concept of the Adiophoria is that it protects the individual from the onslaughts of super moralists who see every action as a possibility of evil. The Christian Church certainly was guilty of this: no work on the Sabbath, no dancing of any kind, beware of all pleasures, guilt for not believing innumerable doctrines about mythological saints who never existed, fear of things classified as evil but were part of human normality. On and on the Church went imposing good and evil upon everything, and the Church itself was the sole arbiter as to what could be done and couldn't be done. Loads of laws and customs plagued man and it was done for control and for the money in order that people would pay to see false relics and the offerings they would make to release relatives bound in purgatory for endless ages. This day you can eat meat and that day you can not eat it, divorce is evil and an attack on holy matrimony--a doctrine created by the Church and even made a sacrament. Personal and natural freedoms taken away from individuals and classified as sacred law. This book can not be read nor can one go to this movie. One game can be played and another can not. This total submission posed as a spiritual and pious regulation of morality and ethics, often with the grossest of hypocrisy, harmed millions of consciences, caused unlimited spiritual discomfort and tension in the souls of sincere believers.

d) Erasmus, Luther and others rebelled against such in the Sixteenth Century, but then one had two general self appointed classifiers of good and evil: Catholicism and Protestantism, both at times at the throats of those under their power in order to get "obedience" out of them. Both claiming to be the hand of the Lord God. The people must constantly demand new reformations of all forms of organized religions because they have a natural tendency, when in power, to impose their control by means of what they claim to be substantial and spiritual necessities, when they are in fact nothing more than self created weapons of control. Ethics and morality are necessary and all such will be discussed in the following chapters, but false morality and poisoned consciences are not the avenues to goodness and happiness but infectious diseases created by the organized religions to kill the spirit and joy of life. Erasmus recommended knowledge and prayer and likewise the studying of the pagans was recommended. "I might also add that a sensible reading of the pagan poets and philosophers is a good preparation..for life." Especially recommended was "the divinely inspired Plato." There are two basic elements to ethics: universal love and tolerance and the idea of the golden rule; do to others what you would want them to do to you or do not do to others what you would not want them to do to you. Again the details of the virtues will follow, but those two basic elements can be very helpful.

127a)

III. RELIGION AS PERSONAL INNER GROWTH: DEVOTIONS, MEDITATIONS, LITANIES, HYMNS, AND PRAYERS

The other great aspect of religion, after the moral life of loving, helping, honoring, and encouraging others, is the inner growth of the individual. This is a type of religious "home base" that gives the strength and power to love and care for others. It is here where the "fire of the Spirit" emits the spiritual energy to learn the good and the courage to do the good. Here is where the emotional spiritual peaks of joy take place that simply can not be shared with others except by love and honor and charity. Paul Tillich in his *The Religious Situation* said "The most important religious movements are developing outside of religion" (p 157). This statement applies to this and the next three sections of this chapter. True religion has always been a personal experience anyway, between a person and that which he believes to be the Life Force that has given him life and upon whom his dreams of meaning and immortality depend. The personal encounter between a man and his God that shuts out and overwhelms every other perspective of one's life, can not be placed outside of his own personal being and put into a community's power or influence. Those encounters or experiences fall, generally speaking into the five categories of this section.

b)

A. Devotion

Karl Jaspers stated in his *Way to Wisdom* "Unlimited devotion to God is the authentic mode of existence. That to which I devote myself in the world, to the point of staking my life, must be constantly tested in relation to God." (p.83). Such devotions are sometimes intense with feelings of joy, humility, freedom and dependence, and awe. There is also connected with such devotion a feeling of comfort, of devoting oneself to the care of God and letting God be God: so to speak, putting the whole world in His hand, including one's personal life and destiny. Hegel in his *Lectures on the Philosophy of Religion* made the following statement about devotion:

c)

"Feeling--the gratification that I am with God in his grace and that God's spirit is alive within me, the consciousness of my union and reconciliation with--this is the innermost feature of the cultus. The first form of the cultus is what is called *devotion* in general. Devotion is not the mere faith that God is, but is present when the faith becomes vivid, when the subject prays and is occupied with this content not merely in objective fashion but becomes immersed therein; the essential thing here is the fire and heat of devotion."11.14

Hegel also declared: "Hence the believer not only has a vision of God, he longs for union with Him. He is moved to devotion to the divine."11.15

d) Friedrich Schleiermacher in his *On Religion* made an attack on what he considered to be a cold dogmatism about which the Church spent all it time arguing, instead of trying to foster a true and devotional feeling in the hearts of people towards God. He accused the priesthood of his day of living like cold robots all concerned with fighting each other about doctrinal issues instead of warmly and joyfully living a life of devotion that is uplifting to their parishioners. They were false priests. This is what he said a true priest would be:

128a)

"He is needed to show to their anxious, restless, self-love, another self-love whereby man in this earthly life and along with it loves the highest and the eternal, and to their restless passionate greed a quiet and sure possession. Acknowledge, then, with me, what a priceless gift the appearance of such a person must be when the higher feeling has risen to inspiration, and can no longer be kept silent, when every pulse-beat of his spiritual life takes communicable form in word or figure...This is the priest of the highest, for he brings it nearer those who are only accustomed to lay hold of the finite and the trivial. The heavenly and eternal he exhibits as an object of enjoyment and agreement.... In this way he strives to awaken the slumbering germ of a better humanity, to kindle love for higher things, to change the common life into a nobler, to reconcile the children of earth with the Heaven that hears them...This is the higher priesthood that announces the inner meaning of all spiritual secrets." 11.16

b)

And again: "Why do you not regard the religious life itself, and first those pious exaltations of the mind in which all other known activities are set aside or almost suppressed, and the whole soul is dissolved in the immediate feeling of the Infinite and Eternal?"11.17

Again: "In itself religion is an affection, a revelation of the Infinite in the finite, God being seen in it and it in God."11.18

Schleiermacher who was very Platonic in thought, was full of charity and feeling for others, but totally undogmatic in terms of evaluating another. He translated the Platonic dialogues into German, and was never the same after being spiritually affected by the Republic. He sympathized with Spinoza for the way he was treated and rejected by theologians and even countries. Of him Schleiermacher had this to say:

c)

"Offer with me reverently a tribute to the manes of the holy, rejected Spinoza. The high World-Spirit pervaded him; the Infinite was his beginning and his end; the Universe was his only and his everlasting love. In holy innocence and in deep humility he beheld himself mirrored in the eternal world, and perceived how he also was its most worthy mirror. He was full of religion, full of the Holy Spirit. Wherefore, he stands there alone and unequalled; master in his art, yet without disciples and without citizenship, sublime above the profane tribe...See in him the power of the enthusiasm and the caution of a pious spirit, and acknowledge that when the philosophers shall become religious and seek God like Spinoza, and the artists be pious and love...the great resurrection shall be celebrated for both worlds."11.19

d)

It was in the deepest felt feelings that Schleiermacher felt religion becomes most alive: "These feelings are the beautiful and sweet scented flowers of religion."11.20 The feelings of sacred reverence and love give the truly religious and joyful life. A longing for love and its continuous renewal within is the center of religion. Thus devotion wrapped in love and joy in the presence of God gives one a taste of true religion.

129a)

B. Meditiation

Meditation is defined as the engagement of continuous and contemplative thought, of musing and pondering about one's being and how it relates to destiny and ultimate reality. Anselm of Canterbury, a Christian Platonist, encouraged his readers to try to get away from the world and meditate upon God and thus draw near to him.

"Come now, little man! Flee for awhile from your tasks, hide yourself for a little space from the turmoil of your thoughts. Come, cast aside your burdensome cares, and put aside your fatiguing pursuits. For a little while give your time to God, and rest in Him. Enter the inner chamber of your mind, shut out all things save God, and whatever may aid you in seeking God; and having barred the door of your chamber, seek Him."11.21

Iamblichus, in speaking of the disciples of Pythagoras, he stated:

b)

"For those who committed themselves to the guidance of his doctrine, acted in the following manner; they performed their morning walks alone, and in places in which there happened to be an appropriate solitude and quiet, and where there were temples and groves, and other things adapted to give delight. For they thought it was not proper to converse with any one, till they had rendered their own soul sedate, and had co-harmonised the reasoning power."11.22

c) The *Corpus Hermeticum*, Libellus IV, states: "For it is man's function to contemplate the works of God; and for this purpose was he made, that he might view the universe with wondering awe, and come to know its Maker." One wonders also if the ancients had access to the Hubble telescope how much wonder and awe they would have, for today man is truly overwhelmed at space and the very distant galaxies. Einstein and von Braun had great glimpses of it, and gave thanks to God. One could say that if man truly sees this grand scale of space and knows himself, he will be awed: the entire universe becomes sacred as Teilhard de Chardin tried so hard to tell us.

Anthony the Great relates how meditation and the peace that follows it put a man's mind at rest, and with that contended mind sleep itself becomes a vision of the sacred.

d)

"When you go to bed with a contented mind, recall the blessings and generous providence of God; be filled with holy thoughts and great joy. Then, while your body sleeps, your soul will keep watch; the closing of your eyes will bring you a true vision of God; your silence will be pregnant with sanctity, and in your sleep you will continue consciously to glorify the God of all with the full strength of your soul. For when evil is absent from man, his thankfulness is by itself more pleasing to God than any lavish sacrifice."11.23

To close out this section, Jeremy Taylor encourages us with these words:

130a)

"When you begin a religious exercise, make an act of adoration; that is, solemnly worship God, place yourself in His presence, and behold Him with the eye of faith. Let your desires focus on Him as the object of your worship, the reason for your hope and the source of your blessing. When you have placed yourself before Him and have knelt in His presence, it is most likely that all the rest of your devotion will be influenced by the wisdom of such an awareness and the glory of such a Presence."11.24

C. Litanies, Psalms and Praise

b) These acts are more formal and often follow a set pattern and repeated by the worshipper, yet they can be very personally encouraging for they have been around a long time or they contain an innate beauty to them that makes them, not only long lasting, but also universally appealing to those who desire to express love for God. The Eighteenth Libellus of the *Corpus Hermeticum* encourages us to praise God even though we are small children who are incapable of speaking to the level of His nobility:

"To God then, the Father of our souls, it is fitting that praise should rise from countless tongues and voices, even though our words cannot be worthy of him, seeing that it is a task beyond our power to tell of him. Even so, little children are not able to worthily to sing their father's praise; but they do what is fitting when they render to him such honour as they can. Nay, this very thing redounds to God's glory, that he greatness transcends the praise of his offspring; and the beginning and middle and end of our praise is to confess that our Father is infinite."

b)

Francis of Assisi, in love with both God and nature, rendered this praise to God for all such blessings.

"Most high omnipotent good Lord,
Yours are the praises, the glory, the honor, and all benediction.
To you alone, Most High, do they belong,
And no man is worthy to mention you.
Be praised, my Lord, with all your creatures.
Especially the honorable Brother Sun,
Who makes the light of day and gives light also to us by you.
And is beautiful and radiant with grand splendor.
Of you, Most High One, he bears significance.
Praise you, my Lord, for Sister Moon and the stars,
In heaven formed, clear, precious, and beautiful.
Be praised, my Lord, for Brother Wind,
And for the air, and clouds, and serenity, and all weather,
Through which, to your creatures, you give sustenance.
Be praised, my Lord, for Sister Water,
Which is of much value and humble and precious and chaste..
Be praised, my Lord, for Brother Fire,
By which you illuminate the night,
And he is beautiful and full and robust and strong.
Be praised, my Lord, for Our Sister Mother Earth,
Who sustains and governs us
And produces diverse fruits and colorful flowers and herbs.
Praise and bless my Lord, and thank him,
And serve him with great humility."

Lorenzo de Medici was a poet who wrote poems immersed in Platonic Love. George Santayana in his *Interpretations of Poetry and Religion* presents this poem of Lorenzo taken from his *Laudi Spirituali*:

c)

"O let this wretched life within me die
  That I may live in thee, my life indeed;
In thee alone, where dwells eternity,
  While hungry multitudes death's hunger feed.
I list within, and hark! Death's stealthy tread!
I look to thee, and nothing then is dead.

Then eyes may see a light invisible
  And ears may hear a voice without a sound,--
A voice and light not harsh, but tempered well,
  Which the mind wakens when the sense is drowned,
Till, wrapped within herself, the soul have flown
To that last good which is her inmost own.

When, sweet and beauteous Master, on that day,
  Reviewing all my loves with aching heart,
  I take from each its bitter self away,
The remnant shall be thou, their better part.
This perfect sweetnes he his single store
Who seeks the good; this faileth nevermore.

A thirst unquenchable is not beguiled
  By draught on draught of any running river,
Whose fiery water feed our pangs for ever,
  But by a living fountain undefiled.
O sacred well, I see thee and were fain
To drink; so should I never thirst again."11.25

d)

Santayana then comments concerning Italian Platonic Poetry: "It is nothing else than the application to passion of that pursuit of something permanent in a world of change, of something absolute in a world of relativity, which was the essence of the Platonic Philosophy."

131a) From the Psalm-Book of Thomas Sternhold and John Hopkins, 1567 CE, one finds this rendition of Psalm 23 of the Hebrew Scriptures in English.

"My shepherd is the living Lord; nothing, therefore, I need.
In pastures fair, with waters calm, he set me for to feed.
He did convert and glad my soul, and brought my mind in frame
To walk in paths of righteousness for his most holy name.

Yea, though I walk in vale of death, yet will I fear none ill;
Thy rod, thy staff doth comfort me, and thou art with me still.
And in the presence of my foes, my table thou has spread;
Thou shalt, O Lord, fill full my cup and eke anoint my head.

Through all my life thy favor is so frankly showed to me
That in thy house forevermore my dwelling place shall be."

b) Because of some of the horrors of organized religion, Karl Jaspers in his *Way to Wisdom*, under the section of *The Independent Philosopher*, urges his reader not to be concretely attached to any one system of thought but to be himself, think for himself, and then seek to find himself as he best relates to truth and the world.

"Let us not pledge ourselves to any philosophical school
or take formulable truth as such for the one and exclusive truth;
Let us be master of our thoughts;
Let us not heap up philosophical possessions,
but apprehend philosophical thought as movement
and seek to deepen it.
Let us acquire the power to learn from all the past
by making it our own;
Let us listen to our contemporaries and remain open
to all possibilities;
Let each of us as an individual immerse himself in his own historicity,

in his origin, in what he has done;
Let him possess himself of what he was, of what he has become,
and of what has been given to him;
Let us not cease to grow though our own historicity
into the historicity of man as a whole
and thus make ourselves into citizens of the world."(p.118)

c)

Since God gave us "the gift of numbers" and reason, He will be delighted if we take that divinity within us (Logos or Reason) and use it as individuals for it is as individuals that we relate to Him and it is as individuals that we can truly "know ourselves." Therefore, the words of Jaspers are a proper "litany" for our own spiritual growth and one that honors the gift of reason that God has so graciously given us.

D. Hymns and Odes

One of the great hymns of antiquity is Cleanthes' Hymn to Zeus, and below a portion of it is presented. Some of Cleanthes' Stoicism will show forth, but basically it is Platonic in nature:

d)

"O God most glorious, called by many a name,
Nature's great King, through endless years the same;
Omnipotence, who by thy just decree
Contollest all, hail, Zeus, for unto thee
Behooves thy creatures in all lands to call,
We are thy children, we alone, of all
On earth's broad ways that wander to and fro,
Bearing thine image whereso'er we go.
Wherefore with songs of praise thy power I will forth show.
Lo! Yonder Heaven, that round the earth is wheeled,
Follows thy guidance, still to thee doth yield
Glad homage; thine unconquerable hand
Such flaming minister, the leven brand
...
Vehicle of the universal Word, that flows
Through all, and in the light celestial glows
Of stars both great and small. A King of Kings
Through ceaseless ages, God whose purpose bring

To birth, whate'er on land or in the sea
Is wrought, or in high heaven's immensity;
....
132a) ....
One Word--whose voice alas! the wicked spurn;
Insatiate for the good their spirits yearn;
Yet seeing see not, neither hearing hear not
God's universal law, which those revere
By reason guided, happiness to win.
The rest, unreasoning, diverse shapes of sin
Self-prompted follow: for an idol name
Vainly they wrestle in the lists of fame:
Other inordinately riches woo,
Or dissolute, the joys of flesh pursue,
Now here, now there they wander, fruitless still,
For ever seeking good and finding ill.
Zeus the all-bountiful, whom darkness shrouds,
whose lightning lightens in the thunder-clouds,
Thy children save from error's deadly sway;
Vouchsafe that unto knowledge they attain;
For thou by knowledge art made strong to reign
O'er all, and all things rulest righteously.
So by thee honored, we will honor thee,
Praising thy works constantly with songs,
As mortals should; no higher meed belongs
E'en to the gods, than justly to adore
The universal law for evermore.

b) Synesius the Neoplatonist of Cyrene wrote many letters and hymns, and one of his, a morning hymn, is here given in part:

"Again light shines forth, again dawn, again day,
after the darkness that roams by night.
Again make supplication to God, O my heart,
in the songs of the morning.
He has given light to the dawn, who has given stars to the night,
the dancing company that encircles the universe.
All things hang upon Thy will, and Thou art the root of things

present, past, future and within.
Thou art Father, art Mother, Thou Male, Thou Female,
c) Thou Voice, Thou Silence, of nature the fruitful nature.
All hail Thee, O king, whenever it be lawful to cry this aloud,
Age of ages, Root of the universe.
All hail to Thee, Center of existing things, Monad of numbers immortal,
of kings that existed not before Thee.
Mayest Thou rejoice greatly, mayest Thou rejoice greatly,
for it is with God that joy is found.
Lend a propitious ear to the hymns of my choirs.
Open the light of wisdom,
pour down the glorious plenty of calm life
pour down its shining grace.
Drive poverty from our midst, and the earthly calamity of wealth.
Drive illness from my limbs,
the disorderly urge of the passions from my life,
and soul-gnawing cares, to the end that
destiny of earth may not weigh down the wings of my soul,
But lifting a free pinion,
may I dance in the ineffable rites of Thy offspring.

d)

What a lovely way to met the dawn and start the day with gratitude and praise to God!

Many people hear both the music and the words to Beethoven's Ninth Symphony, the Choral, but seldom, probably because it is sung in German, are the words understood and the theme understood. The theme is that joy and both God's beauty and presence are not to be separated, and therefore, if all men are to live in joyous harmony, they must do so under the wings of God. The words and theme were written by Schiller who had written much on the purpose, power and beauty of the arts. Those words that are used from his Ode to Joy by Beethoven for his Choral, now used as the uniting hymn of the European Union, are shown here, first in German and then in my English translation.

133a)

Freude, shoener Goetterfunken, Tochter aus Elysium
Wir betreten feuertrunken, Himmlische, dein Heiligtum!
Deine Zauber binden wieder, Was die Mode streng geteilt;

Alle Menschen werden Brueder, Wo dein sanfter Fluegel weilt!

Wem der grosse Wurf gelungen, Eines Freundes Freund zu sein,
Wer ein holdes Weib errungen, Mische seinen Jubel ein!
Ja, wer auch nur eine Seele sein nennt auf dem Erdenrund!
Und ser's nie gekonnt, der stehle Weinend sich aus diesem Bund.

Freude trinken alle Wesen an den Bruesten der Natur;
Alle Guten, alle Boesen Folgen ihrer Rosenspur.
Kusse gab sie uns und Reben, einen Fruend, geprueft in Tod;
Wollust ward dem Wurm gegeben, Und der Cherub steht vor Gott!

Froh, wie seine Sonnen fliegen durch des Himmels praechtgen Plan,
Laufet, Brueder, eure Bahn, freudig, wie ein Held zum Siegen.
Seid umschlungen, Millionen, Diesen Kuss der ganzen Welt!
Brueder! Ueberm Sternenzeit muss ein lieber Vater wohnen.
Ihr stuerzt nieder, Millionen? Ahnest du den Schoepher, Welt?
Such' in ueber'm Sternenzeit! Ueber Sternen muss er wohnen.
b)
Joy, The sparkling beauty of God, Daughter of Elysium,
Fire-inspired, we enter, into the heavens, your sanctuary.
Your magic binds again, all that custom has harshly divided;
All men become brothers, where your tender wings linger.

Whoever has received the abundant gift of friendship,
Whoever has obtained a charming wife, unite in jubilation,
Yes, who also calls only one soul his own upon the round earth!
And he who cannot rejoice, removes himself tearfully from our circle.

All creatures drink of joy on the breasts of nature.
All who are good, all who are bad, follow her sweet smell of roses.
She gave us kisses and the grapevine, a friend proven even in death;
Even the worm was given full joy, and the cherub stands before God.
Cheerfully, as the sun flies its splendid course through the heavens,
So also brothers, run your race happily, as a hero to victory.

You millions, you are embraced, this kiss is for the entire world!
Brothers! Above the canopy over the stars, there must dwell a

Loving Father. Do you kneel before Him, you millions?
World, do you acknowledge your Creator?
Seek Him above the covering of the stars.
It is above the stars He is obligated to reside."

c) E. A Prayer Book

Since prayer is such an important element of one's connection to God, it is without much doubt the center piece of one's religion. It is also a very personal experience for the believer to empty his heart and mind before his God and Maker. The physical part is, of course, secondary, for it does not really matter if one is kneeling, standing, lying down, or even prostrating before a designated sacred object. It is the honesty and humility of the person praying that pleases God. There simply can be no hypocrisy or arrogance in the presence of God, especially during the sanctity of the act of prayer. Following are many prayers that show how the worshippers and lovers of God have prayed in the past, and the reader who can empathize with their words and their spirit will gain much for his own spiritual growth. It should be noted up front that in Plato's dialogues it is stated many times that prayer is of great value and that neither small nor great endeavors are to be undertaken without praying first, for not to seek guidance and help from one's God when he starts an activity is partially foolish and partially arrogant. Coming before God is likened to a sacrifice of one's self by Persius who then asks the one who prays to have a pure heart.

d)

"To the just gods let me present a mind,
Which civil and religious duties bind,
A guileless heart, which no dark secrets knows,
But with the generous love of virtue glows.
Such be the presents, such the gifts I make,
With them I sacrifice a wheaten cake." (Satire II:133-138)

Iamblichus said of even discussing certain things one must consider prayer first: "Since it is usual with all men of sound understanding, to call on Divinity, when entering on any philosophic discussion...". This is the first sentence in his book on Pythagoras. Aratus begins his work *Phaenomena* with these words.

"Let our beginning be from Zeus, for we as mortals never leave him unnamed, for he fills all about us, the streets and marketplaces of men, the seas and the ports. We shall always have need of him, for we are his offspring."

In Boethius' Consolation of Philosophy, he puts into the mouth of Lady Philosophy this prayer as she seeks to guide a suffering Boethius.

134a)

"You who does govern the universe with everlasting law, Founder of earth and heaven who bids time to roll on from age to age, forever firm Yourself, yet giving movement to all things,...grant what we may behold the fount of the Good; grant that, when the light has been discovered, we may set upon You the soul's unblinded eyes. Hurl asunder the heavy clouds of this material world, and shine forth in Your splendor! For You are to the pious a serene and tranquil rest; to know You is our aim. You are our beginning, our progress, our guide, our way, our ending." (Bk III, Meter IX).

b) Prayer is basically a spiritual exercise and not a request for some favoritism from God that relates to material benefits, even for one's health or any bodily benefit. For that cheapens prayer and detracts from the devotional aspect of it. The "I love You, God, now give me something!" type of prayer is insulting to God, because it attacks his impartiality and it is destructive to one's spiritual life, for it puts one's spiritual life and growth upon the success of attaining material and physical benefits. That is what Lady Philosophy had to remind Boethius of. Immanuel Kant was blunt about it: """Concerning the matters of prayers, when they do not have the intention of negotiating a moral mind-set, but they have in view the needs of physical life, then the prayer is never validated" (*Ethica* from his *Vorlesungen ueber Moralphilosophie: (Von Gebet)* R. W. Emerson is even more dogmatic about such prayers:

c)

"Prayer that craves a particular commodity is vicious. Prayer is the contemplation of the facts of life from the highest point of view. It is the soliloquy of a beholding and jubilant soul. It is the spirit of God pronouncing his works good. But prayer as a means to effect a private end is meanness and theft. It supposes dualism and not unity in nature and consciousness. As soon as a man is one with God, he will not beg." 11.26

d)

Maximus of Tyre reminded his readers that the value of prayer is spiritual in his essay entitled *Whether one should pray.* His basic message was that asking and begging have no place in a prayer made to God who is good and gives what we need anyway. Prayer itself is beneficial, but one must remember that it is for the spiritual benefit of being closer to God. As Pythagoras, Socrates and Plato all prayed they knew, as all good philosophers, that prayer is not asking but communion with God. Yet, God is a Father to us, and Kant is quick to remind us that He certainly looks kindly on some prayers for physical benefit due to the weakness of our nature; as when one prays because his ship is sinking at sea.

135a) Jacob Boehme prayed this prayer:

"O Lord...stay with us and in us, and teach us to consider that our external life, on which we trust so much, walks toward evening and its end, and that it is soon over for us. Teach us to travel the right way. Be with us on our pilgrim's path, and lead us home to You."11.27

Michel de Montaigne stated in his essay *Of Solitude*: "And knowing of how uncertain duration these accidental conveniences are, I never forget...to make it my chiefest prayer to Almighty God, that He will please to render me content with myself and the condition wherein I am." Auguste Sabatier taught: "The living expression of the relations of man to his God, prayer is the very soul of religion...Nothing better reveals the worth and moral dignity of a religion than the kind of prayer it puts into the lips of its adherents."11.28

b) One of the most endearing prayers was left us by one of the most endearing men of the West, Francis of Assisi, who gave us this lovely *Peace Prayer.*

Lord make me an instrument of your peace.
Where there is hatred, let me sow love;
Where there is injury, pardon;
Where there is doubt, faith;
Where there is despair, hope;

Where there is darkness, light; and
Where there is sadness, joy.

O Divine Master, grant that I may not so much seek
To be consoled as to console,
To be understood as to understand,
To be loved as to love.

For it is in giving that we receive,
It is in pardoning that we are pardoned,
And it is in dying that we are born to eternal life.

c)
Thomas Browne gives to us this beautiful night prayer:

"The night is come, like to the day,
Depart not Thou, great God, away,
Let not my sins, black as the night,
Eclipse the lustre of Thy light:
Keep still in my horizon; for to me
The Sun makes not the day, but Thee.
Thou, Whose nature cannot sleep,
On my temples centry keep;...
Let no dreams my head infest,...
While I do rest, my soul advance;
Make my sleep a holy trance;
That I may, my rest being wrought,
Awake into some holy thought;
And with as active vigour run
My course, as doth the nimble Sun,
Sleep is a death; O make me try,
By sleeping, what it is to die;
And as gently lay my head
On my grave, as now my bed.
How'ere I rest, great God, let me
Awake again at last with Thee:
And thus assur'd, behold I lie
Securely, or to awake or die.

These are my drowsie days: in vain
I do now wake to sleep again:
O come that hour, when I shall never
Sleep again, but wake for ever."11.29

d)

IV. COMMUNAL WORSHIP

Both Jews and Christians worship in group settings weekly and many find a great benefit from being in and identifying with a worshipping community. For many, such united meetings have been life changing, life supporting, spiritually refreshing, and socially enhancing even to the extent that if one weekly service is missed, participants often feel their week to be unfulfilled and wait with great anticipation for the next communal gathering to be held. For such meetings can be avenues to newly acquired friends who share a similar spiritual base, and empower families to an enhanced feeling of wholeness.

136a) Platonism, especially as it is practiced today, is not community based and has no communal creeds and dogmas, and no huge buildings solely for the purpose of such gatherings. In antiquity the gods were honored by the multitudes at all the city's festivals and games. But a trip to Delphi for an oracle was usually by one individual seeking some type of advice from the appointed Pythia, a female prophetess, who undoubtedly was well educated in the art of spiritual counseling. Likewise there were temples and altars among the Platonists in antiquity, that is, until they were all destroyed by the Christians. Those temples and altars were created with great beauty that a sense of the Holy and the Beautiful was present, and thus a sense of awe and reverence was created by the setting, and the worshipper would feel that there was a presence, **b)** sacred and pure that would bless his worship and help him in his life quest to become a good and honorable person. Such a setting and any ritual of bowing, praying, and offering a wine or other type of sacrifice was performed by the individual. But the essence of Platonism, itself, was more of a philosophical religion, as least among the leaders of the Platonic faith. Gatherings took place, there were some rituals performed, and always a prayer before the activities started. Singing took place and entertainment was presented in the form of dancing and music. But the climax of the gathering was always a discussion of virtue in the hopes of gaining wisdom, that by wise decisions one would learn to live the good life and imitate the goodness and beauty of God himself in their own lives. All participated in the discussion, the meal, the fellowship, and even in the entertainment in which each person might sing a song solo that he had created, both the words and the melody. Most of those gatherings would take place at the house or estate of one of the members of the group.

c) On another level, there were the schools of Platonic thought for those deeply interested in all aspects of human life, and people came to the location and stayed there for such intellectual and spiritual fellowship, and some stayed for years. Aristotle stayed at Plato's Academy for twenty years. The schools often became a setting for living one's life. Well educated and deeply spiritual, some of the members would leave the Academy in Athens and establish similar schools at Rhodes, Pergamum, Alexandria, Antioch, and many other places that people throughout the Greek Oikoumene (the Greek learned "household" of the Mediterranean Sea area). Wherever there was a Greek Gymnasium established there were educators from the Greek schools of thought, especially the Platonic School. What happened to them? The organized Christian Church between 325 CE and 529 CE looted them, destroyed them and burned their books, condemned their teachings, and sometimes killed them as the Church sought total control over the spiritual and intellectual lives of the people of the Mediterranean world. Platonic teachers were classified as heretics and pagans and went underground or disguised themselves as Christians, which, of course was a risky business fraught with dangers. But in all the schools of learning during the Middle Ages and especially during the Renaissance the Platonists were there: in England, at Chartres, in Paris, and openly in Florence where under both the sponsorship and protection of the Medici family a new "Academy" was established openly. But it never became an organized church body that established dogmas, creeds, political power blocks, and never cried out "heresy" for someone in their group discussions who took a contrary

d) view of the group or even of Plato himself, who left most of his dialogues open ended (aporetic). Learning how to think and how to pursue goodness was held to be greatly superior to simply holding certain views, especially if those views had never been under rational criticism and logical discussion and fact gathering analysis. For learning the truth about reality, about oneself, and about the human experience and seeking to apply wisdom for the sake of goodness, purity, beauty, and ethical living was, to the Platonist, worship itself. For, in all honestly, how else can man honor and love God as well as his fellowman. A scientific breakthrough to create a drug or help a disabled person walk again, was an act of worship. The flourishing of the arts and sciences was a sign of Platonic worship. For such sought to bring truth, goodness, and happiness to mankind, and thus imitate the Creator Himself. Gather together to enhance one's capability of being a benefactor to humanity, for such is the only purpose of a communal religion, at least, in the Platonic Tradition.

M

MY

CHAPTER TWELVE
THE COSMOS -- OUR GREATER HOME

I. THE COSMOS IS BEAUTIFUL AND GOOD

137a)

As one looks out into space one can say with many of the ancients as well as with Plato that the universe or cosmos is indeed beautiful, deep beyond comprehension, awe inspiring, and, at least to Plato, good. Also it was believed that it would have had to have been a master craftsman to have made it function the way it did, including the beauty of the earth and its various life forms. It was naturally a subject of interest and discussion by the philosophers as well. Plato proposed his Timaeus as a basis for future discussion. It was humbly based on the best science, mathematics and astronomy that was available to him in the Fourth Century BCE. He calls the Timaeus a most likely μυθος (mythos) which can be translated as myth, account or story. He approached the subject with prayer, and declared "All men, Socrates, who have any degree of right feeling, at the beginning of every enterprise, whether small or great, always call upon God"(Timaeus 27c). When he concluded the first round of discussion and temporary conclusion, he wanted to review it for logical faults, but again, before he started, he stated: "Once more, then, at the commencement of my discourse, I call upon God, and beg him to be our savior out of a strange and unwonted inquiry, and to bring us to the haven of probability"(Timaeus 48 d-e). Thus he set a pattern for discussing the cosmic wonder. Use the best astronomer of the day, Timaeus, use mathematics and logic, seek the truth with scientific precision, and humbly with prayer, and even then one must judge his conclusions only as a probable myth. The question must remain aporetic (open ended for the future discussions).

b) He believed the Maker and Father of the cosmos decided to order the great mass of chaotic substance of the universe into an orderly, beautiful and meaningful arraignment of the matter whereby he could bring to life other rational creatures with whom he could share existence. For he was not a jealous God, but one who desired to share being with others who could enjoy existence, even eternal, but also a material existence for the sake of the pleasures that only being incarnate could produce. That was the motive of a loving and gracious God. God had the forms of existence in his mind as a blue print and set to order the cosmos to make it as beautiful as possible (cosmos actually means the orderly making of something beautiful--much like the purpose of "cosmetics"). When God finished, he was delighted at what he had made, but wanted to improve it to the most perfect order possible. He was limited to the natural laws of the matter itself, and because of such αναγκη (necessity or laws of nature), he could only make it as perfect as those laws would permit. God was powerful and good, but not all powerful and all knowing, for he had limitations and even within those limitations he had to remake it to satisfy himself that that was the best he could do. Plato called this wonderful world the world of becoming, for it was not an ultimate and perfect world and in the future the becoming or evolving would follow its own laws inherent in the material itself.

c) If one were to describe a myth or an account of creation today, following Plato's example, he might say something like this: Some time in the distant past, probably billions of human years ago, the universe was initiated by an explosive event that continued during these many years to expand and form clusters of stars called galaxies, and gradually from these stars appeared large forms of matter that solidified and found themselves in orbit around the stars, and eventually those with the capability of retaining water and warmth began to produce types of growth that evolved through time until, in some places, rational beings appeared, and this would be a delight to the God who had hoped it would turn out in such a manner. Some will doubt the necessity of God's influence upon the development of the universe, others like Plato, Einstein, Otto Hahn, and Werner von Braun chose to believe that there was, and is, a God involved. This work, The Platonic Bible, presupposes the existence of God. Further, in keeping with the Platonic Tradition,

God was good and the cosmos was beautiful and good, and all life in the flesh is good and to be enjoyed.

d) Ovid, the Roman poet, with the world vision of Plato, that is, that the earth was the center of all, in his poem, attributed the ordering of the chaotic mass either to God or to Nature. He knew that it existed and that it always did not have such form, but he wasn't sure why the forming of the earth and universe took place. "Nature was all alike, a shapelessness, Chaos, so-called, all rude and lumpy. Nothing but bulk, inert, in whose confusion discordant atoms warred...Till God, or kindlier Nature, settled all argument." Here, Ovid gives an either/or: God or Nature as to the ordering factor of the formation of the universe. Plato, as shown above included both God and αναγκη (ananke) which was "necessity" or "laws of nature". He himself could not exclude either, for to him both would have been necessary. Many of the ancients followed Plato stressing different elements of Plato's Timaeus: some called the God, Apollo, who is often identified with the power of the sun, others refer to νευς or intellect or mind, the Latins using *mens* (the Latin for intellect or mind), and some make express mention of the motive that it was done out and mixed with love: Plato himself having had used *νευς* some twenty times for God.

138a) Seneca himself follows Plato very closely in his views of the beginning of the universe:

"As Plato has it, then, there are five causes: the material, the agent, the form, the model, and the end....The universe as well, according to Plato, has all these elements. The maker is God; matter is the material; the form is the general character and layout of the universe as we see it; the model naturally enough is the pattern which God adopted for the creation of this stupendous work in all its beauty; the end is what God had in view when he created, and that -- in case you are asking what is the end God has in view -- is goodness."12.1

b) In discussing The Good, Plotinus points to the cosmos (κοσμος), and mentions that it is virtually impossible to look at it and not wonder how it came about, and not be led to think of a Maker:

"But as one that looks up to the heavens and sees the splendor of the stars thinks of the Maker and searches, so whoever has contemplated the Intellectual Universe and known it and wondered for it must search after its Maker too. What Being has raised so noble a fabric? And how? Who has begot such a child, this Intellectual-Principle, this lovely abundance so abundantly endowed?"(III.8.11)

c)

Indeed, wonder was the beginning of philosophy. It still is today. But our scientific knowledge has far exceeded that of the past and our faith must be tied to a modern view, yet that will not take away, but rather enhance, the wonder of the cosmos and its beauty and depth, its goodness and incomprehensibility. For the spiritualization of the universe, one can look to what Einstein or Pierre Teilhard de Chardin had to say about it. Einstein saw religion as the motive to increase our knowledge of the universe: "I maintain that cosmic religious feeling is the strongest and noblest incitement to scientific research." (Words taken from his book *The World As I See It.*) Teilhard de Chardin likewise saw a spiritual lesson in the wonder of the universe:

"Blessed be you, universal matter, immeasurable time, boundless ether, triple abyss of stars and atoms and generations: you who by overflowing and dissolving our narrow standards or measurement reveal to us the dimensions of God." (The Hymn to Matter from his *Hymn of the Universe)*

d) For us, the Platonic teaching that is most important is not how the universe came to be, but that it is good and beautiful and we can enjoy human life in the material body as being a gift from God, from his love, and for the purpose of our pleasure and happiness. That can be an eternal statement, but how the cosmos came about and how it will continue to evolve will be an element of our thought processes that also are in a continuous state of change and flux. We are in the world of "becoming" as Plato would say, as he honored the teachings of Heracleitus: all things change.

II. THE COSMOS IS OUR FRIENDLY HOME

139a) Therefore, since God gave us this creation and we come to be materialized in this earth, then within the greater Cosmos, we find ourselves upon this third planet from our star. While we have come through the ages to be humbled, we are no longer the center of the cosmos, yet in our small and humbled state, we still can experience the tremendous experience of being "in the flesh" and participating in human history. Also, while God can not control the laws of nature, one can still find the universe to be friendly and even more so as we learn more about those laws of nature. Richard Maurice Burke who in 1890 CE became President of the American Medico-Psychological Association published in 1901 CE his book *Cosmic Consciousness*, and was a predecessor of thinkers like Teilhard de Chardin. *Cosmic Consciousness* became the first great investigation of the development of man's mental relationship to the Infinite. But even in antiquity, for example in the Neoplatonists one can see the union of man's soul and mind with the splendor and depth of the universe. Plotinus and Boethius pointed to it emphatically. Nietzsche spoke of the *Tiefe, Tiefe Ewigkeit* -- the deep deep eternity. Yet in the smallness of our existence in this deep deep eternity and the deep deep space, we can immensely enjoy life on this earth, *God's Little Acre.*

b) Looking out from earth, Plato saw the harmony of the universe and believed that there was a divine type of music and even referred to the heavenly bodies as the celestial choir. He also saw a type of eternal serenity to the heavenly choir, and felt that if man could learn from the heavenly bodies how to live a musical, harmonic and serene life he would be very happy. He would be imitating the lower gods and in that sense partake of the eternal nature. To him the cosmos was truly our home, our temple, our fatherland. The Stoics took this element of Plato and used it as a major backbone to their entire philosophy. Follow Nature was their call to those seeking a happy life. That the universe creates music is evident to any thinking person: the earth itself with wind, thunder, volcanic eruptions, the movement of the waters and also all the voices and calls of the animals and the birds. The earth is alive with the sound of music and the entire universe is also, whether we hear it or not. Musical harmony from any source is a comfort and a joy It is the cosmos that is imploring us and encouraging us to come and sing unto the Lord.

c) In Cicero's *The Dream of Scipio* he encourages his readers to look up and grasp the power of the eternal in their own lives:

"Look upwards, then! Contemplate this place which is a habitation for all eternity!...And if there is really a path leading right to the entrance of heaven..the knowledge of this great goal before me will inspire me to redouble my endeavors...Since, therefore, it is plain that the self-moving principle is eternal, the same must evidently apply to the human soul... Use this eternal force, therefore, for the most splendid deeds it is in you to achieve."

d)

Get attached to the cosmos, it is your home, both now and forever, and use that attachment to make your present life joyous and whole.

III. THE COSMOS IS ALIVE AND EVOLVING AND MAN IS EVOLVING WITH IT

Mankind has evolved so much and has come so far, yet, his real completeness is still in the future. For he is part of an evolving cosmos that may be expanding to even farther space, the receptacle for both matter and time. Let mankind join in this progress and let his future come with a spiritualized optimism. Even if the individual man ultimately surrenders his material body, humanity as a whole becomes attached in his destiny in the material realm with the cosmos itself, so that the secular and the sacred are unified in holiness and in testimony to man's future and value. Paul Tillich tries to find such compatibility between the two realms in his *Theology of Culture*:

140a)

"If religion is the state of being grasped by an ultimate concern, this state cannot be restricted to a special realm. The unconditional character of this concern implies that it refers to every moment of our life, to every space and every realm. The universe is God's sanctuary. Every work day is a day of the Lord, every supper a Lord's supper, every work the fulfillment of a divine task, every joy a joy in God. In all preliminary concerns, ultimate concern is present, consecrating them. Essentially the religious and the secular are not separated realms. Rather they are within each other."(p.41)

b) Teilhard de Chardin, after addressing man's growth from his most primitive state to where he is now, points man then to his future, where he going. He believed that man is, like the universe, evolving to an unknown, but a higher state of existence. From his more animal past man is continuing his becoming process to higher levels of spirituality and cosmic consciousness. He held the great hope that man, still being a teenager now, will eventually grow into a full spiritual adult and our present centuries will seem childish to the fully grown man: grown both in body and soul, in intellect and in spirit. Man will truly come to know himself and come to a more full possession of his sphere of action, his strength, his unity, and "will at last have become an adult being; and having reached this apogee of his responsibility and freedom, holding in his hands all his future and all his past" he will have the power to be arrogant or remove himself from the center of all things: both as an individual and as an animal species. The great first step was, of course, moving intellectually from an earth centered universe to a solar system, **c)** and now on the rim of one of perhaps millions of galaxies. We have already taken a giant step to the reality of our place in the universe. Yet, spiritually we are connected to it all by a spiritual gravitational pull, and the vastness of the universe only increases the scope of our existence. Let us expand our awareness and become acquainted with the many rooms in our Cosmic Mansion, our Eternal Garden of Eden. Man himself is obligated to participate in this evolutionary process both by the deepening of the spirit with the discoveries of science: the spiritual longing and the power of science and mathematics were central in Platonic thinking and they are central in our needs today so that we can continue our progress in this world of becoming. While there may be an end to the present form of our material world it is still part of the great experience of the history of mankind, an experience God willed us to have before returning to the invisible and spiritual world. Let us then, imitate the Father and Maker of the cosmos and participate in the evolutionary development of the history of mankind. From walking upright to flying to the moon has been an incredible feat of human progress, how much more can be anticipated in the vast extended future of our existence. The cosmos is material man's home, let us adorn it with **d)** the greatest of goodness and beauty for it, although temporary for the individual, will give great joy to that divine and eternal part of our nature. Simply stated by A.N. Whitehead in his Process and Reality is the declaration that "the actual world is a process, and the process is the becoming of actual entities." (p.22)

It is no wonder that the Stoics took this teaching of Plato and make it central to their entire philosophy: follow nature--seek harmony with the cosmos.

IV. MAN'S ECOLOGICAL RESPONSIBILITY

141a) Since man has been placed and developed upon this planet, earth, it is his responsibility in being part of the evolutionary process of the cosmos to take care and nourish the beauties of his own backyard.

A. Nature

For millennia humans have loved and admired the beauty of nature on the one hand, but have also plundered and destroyed it on the other. Much of the problem comes with population growth and that will be in a later section. But for now let us look at the beauty of nature, perhaps not equaled anywhere else in the entire universe. At least we are not assured by our present discoveries of space that another example equal to earth is guaranteed. Plato established his Academy at a grove sacred to Akademos as a delightful setting outside the hustle of the activities of Athens and often in the dialogues people have the discussions while they are walking: in the Republic to the Piraeus--about eight or ten miles one way. Greeks in general had an appreciation for the beauty of nature. Some of the comments made by Walter Burkert are appropriate here

b) "Modern experience of a Greek sanctuary is indissolublely fused with Greek landscape. Something of this even touched the ancients: they speak of the towering heights, the rocky cliffs of Delphi, and the sweet charm of sacred groves with their rustling leaves, singing birds, and murmuring brooks...The shade-giving tree epitomizes both beauty and continuity across the generations. Most sanctuaries have their special tree. In Athens the carefully tended olive tree stands on the Acropolis...In the Hera sanctuary on Samos the willow tree remained always at the same spot and was even incorporated into the great altar...On Delos the palm tree...In Didyma there stood the laurel tree of Apollo...In Olympia it was a wild olive tree...the oak of Dodona...water for drinking and water for the animals was still more important."12.2

Lactantius, a pompous, judgmental, ignorant of the Greek language and of the Greek culture, a narrow Roman Christian, made this foolish and unappreciative of nature statement:

"The Stoics, failing to discern the truth, reply most clumsily that among plants and animals there are many whose usefulness has up to now gone unnoticed; but that this will be discovered in the course of time, just as numerous things unknown in earlier centuries have been discovered by necessity and use" 12.3

c)

This statement says much about both many Romans and Early Christians about their lack of knowledge and interest in nature. The Stoics, of course, were right and we continue to this day making wonderful discoveries of the value of the plants and animals that have evolved and grown upon the earth. The Romans and Christians did not have the same appreciation of the scientific discovery within ecological realm and the love of nature as did the Greeks. Aristotle had Alexander the Great in his conquests and travels send back animals and plants unknown to the Greeks in Greece, that he might study and classify them. The Romans on the contrary wiped out the large animal population of Northern Africa by bringing them to Rome only to slaughter them in the arenas as they slaughtered the gladiators, captured in their expansive wars.

d) One Roman, Marcus Aurelius, emperor by profession but Stoic by philosophy was thankful to mother earth and gave this ode of praise to her.

"I travel the roads of nature until the hour when I shall lie down and be at rest; yielding back my last breath into the air from which I have drawn it daily, and sinking down upon the earth from which my father derived the seed, my mother the blood, and my nurse the milk of my being -- the earth which for so many years has furnished my daily meat and drink, and, though so grievously abused, still suffers me to tread its surface." 12.4

142a) Plutarch in rejecting artificially made smells and colors points his readers to the natural beauties of nature's flowers, which give both pleasure to the sense of smell and the sense of sight: "these natural smells and colors are pure and simple as fruits themselves, and without expense or the curiosity of art...nature gives according to the seasons smells and colors that blossom with delight...even if they bore no fruit, they would be a delight for us by means of their smells and varieties of colors." 12.5

Proclus in his commentary on Plato's *Timaeus* praises mother earth this way:

"Such then being the nature of Earth herself, she is said to be our nurse; in the first place indeed, as possessing a power in a certain respect equivalent to Heaven. For as that comprehends in itself divine animals, thus also Earth is seen to contain terrestrial animals. But in the second place, she is our nurse, as inspiring our lives from her own proper life. For she not only produces fruits, and nourishes our bodies through these, but she also fills our souls with the illuminations of herself. For being a divine animal, and generating us who are partial animals, through her own body indeed, she nourishes and connectedly contains our bulk. But from her own soul perfects ours. By her own intellect likewise, she exits the intellect which is in us."12.6

b)

He later refers to Plato's words in the *Timaeus* myth, indicating that God wanted a nice balance of species to share the earth:

"Three genera of mortals yet remain to be produced. Without the generation of these therefore, the universe will be imperfect; for it will not contain in itself all the genera of animals. But it ought to contain them, that it may be sufficiently whole."

Plato was saying that all the animals fulfill a purpose in balancing out the beauty and variety of life that God wanted upon the earth. Therefore, for us today, each lost species is a tragedy for it brought balance to the earth and now it can never again be reclaimed. The human animal has not had much love for its own kind, and has even less for the other of nature's creatures. It is not only a finite transgression, it is an infinite one and a spiritual one.

c) The mystic Henry Suso, as many mystics, had an attachment to the sacredness of all nature and thought much of it. He stated:

"I contemplate the angels of heaven, the beasts of the forest, the dwellers in the waters, the plants of the earth, the sand of the sea, the tiny motes which float in each ray of sunshine, the snowflakes, the drops of rain, the diamonds of dew. I consider that, even in the farthest ends of creation, every creature obeys God and contributes, in so far as it is able, to the mysterious harmony which ascends without pause to praise and bless the Creator. I picture myself in the midst of this chorus."12.7

Again we see here a spiritual soul awakened by the beauty of nature, all living creatures teach us how to rend a hymn to God, and all we need to do is join the chorus.

John Moschus (d. ca. 620CE), wrote a book by the name of *The Spiritual Meadow* in which the delight of the flowers of the earth lifted his soul up to heaven. A part of it reads:

d)

"The aspect of the meadows in springtime, dearest Sophronius, is very beautiful, owing to the great variety of their flowers. The eye is attracted, the passer-by is charmed, by the ever-varied color. The sight and perfume alike are most pleasing. On one side the meadows are resplendent with the color of the rose, and on the other the eye is attracted by the whiteness of the lily, standing out in contrast with the rosier hues. Elsewhere is seen the deeper red, calling to mind the royal purple."12.8

The name Sophronius is probably fictitious and is Greek derived, meaning one of prudence and self-control. One of Plato's four cardinal virtues was Sophrosyne--temperance, and Socrates' father's name was Sophroniscus, one of temperance and self-control. The description of the meadow makes the city dwellers of the Twenty First Century envious that those a thousand years ago could have such surroundings in their natural habitats. It is up to man that such must be retained even if only in miniature. Even two hundred years ago Goethe began the Second Part of his *Faust* with a lovely section called "A Pleasant Landscape" which describes the beauty and loveliness of both the night and the new day which follows. He speaks of the twilight which gently closes the day by bringing with it the sweet fragrance that softly whispers peace...and rocks the heartfelt concerns to a childlike rest, closing softly the eyelids, gates of the daylight. The stars begin to appear, some brightly, others dimly, and with them and their gleam from afar appear their reflections that glitter upon the lakes. While man is enjoying his deepest rest, the moon **143a)** lights up the heavens and manifests its full majesty. Daybreak approaches and man, who is refreshed anew, sees the beauty of the sunrise, and this new fresh adorning of nature 'wraps me round with gladness thrilling'..All earth comes alive and even the deepest gorges are given the light from heaven to awaken the flowers of the earth: 'all around me is a Paradise appearing'. He feels a hope that is supreme and transcending so that he experiences a great flame with wonder burning within, calling out to it 'embrace me', viewing it all with rapture growing in amazement. He views with joy the many-colored rainbow as it slowly changes and mirrors human goals and activities: 'Think, and more clearly will you grasp it, seeing life is but light in many-hued reflection'. What loveliness of thought Goethe has given us! Let us be absorbed therein!

b) A letter written by Teilhard de Chardin on April 27, 1923 exudes in his appreciation of the "charm of Ceylon". He wrote:

"The real charm of Ceylon lies in its vegetation: the heavy opulence of the foliage, the luxuriance of the flowers. On landing, you first notice the acacias. lebeks, with their large mimosa-like blossoms, the 'flamboyant' smothered scarlet blossoms as big as nasturtiums, and other trees with cluster of golden yellow splashed with purple which, with the coconut palms, provide most of the shade. I went to admire this splendid flora in Victoria Park--the public gardens. Gorgeous butterflies hovered over the blooms, and small gray striped squirrels ran about in the branches; and instead of gardeners, it was a surprise to see little copper-skinned Hindu girls, draped in pink, walking between the clumps of flowers, or little ragamuffins begging for a few pennies in exchange for fallen blossoms, their gestures astonishingly graceful, and so quaint with their velvet eyes."12.9

c)

B.. The Earth's Animals

As mentioned above the Platonic Tradition from the time of Plato onwards has always taught that all the animals of the earth play a role in God's plan and design. One must then ask, "Why does God let some animals become extinct?" The answer can also be found above: basically two reasons. The first is that this is a material world with its own laws of nature in which God does not interfere, and the second is that He leaves it to the reason and wisdom of men to be a type of divinity on earth. In other words, the laws of nature (ananke) are established and man must work within those laws in the upkeep of the creation the way that God himself in the ordering of the universe had to work within them. Remember, one of the ideas and motives of God in the beginning was to make another creature that had rational powers so that He would not be alone in the universe in that respect. He was gracious and good and gave **d)** to us intellect (nous), reason (logos), and the "gift of numbers". We are to use them in governing the same way and with the same spirit with which God made and governs us. With the spirit that we do not want to be alone without the companionship of all the wonderful other animals of the earth. They are our brother and sister creatures. They are not "distant and irrelevant" relatives. We, and our happiness and their's, are linked together. Together we are to share this good earth.

144a) Dolphins in antiquity were loved and honored as a friendly and helpful mate to mankind and their many attempts at saving drowning humans were so well known that it was almost proverbial to speak of them as man's friend at sea. Plato put into Socrates' mouth these words while speaking to Glaucon: "Then we, also, must swim and try to escape out of the sea of argument in the hope that either some dolphin will take us on its back or some other desperate rescue" (Republic V 453d). In the mythology of many ancients the progenitor of a hero race himself is often cared for and fed by animals. This is not so absurd as some might think, for today we find one species of animal nursing an infant of another animal, and most people in America witnessed via television an ape who cuddled a human child that fell several feet to a hard surface and lay unconscious in the bottom of the area set aside for apes in the zoo. The ape was absolutely tender with the child and turned him over to the zoo keeper.

b) Pliny the Elder, in praise of the loyalty of dogs mentions several occasions, some during his own life time, when dogs risked their own lives in defense of their master or died trying to save them from a hopeless situation. He reported:

"A dog to which Darius gives the name of Hyrcanus, upon the funeral pile of King Lysimachus being lighted, threw itself into the flames, and the dog of King Hiero did the same. Philistus also gives a similar account of Pyrrhus, the dog of the tyrant Gelon...Amone ourselves Volcatius...as he was riding on his Asturian jennet towards evening from his country-house was attacked by a robber and was only saved by his dog... (about another dog who was howling next his dead master) when some one threw a piece of bread to it the animal carried it to the mouth of its master...the dog swam into the river (his dead master had been dumped into it) and endeavored to raise it our of the water.12.10

"There is a very famous story about an eagle at the city of Sestos. Having been reared by a little girl, it used to testify its gratitude for her kindness, first by bringing her birds, and in due time various kinds of prey: (she died as a child and her body was in the process of bring burned)...and the bird threw itself on the lighted pile and was consumed by the fire (in an obvious attempt at rescue despite the flames)."12.11

Pliny the Younger in his letter to Caninius Rufus told the story of a dolphin that came to shore and entertained the children there, and eventually letting them swim with him and even touched and stroked it. One boy in particular formed a friendship with the dolphin and even mounted it, and one day the dolphin took him out further into the sea and then returned him to shore in the company of another dolphin:

c)
"...the boy, in particular, who first made the experiment, swam by the side of him, and leaping upon his back, was carried to and fro in that manner: he fancies the dolphin knows and is fond of him, and he returns its fondness...All the magistrates round the country flocked hither to view this sight, the entertainment of whom upon their arrival...was an additional expense [When Roman officials came to a town, the town had to feed and shelter them at the town's expense]...which this little community could ill afford. It was thought proper therefore to remove the occasion of this concourse by privately killing the poor dolphin. And now, how will your genius adorn and heighten this moving story! Though, indeed, it does not require any fictitious embellishments."12.12

d) Immanuel Kant (1724-1804 CE) in his *Vorlesungen ueber Moralphilosophie: Ethica* (in the section titled *Von den Plichten gegen*

Thiere und Geister) takes an indirect approach in his judgment of man's neglect of duty to animals, for he feels that animals are to be respected indirectly because of the human traits which they exemplify. But even this indirect duty of man is a powerful teaching of human morals towards animals, and it is much more as one can see from his words.

145a)

"Because the animals are relatives (relative to man -- '*analogon*') of mankind, we observe our duties towards mankind, when we also observe our duties to these same relatives, and by means of such duties to these same animals we carry out our duties to mankind. For example, when a dog has long and faithfully served his master, in that very manner it is an analogy of having his rights to wages; and on account of that very service I must reward the dog, even if he no longer can serve, and maintain him until the end; therewith I have then observed my duty to humankind...Likewise if someone shoots dead his dog, because he cannot serve him anymore, he acts not at all against his duty towards the dog, because the dog cannot play judge, he only harms, through such action, the affability (*Leutseeligkeit*) and humanness in himself, which he in regard to his duty to humanity should exercise. Therewith man should not destroy, rather he ought to practice goodness towards the animals. For a man who readily practices such cruelty towards animals, is also in the same way hardened against mankind. Man can already know the human heart of another as he consider his actions towards animals (trans.JDE)2.6 BL

b)

Kant then goes on to refer to a copper engraving of Hogarth that pictures the stages in which a child, from abusing a dog or a cat escalates, with the years, his types of cruelties until he ends up murdering someone. He continues by pointing out the tenderness of animals towards their young, yes, even the wolf. Man would do well, said Kant, to acknowledge that if we have genuine feelings of kindness for the animals, we also will have similar feeling towards other humans. Kant, then, develops here two themes: how we treat animals is the way we treat human beings, although it is indirectly; and how we treat animals is how we develop our own virtue and dignity as human beings. One then easily concludes that man harms himself spiritually and psychologically when he harms an animal, and this harm deposits nourishment to his evil nature and thereby excludes him from moral goodness and with that eliminates any chance for personal happiness. We are all familiar with John Donne's statement that no man is an island. Kant is telling us that no animal (man is one species of animal) is an island. When an animal dies, the bell tolls for mankind also.

c) Iamblichus said of Pythagoras:

"Wishing therefore to insert this familiarity from afar in men, he also ordained that his disciples should extend it to animals of the same genus, and commanded them to consider these as their familiars and friends; so as neither to injure, nor slay, nor eat any one of them. He therefore who associates men with animals, because they consist of the elements as we do, and participate with us of a more common life, will in a much greater degree establish fellowship with those who partake of a soul of the same species, and also of a rational soul. From this also it is evident that he introduced justice produced from the most proper principle".12.14

d)

Pythagoras also believed that some animals, blessed with reason, and therefore free choice for virtue, could also experience happiness, for virtue is the basis of happiness. Plato also had no desires to participate in the animals sacrifices, for such were cruel to the animals, and also he considered them a bribe so that God would tolerate their immoral lives. Animals are our kinfolk. But few humans have tried hard to make it so: the legends of Orpheus gathering animals together by the attraction of his music, of Francis of Assisi and the Spanish Carmelites preaching and blessing the animals, the many stories of dolphins, dogs, eagles and many other friends and pets risking their lives for their human companions are all such evidence that man can, if he wants to, make friendships with the animals. Michel de Montaigne pointed to a type of universal acknowledgment of the inclination of men and animals to feel like near relatives. He stated:

146a)

"We owe justice to men, and graciousness and benignity to other creatures that are capable of it; there is a certain commerce and mutual obligation betwixt them and us. Nor shall I be afraid to confess the tenderness of my nature so childish, that I cannot well refuse to play with my dog, when he the most unseasonably importunes me so to do. The Turks have alms and hospitals for beasts. The Romans had public care to then nourishment of geese, by whose vigilance their Capitol had been preserved. The Athenians made a decree that the mules and moyls which had served at the building of the temple called Hecatompedon should be free and suffered to pasture at their own choice, without hindrance. The Agrigentines had a common use solemnly to inter the beasts they had a kindness for, as horse of some rare quality, dogs, and useful birds, and even those that had only been kept to divert their children; and the magnificence that was ordinary with them in all other things, also particularly appeared in the sumptuosity and numbers of monuments erected to this end, and which remained in the beauty several ages after. The Egyptians buried wolves, bears, crocodiles, dogs, and cats in sacred places, embalmed their bodies, and put on mourning at their death. Cimon gave an honorable sepulture to the mares with which he had three times gained the prize of the course at the Olympic Games."12.15

b)

Jeremy Taylor, a Cambridge Platonist, said:

"God is in every creature. Be cruel towards none, neither abuse any by intemperance. Remember that the creatures and every member of your own body are 'receptacles of God,' because God has blessed them with His presence, hallowed them by His touch and separated them from unholy use by making them to belong to His dwelling."12.16

In the world today there are many ways in which humans have been self-centered, destructive, and cruel to the animal world. And, how noticefully absent are the leaders of any nation about this human slaughter and torture of animals. Politicians simply do not care, at least in any significant size that would actually change things. Money and re-election, ego, and power to manipulate the economy for their own benefit **c)** are the elements that go into making a modern politician. The few who know what is right simply do not have the courage to pursue what it would take to change the relationship between humans and animals in any significant degree. Stop the pollution of the land and the oceans, ha! that would slow down the economy and attach our profits. Many of these famous families who stored up money to run for office have ancestors that killed animals as trophies or to have their head stuffed in a cottage some where. They were adventurers! No! They were murderers for play. They did not go gaming for necessary food; they went to slaughter an animal to prove that they had testicles. How embarrassing that a man could sink so low and yet to think he would gain history's praise and recognition for such a thing. England's ridiculous fox hunt by "honorable" upper and middle class "gents" using dogs to frighten and then kill a fox. How many animals suffered because of perfume experiments? Why can a human being rape and kill several people but in no way suffer an ounce of physical punishment while innocent dogs and **d)** other animals suffer unto death because of the competition of the toiletries? Animals do suffer pain. See their eyes torn with pain. See them limp, stagger, and then die because of human cruelty. And where is the Judeo-Christian religion in all this? Animals use the mental capacities they have to struggle to survive but one by one, daily see their species come to an end. Animals too have a sense of tender touch, a care for their young for whom they will die, a sense of play, and a sense of reason in grooming each other and in building little homes for their young ones. Let's face it, a dog is more faithful than many a so-called human friends who will tear apart a relationship because of a political disagreement, a competitive quest for man or woman, a poker game, which football team they root for, or a social status change. No dog has rejected a person because he is tall or short, skinny or fat, or because of his wealth or color of his skin. They just do not want to be abused and beaten. If men could only learn from the animals. The real beast, as it has played out in terms of human harmony and man's relationship to animals is man himself. Can we not share the earth with our animal friends and relatives. Too long religion in the West has made an unnecessary huge distinction and division between humans and animals. Arrogance! Probably the real reason Darwin is still so hated and rejected by Judeo-Christianity is that he reminded us that we are animals too. Goodbye to the dusky seaside sparrow, we will miss you, your chirping and quick jumps into flight. Good bye to the wild wolves who have been killed simply to save game for the hunters, who did not need the food, but wanted to play "kill the innocent animal". One can tell much about a person by the way he or she relates to animals and one can tell much about a religion by the way it also treats the animal world.

147a)

C. Man's Overpopulation as The Major Cause of Human and Animal Suffering and the Ecological Destruction of Nature.

Plato believed in population control of the city and its surroundings and stipulated that a city ought not to have more than about 25,000 people. As a result, he recommended limited child birth and only the best ages for such child births, even if it necessitated abortion.

1. Overpopulation

In the last century because of great jumps in science and abundant food supply, the world population exploded from about 1.2 billion people in 1900 to 6 billion in 2000 . From about 1800 to 1900 the population grew only from 1 billion to 1.2 billion, an increase of 20%, but from 1900 to 2000 grew 500%. To give two examples: in Mexico in 1930 the population was 16.6 million people and by 1991 it was 91.1 million, and it was estimated at 100 million at the year 2000. In only 70 years the population grew almost 600%. In China in 1953 there were 588 million people and in 2000 there were 1270 million people (1.27 billion); and this was despite at least two decades of a one child per couple policy that the government tried to enforce. In other words China alone had more people in 2000 than the entire world in 1900.

b)

1800 1900 1927 1960 1987 2000

O X X X X X X X X X O X X X X X X X X X O

1 billion 2 billion 3 billion 5 bil 6billion

The European countries and Japan have made a successful lowering of the rate of reproduction. The ten lowest are: (children per woman--1999)

Spain 1.15 Romania 1.17 Czech Rep. 1.19 Italy 1.2 Bulgaria 1.23
Latvia 1.25 Slovenia 1.26 Greece 1.28 Estonia 1.29 Germany 1.30

But on the bottom are these rates for children born per woman:

Yemen 7.6 Somalia 7.25 Uganda 7.10 Afghanistan 6.9 Nigeria 6.84
Angola 6.8 Malawi 6.75 Mali 6.50 Burkina Faso 6.57 Ethiopia 6.30

These countries are more than tripling their population every generation (40 years).

2. What Problems Are Caused By Overpopulation?

c) The cities of the world, once a nice place to live, are now overcome with noise, polluted air, impossible traffic, areas of no space to separate from each other, massive areas of poverty and crime, impoverishment of all elements of life, high potential of spread of viruses and other contagious diseases, cost of living, tension at the work place and at home, business competition that escalates to constant tension, lack of parks and places to get necessary yet natural exercise and host of other uncomfortable and irritating conditions.

The improvement of the entire globe, especially in those countries with high birth rates and the impossibility of satisfying six billion people with enough food, enough water and enough space to live a happy and secure life. Territorial conflicts and wars over the shortage of the earth's resources for so many people: oil, water, minerals, wood, coal and many other, for some people, absolutely necessary things for their livelihood. The forests are being stripped, the Amazon valley being raided by people, natural beauties destroyed, and global warming.

d) Added to these two is the pollution man has created: nuclear waste, no rivers from which to drink, clean air is a rarity, and the oceans are full of poisons and pollutants. Beaches are dirty, oil spills destroy the ecology, and man lives in the asphalt jungle. The food shortage only increases each year with the 80 million more people born each year than the number that dies. Life expectancy increases in the countries that face the problem the best, but massive numbers of children die in those countries that continue to produce more than 2.5 children per woman. As of 1990 the USA ranked 17th in the world in life expectancy with Japan, Switzerland, Iceland, Sweden, and Spain the top five in that order. 40,000 to 50,000 people die every day because of not enough food, and death by starvation is one of the most brutal ways to die. People suffer more from natural disasters because they are forced to live in the worst areas, for the best ones have all been taken. Humans live in flood prone areas, wildfire areas, the desert, and earthquake prone areas, and then they can not purchase insurance for their homes or, if they can, its price is costly. They can not leisurely drive on the freeways, or go to work in 15 minutes.

148a) Fourthly, mankind is slowing killing mother earth and all her creatures. Man has not shared the earth with the creatures of the air, the sea, or the land. Asian debris takes six months to cross the Pacific Ocean and reach the United States, all the while killing off much of the sea life and sea birds that try to digest it, thinking it to be food. Killing off the marine life also kills off the birds that depend on them for food. 200,000 albatross die of starvation each year and tens of thousands die because they suffocate trying to digest plastic.

3. Religious Hindrance to Rational Living and Happiness

b) As mentioned earlier, one can tell what people are like by the way they treat their animal kinfolk on earth and how they treat mother earth itself. One also can judge a religion by whether or not it is willing to sacrifice to care for other people, other living things, and the entire ecological system. Those who seek to grow by a high birth rate are a total discredit to science, logic, ethics, and the God whom they claim to honor and worship. All religions must get out of the competitive numbers game and ought to try love and kindness, some personal self-sacrifices, and a logical and ethical economic and ecological way of life. Let sexual pleasure live, but separate it from the doctrines of necessitated procreation. It seems to becoming evident that the worst religions of the earth are the ones with the most people. None are without great guilt: Christianity, Islam, Hinduism, and Confucianism. The smaller religions are also part of the problem. Europe and Japan have grown up and faced and actually decreased in population in the last ten years--if one does not count the many immigrants from the irresponsible countries coming into their land. But in the Western Hemisphere growth is rampant and mostly **c)** Christian. The Islamic countries likewise rejoice in internal growth: Osimah Bin Laden is one of 50 children. Conservative Protestants in America and Roman Catholics have no tolerance for intellect, reason, and the future of the world. Every clergyman rejoices when his congregation grows and the budget soars upward--hardly a spiritual achievement.

4. Political Cowardice

d) An honest man in politics with courage? No way! If one mentions serious measures for controlling the population of one's country, he is laughed at. Personal rights to have 25 children; personal rights to use fertility drugs, personal rights for dead beat dad's with ten children spread across the nation will stop a legally imposed vasectomy every time. Industrialists like to grow and make big profits and they sponsor people running for office and then lobby them after they get in office. These are the bribes that Plato talked about, and also why Plato taught that the decision makers of the city or state can never own property or have any type of personal wealth during their lives. He knew that men of decision making power will always be subject to the temptation of bribery. The best of people--by intellect and virtue, including courage, are to be set aside, both of men and women, and they, for the rest of their lives can never "own" anything; even the children they produce will be raised by the city or state and placed into the proper category according to their natural talents after they have grown. They will have the satisfaction of having lived for and serviced their city or state with the talents they received from above. They would be men and women for others, but also, they above everyone else, because of their virtue, would feel the greatest happiness and be spiritually united to their people, their state, and their God. Only when politicians become philosophers who have loved wisdom and goodness, will states become good and righteous and work honorably for their people, their land, and their earth. If they are married to money and glory, they are not fit nor capable of being a philosophical politician.

149a)

5. Are There Any Solutions That Can Work?

First of all is to, in some inconceivable way, install knowledge and wisdom into the heads of politicians, and to pray and beseech them to have courage enough to face the facts. Also the politicians will need the wisdom to implement strong, even harsh, measures and laws that will stop population growth.

The major measures would be to convince the citizens that they must acknowledge the problem and the benefit it would be for their own children and for the future of the United States. Then to set a law that no woman be permitted to have more than two children, and after having the second to automatically be sterilized at the time of the birth of the second child. Men who have participated in the insemination of two children must be sterilized by means of a vasectomy. If he avoids it, and inseminates another woman, the woman shall have an abortion and the man will be given a forced vasectomy and a prison term of 5 years for having caused a woman to have an abortion. If the man avoids detection and the woman will not tell who it is, then she shall be imprisoned until she does, and when found the man will be given ten years. Draconian laws for the most desperate times that humanity has ever faced. For individuals who do not give a damn for the rest of society or the future of the human race, such punishment and laws are appropriate. If they do not like the laws, let them immigrate to a country that doesn't care about its future. This brings the subject to the topic of immigration.

b) Each country must solve its own problems first and in order to do it, it must close completely its borders to all immigrants, both legal and illegal. The politicians want votes and their supporters in big business want more consumption, more people, and more immigrants for cheap labor. They are likewise arrogant money hungry people who do not care about human welfare, standard of living, and a personal sacrifice of the immoral passion of greed. Those caught hiring non-citizens should be fined $100,000 for each immigrant for each year that he has worked and those in the corporation who are responsible for keeping the laws, in addition to the fines, are to spend one year in prison for each year they have disobeyed the laws of their country. Ten years of using ten immigrants would cost the company 10 million dollars and put its executives in prison for ten years. The punishments of the new law would not be retroactive, but the non-citizens would have to leave when the law is past. Just pass the law and it will work!

c) Volunteers to be responsible are not enough. Religious leaders who have no concept of doing unto mother earth and animals as they would want done unto them are to be held accountable, possibly even for treason if they do not conform. The world no longer needs the "leadership" of such "holy men". They are as self-centered and irresponsible as the industrialists and capitalists who insist on growth and profit.

There have been good men who have tried desperately to blow the horn of desperation to the masses and to the politicians. And while many individuals have learned and been converted to care about the earth, other people and all the animals, it simply has not been enough. In 1960 Julian Huxley published a book by the name of *Knowledge, Morality, and Destiny*, in which a chapter was titled Population and Human Fulfilment. He starts the chapter with these words:

"Population is the problem of our age. The increase of population, and its relation to resources and to fulness of life, inevitably obtrudes itself on anyone who, like myself happens to travel round the world in the middle of the twentieth century. The traveler is struck by sheer numbers...---the fact that the increase of human numbers has initiated a new and critical phase in the history of our species."

Paul R. Ehrlich of Stanford University has, since 1968 published books, spoken on late night television, written many articles, but there are still, even politicians and religious leaders who have never heard of him, despite his *Population Bomb* in 1968, with many reprintings and his revised edition of 1971 that had likewise many reprintings, 10 already by 1974. Even the Sierra Club has not been coordinated and expressive enough in opposing immigration and overpopulation as was pointed out by UCLA professor Ben Zuckerman in an article in the Los Angeles Times Magazine, June 9, 2002. Do they really think that nature can be preserved in great beauty and animal life restored to where it was a century ago if the population growth is not stopped? Even Zero Population Growth (ZPG) is not enough. America and the world must reduce its population to where it was in the past if it seeks to live in the country like it was in the past.

d) There are many racist activists that want more "of their own kind of people" to be born and see any type of stoppage of immigration as an assault upon "their people", and do not care about what kind of assault "their people" are bringing to the ecological nature of America. Like the religious leaders and the industrialists who also do not care about the health of mother earth, they are concerned only about themselves, their growth, their wealth, and their power and influence upon the decision making of the politicians, who crave reelection more than they care about making life in America better for all. All of them should be forced to go down to where the rivers and canals dump their industrialized polluted waters into the ocean, and be forced to drink the water for a month. If any survived, he might get the message, but even then his reelection interest would probably control his future decisions. I, personally am not a hypocrite in these matters: I have no children, despite a marriage that lasted 13 years, one vasectomy, a small sedan that gets over 30 miles a gallon and buy only those things essential to basic living. Yet I am a happy person and feel that my life has not been limited in any way that would lessen my personal happiness. I have given up the American Idols, and live in an average size apartment, and feel a sense of personal worth and liberation from all the vendors on TV, religious leaders who want their churches to grow, and the disgusting "status symbols" that the insecure and inferior complexed people depend on to give them a sense of personal worth. I try to live in the way of the Platonic Tradition and consider this life a wonderful experience, especially in being detachment from the lure of the material toys and large clans of relatives that appeal to others. The things that people will need to give up and release from their minds are not the things that can offer happiness in the first place, and to know that they are participating in the saving of many species, the restoring of land for the wild animals, and the healthy air of the wilderness that offers all the wonder of nature in its real beauty, is so emotionally and ethically fulfilling that he can feel the depth of his worth and commitment to the dignity of man. He has found his nobility. To each, one can say, your are totally free when you chose of your own accord to do that which is right and moral in the first place, without having to be forced to by law. Freedom is total, when it is used to enhance the human experience on earth and to honor the other animal kin with which we share the planet. Then man can rise up with joy and recognize the divinity within himself.

N

NY

CHAPTER THIRTEEN
PLATO'S CARDINAL VIRTUES

I. WISDOM

150a) A. Plato established four cardinal virtues which he called heavenly (divine or godlike) virtues: wisdom (φρονησις - phronesis or σοφια - sophia), courage (ανδρεια - andrea) , temperance (σωφρωσυην - sophrosyne) and justice (δικαιοσυνη - dikaiosune). He also designated four secondary virtues which he called human virtues because they were involved with man's earthly life only: health, beauty, strength, and wealth in that order. All of the secondary virtues were subordinate to the four heavenly virtues, also in corresponding order. For example, health is superior than all the other earthly virtues, but it in turn is subordinate to the heavenly virtues which have eternal significance as well as being the ideal foundations for all knowledge, happiness and goodness. Wisdom is the greatest virtue and wealth the least of all virtues.

b) Wisdom was defined as the most appropriate way to utilize knowledge, in every occasion, every pursuit, every quest, in every decision, and in every action. Everything else was subjected to it. Wisdom involved the intellect, logic, reason, mathematics and any other way in which one first attained knowledge and then the way in which knowledge was used for the good and the happiness of the individual or the state. It was supreme and the man who sought out of love this wisdom was a φιλος σοφια a philosopher. It is for this reason that within the Platonic Tradition that philosophy is always the highest virtue and the one that can bring the most goodness and happiness to man.

c) Wisdom is the product of man's intellect or mind (νους - nous) and reason (λογος - logos) and therefore they are the features in man's being that gives him the power of being the greatest of the animals, because he has a greater portion of reasoning powers than the other animals, and since the intellect is located in the head, the head is the "castle" of the body. Nous was a word that Plato even used many times for God himself. He was the Intellect of the universe. Therefore, reason (logos) and intellect (nous) are the divinity within man. In each man this divine element is incarnate, and by it he has the power to lift up his virtuous nature to reflect God's goodness, i.e. to be like God as much as it is possible. Plutarch in his essay *On Listening* wrote:

"You, on the other hand, have often been told that following God and listening to reason are identical; so bear in mind that for intelligent people the passage from childhood to adulthood is not an abandonment of rules, but a change of ruler: instead of someone whose services are hired and bought, they accept in their lives the divine leadership of reason - and it is only those who follow reason who deserve to be regarded as free. For they alone live as they want, since they have learned to want only what is necessary."13.1

d)

Philo of Alexandria in his *On The Creation* stated concerning man's head in the creation of it:

"...for a sacred dwelling-place or shrine was being fashioned for the reasonable soul, which man was to carry as a holy image, or all images the most Godlike...God made man then in his own likeness and imitation, that is reason-like, for he had a rational or logical soul (Ψυχης λογικης). For God had installed the kingly or royal reason (βασιλεα λογισμον) in the soul, the royal part of man."(139).

Polus in his treatise *On Justice* stated:

"Man was generated by far the wisest of animals. For he is able to contemplate the things which exist, and to obtain from all things, science and wisdom. To which also it may be added, that divinity has engraved and exhibited in him the system of universal reason, in which all the forms of things in existence are distributed, and the significations of nouns and verbs."

151a)

Ficino reminds his readers that "Of all the powers of the soul that are concerned with knowing, the highest are intellect and reason."13.2 He also reminds his readers to think. "The best principle for living is to think, and to do your utmost to live in harmony with the intellect, for this is to live forever and to live happily. For it is in the mind that stability and peace are found."13.3

Giovanni Pico Della Mirandola in his *Oration on the Dignity of Man* alludes to reason as the factor that lifts man from an earthly creature to a heavenly one. "If, however, you see a philosopher, judging and distinguishing all things according to the rule of reason, him shall you hold in veneration, for he is a creature of heaven and not of earth."

Thomas Browne in his *Religio Medici* also praised reason:

b)

"Search while thou wilt, and let thy Reason go,
To ransome Truth, even to th' Abyss below;
Rally the scattered Causes; and that line,
Which Nature twists, be able to untwine.
It is thy Makers will, for unto none
But unto Reason can He e'er be known.13.4

Nathaniel Culverwell, a Cambridge Platonist, had this Platonic advice to give:

"The light of reason is 'a calm and friendly light', it is a candle, not a comet--a quiet and peaceable light. And though this 'candle of the Lord' may be too hot for some, yet the lamp is maintained only with soft and peaceable oil. There is no jarring in pure intellectuals; if men were tuned and regulated by reason more, there would be more concord and harmony in the world. As man himself is a sociable creature, so his reason also is a sociable light. This candle would shine more clearly and equally, if the winds of passion were not injurious to it."13.5

c) William James in his lecture *The Dilemma of Determinism* urged his Harvard students to carefully use their reason in the choices they make in life, for each choice establishes an entirely new set of circumstances by which one approaches all the other decisions that will be made in the future. Each step in free choice, determines, to a degree the options for future choices. James is correct, of course. Perhaps one can think of life as a game of chess: each move changes all the circumstances for the following moves. Therefore, to win one must be rational in each move, trying one's best to foresee what each particular move means for the future. Man by his free choice makes his own determined future situations.

Thomas Jefferson points man, not to any "authorized book", but to reason in examining one's life and making decisions: "Read the Bible, then, as you would read Livy or Tacitus. Your own reason is the only oracle given you by heaven, and you are answerable, not for the rightness, but uprightness of the decision."13.6

d) G. E. Moore in his *Principia Ethica* encouraged us to rationally weigh our decisions and the circumstances we find ourselves.

"With regard to actions of which the general utility is thus proved, the individual should always perform them; but in other cases, where rules are commonly offered, he should rather judge of the probable results in his particular case, guided by a correct conception of what things are intrinsically good or bad."13.7

Paul Tillich in his book *The Courage To Be* argues that man, at least in his best character, is his reason, and he needs the courage to be reasonable against the strong emotions that battle against his reason (this, of course, sounds like Plato's Phaedrus and other writings). Tillich said:

152a)

"Reason...is the Logos, the meaningful structure of reality, as a whole and of the human mind in particular. 'If there is,' says Seneca, 'no other attribute which belongs to man as man except reason, then reason will be his one good, worth all the rest put together.' This means that reason is man's true or essential nature, in comparison with which everything else is accidental. The courage to be is the courage to affirm one's own reasonable nature over against what is accidental in us. It is obvious that reason in this sense points to the person in his center and includes all mental functions. Reasoning as a limited cognitive function, detached from the personal center, never could create courage."

It is interesting that Tillich would link courage, one of Plato's four cardinal virtues, with and under the ability of man to think authentically from the center of his existence. This is in total harmony with Plato who puts wisdom as the primary and controlling virtue of the four cardinal virtues. The "courage to be" must be based on wisdom reached by means of reason.

b)

B. KNOWLEDGE AND NUMBERS

By means of reason, man alone can reach such heights of abstract knowledge, as in all abstract concepts like love and justice. Likewise, he receives the "gift of numbers" sometimes used similarly with the gift of reason by Plato. For no animal, other than man, learned to divide fractions. Therefore, these two fruits of reason, knowledge and mathematics are two of the foundation stones upon which Plato builds his entire educational system and upon which all future science is based. Man's intellect when working rationally brings him to a higher level of existence than any other creature and gives him theories of reality by which he can understand the cosmos, the nature of earth and material laws. This empowers him to participate in the evolving material universe at least on his own little planet, but even this is an absolute and joyous wonder. Memory on which the possibility of retained knowledge rests is in itself a wonder, and many have marveled at it's abilities to recall so much of what went before. Man, in many ways, becomes his memory, for without it his identity and powers of thought would be lost. We are told today to keep using our rational facilities for that keeps the physical brain in shape and may ward off senility in later years.

c) Even with good reason and mathematics our knowledge is seldom complete, but rather offers to us a probability as to the truth of events and the laws of nature. This was certainly understood by Thucydides, Plato and Aristotle and they cautioned that even correct opinion was not knowledge: for knowledge had four components: the truth that something is, why it is, how it is and that it cannot be otherwise. If those four steps can not be proven with the rational accuracy of that in mathematics, then one has opinion and not knowledge. Thucydides in his great work *The History of the War Between Athens and Sparta*, attesting to his attempted accuracy of the speeches given, makes this statement: "As to the speeches that were made by several men..., it has been difficult to recall with strict accuracy the words actually spoken...Therefore they are given in the language in which, as it seemed to me, the several speakers would express, on the subjects under consideration, the sentiments most befitting the occasion"(I.22) Plato himself also felt the written word to be inferior than the actual dialogues themselves, and his attempt at definition of words and virtues, an attempt at making the definitions as accurate as the **d)** numbers in mathematics, simply could not be done. But the attempt to clarify speech and words was a great leap forward in the communication of knowledge from one person to another. Plato often used the concept of myth to explain himself when he acknowledged that the subject itself was beyond the accuracy of the words and knowledge available. The answer to such difficult questions simply could not be put to or proven by dialectical proof. Therefore in speaking about the absolutes, the virtues, and the material universe where knowledge was simply not available, it was necessary to speak about what is likely to be the best account (mythus) of the probability of knowing. This applies to all his writings: about politics, the cause of the universe, the "forms" of the virtues, and the exact definition of words. He had the greatest trust in the proofs of mathematics, for he considered numbers to be the most perfect symbols of truth. "If you do not know mathematics, do not come in" was at the entrance of his Academy.

153a) Nevertheless, to strive to be accurate and to attain knowledge as much as possible in every field of study was a necessary quest for man, and for that purpose, man was given intellect (nous) and reason or logic (logos). Thus it was first at the Academy and then to all the other schools established by its students throughout the Mediterranean rim that the greatest advancements in antiquity in all subjects took place. This was the foundation of Western thinking and advancement, hindered by the Christian Church for a thousand years, but reborn in the Renaissance that gave the Western World its great progress in every field of study. As Edith Hamilton aptly said,"It was the Greeks who taught us how to think". Archytas stated in his *The Good and Happy Man*, "Intellect is the satellite of the Deity". For the Greeks knew that the more rational a thought was expressed, the better it could be understood. For if each

culture spoke only by means of myths without the framework of reason, communication between the cultures would be near impossible.
b) Robert Grosseteste had to point out that even though the immortals were called gods, it was not true that all eternal things were gods: "Seven and three are ten" but they, even though one is not the other and both are eternal as also is the proposition, numbers are not gods. This is truly Platonic. Mathematics are the closest thing to God himself as to the virtues of eternalness and reliability, and thus they are the closest thing man can have to truth. Roger Bacon, another Platonist like Grosseteste, was also aware that mathematics was the key to the quest of real knowledge. Richard McKeon, in introducing Albert the Great's works stated:

"Bacon even admits that Albert was a man of infinite energy and study, who had collected a vast number of things from the ocean of facts; yet Bacon esteemed that on the whole his influence was bad, since he like Thomas Aquinas, for all his assiduity and metaphysics, was ignorant of mathematics and science and perspective, and had begun to teach before he had learned." 13.8
c)
This is really symbolic of the way Platonists viewed all the Church Fathers who taught about metaphysics, that they never tried to rise above opinion to seek actual knowledge, while at the same time, declaring that they had the keys to eternal truth. Bacon was right, their influence, no matter how impressive, was bad, because it lacked mathematics, and science and perspective. And, unfortunately, what it lacked it condemned. Like Albert they began to teach, even pontificate, before they had learned.

The Renaissance reached England and the gift of numbers was reborn there. Thomas Hobbes (1588-1679), who lived 90 years, was one of the great English thinkers and one of it's earliest philosophers. At age 40 he discovered Euclid, and, at first rejected the conclusion of the 47th Element of Book I, but after more study realized, it's correctness and the value of numbers in every human endeavor and his thinking was changed for the rest of his life. Twenty Three years after discovering Euclid he published his Leviathan, and from it Part One, Chapter Five the following is taken:

"When a man reasons, he does nothing else but conceive a sum total, from addition of parcels, or conceive a remainder, from subtraction of one sum from another; which, if it be done by words, is conceiving of the consequence of the names of all the parts, to the name of the whole; or from the names of the whole and one part, to the name of the other part. **d)** And though in some things, as in numbers, besides adding and subtracting, men name other operations, as multiplying and dividing, yet they are the same; for multiplication is but adding together of things equal; and division, but subtracting of one thing as often as we can. These operations are not incident to numbers only, but to all manner of things that can be added together and taken one out of another. For as arithmeticians teach to add and subtract in numbers; so the geometricians teach the same in lines, figures solid and superficial, angles, proportions, times, degrees of swiftness, force, power, and the like; the logicians teach the same in consequences of words; adding together the names to make an affirmation, and two affirmations to make a syllogism, and many syllogisms to make a demonstration; and from the sum or conclusion of a syllogism, they subtract one proposition to find the other. Writers of politics add together pactions (agreements) to find men's duties; and lawyers, laws and facts, to find what is right and wrong in the actions of private men. In sum, in what matter so ever there is place for addition and subtraction, there also is place for reason; and where these have no place, there reason has nothing at all to do.
154a) Out of all which we may define, that is to say determine, what that is which is meant by this word *reason*, when we reckon it amongst the faculties of the mind. For reason, in this sense, is nothing but reckoning, that is adding and subtracting, of the consequences of general names agreed upon, for the marking and signifying of our thoughts. I say marking them when we reckon by our selves, and signifying when we demonstrate, or approve our reckoning to other men."

This long quotation of Hobbes perhaps can be illustrated by this simple way of thinking. Just think how many times one has rejected an argument by stating that the other person's argument "just doesn't add up". Or the way we might say, "I reckon so". Reckon of course means to calculate something, as calculate itself is related to numeration. One computes and makes a rational decision. One can see why Plato tied together the gift of reason and the gift of numbers. Because that is the

way intellect functions when it functions logically. Critics have kidded about Plato's God being a Geometer, but, in fact, that was Plato's way of expressing the rational and carefully planning of ordering the universe, just as any carpenter or builder would be lost without the gift of numbers and measurements. Thus all knowledge in one way or another is related **b)** to reason, the gift of numbers. To Leibniz, a Platonist was a mathematician. The role of dialectic with Plato is also the art of weighing the validity of arguments the way one would weigh an amount of gold to find its value. It is the careful bringing in of all the facts, and then weighing them. That is the way that men attain the knowledge that is available for them. Immanuel Kant, in his work *Religion within the Boundaries of Mere Reason*, simply weighs the arguments for the various reasons why one may or not believe in God, and concludes that there is an abundance of issues concerned about morality and the necessary basis for morally verifiable standards that God exists, for man needs an absolute standard of virtue to make moral quests and judgments. His main argument against prevailing religion of his day was that it was largely irrational in many of it precepts, its censorships, and its limitations put upon science. Despite being deeply religious himself, he avoided attending public worship. His quest was for a logical and moral reason to believe in God, and the Church offered neither. But the practical result of his rational need for morality led him to believe that there must exist a source and ground for moral purity itself, and that Ground was God. His words from the Preface to the First Edition were:
c)
"Morality thus inevitably leads to religion, and through religion it extends itself to the idea of a Mighty Moral Lawgiver outside the human being, in whose will the ultimate goal is what can and at the same time ought to be the ultimate human goal...Over against biblical theology, however, there stands on the side of the sciences a philosophical theology which is a property held in trust by another faculty. This theology must have complete freedom to expand as far as its science reaches, provided that it stays within the boundaries of mere reason."

Against holy books, like the Judeo-Christian Bible, and councils and edicts and creeds he declared that all teachings must be based on reason: "...they can surely be none other than pure doctrines of reason, for these alone carry their own proof and on which, therefore, the accreditation of any other must principally rest."(6:159)

The life of reason alone is free from superstition. For knowledge is not available without it.

d)

C. PHILOSOPHY IS THE CLIMATIC UNION OF REASON AND KNOWLEDGE

The love of wisdom - philosophy - is the great quest of the rational ordering of knowledge into a wisdom that gives life its beauty and adorns it in goodness and happiness. It is a seeking of the Absolute and Ultimate Goodness and Spirit of the universe. It is here where one finds rational answers to questions like: What is the meaning of life? Is there really a distinction between what is good and what is bad? Are such abstracts as love, joy, justice, and human kindness only a figment of imagination or are they real and effective in bringing happiness and meaning to men and women? Can a person really harm himself in any way by lying, cheating and stealing - or even by murdering? Is there an actual moral basis for making decisions? If I am mortal, why should I care about anything at all? In reality, many have come to feel greatly enhanced in spirit with uplifted psyche and attitude for life and finding great meaning to it when they become acquainted with the wisdom of the Platonic Tradition.

Cicero gives an ode of praise to philosophy in his *Fifth Discussion at Tusculum.*

155a)

"Philosophy! The guide of our lives, the explorer of all that is good in us, exterminator of all evil! Had it not been for your guidance, what would I ever have amounted to - and what indeed, would have become of all human life?...Inventor of laws, teacher of morals, creator of order! You were all these things. And now, you are my refuge and rescuer. I have already relied on you so much in past years; and now my dependence is total and complete. One day well spent in obeying your rules is better than an eternity of error. Your aid is the most precious in all the world. It is you who have brought peace into our lives, you who have relieved us of the fear of death."13.9

In his *The Nature of the Gods*, Cicero admits that even philosophy has not answered completely all questions, yet it has been his mainstay in life:

"I have not become a philosopher overnight. I have been much interested and engaged in philosophical studies from my earliest years. And I was often most the philosopher when I seemed least interested in philosophy. Witness my speeches, which are full of philosophical aphorisms, and my friendship with men of learning, who were never absent from our house, as well as those eminent philosophers Diodatus [a Stoic], Philo [head of Plato's Academy], Antiochus [head of Plato's Academy] and Posidonius [Platonist Stoic], who have been my tutors in this subject."13.10

b) Seneca in one of his letters stated:

"Why 'liberal studies' are so called is obvious: it is because they are the ones considered worthy of a free man (liber). But there is really only one liberal study that deserves the name - because it makes a person free - and that is the pursuit of wisdom. It's high ideals, its steadfastness and spirit make all other studies puerile and puny in comparison."13.11

Plutarch believed that active philosophy was the substance of pleasure and true happiness, and he gives the names of Plato, Aristotle, Theophrastus and Phidias as examples. For to him philosophy builds and raises men to the highest of levels. He stated:

"True philosophy...is a spring and principle of motion wherever it appears; it makes men active and industrious, it sets every wheel and faculty in motion, it stores our minds with axioms and rule by which to make a sound judgment, it determines the will to the choice of what is honorable and just; and it wings all our faculties to the swiftest prosecution of it. It is accompanied with an elevation and nobleness of mind, joined with a coolness and sweetness of behavior, and backed with a becoming assurance and inflexible resolution."13.12

c)

Plutarch thought that philosophy should be divided into three levels: the logical, the ethical, and the spiritual. The first level was that of logic, reason, and the power of correct thinking; the second level that of ethics build upon such correct thinking that habits of doing good become the nature of man; and thus equipped with reason and goodness man could contemplate and philosophize about the spiritual realm and God himself. A good lesson from this pyramid of order is that all teachings about God must be based upon reason and logic first and second upon goodness. The irrational and immoral have no claim upon the knowledge of the spiritual realm and of God himself. If one's theology is in conflict with the logical results of scientific knowledge or based upon immoral tenets then one's theology is polluted. If one's mathematics can not add two and two and get four, then he can not presume to know about God.

Lady Philosophy, after declaring that the Good was nothing other than God himself, bids Boethius and all others to come to her and be comforted:

156a)

"Come hither, all who are the prey of passions, bound by their ruthless chains, those deceitful passions which dwell in the minds of men. Here you shall find rest from your labors, here a haven lying in tranquil peace, open to receive within itself all the miserable of the earth."(Bk III, Meter X)

Reading Pico della Mirandola's *Oration on the Dignity of Man*, one would think that he copied Plutarch:

"We, therefore, imitating the life of the Cherubim here on earth, by refraining the impulses of our passions through moral science, by dissipating the darkness of reason by dialectic--thus washing away, so to speak, the filth of ignorance and vice--may likewise purify our souls, so that the passions may never run rampant, nor reason, lacking restraint, range beyond its natural limits. Then may we suffuse our purified souls with the light of natural philosophy, bringing it to final perfection by the knowledge of divine things."

Ficino, in a speech in praise of philosophy declared:

b)

"Since she is a gift from heaven, philosophy drives earthly vices far away; firmly subdues fortune; marvelously softens fate; uses mortal gifts most rightly; and bestows immortal gifts according to desire...O surest guide for human life...she frees men from this earthly exile and restores them to their celestial homeland in the fullness of truth and happiness."13.13

In Hegel's lecture on Absolute Spirit, he presents three levels to reaching that Absolute Spirit: Art, Religion, and Philosophy. Each is valid, but Art is the lowest, Religion the middle form, and the highest and climatic is Philosophy. He concluded:

"So we move to the highest form of absolute knowledge--Philosophy. Philosophy when it reaches its fullest development expresses the same content as religion--the deep speculative truths we have found in the absolute religion--but in another form. This is the form of thought."13.14

c)

Hegel goes on and declares that it is only in philosophy were the Spirit is truly itself and is totally free. This is the peak experience of thought, a type of mental rapture that brings man into life in its greatest and purist form. Philosophy, said Plato, begins in wonder, and it might be added that it ends in wonder also. Claudius Ptolemaeus composed this noble epigram:

"I know that I am mortal and ephemeral; but when I see the multitudinous circling spirals of the stars, no longer do I touch earth with my feet, but sit with Zeus himself, and take my fill of the ambrosial food of the gods."

d) Josiah Royce in his *The Religious Aspect of Philosophy* concludes his work with these words: "This Universal Thought is what we have ventured, for the sake of convenience, to call God. It is not the God of very much of the traditional theology. It is the God of the idealistic tradition from Plato downwards."

D. KNOW YOURSELF

The full validation of one's philosophy is to know himself and his role and value in the great creation. γνωθι σαυτον, at the entrance of the temple at Delphi, and μηδεν `αγαν, were the two great proclamations for the Greek individual seeking help from the Pythia, the prophetess who gave the oracles of Apollo. Gnothi Sauton and meden agan, know yourself and nothing in excess: self-knowledge and self-control were absolutely essential for spiritual growth as well as understanding what was proper and fulfilling in the present life for wholeness and happiness. "Who am I?" was the question.What is my role here and now in this place among these people and this time in human history? Persius in his Satire III says it beautifully:

"Contemplate well this theatre of man;
Observe the drama, and its moral plan;
Study of things the causes and the ends;
Whence is our being, and to what it tends;
Of fortune's gifts appreciate the worth,
And mark how good and evil mix on earth:
Observe what stands as relative to you,
What to your country, parents, friends, is due:
Consider God as boundless matter's soul,
Yourself a part of the stupendous whole;
Think that existence has an endless reign,
Yourself a line in the eternal chain.
Weight these things well.(103-115)

Again Persius laments that people seek, as busy-bodies, to know all about their neighbors, but forget to look at themselves.

"None looks at home; none seeks himself to know
...
But each intent regards his neighbor's mind,
Sees other's faults, and to his own is blind." (IV. 35-38)
157a)

Seneca in one of his letters stated:

"'A consciousness of wrongdoing is the first step to salvation.' This remark of Epicurus' is to me a very good one, for a person who is not aware that he is doing anything wrong has no desire to be put right. You have to catch yourself doing it before you can reform. Some people boast about their failings: can you imagine someone who counts his faults as merits....demonstrate your own guilt, conduct inquiries of your own into all the evidence against yourself. Play the part first of prosecutor, then of judge and finally of pleader in mitigation. Be harsh with yourself at times."13.15

b) In another statement Seneca addresses the person who is unhappy and seeks to find happiness by traveling throughout the world as an exciting adventure.

"Do you think you are the only one this has happened to? Do you find it uniquely extraordinary that such extensive travel and such a variety of scenery have not shaken off your melancholy and heaviness of spirit? It is your soul you need to change, not your climate...If you ask why escape is not feasible, you are escaping with yourself. You must lay down the weight on your soul."13.16

If you are an unhappy person, a different city or country will not change the fact, because wherever you go--You will be there, and You are the problem. You must examine yourself and change--for an unexamined life is not worth living as well said by Socrates.

Hipparchus in his treatise *On Tranquillity* reminded people that they must accept the brevity of bodily life, for to know this and accept this gives a foundation on which one can build a peaceful and joyous attitude towards this life.

c)

"Since men live but for a very short period, if their life is compared with the whole of time, they will make a most beautiful journey as it were, if they pass through life with tranquillity. This however they will possess in the most eminent degree, if they accurately and scientifically know themselves, viz. if they know that they are mortal and of a fleshly nature, and that they have a body which is corruptible and can be easily injured, and which is exposed to every thing most grievous and severe, even to their last breath."

Lady Philosophy had to remind Boethius that "For in other animals ignorance of self is natural, in men it is a moral defect." (II. Prose V) Lady Philosophy also makes it clear to Boethius that he is not the center of the universe.

"As you have learned from astronomical demonstrations, the whole circumference of the earth is only a pin point compared with the expanse of the heavens; that is to say, when compared with the circle of the universe, it must be reckoned as of no size at all...And you, so firmly restricted to this infinitesimal point within a point, are thinking of proclaiming your fame and publicizing your name! What size and magnificence can fame have when shut in by such close and narrow limits?"(II. Prose VII).

d) Know yourself within the cosmos and you will not be so self-centered and big headed, rather be humbled and recognize who you are. Yet you have value, moral value and integrity and that is worth much before God. Do not sell that which is of value so cheaply. Epictetus warns us: "For it is you who know yourself, how much you are worth to yourself, and at what price you sell yourself; for men sell themselves at various prices." (Discourses I.2) It is one of the great inconsistencies of many "religious" people to look down on others for selling their bodies to others, yet they sell the divinity within them for a few dollars, they forfeit their souls and their eternal beauty for the sake of glory or wealth or status. Know yourself and how do you value yourself?

158a) Immanuel Kant addressed the same question in his *Lectures on Ethics:*

"The supreme rule is this: Give good, practical proof of yourselves in your lives by your actions; not by set prayers, but by doing good acts, by work and steadiness, and in particular by righteousness and active benevolence towards your neighbor; then you can see whether you are good. Just as one does not get to know a friend from conversation, but from having dealings with him, so also it is not easy to get to know oneself from any opinion one has about oneself. In any case it is not so easy to know yourself."

Gabriel Marcel speaks of traveling about the world, and as one comes to a strange town where he expects to stay for some time, he ventures out each day to get to know the town better: where to find relaxation, where to buy clothes or food, what kind of cafes and restaurants there are and what are the prices of things, and to know the pleasures and the people, and the means of transportation. Only after knowing well the city does one relax and truly enjoy it and its country side. But then he continues:

b)

"We must now continue with our process of turning our awareness of the outer world inwards, and ask ourselves what it is to reconnoitre, or to fail to reconnoitre, at the level of our own lives; what it is to find our way, or not to find our way, in ourselves."

II. COURAGE

Plato discusses courage in his Laches, a very easy dialogue to read for those beginning to read him. In this dialogue the usual ancient idea is that courage is holding your position, whether winning or losing, in a war. And it is in this sense of imminent danger of death that they did and many do today think of the concept of courage. Ανδρεια (andreia), being a man, however was much more than a virtue for battle. Indeed, the Laches continues to speak of other ways in which courage is displayed in danger. Another example would be of a woman in childbirth, for in those days it was indeed a danger to a woman every time she bore a child. Thus, being a man, was, perhaps, not the best way to describe the virtue. The discussion goes on and states that courage also has the other virtues, self-control and wisdom, for if a man rushes into danger recklessly, it is rashness, not courage: or some would say stupid. Thus it meant a firm and committed mind to face a necessary danger. The statement is made in the dialogue that "A man whose actions do not agree with his words is an annoyance to me, and the better he speaks the more I hate him." For many are brave with words, but few are brave in face of a necessary danger. A man can cry "Give me liberty or give me death" and still be a coward if his own life is not involved. Politicians seem to have this problem in the modern world. And they are truly an annoyance, and the more they talk the more the masses tend to hate them. For the teacher is to teach the student by representing the virtues himself, and if he can not do that then he is a hypocrite. Socrates declares to Laches the type of definition of courage that he wants:

"For I meant to ask you not only about the courage of the heavy-armed soldiers, but about the courage of cavalry, and every other style of soldier--and not only who are courageous in war, but who are courageous in perils by sea, and who in disease, or in poverty, or again in politics are courageous, and not only who are courageous against pain or fear, but mighty to contend against desires and pleasures, either fixed in their rank or turning upon their enemy."(191d)

c)

Thus courage has many faces: in women, in men, in children, and even in some animals as shown by females protecting their young and fighting much larger and stronger animals to protect them.

Plutarch in his *Life of Timoleon* tells of one Aristides of Locrain, one of Plato's companions, while he was in Syracuse visiting Dionysius the Tyrant. Dionysius saw the beauty of a daughter of Aristides and asked for her in marriage, and Aristides, who despised tyranny, said: "I had rather see my virgin girl in her grave than in the palace of a tyrant." He wanted to protect his daughter at any cost, but the cost was heavy as other of his children were then executed. Dionysius then asked if he thought well of his words that brought on the death of his children, the reply by Aristides was: "I can not but grieve at the cruelty of your deeds, but I am not sorry for the freedom of my own words." The cost of courage was always dangerous when expressed against the request of tyrants, but many have lost loved ones as well as their own lives. Plato himself lectured Dionysius and was put on a ship that took him to an island and there Plato was put on the slave block and sold as a slave. Fortunately he was recognized by another Athenian who then purchased him and released him to his own freedom. In Plutarch's *Life of Cato the Younger*, he tells of a request of Lucius Caesar, Julius Caesar's kin, to prepare a speech for him. Cato said no, for he had no love for the Caesars. He was then condemned to death by means of suicide. Cato then bathed had a walk with his friends, and before committing suicide, read Plato's dialogue on the soul, the Phaedo, and by means of a sword killed himself. He simply could not face life if he complied with Lucius Caesar's request to give him words that would impress the multitude, for that would be supporting what he considered the tyranny of the Caesars.

d) There is the well known story of Diogenes (Born of God) of Sinope, the founder of the Cynics, and his meeting with Alexander of Macedon, who never took no for an answer unless he, in some way, was impressed by the person. He came to Diogenes, who was lying in mud and sun bathing, and asked him what he could do for him. Diogenes, simply said, "Remove yourself, you are blocking the sun". Alexander did, and as he was walking away said that if that had been anyone else but Diogenes, he would be dead now. The point is that Diogenes, at the risk of insulting the most powerful man on earth, stayed true to his Cynic philosophy. Some would say that he was a little stupid and caused a tension that could have been swept aside by a little politeness, but history has honored him as a man of courage whose life matched his words.

159a) Karl Jaspers in his *Way to Wisdom* has a chapter titled "The Unconditional Imperative" in which he expresses the view that a person must, if he wants to authenticate his own being, follow the unconditional imperative which is the eternal element that attaches man to the love of and the loyalty to truth and ultimate ideals. He believed that Socrates was the purest example for he gave his life. A non Christian can see Jesus the same way, who preferred death over renouncing his call from God. Jaspers continues on naming as examples: Seneca, Thomas More, Luther, Boethius and Bruno. Jaspers declared: "The unconditional imperative comes to me as the command of my authentic self to my mere empirical existence. I become aware of myself as of that which I myself am, because it is what I ought to be." This sounds like a page of Kant and the absolute and divine imperatives he taught. The "ought to be" is the driving force that gives one courage to be in harmony with one's "oughts". To go against the "oughts" within is self destructive. But it takes courage to say no to that which is destructive and yes to that that authenticates one's true being and lifts his spirit to the eternal and divine.

b) Concerning courageous action, Dietrich Bonhoeffer, who suffered martyrdom under Hitler, at the beginning of his book *Ethics* stated the following about courageous action:

"Do and dare what is right, not swayed by the whim of the moment.
Bravely take hold of the real, not dallying now with what might be.
Not in the flight of ides but only in action is freedom.
Make up your mind and come out into the tempest of living.
God's command is enough and your faith in him to sustain you.
Then at last freedom will welcome your spirit amid great rejoicing."

c) Eugene V. Debs was an American who cared about the working poor and about the destructiveness of war. He was strongly against the United States entering World War One against Germany, a betrayal by President Wilson who had promised not to enter into the war. The lower classes always suffer the most in war, and if won, the upper classes always have the most to gain: the war profits. Being against both war and war profits and also against the powerful using the poorer people to work in the industries and also to fight the wars the leaders started, he started his campaign against America's participation in a foreign war fought for control of the poor people of the world, the so called colonies owned by the Europeans and Americans. It was risky business, because in the "land of the free" it was prison time to oppose a war. In 1918, on June 16, on a Sunday afternoon in Canton, Ohio, he gave his "Canton, Ohio, Speech." After the speech he was sentenced to ten years in prison. He knew it was coming, but to back away from his deepest convictions would have been an act of cowardice. Instead he showed his courage. Below are some of the excerpts from the speech.

d)

"I would rather a thousand times be a free soul in jail than to be a sycophant and coward in the streets.

If it had not been for the men and women, who, in the past, have had the moral courage to go to jail, we would still be in the jungles.

To whom do the Wall Street junkers in our country marry their daughters? After they have wrung their countless millions from your sweat, your agony and your life's blood, in time of war as in time of peace, they invest these untold millions...(basically in status titles).

A Man of Galilee, the Carpenter, the workingman who became the revolutionary agitator of his day soon found himself to be an undesirable citizen in the eyes of the ruling knaves and they had him crucified.

These treaties have never been denied nor repudiated. Very little has been said about them in the American press. I have a copy of these treaties, showing that the purpose of the Allies is exactly the purpose of the Central Powers, and that is the conquest and spoliation of the weaker nations that has always been the purpose of war. [All "advanced" nations wanted colonies to suck dry of natural minerals--thus making both the Allies and Central Powers equals in crime, and equals in using the low economic classes to fight to the death to enhance the wealth of their leaders]

160a)

Rose Pastor Stokes! And when I mention her name I take off my hat. Here we have another heroic and inspiring comrade. She had her millions of dollars at command. Did her wealth restrain her an instant? On the contrary her supreme devotion to the cause outweighed all considerations of a financial or social nature. She went out boldly to plead the cause of the working class and they rewarded her high courage with a ten years' sentence to the penitentiary. Think of it! Ten years!"

Of course, Debs too was rewarded with a ten year sentence. The leaders who lied about the causes of the war (world safe for democracy) were praised, the truly courageous were sent to prison. Norman Thomas in 1961, on the verge of the escalations of the Viet Nam conflict, wrote a book praising those who had the courage in the past to dissent and it was called *Great Dissenters*. The five lives he discussed were those of: Socrates, Galileo, Thomas Paine, Wendell Phillips, and Gandhi. In 1941 A.J. Muste warned about America's leaders getting the USA into another war, for it was obvious the sides were already chosen, and all that was needed was an "incident" like the Lusitania. Another book worth reading to find individuals standing alone with courage and loyalty to honesty and peace is Barrows Dunham's *Heroes and Heretics: A Social History of Dissent,* 1963. Erasmus was frustrated that in "Christian" Europe all the princes and kings were willing to kill each other for land and materials, and wrote *The Education of a Christian Prince*. In it he said.

b)

"So I am led to declare boldly that the god-fearing prince will be far more astute to maintain peace, however unfair, than to embark on even the most advantageous war; for such a war will be preceded, accompanied, and followed by such an ocean of ills, so vast a swamp of wickedness, so black a plague of immorality."

One can notice that he said "god-fearing prince" for he obviously doubted that those claiming to be Christians would be, since they had not been "god-fearing" in the past.

Courage has many faces and is put to the test in many ways for the person who wants truly to be honest with himself and authenticate his soul as something divine and celestial. It really makes a man examine himself and see if he is clothed in virtuous garments or if he is a wolf in goatskin.

III. TEMPERANCE

c) The word that Plato used for the third of his four cardinal virtues was σωφρωσυνη - sophrosyne, and it has been translated three different ways: temperance, moderation, and self-control. It fulfills the Delphi Oracle's command μηδεν αγαν - meden agan, nothing too much or nothing in excess. It is a type of sobriety, that is the opposite of being "drunk with the passions", such as anger, envy, jealousy, hatred, sloth, lust and greed. Such must always be controlled, for any one of them that runs loose in a person's actions can destroy the entire person: soul and mental harmony will be discordant and the balance of the virtues will be nullified. Man will be internally rent asunder and his psychological equilibrium will be so erratic that he can not meet the day's necessary challenges without imploding. Sophrosyne keeps everything in the human mind and character in balance that life can be lived smoothly and in harmony with his highest ideals.

Persius speaks of the effects of unbridled passions:

d)

"Unhappy man takes passion for his guide,
And sighs for bliss to sated sense denied;
Untamed desires impel the vicious mind,
To God, to Virtue, and to Nature blind." (IV. 75-80)

And later in his Fifth Satire he declared that only the man who has command of himself is free.

Philo of Alexandria also speaks of the necessity of sophrosyne, translated by Colson and Whitaker as self-mastery, for the man who desires to feel the joy of being beloved of God. "But the principle of self-mastery, being forcible and unyielding [to the passions], is likened to the strong and firm substance of brass, perhaps also because, whereas the self-mastery found in the man beloved of God is most precious and like gold." (*Allegorical Interpretation* II.80-81)." He continues to speak of sophrosyne as "the beauty of self-mastery" (σωοφροσυνης καλλος), and plays a role similar to dominant wisdom (απχουσα σοφια).

161a) Plutarch spoke of the need of schooling the emotions, taming and disciplining them so that one could avoid being irrational in judgments and actions. Plutarch also, writing on love, praised Alexander the Great for not letting his desire of beautiful women ruin established romances.

"It is told of Alexander that he wrote to Theodorus, brother of Proteus: 'Send me that music girl and accept ten talents, that is, unless your are in love with her.' Another of Alexander's companions, Antipatrides, once came to a banquet with a lutenist, and Alexander was amorously inclined to the girl. He asked Antipatrides, 'You don't happen to be in love with her?' When Antipatrides answered that he was very much in love with her, Alexander said 'A thousand plagues on you!'--but he refrained himself and did not lay a finger on the woman."13.18

b) One of the more difficult experiences in life is the death of a loved one. One's self-control is strongly challenged, for grief can be deep and penetrating, and often it paralyzes the survivor. The death of one's child or parent or mate not only hurts, but causes such a great frustration because of the inability of the lover to do anything or "turn back the clock". Libanius, a Platonist of the Fourth Century of the common era mentions such grief in two of his letters: the first the grief of a dear friend whose wife had died and the second his own grief over the death of his friend, the Emperor Julian, a fellow Platonist who was seen as the only hope against the rising and destructive power of the Christian Church that condemned and persecuted all but their own. The first a letter to Aristaenetus:

c)

"The style of your letter induces me to believe that you are a pupil of Plato, but the continued growth of your despondency within you, your hair let down in sorrow, and the appearance of your household, as though your wife's death occurred but yesterday--all this is certainly not like a devotee of Plato. Indeed, it would be far better if you attended more to your attitude than to your eloquence. You believe that your present behaviour is in harmony with your attitude towards her while she was alive, and that this is as pleasing to her now as that was then. Yet it seems to me that, though you never gave her cause for pain during her life, you are certainly doing so now after her death; for if she saw how you are ruining yourself, she would deeply lament that she gave occasion for such misfortune."(LCL p.379)

d)

And about his own grief when he heard that Emperor Julian had been killed in battle with the Persians at age of 31, when he had hoped that he would have lived long enough to restore freedom of religion to the empire and laid a foundation for its permanence.

"My first impulse was to look to my sword, for life would be harder to bear than death. Then I reminded myself of Plato's maxim that one must not seek such relief, and that if I met Julian in the other world, he would hold me guilty for dying so, for he would have no good word to say for a man who had not waited for orders from heaven."(LCL p.203)

Basil the Great, both Christian and Platonist, writes to a friend, Candidianus, who is under great pressure and in crisis, but who did not complain about it in his letter to Basil, and Basil honors him for such personal control.

162a)

"But, as Plato says, in 'the storm and stress' of affairs you, 'withdrawing', as it were, 'under some strong wall', remain untroubled amid the tumult, nay more, you do not, according to your power, even allow others to be disturbed. And indeed, such conduct on your part seems great and admirable even to casual observers, though it is not astonishing to one who judges it in comparison with the whole policy of your life."13.19

Those influenced by Plato knew that in life there were numerous occasions for desire, fear, pleasure, regret and sorrow to become pathological states. By the power of moderating and controlling such passions man could free himself from them and reach the goal of imperturbability (απαθεια or αταραξια) and calmness and impassiveness. The Stoics stressed such self-control, and even the expression "to be stoical" about such matters was to have them under control. One can also combat certain matters by returning to the virtues in order to put up a wall between both tragedies and passion and oneself. Be active against the sufferings of life with the positive elements of philosophy. For example, if there is a tremendous and fearful storm, take cover in one's house or elsewhere, stay warm and dry and get near a fire. The storm will pass and one will not be damaged. In Beethoven's Sixth Symphony the calmness, beauty and gradually increasing strength of the **b)** music after the storm scene is so emotionally uplifting that one forgets that there was a storm preceding such beauty. This virtue of self-moderation leads to this apatheia that is impregnable against the emotions and passions of life, and when a person develops such strength he becomes an αυταρκες -- that is, a self-sufficient one, one who has within the necessities of power to the extent that other powers from the outside stay on the outside and do not penetrate his calmness and control of his own life. In the quest for true freedom, a person must understand above everything else, that he must master and control the lowest element of his soul, the emotive element, otherwise the undisciplined emotions will bounce him back and forth and lead him this way and that way with emotive instability. It is by way of self control that freedom is finally attained, regardless of the circumstances and tragedies of life.

IV. JUSTICE

c) Justice, like the other three virtues, has both social and individual functions. Δικαιοσυνη (Dikaiosyne) sought both social and individual unity and harmony. To Plato a just city was one in which each would play his role or function for the betterment and unification of the city's effort to make life peaceful and fulfilling for all of its citizens. For the individual, Plato divided the soul into three parts; the proper functions of those parts were played by wisdom, courage and temperance. If all three functioned properly according to each's role then the individual would have a unified peacefulness within, and that Plato called justice. Justice then is a unity of all virtues. Most of Plato's dialogues dealt with individual virtues, but the four cardinal virtues had a duel role laying the foundation for both the happy individual and the happy city. This presentation will include both, but will be focused mainly on the individual's self improvement for his spiritual well being.

A. Personal Responsibility.

d) First of all, it is important to recognize the call for personal responsibility for all. One makes his own spiritual unity, for it can not come from the outside, nor by laws of a state, nor by rituals of a religion. If, in life, one does not "have it all together", the blame is his: not God's and not his country's. One must examine his own life, put on the clothes of the virtues, each in its proper place (one does not put his shoes on his ears), and then each will clothe the person in justice or unified well being. The doctrines of some Stoics are in conflict with such Platonic premises, for they believe that fate or destiny is going to be the chief controlling factor in one's life. This is not true of Platonism. While it is necessary to admit that where, to whom, and when we were born and into what gender we were born was out of our control. But to believe that one can not be happy because he was born a male, or in Iceland, or in the 12th Century CE, or to parents who were middle class is just a series of excuses that avoids the decree of personal responsibility for one's virtues of wisdom, courage, and self-control. If one is experiencing a destruction of his life, he needs to look into the mirror and declare, "The enemy is me." If a football team is declared a winner before the game "by destiny", and does not play responsibly, it will lose. It is the same with the battle of being good and happy. It is in the individual's hands. Related to this is the Platonic teaching of man's free will. Again, he can not decide to be seven feet tall. But about his goodness and happiness there is his free will to choose the ways he shall go and the thoughts he thinks and the actions he chooses to do. In other words, the divine virtues are open to all. The human virtues are more fated, but they are temporal and need not have power over the ability for one to excel in the cardinal virtues. I may not have wealth, but that does not mean I cannot have purity of heart or the ability to experience friendship based upon human goodness.

163a) Contrary to the Judeo-Christian scriptures, God does not "harden man's heart" to do evil. The Platonic God constantly rejoices in all good actions, for he, when it comes to evil, is `ο θεος αναιτιος, (ho theos anaitios) the God who is not the cause or at fault for anything bad. If something happens that is harmful or evil, it is not the will of God, but either the laws of nature or the makings of humans. God is blameless. The individual must chose his own actions. Mahatma Gandhi made many difficult decisions in his life and expressed the following: "There are moments in your life when you must act even though you cannot carry your best friends with you. The still small voice within you must always be the final arbiter when there is a conflict of duty."13.20 Gandhi was no soft hearted liberal, but a man of strict personal responsibility. He declared: "God created man to work for his food and said that those who ate without work were thieves. Eighty percent of India are compulsorily thieves half the year. Is it any wonder if India has become one vast prison?"13.21 Later he repeated: "We dare not support able-bodied members of the family--men or women--who will not work."13.22

b) Dietrich Bonhoeffer chose to go back to Germany after his stay in the United States, even though others encouraged him to stay because of the danger of the Nazi Gestapo. He declared that if he did not return to his Germany then and work against Hitler, he would forfeit his right to help rebuild Germany after the Nazi reign. "I know which of these alternatives I must choose; but I cannot make this choice concerned with my security...You must never doubt that I am thankful and glad to go the way which I am being led. My past life is abundantly full of God's mercy and, above all sin, stands the forgiving love." On April 5, 1943, he, his sister and her husband were arrested and imprisoned by the Gestapo. He never left prison and on April 9, 1945, at the personal command by Himmler he was executed just a few days before the war ended. He was 39 years old. He had free will and took his personal responsibility seriously, for it was essential to him to have justice, peace and harmony, within.

R. W. Emerson ended his essay on Self Reliance with this sentence: "Nothing can bring you peace, but yourself. Nothing can bring you peace but the triumph of principles."

c) B. Man in Society

The individual in society has basically three different roles that he might play: two or a sort of guardianship of the state divided between the decision makers whose virtue is wisdom and the protectors of the city whose virtue is courage. The third role is that of the artisans, farmers, builders and others, and their virtue is temperance. The first two, who have the power of the decisions and military are totally committed to the welfare of the city and can own no property, no sexual mate, and the children that they have will probably become future guardians themselves. They will live a good and prosperous life for their service, but, again, they can have no possessions of any kind for their own. Plato was convinced that even the wisest and best, the strongest and most courageous, of all men and women are not immune to the temptation of bribery for the sake of a favorable decision to some wealthy artisan. The guardians, as said above, will live well and be equally divided between men and women, at least the decision making guardians. This implies that Plato saw no difference between the mental capacities of men and women. He was not gender bias; he simply wanted the wisest of the city to run the city.

d) The third class of builders, artisans and farmers could have possessions of all genera: property, relics and artifacts, statues, gold, and they would have traditional families. Some would be wealthier than others, but it would be because they worked harder and smarter, not because they received favoritism from the guardians. The guardians, when they procreated, would not be informed who their children were and the children would be raised apart from them by the city. In that way, the guardians could not, even if they wanted to, have a favoritism in ruling for their relatives, whose identity they would not know. The third class would have more freedoms and that is why their virtue would be self-control, temperance, and moderation. All classes would fill the function for which they were, by nature, most qualified, although one from the higher classes, one and two, could go down, but none, unless qualified, could go up a class. Likewise, two artisans may have a brilliant child and he may be qualified to move up. There was some mobility, if it were good for the city as a whole. When all 3 classes representing the three virtues executed their proper function for the city, then justice, the fourth cardinal virtue, for the entire city would become a reality. In Plato's Republic there is no room for slaves, an institution he called despicable.

164a) For man today, regardless of the form of the government in which he lives, his role in society is, of course, one of being just also. But the justice can come in many forms for the individual. He tries to stay in tune with the societal laws in as much as they themselves are fair and just, if not he is to seek to change them. There is to be economic fairness, equality of opportunity, and individual freedoms as long as they do not harm others. The freedoms must cover the quest of happiness, the right to speak and write one's views, the right to be formally religious or not religious, and also freedom from all imposed forms of religion, and be educated for the sake of goodness, success, and the ability to be of economic and cultural value to others. Education also should make each person capable of being agents of grace and comfort to each other. Plato did stress the comprehensiveness of education in every field so that each could become a type of Renaissance man, that is, that each one has the opportunity to become functional in all the arts and sciences that the fulness of life could be experienced by each individual: that in every part of man-- mental, physical, moral, spiritual, artistic--he or she would have harmony and balance.

b)

Thirteen Basic Principles For The Individual In Society

1. Know yourself.
2. Treat others as you would like to be treated.
3. How one treats those weaker than himself, displays his character.
4. Face life with courage, you are an eternal being.
5. Put all virtues in motion with love.
6. Let your intellect order and control your emotions.
7. Respect the life of another, for it is as sacred as your own.
8. Purifying oneself is holy, judging others is vulgar.
9. When necessary or possible, be an agent of grace and kindness.
10. Honor Mother Earth and all her children.
11. Do something personal for, and enjoy, your animal kinfolk.
12. Never lessen the dignity of God by the way you speak of Him.
13. Seek to be, as much as possible, like God: Absolute Goodness, Beauty Itself, and The Eternal.

V. PLATO'S FOUR HUMAN (EARTHLY) VIRTUES

c)

A. Health

The first and foremost of the earthly virtues is health. There are many different aspects to staying healthy, and most are well known: eat right, exercise, avoid danger habits, laugh and enjoy oneself with the natural pleasures. The main point that Plato is trying to make is that health is far more important than the other earthly blessings: comeliness, strength, and wealth. Yet, most people have the four in reverse and that can be devastating.

B. Comeliness or Beauty

Of course, every man desires to be handsome and every woman attractive or beautiful. But a man combing his hair all the time and looking into the mirror rather than doing some exercise and playful activity will look good when they bury him at age 50. The women, especially when young, who depend on cosmetics more than on good health by what they eat and how they exercise are also going to look good when they get out with their walkers at age 50.

d)

C. Strength

Strength is important. For each wants to have the strength to do the things necessary for one's health and mobility. But to pump up with drugs or countless hours of lifting weights for the sake of abnormal muscle tone, is foolish and destructive. Great strength is mainly a male macho problem or one of glory and money, such as the doped up athletes of the professional athletic contests in the industrial world, misnamed "sports". Even the brutality of such contests must be questioned by rational men. Today in America there are numerous athletes that, with age, have become prematurely crippled, mangled, and in other ways disabled with pain because of the damage done in the professional contests that offer much wealth. Some are wise and leave when they have met rational goals and before their body is too battered. There is nothing innately wrong with such contests as long as the person "knows himself" and rationally makes a decision to leave at the proper time, as much as possible. Here it is necessary to caution also the young female athletes who are focussing on professional athletic contests. Be good to your body and do not destroy it for the sake of money.

165a) D. Wealth

Wealth is the least important and yet the other three human virtues are often sacrificed for its sake. In business a man will work so hard to make it big, he will forfeit his health, his loved ones, his looks and his strength. It is not worth it to be wealthy and sickly, weak, unhappy, and lonely during the latter years of one's life. Money is good, and enough of it should be made to lead as life without fear of poverty and to do the pleasurable things a person wants to do with his loved ones. But beyond that there always lurks an evil outcome in the love of money and its power to do those things that are totally unnecessary for the three more important earthly virtues.

In summary of the earthly virtues, one must remember for the philosophical life of happiness they are supplementary and inferior to the spiritual or heavenly virtues. A man who has health, good looks, strength and wealth, but who is paranoid and filled with cowardice and totally lacking in courage to live, love, experience and face life, is not a happy man. Likewise for the unjust, the unwise and the intemperate who simply can not control any of his emotions. For Plato's virtues, the order is obviously a wise one if one is really seeking happiness and a calm and spiritual life of fulfillment.

Ξ

ΞΙ

CHAPTER FOURTEEN
GOODNESS, THE MOTHER OF HAPPINESS

I. GOODNESS IS THE FOUNDATION OF HAPPINESS

166a) A Basic teaching of Plato was the impossibility of happiness unless it was built upon a person's moral and ethical goodness. In fact, the idea that man was to imitate God if he were to be happy like God, was constructed upon the precept that God was the Good (το αγαθον) beyond being. God was the unity of all the virtues and thus His very nature was goodness. If one were to say, what one thing is God above everything else, the answer would be that He is the Good. Sometimes Plato used the word kallos (καλλος) which is usually translated "beautiful", but is often used for the concept of the good (το αγαθον - to agathon). There is some overlapping, and many Platonists use them almost interchangeably. For Plato there is a purity and awe to both words and they were used to inspire one spiritually as an attraction for man's love, which would be restless and unfulfilled without an assimilation to such beauty and goodness. In both the *Symposium* and *Phaedrus* this idea is fully developed. This theme is shone in many variations by Platonists of all ages and all cultures.

P.E. More stated it this way:

b)

"To honour the soul is to make righteousness the end (goal) of life, and the reward at once and measure of righteousness is happiness. That would seem to be the full circle of Plato's philosophy so far as it belongs to religion--a thesis so simple in appearance that many may pass it by as commonplace or reject it as insignificant."(*The Religion of Plato*, Ch.XI)

"He who thus believes will be filled with awe and admiration of the divine nature; he will desire to be beloved of God even as he loves God, and will endeavour to make himself worthy of God's love by imitation of God's holiness...the life of the religious man will be flight from evil and an assimilation of the human to the divine nature, in so far as this is possible, by rendering himself just and righteous, even as God is free from all injustice and unrighteousness." (Ibid)

c) Moral goodness naturally includes wisdom, courage and moderation, and all basic virtues, and, by means of them, when one experiences ups and downs, accidents and tragedies, and other of life's unsuspecting difficulties his basic nature will understand and address such occurrences with philosophical calmness and not let them affect one's basic and natural character of happiness that has been implanted by the virtues. For moral goodness gives the person, not only control of such disasters, but power over them and freedom from them. Cicero said, "Whereas moral goodness, according to my interpretation, is essentially something free and undefeated: the whole point of morality is its independence."(Discussions at Tusculum V) Cicero went on to declare that "good men are always happy...if they stop being enamored with physical strength, health, beauty, riches, honors and possessions." The temporal "virtues" must not try to replace the eternal virtues, for if that happens, man is seeking goodness in the wrong things and he will not find happiness there.

d) Plotinus in I.4, the Tractate on Happiness, in many ways says basically Plato's simple theme: Being like God is man's supreme goal, and happiness comes with imaging God. "Such a one will possess not merely the good, but the Supreme Good...in the realm of existents the Supreme Good can be no other than an authentic living, which is life in its absolute fullness, a life that has the necessary quality within itself, having possessed the good...the avenue to happiness is paved with goodness." In Boethius' struggles in prison, Lady Philosophy must remind him that as long as he is good and tries to imitate God, nothing can take away his happiness. "Since happiness is the absolute Good, it is clear that all good men are made happy by virtue of the very fact that they are good. But we agreed that happy men are God-like. Therefore this is the reward of the good, which no time can ravage, no man's power lessen, no man's wickedness obscure: they become God-like." (IV Prose III)

167a) Ficino after declaring that virtue was the quality of the soul that led man to bliss, then divided the virtues into the rational and the moral. The rational were those of reflection and meditation; wisdom, science--the study of natural laws, prudence or logical application of knowledge in conducting one's personal and social lives. The moral virtues were justice, courage, and temperance. These virtues led to goodness and goodness led to bliss. (A letter to Antonio Calderini)

Hegel in his *Phenomenology of the Spirit*, in the section "The Moral View of the World", basically elaborates on the idea that The Perfect Being bestows happiness to those seeking moral perfection, that is, those who actualize the souls as much as possible to that level of moral perfection. The three, as in Plato, are bound together: morality, happiness, and God.

Moritz Schlick (1882-1936) in his *Problems Of Ethics* stated:

b)

"...this means that virtue and happiness have the same causes, that they must go hand in hand. I am firmly convinced that experience clearly demonstrates this dependence. I have never been able to conceive how this can be denied, and am always astonished at the superficiality of the observations and arguments by which men seek to prove that happiness and morality have nothing to do with one another."14.1

That is a nice tribute to the Platonic Tradition by the Logical Positivist leader of the "Vienna Circle."

Moral being establishes character and only with character can one have a blissful identity that rides above everything else and affirms one's authentic being. If a man is moral, regardless of what happens in life, he still has a character of nobility, but those who identify themselves with the lesser virtues, like wealth, popularity, good looks and strength are prone to lose their own value when they lose the lesser virtues upon which they placed their value. Men of wealth have committed suicide after losing all their money. Great athletes who quit playing and are lost to the new generation of sports fans who used to nearly worship them previously, often lose all their identity. Glamorous actresses who have lost their beauty hide from public appearances. But the moral person always remains moral and in whatever condition in life, he is still authentic to those who honored him in the past, and his happiness is not diminished because it was always a child of his morality. For all Platonists, happiness is a strong and joyous pleasure of each of their mind-souls, which it enjoys from knowing that virtue reigns in their thoughts and lives, being reflected in the works of love that they render to their fellow humans. It is a consciousness of the beauty and purity of their soul and the awareness that people see a glimmer of the divine in their own lives. They can desire nothing better, their soul is blissfully full.

b)

II. GRATITUDE

An attached virtue to happiness is that of gratitude. The unthankful person is seldom a happy person. Ingratitude is a vice, not a virtue, and it is one vice that has plagued 20th Century mankind. Never before in history had man created so many benefits to relieve human suffering and physical work, yet the biggest and most destructive wars in history were fought because Europeans and Americans and Japanese wanted more and were willing to kill each other to see who could plunder the wealth of the weaker nations. Virtually every "Christian" nation was in on the greed of plundering others. Total ingratitude! And this plague of ingratitude seeped down from the leaders to the individuals of each of the participating nations: bigger cars, bigger houses, more pleasures and more entertainment, more wealth and more ego. Television commercials nourished such possessiveness and status symbols ruled the **c)** day. All of this was a symptom of ingratitude for the simple, the necessary and the pure. A man of ingratitude automatically disconnects himself from God because he spurns His gifts. Children picked up the greed element from their parents and wanted more, and an entire culture of grasping and ingratitude was born, paradoxically in the nations with the most wealth to begin with. People learned to cheat, to lie, and to deceive to "get ahead" in life, in school work, in their professions and in their businesses--all to get a little more. And the were unhappy.

d) "Plato, when he saw his death approaching, thanked the guiding providence and fortune of his life, first, that he was born a man [not an animal with less reason], and that he was born in Greece [where reason flourished] and not a barbarian or a brute [those without the Greek educational system], and finally that he happened to live in the same age as Socrates [who, Plato believed, was the most righteous and moral man of his era]." Those words are from Plutarch (14.2) except those explanatory words of mine that were bracketed.

The "Prince of Stoics", Epictetus, had a difficult life as a slave, for he was beaten by a master who was always out of control, and beaten so badly that he was basically crippled. Yet he survived in the arms of philosophy, his being a Platonized Stoicism. Still, he had difficulties with people who complained about the hardness of some things in life. These are his words and testimony of life that reflect his wonderful virtue of gratitude:

168a)

"For if we had understanding, ought we to do anything else both jointly and severally than to sing hymns and bless the deity, and to tell of his benefits? Ought we not when we are digging and ploughing and eating to sing this hymn to God?

'Great is God, who has given us such implements
with which we shall cultivate the earth:
Great is God who has given us hands,
the power of swallowing, a stomach,
imperceptible growth, and the power of breathing
while we sleep.'

This is what we ought to sing on every occasion, and to sing the greatest and most divine hymn for giving us the faculty of comprehending these things and using a proper way. Well then, since most of you have become blind [they can not see the blessings], ought there not to be some man to fill this office, and on behalf of all to sing the hymn to God? For what else can I do a lame old man, than sing hymns to God? If then I was **b)** a nightingale, I would do the part of a nightingale: if I were a swan, I would do like a swan. But now I am a rational creature, and I ought to praise God: this is my work; I do it, nor will I desert this post, so long as I am allowed to keep it ; and I exhort you to join in this same song."14.3

Just the basics, and even less since he was crippled, were the only desires and needs for Epictetus to break out in joyous song to God. How very much we can learn from him! He did not have physical freedom from slavery much of his life, and his beaten condition caused him much pain and sickness. But he always was content. "Have I not always approached **c)** Thee with a cheerful countenance, ready to do Thy commands and to obey Thy signals? Is it now Thy will that I should depart from the assemblage of men? I depart. I give Thee all thanks that Thou hast allowed me to join in this Thy assemblage of men and to see Thy work and to comprehend this Thy administration."14.4 Throughout all of his works this tone of gratitude for having experienced human history and been able to see the skies with such wonder and depth and the beauty of the earth. If only all humans could have spent some time with him!

O

OMIXPON

CHAPTER FIFTEEN
WOMEN

169a)

For almost all the world of antiquity women were the vessels through which men had children in order to create a family and even a small clan, sometimes it took two to five women, even for the poorer of men in order to do so because many women died in childbirth. Yes, there often was love, even romantic love. But in general getting a wife was a business transaction with the woman's father. In some cultures women were more highly prized than in others, especially if she were good looking, which indicates that romance was not completely absent in the eyes of men. But woman's greatest fear was not that she wasn't beautiful, but that she might be barren--or bear only females. Plato was different, and probably was influenced by Euripides who, in his tragic plays, often showed respect and tenderness for the women in his era. Perhaps it was his mother, Perictione, or his sister, Potone, who married Speusippus who followed him as head of the Academy, that planted the concept in his mind that women were just as capable of thought and reason as men. Or perhaps it was because Aristippus, a Sophist who was about 20 years older than Plato and was drawn to Athens to be a student of Socrates, for **b)** he had a daughter name Arete (αρητη) which means virtue or excellence. This daughter he educated into philosophy and she herself had become a Sophist and drew students to her, including Anniceris, who was the person who ransomed Plato from the slave block. That, undoubtedly, impressed Plato. At any rate, women were welcome to his Academy, if they knew their mathematics, and two of them became "permanent" students, maybe not like Aristotle who stayed at the Academy for 20 years, but still they were listed among his official historical 22 students: Lastheneis and Axiothea (worthy goddess). But I know of no other permanently established school like Plato's who welcomed women. However, it should be mentioned, the Pythagoreans listed 17 female philosophers among them historically of about 300 male philosophers. But they did not have an contiuously established school similar to Plato's Academy in Athens.

c) Evidence of Plato's acceptance of women's capabilities, in his ideal city, the Republic, he recommended that the decision makers, the guardians (phylakes), be evenly numbered between the men and the women and also the priesthood was to have even numbers of both sexes. This was far beyond the reality and thinking of any ancient culture, and is still beyond the thinking of even the most liberal of traditional governments and traditional churches. The Christian Church of Rome has more than one billion people, and women are still not welcome in the priesthood. In the Protestant churches there has been many breakthroughs, but men seem to be preferred by far too many parishes. States have had female leaders, Elizabeth and Victoria and recently Thatcher, and even now Germany with Angela Merkel, but the Houses of Lords and Commons and the Congress of the United States still have a long way to go to have an even numbered men and women count. Plato still has much to teach us in the governing of the modern states, and even more to teach us about an honorable respect for the mind of women.

d) Plato judged people by virtue and by rationality only: sexual gender, race, wealth, and comeliness were all accidental to man's being, and had no relationship with the true substance of man's goodness or function in human society. There are good people and there are wise people, and it is to the good and wise ones that the leadership of humanity should be given. Therefore, all people should be treated impartially as to sexual gender, racial status, wealth, and looks in the search for the truly good, wise, and excellent who are to lead the others. Here, again, Plato is far beyond his contemporaries and the rest of mankind by two thousand years and more. From the dialogue in the Republic is the following.

170a)

"Then, if women are to have the same duties as men, they must have the same nurture and education? Yes. The education which was assigned to the men was music and gymnastics. Yes. Then women must be taught music and gymnastics and also the art of war, which they must practice like the men? This is the inference."(Republic V 452a)

Each is to be treated according to his/her natural talent and its appropriate function.

"...that a physician and one who is in mind a physician may be said to have the same nature. True. Whereas the physician and the carpenter have different natures? Certainly. And if, I said, the male and the female sex appear to differ in their fitness or any art of pursuit, we should say that such pursuit or art ought to be assigned to one or the other of them" (Republic V 454c)

b)

"Then are we to impose all our enactments on men and none of them on women? That would never do. One woman has a gift of healing, another not; one is a musician, and another has no music in her nature? Very true. And one woman has a turn for gymnastics and military exercises, and another is unwarlike and hates gymnastics? Certainly. And one woman is a philosopher, and another is an enemy of philosophy; one has spirit, and another is without spirit? That is also true. Then one woman will have the temper of a guardian, and another not. Was not the selection of the male guardians determined by differences of this sort:? Yes. Men and women alike possess the qualities which make a guardian; they differ only in their comparative strength or weakness [i.e. physical strength or weakness]. Obviously."(Republic V 455c-456b).

c) Unfortunately Aristotle, his student of twenty years, simply could not get it, and his words plagued women in the West almost as much as Christianity did. Let us hear some of those non-platonic words that to us today seem quite insulting to us. Aristotle said:

"...That is why her pallor and the absence of prominent blood-vessels is always most conspicuous, and the deficient development of her body compared with a man's is obvious."(727a 20-25)

"Now a boy is like a woman in form and the woman is as it were an impotent male, for it is through a certain incapacity that the female is

female, being incapable of concocting the nutriment in its last stage into semen owing to the coldness of her nature." (728a 16-22)
d)
"For females are weaker and colder in nature and we must look upon the female character as being a sort of natural deficiency. Accordingly while it is within the mother it develops slowly because of its coldness,...but after birth it quickly arrives at maturity and old age on account of its weakness, for all inferior things come sooner to their perfection" (774a 10-20) [Contrary to our own age, females died younger from household overwork and multiple child births]

171a) In the following passages he rejects Plato's doctrine (using Socrates as a spokesman for Plato) that women are men's equal in the virtues:

"Clearly, then, excellence of character belongs to all of them; but the temperance of a man and of a woman, or the courage and justice of a man and of a woman, are not, as Socrates maintained, the same; the courage of a man is shown in commanding, of a woman in obeying." (1260a 18-22)

"All classes must be deemed to have their special attributes: as the poet says of women,

'Silence is a woman's glory.'

But this is not equally the glory of man." (1260a 28-32)
b)
Sparta, which Plato admired, partly because of the freedom given women, is seen as a city in decay by Aristotle, for it gives women too much freedom.

"Again, the license of the Lacedaemonian women defeats the intention of the Spartan constitution, and is adverse to the happiness of the state...in those states in which the condition of the women is bad [that is that they have too much control over their own lives], half the city may be regarded as having no laws. And that is what has actually happened at Sparta; the legislator wanted to make the whole state hardy, and he has carried out his intention in the case of the men, but he has neglected the women, who live in every sort of intemperance and luxury. The consequence is that in such a state wealth is too highly valued, especially if the citizens fall under the dominion of their wives."

c) Of course there was little luxury in Sparta and Aristotle exaggerates their "easy" lives, for the Spartan women were trained in gymnastics more than any other Greek state. In fact the women of Sparta were the first women to win victories in the equestrian events at Olympia, not against other women, but against the men.They did not lie around in luxury. Also women were not generally allowed at the Olympic games as spectators, for the men competed in the nude. But the Spartans let their women come to the games. For the Spartan women actually had a much better understanding of physical competition and excellence than the other cities of Greece. Because the Spartans also permitted women to receive a part of a family's inheritance as their own possession, to one male-only man like Aritstotle it seemed horrifying that women should be in control of so much of the finances of the city. "And nearly two-fifths of the whole country are held by women; this is owing to the number of heiresses and to the large dowries which are customary."(1270a 21-25). For Aristotle, women, like slaves and children, are to be under the control of men. The Christian Church loved his advice and implemented it. Plato made the adult men and women equal in his *Republic* and also had no slaves. The Christian Church for nearly two thousand years subjected women to men and for eighteen hundred years sponsored slavery. They were Aristotelians in their practical theology.

d) Plutarch reacted strongly against Aristotelian views about women, he proudly affirmed: "To declare that women have no share in excellence is therefore an absurdity. What need to speak of their prudence and understanding or even of their faith and justice, when so many of them have manifested courage and fortitude and greatness of spirit?" (On Love 23-24). In a letter to one Eurydice, called "Marriage Council", Plutarch comforted her about her marriage. Eurydice was not a wealthy woman and had no wealth, no pearls, and no foreign silks to offer, and Plutarch let her know that with her education and knowledge of the arts, culture and philosophy she was a tremendous cause for joy for her husband. He reminded her of the other wise women that history had honored: Aglaonice who could predict eclipses; Theano, Cleobulina, Timoclea, Claudia and Cornelia the daughter of Scipio--all who were cultured, knowledgeable, and famous and gave so much to their husbands and fathers, without being rich. He even mentions Sappho who ridiculed a pompous wealthy women of her own day as one who would die and be buried and no one would remember her, but that her (Sappho's) own poems would give her life in the distant future, and she would be the one remembered and honored.

172a) Plutarch also wrote an essay called *The Banquet of the Seven Wise Men*, a fictitious writing, but one of interest in as much as he mentions a daughter of one of the wise men, Cleobulus, who was named Cleobulina, after her father who greeted the others to the banquet. One did not know her and the following conversation took place:

"When I was curious to inquire who this lady was, he said. 'Do you not yet know the wise and famous Eumetis? For so her father calls her, though others call her after her father's name Cleobulina. Doubtless, said Niloxenus, they call her by this name to commend her judgment and wit, and her reach into the more abstruse and recondite part of learning; for I have myself in Egypt seen and read some problems first started and discussed by her. Not so, said Thales, for she plays with these as with cockal-bones, and deals boldly with all she meets; she is a person of an admirable understanding, of a shrewd capacious mind, of a very obliging conversation, and one that prevails upon her father to govern his subjects with the greatest mildness. How democratic she is appears, said Niloxenus, plainly to any that observes her simple innocent garb. But pray, continues he, wherefore is it that she shows such affection to Anacharsis? Because, replied Thales, he is a termperate and learned men, who fully and freely makes known to her those mysterious ways of dieting and physicing the sick which are now in use among the Scythians; and I doubt not she now coaxes and courts the old gentlemen at the rate you see, taking this opportunity to discourse with him and learn something of him."

b)

How different this is from Aristotle, and how like it is to Plato. Of course, since Plutarch is a strong Platonist, this is to be expected. Still it is delightful to see a woman portrayed at a man's banquet, one that takes place fictionally, but of the Seven Wise Men of antiquity. She is there, she is honored by them, and she corners the older man who can teach her something of the dietary and medical practices of the Scythians (Russians today). If one remembers that the banquet "took place" in Alexandria, Egypt at her father's house, then her desire to hear what medical knowledge she could gain by learning about the Scythians, only indicates a great avaricious appetite for knowledge, a lover of wisdom, a philosopher. Plutarch must oppose Aristotle, which he does in his *Life of Lycurgus*: "For Aristotle is wrong in saying, that, after he had tried all ways to reduce women to more modesty and sobriety, he was at last forced to leave them as they were." What a relief for the women to get rid of Aristotle, who tried to run their lives according to his idea that they were deficient humans who were to be treated intellectually like "slaves and children." Too bad Aristotle was not around when the Romans made slaves of the Greeks, for he despised slaves simply because they had been conquered in war and were forced into slavery. To Aristotle, slavery was part of the natural order claiming that Syrians, Jews and Egyptians were born slaves and slavery was their natural role. What a difference between the Master, Plato, and his student Aristotle. Plato simply thought much deeper and with a profound sense of spiritual and moral beauty.

c) Diogenes Laertius claimed that Pythagoras' wife, Theano, was literate and wrote some things. She also, according to Laertius, seemed to be quick witted when it was necessary. He related: "Further, a story is told that being asked how many days it was before a woman becomes pure [i.e. clean enough for sexual intercourse again] after intercourse, she replied, 'With her own husband at once, with another man never.'"

In general the Greeks themselves in their myths gave women many roles: goddesses and muses. In fact all 9 muses were female goddesses. They were representative of the spirit behind the arts and as a result English gets the words museum and music from them. Their names were Cleio, Euterpe, Thaleia, Melpomene, Terpsichore, Erato, Polyhymnia, Urania, and Calliope. But Pausanias refers also to Melete, Mneme, and Aoede. Also there were the females goddesses such as Hera, Athena, and Aphrodite. The Graces were also female personifications of **d)** beauty and grace. The heavens were filled with the female element, whereas in the Abrahamic based religions there is only one and it is male: and even the named angels are male. While Plato taught monotheism, and called God on occasion, Father, he also refers to non-sexual name such as Maker and First Cause, and ultimately said that God is the Good, beyond being as we know it: putting God beyond sexual gender. Therefore he could accept the "lower gods" as being the children of the Good and being of both genders. For the priesthood and the guardians then, earth was to imitate heaven and have both males and females in equal number administering the material and spiritual life to humans.

173a) Eunapius, in his Lives of the Philosophers speaks of one "renowned" Eustathius who married a woman by the name of Sosipatra, "who by her surpassing wisdom made her own husband seem inferior and insignificant". Sosipatra was renowned herself even as a youth who was quite precocious and Eunapius says of her: "Now beyond dispute Eustathius of all living men was alone worthy to wed her." After Eustathius died, she returned to her native city of Pergamon and set up a chair of philosophy in her own home, rivaling the school of Aedesius. Besides this school at Pergamon there were other schools established and governed by women: Sappho, Andromeda, and Gorgo all had schools. But none of them compared to the great schools of Athens, like Plato's Academy or the School at Alexandria, although Hypatia became its head. It is noteworthy that the Platonists had no difficulty acknowledging the brilliance of women, even when it was superior to men of the same school. By mutual consensus Hypatia was leading Platonist of her era and taught in Alexandria, until murdered by the Christian monks, maybe even under the orders of Cyprian, bishop of Alexandria, for he certainly did not punish the monks for the atrocity which they committed, and it was well rumored that he was jealous of her wisdom and popularity. That tragic year was 415 CE, and one does not hear much about women in the Western Church again until the Renaissance, and the ones that are known hid themselves in mysticism. In Padua during the Renaissance women seemed to be well educated in the arts according to the work of Scardeonius. And here and there women slowly became part of the intellectual world again. But even as late as Luther many were wondering **b)** why he wanted to educate the girls and who would pay for it. He answered, "The Prince". By and large the destruction of Platonism by the Church diminished greatly the role of women and held them down for a thousand years. To read an "energized" account of this suppression, one can purchase the recent book by Uta Ranke-Heinemann *Eunuchs for the Kingdom of Heaven*, 1988 in German and 1990 in English. In Islam, the second largest "Abrahamic" religion, it was even worse. One Arab of the Twelfth Century by the name of Usamah wrote:

"The Franks are void of all zeal and jealousy. One of them may be walking along with his wife. He meets another man who takes the wife by the hand and steps aside to converse with her while the husband is standing on one side waiting for his wife to conclude the conversation. If she lingers too long for him, he leaves her alone with the conversant and goes away." But he admits that he based this idea on just one or two witnessed occasions. Image how bad it must have been in Islam, if one of their historians thought that women in Christianity in the West were too **c)** free? All the Abahamic religions with their "We alone are God's people"-- as all three must claim also to have had a very poor historical record in the way that women were kept out of the center of mental activities and the responsibilities of running the village, the city, the state, or of their nation. Not till 1900 CE did things start to change. Even Kant when talking about the beautiful morality and charms of women sounded like a modern educator when he hesitated to think that women could understand the deep principles of thought. He did his best in metaphysical and philosophical thought to be a Platonist, but he fell short, a mental defect in one sometimes called the Incarnation of Reason. But an Englishman by the name of John Stuart Mill had the spirit of courage, the true manliness, to confront the issue in his book *On the Subjection of Women.* In 1869 Mill stated these words:
d)
"The legal subordination of one sex to the other--is wrong in itself, and now one of the chief hindrances to human improvement; and that it ought to be replaced by a principle of perfect equality, admitting no power or privilege on the one side, nor disability on the other" (Ch.One)

He spoke of the difficulty of proposing something that was contrary to the universal opinion. "In every respect the burthen is hard on those who attack an almost universal opinion."(Ch.One)

"If people are mostly so little aware how completely during the greater part of the duration of our species, the law of force was the avowed rule of general conduct...Less than forty years ago, Englishmen might still by law hold human beings in bondage as saleable property: within the present century they might kidnap them and carry them off, and work them literally to death...was the law of civilised and Christian England within the memory of persons now living...for the motive was love of gain."(Ch.One)

174a)

"That Aristotle...that Greeks were of a free nature, the barbarian races of Thracians and Asiatic of a slave nature. But why need we go back to Aristotle? Did not the slave-owners of the Southern United States maintain the same doctrine, with all the fanaticism with which men cling to the theories that justify their passions and legitimate their personal interests?" (Ch.One)

"The independence of women seemed rather less unnatural to the Greeks than to other ancients, on account of the fabulous Amazons, and the partial example afforded by the Spartan women; who though no less subordinate by law than in other Greek states, were more free in fact, and being trained to bodily exercises in the same manner with men, gave ample proof that they were not naturally disqualified for them. There can be little doubt that Spartan experience suggested to Plato, among many other of his doctrines, that of the social and political equality of the two sexes." (Ch. One)

b)

"At present...the disabilities of women are the only case...in which laws and institutions take persons at their birth, and ordain that they shall never in all their lives be allowed to compete for certain things." (Ch. One)

Mill attacks "those who attempt to force women into marriage by closing all other doors against them". John Stuart Mill knew the difference between Aristotle and Plato, but the Christian Church refused, perhaps out of ignorance in some cases, to acknowledge that they preferred the philosopher who taught them that slavery and subjection of women were both natural and God-pleasing. America's "Bible Belt" consists of previous slave states and also those states that opposed the more recent equal rights for women amendment. In Chapter Five much of the Church's abuse of women was mentioned and will not be repeated here, **c)** but it was gruesome, horrible, and yes ungodly, from the Vatican, down through the inquisitors and to the Protestants likewise. They grabbed and enfolded with all piety their Papal Bulls and Bibles in their arms so that they would feel God's blessing upon their enforced slavery of men and the cruel control of women. They did the same things to justify their aggressive wars to control the weaker nations of the world.

Perhaps one of the reasons that George Fox and his followers, the Quakers, were so persecuted is that they had the courage to give women a higher status in their fellowship than the other traditional churches did. From Hans J. Hillebrand's *A Fellowship of Discontent* this statement is taken.

"When John Bunyan insisted--in line with a wide spread concensus--that women "are not the image and glory of God, as men are," George Fox asserted the contrary. Subsequently Margaret Fell, Mary Fisher, Mary Dyer, Elizabeth Hooton, and others became important figures in the story of the early Quakers...The several female Quaker martyrs show this quite succinctly. Twelve of the so-called 'Valiant Sixty' were women....Anne Knight, the writer of the first pamphlet on women's suffrage, was a Quaker, and this was surely more than coincidence."15.1

d)

Fox, like Socrates, listened to the spiritual daimon within him, and he did not betray it. The Church had no control over him because he did not need their sacraments, their creeds, their buildings, and, most of all, their inquisitions and witch and heresy hunts. He met God in his own way, and he let the infused Spirit control his life. He, whether he knew it or not, fell into the Platonic Tradition. As she joined Plato's Academy, let Axiothea (the Goddess is worthy) join us today in our religion, our work, our society, and in our homes. When men see a woman with the same mind-set that he would have upon seeing and acknowledging any other beautiful, rational, and equal being to himself, then, and only then, will the earth have good men. Tyrants are not good.

Π

ΠΙ

CHAPTER SIXTEEN
FRIENDSHIP

175a) Friendship among Greeks was a sacred relationship, one of love and intimacy. The very flexibility of the word friend philos (φιλος) and its cognates shows the breadth and depth of the concept. Philos is the word for friend, philia (φιλια) was friendship, philanthropia (φιλανθροπια) was philanthropy or loving kindness. But in addition, phileo (φιλεω) was both to be a friend and to kiss, for philema (φιλημα) was a kiss. To kiss someone indicated one's friendship with them. To betray another by a kiss would be the greatest of disloyalities, and that is what the three Synoptic Christian Gospels claim that Judas did to Jesus, thus casting him into an almost diabolic light.

b) Naturally such a concept as friendship would call for a dialogue to be written about it by Plato. In the Lysis, Socrates sees two boys playing and they claim to be friends, and Socrates, being Socrates, can not leave it alone at that. He asked them what they meant by being friends or friendship. To them it may not have meant more than that they hung around together to play knucklebones (a Greek game for children that the two boys happened to be playing when Socrates came upon them). Others, adults, came and the full setting was established for a discussion about friendship, but basically addressed to the two boys. In the course of the discussion one element of being a friend was to be useful for something. Playing knucklebones all their lives would not be the substance of a lasting friendship. Socrates asked the boys, "Will anyone, then, count us his friends, will anyone love us in those matters in which we are of no use?" They say, "No!" Socrates proceeds, "If, therefore, you acquire knowledge, my son, all men will be friendly to you, all men will be attached to you, for you will be useful and good. If not, you will have no friend in anyone, not even in your father or mother, or any of your own family." Knowledge, usefulness, and goodness become the ingredients of a man that would qualify for friendship. Those who do not know this, have no idea what is necessary in order to be a friend. For love is attracted to the good and useful, and each person must be so, for there is no friendship when only one of the two loves. For like are drawn towards like: a good and useful person is drawn to another who is good and useful. Socrates then talks about the proverb that "the beautiful is friendly", and explains that one can not have a beautiful soul if one is not good. Throughout Plato one will see the idea that beauty and **c)** goodness are twin sisters and are born together. One can not exist without the other, for he is talking about virtue and not about physical looks. Beauty and wisdom are loving and altruistic, but the ugly and ignorant are self-centered. No friendship can exist without knowledge (usefulness), loving kindness, and inner beauty and goodness. Playing knucklebones, watching a football game or going shopping together do not make a friendship regardless of how many times they take place with the same person. The boys, Lysis and Menexenus, and the old man, Socrates, have had a discussion of great value, but Socrates, as usual, leaves the concept open for future discussions "for we have not as of yet been able to discover what we mean by a friend." As in all Plato's early dialogues, it is left open-ended and non dogmatic as to what something, like friendship, is. But he lays out all the necessary ingredients that are necessary for the discussion, and in this he makes us think, and here he makes us think about what friendship is. One thing is clear: without knowledge, usefulness, inner beauty and moral goodness there will be no friendship possible. Only good people can be friends.

Cicero follows Plato very closely in his *Laelius: On Friendship*:

d)

"Friendship may be defined as...an identity which is strengthened by mutual goodwill and affection. With the single exception of wisdom, I am inclined to regard it as the greatest of all the gifts the gods have bestowed upon mankind. Some people, I know, give preference to riches, or good health, or power, or public honours. And many rank sensuous pleasure highest of all. But feelings of that kind are something which any animal can experience; and the other items in that list, too, are thoroughly transient and uncertain....Another school of thought believes that the supreme blessing is moral goodness; and this is the right view. Moreover, this is the quality to which friendship owes its entire origin and character. Without goodness, it cannot even exist."

"For goodwill is established by love, quite independently of any calculation of profit: and it is from love, amor (philia in Greek), that the word for friendship, amicitia (philia), is derived...When there is real friendship, no element of falsity or pretence can possibly enter into the matter. Friendship simply cannot help being genuine and sincere all through."

176a)

"What unites friends in the first place, Fannius and Scaevola, and what keeps them friends, is goodness of character."

It should not be a surprise that Cicero, a Roman, studied in Athens. Seneca in his treatise *Tranquillity* also praised friendship:

"But nothing can equal the pleasures of faithful and congenial friendship. How good it is to have willing hearts as safe repositories for your every secret, whose privity you fear less than your own, whose conversation allays your anxiety, whose counsel promotes your plans, whose cheerfulness dissipates your gloom, whose very appearance give you joy! But we must choose friends who are, so far as possible, free from passions."

b)

Plutarch felt that in order to develop a diversity of character one should have, if possible, a diversity of friendships held together simply by a mutual moral bond of goodness. He felt that even the good man can be made happier with friends because it is a socialized goodness. Iamblichus' *Life of Pythagoras* presented the Pythagoreans as never rejecting a friend for misfortune or any imbecility which happens to human life. The only reason to reject a friend is his participation in vices. This is an acknowledgment that Plato's counsel was correct, that friendship is based on goodness and outside of goodness there can be no friendship. What Iamblichus, a Platonist, liked in addition about Pythagoras is that he extended his friendship to animals. He wanted for them a justice and the right of association that good men render to other good men. Diogenes Laertius in his life of Pythagoras stated that he was the first to say, "Friends have all things in common" and "Friendship is equality."

c) According to Philostratus in his *Lives of the Sophists*, the Emperor Marcus Aurelius, fearful that he had offended Herodes, assured him of his continued friendship and apologized for any harmful words on his part in the past. Philostratus declared: "Such was the apology of Marcus, of human loving kindness (φιλανθρωπος--philanthropos) and so firm." Even Emperors, if wise, do not want to lose friends.

According to Diogenes Laertius in his *Lives of Eminent Philosophers* (Aristippus 96) the philosopher Anniceris taught that friendship is in part based upon one's utility, but not entirely, for if a friend's ability fails, his friendship is still to be retained because of his goodness, and for the sake of his goodness, one will retain the friendship even if it costs something and causes some hardship. Laertius also related the story that Phaedo was captured and Socrates induced Alcibiades and Crito and some other friends to ransom him. Being ransomed was the beginning of his life of philosophy in the circle around Socrates.

d) When a young Pico della Mirandola entered the Florentine Academy well established under the leadership of Ficino, who was thirty years older, they disagreed on many things, including some important aspects of teaching, but it never harmed their friendship in any way. Their basic bond was the goodness of being and of soul, for they both looked to Platonism, Ficino much more so than Pico, but it was still a common basis for both of them.

The friendship of Goethe and Schiller are well known, but the intensity of it in Schiller's mind is often overlooked. One could say that the friendship, in Schiller's view, was the greatest experience in his life. He stated:

177a)

"If it were not that, to me, he is of greater worth as a human being than anyone I ever knew, I would be content with admiring his genius from afar. I may say that in all the six years that I have lived together with him I never had reason to doubt the integrity of his character for one moment. There is exalted truth and uprightness in his nature and the highest seriousness for what is right and good."16.1

Immanuel Kant had some words for those who have trouble finding friends. He pointed out that one must make himself lovable, for an unlovable and indecent person is in a dream world if he thinks he can attract another for a true friend. He stated:

b)

"Uprightness of disposition, sincerity, trust worthiness, conduct devoid of all falsehood and spite, and a sweet, cheerful and happy temper, these are the elements which make up the character of a perfect friend; and once we have made ourselves fit objects of friendship we may be sure that we shall find some one who will take a liking to us and choose us for a friend, and that on closer contact our friendship will grow and become more and more intimate."16.2

Be capable of friendship, and that means be of good quality, genuine and honest, able and helpful, kind and generous, and friendship will follow, and it will come with another who has the same qualities that are also capable of such friendship.

Finally, some thoughts of Emerson from his essay "Friendship":

c)

"Friendship, like the immortality of the soul, is too good to be believed

(but, of course, he believed in both).

"My friends have come to me unsought. The great God gave them to me. By oldest right, by the divine affinity of virtue with itself, I find them, or rather not I, but the Deity in me and in them derides and cancels the thick walls of individual character, relation, age, sex, circumstance, at which he usually connives, and now makes many one"

"Happy is the house that shelters a friend."

"A friend is a person with whom I may be sincere. Before him I may think aloud"

"He only is fit for this society [friendship] who is magnanimous; who is sure that greatness and goodness are always economy."

"The only reward of virtue is virtue; the only way to have a friend is to be one."

Emerson also, throughout the essay, stressed the elements for friendship were truth, sincerity and tenderness.

P

PO

CHAPTER SEVENTEEN
HUMAN INTIMACY

I. THE NATURAL SEXUALITY OF HUMANS

178a)

In no other area of human life has the Christian Church inflicted more harm, frustration and guilt. By limiting sex to marriage and only for the purpose of having children, while at the same time having to say penance for any possible enjoyment during any of the acts of sexuality, the Church attacked with such cruel despotism the most natural of physical pleasures that God had given men. In addition, to complete the total control of human sexuality, the Church made this necessary marriage to one man and one woman a sacrament and classified it as "holy matrimony", and, of course the Church had complete control of all of the "sacraments", basically declaring, not only is there no salvation outside of the Church, there is also no sex to be had outside the Church. The fear of hell or just the burning at the stake would suffice to enforce their narrow and arrogant despotism upon all of Western Society for more than a millennium and is still trying to shame people today who do **b)** not confine themselves to their dictates, whether made in snobbish self-righteousness, or for power, or just plain double standard hypocrisy. For hypocrisy see *Sex Lives of the Popes* by Nigel Cawthorne. In the earlier chapters of this book much of the Church abuse in sexual matters was discussed, but going into this chapter this brief reminder of the Church's cruel despotism has been appropriate. In the last century and a half, the yearning to be free from both Roman Catholic and Protestant Churches has come out in force by the thinking people of the West, and with it the liberation of women and slaves. Friedrich Nietzsche in his *Twilight of* the *Idols* (also named *How to Philosophise with a Hammer*) started out with the chapter entitled "Morality as Antinaturalness". He is embittered by the Church's attempt at "castrating" man's normal sexuality:

"The Church fights against passion with excision in every sense: its practice, its 'cure' is castration. It never asks, 'How to spiritualise, beautify, and deify a desire?'--it has, at all times, laid the emphasis of discipline upon extermination of sensuality...[the Church's} antinatural morality, on the other hand...directs itself straight against the instincts of life,--it condemns those instincts, sometimes secretly, at other times loudly and insolently...the saint in whom God finds his highest satisfaction is the ideal castrate...the wickedness of such a mutiny against life has become almost sacrosanct in Christian morality."

c)

Nietzsche continues stating that the Church's stated purpose was to improve man, but instead weakened him, and in this way it could control him. The Church has destroyed the most primal form of ecstasy, that of sexual excitement. He properly stated that the Greeks brought forth the greatness of civilization, but the Church has done the opposite.

"It is on that account that the Greeks are the leading event in the history of civilization: they knew, they did what was necessary; Christianity, which despised the body, has hitherto been the greatest misfortune for the human race."

How differently, from Christianity, did he feel about Goethe:

"Goethe,--no mere German event, but a European event, a grand attempt to surmount the eighteenth century, by a return to nature, by an ascension to the naturalness of the Renaissance, a kind of self-surmounting on the part of that century--He possessed its strongest instincts: its sentimentality, it honoring of nature, etc."

d)

Nietzsche completes his *Twilight of the Idols* with these words:

"It is only Christianity, with its resentment against life at the bottom, which has caused sexuality to be regarded as something impure: it cast dirt on the commencement, on the pre-requisite of our life."

In *The Antichrist*, Nietzsche claims: "The hatred of the intellect, pride, courage, freedom and the freedom of the intellect, is Christian: the hatred of the senses, of the delights of the senses, of all delight, is Christian."

Even those who respect Nietzsche often feel he is somewhat unfair to Christianity, yet what he said is not contrary to fact and the history of the Church in the West. Those facts were hard, and are still hard, for the dedicated Christian believer to swallow, but they are there, and one must honor his honesty and his courage. He was, unfortunately against all idealism that was metaphysical and he did not believe in the existence of God, and in those respects he also waged war on Platonism, and it is this, his determination to limit all men's goals and dreams to the earthly life of a material body in which he also is guilty of damaging the highest ideals of the minds, hearts, souls, and spirits of mankind. But the passages listed above that describe his anger are valid. Instead of the Church looking at and praising the beauty of intimacy and the joyous excitement of all sexual acts, it has put them in a cage and classified them as evil, and infused by indoctrination and threats such negativity towards the wonder and euphoria of the sensitiveness of the body. Human intimacy is a human right, and its personal action should be left to the individuals engaged in it to find its many aspects of joy and sensuality.

179a) In the Twentieth Century Wilhelm Reich also exploded against the "puritan" war against the physical pleasure of human intimacy. He wrote many things including two books that aim at and hit the subject with powerful words: *The Invasion of Compulsory Sex-Morality* and *The Murder of Christ*. Reich's very nature was one of independence: in his thoughts, his psychological views, his attitude towards sex and religion. As a result he moved from Austria to Germany, from Germany when Hilter came into power to Denmark, from Denmark to Sweden, from Sweden to Norway where he had a relatively calm period in his life and stayed there from 1934 to 1939, but then came to the United States where he was sentenced to two years in prison where he died shortly after at age 60. His life went from communism and after rejecting it, to psychoanalytic therapy to applying it to man's sexual nature. In both his communistic and sexual therapy age he attacked religion as being the problem to happiness, especially in the sexual realm. His views were often rejected by the authorities in both psychology and sexual therapy, but he did have followings and the repression of his works were totally uncalled for and so many untruths were spread about the man that he was truly a martyr. Before he was sentenced to prison his books were burned or impounded. It is to his concern about sexual freedom and enjoyment that is of interest for this chapter. From his book of 1931 The Invasion of Compulsory Sex-Morality some thoughts are taken and here presented.

b)

"The sexual misery in authoritarian, patriarchal society is a result of its intrinsic sexual negation and suppression which create sexual stasis, which in turn begets neuroses, perversions, and sexual crime."

He then refers to Malinowski's work among the Trobrianders and recommends that we ought to follow some of the primitive sexual policies of that tribe. He sees also a repression of women -- for the Church was an enemy of female gymnastics (1931) much like Islam today. He also complained about the tradition from many millennia back of the marriage gift ("Who gives this woman to be married to this man?" is a vestige of antiquity when women were commercially purchased to be wives). It was only about 10 years ago I read a report coming out of Africa that a man turned down the purchase of a woman for wife, stating, "No woman is worth four cows." Reich complains of this tradition of merchandising women and that it is still part of man's attitude towards them. He was against marriages established as the only way man or woman could have sexual intimacy. He ran into much conflict with the established Christian religion.

c)

"A sexual misery is a result of the compulsive regulation of genital life, we always come across it where considerations of compulsory monogamous marriage determine genital life."

In *The Murder of Christ*, he opens his Introduction with these words: "The social crisis we are living through is basically due to the inability of people in general to govern their own lives." He goes on to posit the existence of God in nature itself, and that nature gives to us the natural pleasures which are to be utilized and enjoyed. He brings together four elements that are necessary for our well being: God, nature, goodness, and sex and to attack the purity and joy of any of them is to commit blasphemy. He opens the First Chapter with "Man is born free; and everywhere he is in chains." Besides the Western Colonialization of people and suppressing them, Reich also lived through Hilter's Fascism and Stalin's Communism. Yes, he thought, "Man is born free, and everywhere he is in chains." If he escapes them, then religion subdues him. "Humanity has developed many kinds of religions. Every single kind of religion turned into another way of suppression and misery." Yet, he was somewhat optimistic: "It is possible to get out of the trap." He wants it possible that when two people become very good friends and desire the "genital embrace" they ought to be free to do so, without the State's approval or without the Church's approve. Let people express their affection for each other when they want to and how they want to. In **d)** this he is Platonic, and that freedom of the most intimate element of man's and woman's feelings can be effected without guilt and without hidden secrecy. But the Church preaches guilt and the State cries illegality and the friends who are not yet freed from either condemn them. This is the cause of neuroses in Reich's mind. To him human intimacy is the natural end and climax of a friendship, and it further binds the friendship because then each is fully known to the other. He claims: "Christ knew love in the body and women as he knew so many other things natural." To deny that is to deny the person of Christ in the body. Further it is "*The Murder of Christ*."

180a) Bertrand Russell, one of the Twentieth Century's great philosophers also had his complaints about Christianity's control over man's sexual life and his conscience. He wrote three books that spoke to the point: *Why I am not a Christian*, *Marriage and Morals*, and *Bertrand Russell Speaks His Mind.* In his Marriage and Morals, he recommends that boys and girls who are at the age of sexual frustration, but that can not wisely get married yet, such as university and graduate students, should be encouraged to have intimate relationships with their chosen mate:

"They would in this way be freed from the obsession of sex which at present greatly interferes with work. They would acquire that experience of the other sex which is desirable as a prelude to the serious partnership of a marriage with children. And they would be free to experience love without the concomitants of subterfuge, concealment, and dread of disease, which at present poison youthful adventures."17.1

b)

This was written in 1929, and today it has become a reality for many for the very reasons he gave. Yet at the time he was hated and condemned by the "moralists" of the day. In the 1920s in England they preferred to imprison unmarried mothers for life, which they did. In the Kansas City Star newspaper, May 22, 1972, an article appeared that announced the release from prison of three English women: Lucy Baker 74, Annie Kitson 66, and a third woman 68. Their crime had been to have a child out of wedlock. The third woman was 19 years old at the time of her "crime" of having a child without being married, and was imprisoned 49 years. Annie Kitson was 22, and was imprisoned 44 years. Lucy Baker was 26, and was in prison 48 years. "The three perfectly sane women were committed to a mental hospital as 'immoral mental defectives'." This was Christian England, Victorian and Puritan Christian England, who supported the conquering and destruction of freedom for the weaker countries of the world in order to make them colonies and drain them of **c)** all of their natural resources, and the Church of England never condemned one such "glorious victory." It was the same everywhere the "puritans" went, including Salem, Massachusetts. It did not matter that in England in the 1920 there were 2,000,000 more women than men. Better that two million women be forced into celibacy with no chance of human intimacy, than to be sane or kind or rational about it. Human intimacy is a right, a divine right, and Churches and Nations that take that away from their people are the cause of an unbelievable amount of suffering and neuroses.

In Plato's time, and it was never condemned at all by Plato, or his followers; there was a sexual liberty for men and some women, especially in Sparta. Plato liked the situation in Sparta, for he knew that any idealistic spiritual guide would have to be fair and just for both sexes. In his *Republic* the guardians were to have a type of group marriage in the sense that the changing of partners or the selection of couples for procreation was not a permanent and unbreakable arraignment. Platonists have in general been somewhat in a liberal stance sometimes resembling a traditional family but with freedoms for the individual in terms of human intimacy that far exceed anything else in the West. Of course, they were controlled by the Platonic virtues, wisdom, moderation, courage and honesty, and justice.

d) The recent death of Albert Ellis is the loss of a campaigner, for "Sex Without Guilt" written in 1958 and probably played a bigger role in the sexual revolution of the 1960s than most people realize. Here was a case where the ground root people demanded more sexual freedom for themselves. And it has been a blessing, for the world has changed since, but the Church still holds out for its "Holy Matrimony" a "Christ Instituted Sacrament of Salvation" controlled by the Church in order to control the lives, or at least the consciences, of the people. It's time for the liberal clergy to quit calling a child out of wedlock a "miracle baby" and simply call it the fruit of human intimacy. Of course, "miracle baby" was certainly of a more open mind than simply calling the child a bastard which is still prevalent in conservative minds. Bastard, of course, is a legitimate word, but it has very negative connotations and is a kind of expression of arrogant judgmentalism.

181a) The right of human intimacy was even taken away from the common cleric of the Church by the hierarchy. As early as 306 CE the bishops at the Synod of Elvira declared that celibacy was expected among the clergy. There was very little success of that declaration. Even the Papacy was open, for in 867 Adrian II who was married became the Pope. But the Church kept insisting that its clergy be celibate. It was the two Lateran Councils that marriage was definitely, without exception, outlawed, 1132 and 1139. But then the greatest hypocrisy took over as Popes and clergy disobeyed the rules constantly. For the Popes, again, I refer to Nigel Cawthorne's *Sex Lives of the Popes*. And for the clergy in general I refer to Henri Daniel-Rops who estimated that in Burgundy, during the 1400s, half of the children born "bastards", outside of marriage, were children of the priests. Today it is being revealed that the Roman Catholic clergy is still having trouble with their cruelly imposed "celibacy" upon them, and their parishioners are being betrayed and abused. The Church does not seem able to understand that God "sexed" mankind for a blessing, and that human intimacy is a natural and necessary right of all.

II. SEXUAL GENDER COMPLEXITIES

b) From the very first of literary history there are recordings of people who have not fallen into the strict male-female gender role. In Pliny's *Natural History* he speaks of the many people who are born different from the all-man and all-women gender. Under the section he called "Marvelous Births" he stated:

"Individuals are occasionally born who belong to both sexes, such persons we call by the name of hermaphrodites. They were formerly called Androgyni and were looked upon as monsters, but at the present day they are employed for sensual purposes."

The saddest thing about this was the reaction of the people, to call a man/women a monster was certainly a primitive reaction. To have documented it and categorized it for study and how the person progressed in life as an ordinary citizen would have been a Platonic reaction, but Pliny the Elder was certainly no Platonist.. A further tragedy is how he/she was later in history utilized, as a sex object. How could, under those circumstances, this person ever find an identity and have a social dignity? It was no problem for Plato, for in his Symposium, Aristophanes speaks of three sexes: male, female and hermaphrodites. Unfortunately, today there are still passions of hatred and judgmentalism towards those born in the inter-sex spectrum, who are simply trying to be **c)** good people and find their identity. Fortunately many now have the courage to tell society and in many cases the Church that they are not bothered by such bigotry. They, by faith, a modern faith, know that God loves the moral and good person who seeks his/her usefulness in society without regard to the way that the bigoted look upon them. The inter-sex spectrum is also in the mental framework of the person, even without physical signs so indicating. The poet Phaedrus in his fables, tries to explain this inter-sex group by saying that Promethius caused the inter-sex people. That is the purpose of a fable, to give a fictional account of something that science does not yet know. All Phaedrus knew was that nature had produced tribads (extraordinary lustful women) and effeminate males. They, to him, were different.

d) Sadly the 20th Century showed only a thin veneer of understanding toward people who were sexually attracted to their own sex, and good old England, Victorian England, as they had treated the three unwed mothers and numerous others also treated male homosexuals with the same vulgar and hateful attitude. Most people are aware of Oscar Wilde's (1856-1900) imprisonment for his sexual relationship with Lord Alfred Douglas, son of the Marquess of Queensbury. He was accused of having an "unnatural association". "Unnatural" probably meant that no child could be born of the activity, a hangover requirement for virtue that the Church sponsors and enforced for 1700 years or more.

Bertrand Russell in his *Marriage and Morals*, 1929, in his section "Taboo on Sex Knowledge", stated:

182a)

"Homosexuality between men, though not between women, is illegal in England...And yet every person who has taken the trouble to study the subject knows that this law is the effect of a barbarous and ignorant superstition, in favour of which no rational argument of any sort or kind can be advanced."

As usual, reason and science do not count, only emotion and superstition. What a way to treat one's citizens! Be unreasonable and superstitious and harm people and do it with a sense of self-righteousness. Benjamin Karpman, in his *The Sexual Offender and His Offenses*, 1954, made this observation, basically that it is the constitutional makeup of the individual that leads him toward homosexuality, and that it is not a perversion. He goes on to state that this "has been a matter of scientific and clinical knowledge for many years, but such knowledge has not affected the popular view which is guided more by unreasoning emotions than by rational thinking." 17.2 He continues in the next couple of pages with these angry words:

b)

"They, the persecutors of homosexuals, have inaugurated a witch-hunt which is reminiscent of Old Salem. Then, in ignorance of natural law and inspired by leaders of a sadistic and diabolical religion, the population hunted "witches"; now, in ignorance of natural and psychological law, and inspired by leaders whose motives are open to question, they propose to hunt the "perverts."

The homosexual population has no need of "salvation", it is a judgmental society that is in danger of losing its soul. Karchadourian and Lunde in their *Fundatmentals of Human Sexuality*, 1972, in speaking of the many who are born inter-sex, tell of all the operations and medications doctors gave to the child, without the parents' knowledge, and by the operations virtually determined the sex of the person born into the inter-sex spectrum. It was not until about the 1970s or1980s that the doctors came clean about the situation and consulted the parents who then made the decision to operate and choose a sex or to let the child go and make his/her own decision later. They speak of many situations: the hermaphroditus verus -- the true hermaphrodite; the triple X syndrome; the Klinefelter's syndrome --XXY; the Turner's syndrome XO, and the unnamed XYY syndrome. All of these have sexual variables that affect **c)** the individual. They speak further about bi-sexuals, homosexuals, and trans-sexuals as a chemical reality. Another enlightened book about the matter was put together by Carlfred Broderick and Jessie Bernard called *The Individual, Sex, and Society*, 1969, in which much of the above and more is presented.

Even above all these scientific presentations, a good person will allow another person to pick his or her own partner in human intimacy, and drop the self-righteous act or even worse quote something written about 2000 years ago by some of the most unscientific people in the Mediterranean World, the Tanak and the Christian Canon. The Greeks, by far the most scientific people of the Mediterranean World, accepted both male homosexuality and female homosexuality, although not all preferred it, but it was of the accepted culture of both the military and the **d)** many of the philosophers, we know that Socrates, despite being married and loving his small children, had his lovers, but was very self-controlled if tempted. Sappho's school for women taught the art of sexual intimacy and had her female students practice on each other. Sex to them was a wonderful pleasure and learning the art of it, was another way of seeking the wisdom to live the best life possible. Let each be free to choose, and let each rejoice when he sees another who has that romantic feeling and is fulfilled with the grace and goodness of sexual intimacy.

III. SEXUAL INTIMACY LIBERATED FROM THE "LEGAL MARRIAGE" OF THE STATE AND THE CANON LAWS OF THE CHURCH.

183a)

Marriage has been in the history of mankind an institution of many varied composites. There have been so many different forms of the union of man and woman that one can not say the "traditional marriage" and actually mean something, at least to an ancient historian. Because in the West the Abrahamic source of religion has been prominent, one first looks at the history of ancient Israel to see the distant foundation upon which the Western view of marriage was ultimately built. If one looks at the ancient Jewish Scriptures one can designate seven different forms of marriage that were practiced within the early Hebrew community: matriarchal marriage, patriarchal marriage, polygamy (in the form of polygyny), monogamy, exogamy, endogamy, and the Levirate marriage. And if one adds to those the variations of including concubines, maids, and slaves, one can see a very far different world than what seems today **b)** to be normal in the very Hebrew Scriptures, which are part of the Judeo-Christian Bible. Five of the focal figures in Ancient Israel: Abraham, Jacob, Moses, David, and Solomon were polygamous. Abraham had a wife, Sarah, and she had an Egyptian maid, and Abraham bore children by both of them. After Sarah died, Abraham took Keturah to be his wife and she bore him six male children (only males were counted). Abraham also had concubines, but their number and names are not mentioned. So he certainly had an extended family. Jacob had two wives Leah and Rachel, and showed favoritism towards Rachel, but Leah was more fertile, so Rachel asked Jacob to plant the seed of life in her maid Bildah, and Leah, not to be equaled, gave her maid Zilpah also to Jacob for child bearing: twelve boys and at least one girl, Dinah. Moses was known to have married Jethro's daughter, Zipporah, and the Cushite woman. David seemed much more desirous of women than his predecessors. He seemed to have wives everywhere: Michal, Abigail, Ahin'oam, Ma'acah, Haggith, Abital, Eglanh, and let 2 Samuel 5:13 suffice for the rest: "And David took more concubines and wives from Jerusalem, after he came from Hebron." Yet, in his self-centeredness he committed adultery with Bathsheba and had her husband murdered. His **c)** adultery was not having sex outside of his many marriages and concubines. The Jewish man was never bound to his wives sexually, but his adultery was that he had sexual intercourse with another man's wife. That was adultery. Adultery could happen only when a married woman or engaged woman participated in sex with one other than her husband or betrothed. The man was totally free, but he could not enter into another man's domain. The woman, on the other hand, was totally bound to her husband. The laws were very slanted against the woman. In fact, they were totally unjust. Look at Solomon, while the numbers are exaggerated and rounded off, yet 700 wives and 300 concubines, even though he was the king, still seemed far beyond reason and had no room for respect and affection with his wives on a truly personal basis. Even in Jesus' day Herod the Great had ten wives and eight of their names are known. Also we know the names of fifteen of his children. Those who base their marriage laws upon the Hebrew Scriptures tend to be more open to polygamy: the Mormon Church and Islam. Brigham Young was said to have had '19 sisters in the Lord", and Osamah Bin Laden's father had 20 wives and 50 children.

d) It does appear that the ancient Greeks practiced some polygamy, at least on a somewhat minor scale, but outside of marriage they were freed to be with other women who were not married, who were generally hetairai, who were professional entertainers and courtesans, who were freedwomen, foreigners, and often well educated slaves. Sappho's school trained them to be knowledgeable, artistic, entertaining and pleasant. Aspasia, a former hetaira, married Perikles and became a queen. The Greeks saw absolutely no problem with this, for she was honored. Greeks also had female slaves which were available for human intimacy. Little is known about Plato in regard to his acts of human intimacy. We know that he despised slavery and he would have never used someone against their will for his own pleasure. But Diogenes Laertius, who flourished 225-250 CE, about 600 years after Plato, said that he had two female lovers based on some inscriptions: Archeanassa and a Xanthippe. It is also possible that he had male lovers: Aster, Dion, and Alexis. But all of these lovers, both female and male, were those who probably shared a great affection with Plato; although Archeanassa, may have been favored, and is called directly his "mistress". We have no account of his being married or having children. He always felt the highest pleasures to be mental, yet it is almost certain that he shared in physical intimacy with the above named people. None of the Greeks felt sexual relations were anything but good, as long as man did not lose control of his passions and become addicted to such relations. Nothing too much! In the *Symposium* which speaks of love, many forms of sexual intimacy are discussed and none of them were disapproved. In the *Republic* the hetairai are to be excluded, but remember that the two groups who usually could afford them, the two higher classes, themselves would be living in an open-ended communal marriage and there would be absolutely no need of the hetairai.

184a) In Sparta the married woman were the queens of the household, and the men were not the kings. She ruled completely the household economy and control. If a man came home drunk, she had the right to lock him out for the night, or if he returned disgraced from battle, she could keep him out of the house until in some way he restored his dignity with a proof of his courage. When a man went to battle she gave him his shield and told him to come back with it or on it; which meant that if he fled battle and discarded his shield to flee faster he would not be welcomed back into the house. If he were killed in battle, he was carried back on it and she would honor him. When she decided to have a child, she would look at other men, and if she found one stronger and healthier, she would choose him to impregnate herself. As mentioned in Chapter 15, the Spartan woman, at the time of Aristotle, owned two-fifths of the city's wealth. Plato saw above all other Greek cities an equality of men and women in Sparta and upon it largely based his *Republic*. But, Sparta was extraordinary and few cities or states in past history followed them.

b) To look at the marriage contract itself, it will be well to look at a couple of extant marriage contract that have been found in Aramaic, one from 459 BCE and the other from 440 BCE. The first is titled "Mibtahiah's First Marriage" and is a Jewish document. It describes a house that the father has given to a man who has married his daughter, and the man is told to improve it and live in it with his new wife. The house is not to be sold, but is to be used as a residence for the two of them and their children that will be born of the marriage. If his daughter leaves the marriage the house her right to the house is forfeited. The house then falls into the hands of the children that they had during marriage. If he leaves her, because of the work he has done he will receive rights to one half of the house which will go to their children when he dies. There is also a provision for repossessing the man's part of the house for 10 "karshin" by royal weight, if living arraignments are not working out. The Temple or Synogogue or the government of

Elephantine have absolutely nothing to do with the "legality" of the marriage. It was a private prenuptial contract between the man and the daughter's father. Another contract, again with Mibtahiah, describes her third marriage. The man declares that she will be his wife forever, and pays 5 shekels of royal weight to purchase her. He promises that he will have no other children than by his wife, to assure that the inheritance goes to their children alone. But there are also provisions made for a divorce. Again the contract is a personal prenuptial one between the father of the bride and the man who seeks to purchase her.17.3

c) A marriage contract from 13 BCE appears to be a Greek one by the names indicated. The dowry is given to the man, and he pledges made not to ill-treat her or cast her out from his house. If he does he must return the dowry plus fifty percent more. The woman makes a pledge to stay at home unless given permission to leave "shall not absent herself from the house for a night or a day without the consent of Apollonius, nor dishonor nor injure their common home nor consort with another man." If she does any of the following she is cast out and forfeits her dowry. The man evidently can have other relationships, but he can not have another wife. Again: a private agreement in prenuptial form.17.4

d) The purpose in presenting to the reader the ancient documents of marriage is to show that marriage for the far greater period of man's history has been a personal thing, without any involvement by either the Church or the State. But both finally encroached upon this freedom of the individuals to try to control their most important decisions. The Church for power over them, and the State for various purposes. Actually the first State ordained marriage contract was not until 1580 CE in the Netherlands and it was to free the individuals from the power of the Church over "Holy Matrimony". Unfortunately, things turned out that now both of them try to control people's human intimacy and children. The State entangles many benefits for those "legally married" so that the State can control a couple's finances: Social Security benefits, discounts for children of married couples, inheritance benefits, alimony benefits which only encourages gold diggers of either sex looking for a good life-time settlement after a brief marriage. Divorce lawyers fighting with each other, and the divorces themselves become "wars of the roses". The purchasing of women was abominable in the past, and the present marriages are so mangled and controlled by the State and its legal system that it makes divorced couples poor and lawyers rich. In today's world it should be illegal for a father ever to sell his daughter, and any women from sixteen or maybe eighteen years of age should be able to make her **185a)** own prenuptial contracts. Of course, some family counseling courses should be included in high school classes, for knowledge is the basis of good decisions. People would be free to make any contract they want to and to incorporate any type of marriage they want to, and the Church and the State should leave them their freedom to do so. Likewise contracts should not even be necessary unless the marriage is seen as a business or for the procreation of children. Couples without contracts simply keep their own financial benefits separate and when they separate there will be no problems. If they both invest in a common material benefit, then it should be drawn up as any other partnership contract and notarized.

b) Pope Gregory issued many laws concerning marriage to Augustine of Canterbury and they became Church doctrine and, of course, came with the threat of hell: "Warn them of the terrible judgment of God lest their bodily desires incur the pains of eternal punishment." He also stipulated when the married couple could have sexual relations. And "lawful intercourse should be for the procreation of offspring, and not for mere pleasure; to obtain children, and not to satisfy lust." A half century later, Archbishop Theodore gave more Church decrees, one of them read:

"That lawful wedlock alone is permissible; incest is forbidden; and no man may leave his lawful wife except, as the gospel provides, for fornication. And if a man puts away his own wife who is joined to him in lawful marriage, he may not take another if he wishes to be a good Christian. He must either remain as he is, or else be reconciled to his wife."

c)

In some of this there are some valid limitations on man's freely discarding his wife. Why is there no warning against a woman abusing her powers? Simple. She had no authority or powers. The above are taken from Bede's *A History of the English Church and People*.

The Romans did not have a very good early history on how the man treated his wife or wives or children. He was totally omnipotent over them as was labeled a "Pater Familias". Things did get better gradually in Rome for the women, but even in Cato the Younger's days an attitude of ownership over the women was very strong. Cato was a very close friend of Quintus Hortensius who wanted to marry Cato's daughter, Porcia, but she was already married to Biblus. But Quintus, desirous of children then asked for Cato's own, second, wife who had had children and was still "fertile", and as Quintus, a "man of high repute and virtue" but without children, pleaded that a "woman in the prime of her youth should not lie useless, and lose the fruit of her womb." Cato then asked Marcia's (his wife) father if it would meet his approval to let Quintus breed with Marica, and upon consent of Marcia's father, Cato let **d)** Quintus mate with his wife, Marcia 17.5 Now there was nothing wrong with Marcia, since she was offered, to have a sexual relationship with someone other than her husband. What was wrong, was that she never seemed to have any say in it: all the decisions as to whom she would sleep with were made by men. That is the disease men suffered, acting as if they had ownership of "their" women. However well intentioned and charitably sharing such an act was by Cato, it was a brutal offense to the dignity of Marcia. Perhaps Marcia was even eager to do such a thing, but Plutarch never mentions that, and it should have been mentioned that she wanted to do it. The fact that it is not mentioned is probably because she did not have a say in the matter. From Plutarch's letters to his own wife, it seems most likely he himself would have never considered such a request, much less imposed it. Plutarch himself was strongly monogamus. Also, Porphyry's letter to his wife Marcella also shows the intimacy between them and his love of her learning and making of such a great wife. Marriage can be very flexible and very moral, but only if it is a marriage between good people who treat their mates as equals.

186a) The flexibility of human intimacies should be liberated from the laws of the Church and of the State and given into the hands and decisions of the people who are actually experiencing such relationships. In the 12th Century Andreas Capellanus in his *Rules of Courtly Love* included:

vii. No one should be deprived of love without the very best of reasons.

xxxi. Nothing forbids one woman being loved by two men or one man by two women.

He, of course, "retracted" his statement to "Walter" at the end of the book, for he did not want to be burned at the stake.

b) A masterful overview of the history of marriage and *The Future of Marriage* by Jessie Bernard gives the reader a comprehensive summary of all the variations available for human beings to share intimacy with one another. Also the various kinds of commitments that are available between people, public and private commitments, the function of the commitment, anti-establishment commitments, the duration of a commitment, costs and benefits of the commitments. She also gives a full overview of the diversity of relationships that are possible and have been used in human history; eleven by number. She states:

c)

"Almost every kind of relationship has occurred somewhere, sometime--monogamy, polygyny, polyandry, exogamy, endogamy, matrilocal residence, neolocal residence, arranged marriages, self-selection of mates, parental selection of mates, marriage for love, marriage for convenience...There is literally nothing about marriage that anyone can imagine that has not in fact taken place, whether prescribed, proscribed, or optional. All these variations seemed quite natural to those who lived with them. If any of them offends our "human nature," we have to remind ourselves that "human nature" as we know it this moment in our country is only one kind of human nature."17.6

And this list does not even cover other forms of marriage covered in her book. Bertrand Russell in his *Marriage and Morals* stated:

d)

"For my part, while I am quite convinced that companionate marriage would be a step in the right direction, and would do a great deal of good. I do not think it goes far enough. I think that all sex relations which do not involve children should be regarded as a purely private affair, and that if a man and a woman choose to live together without having children, that should be no one's business but their own."

And in his *Bertrand Russell Speaks His Mind*, he stated:

"I should like to say that if what you're doing does no harm to anybody there's no reason to condemn it. And you shouldn't condemn it merely because some ancient taboo has said that it is wrong. You should look into whether it does any harm or not, and that's the basis of sexual morality as of all other."

187a)

Julian Huxley in his *Knowledge, Morality, and Destiny* stated: "The relationship between love and marriage urgently needs reconsideration." Thomas Browne in his *Religio Medici* advocated the times and needs of the times should be considered: such as a great inequality of numbers between the sexes.

In conclusion to this section the rational and Platonic view of human intimacy is that, first of all, it is a human right for every one. Secondly, all people should be treated equally, all decisions voluntary and not coerced, and all forms of human intimacy permitted. Thirdly, keeping with basic honesty and morality, one should never break a trust or pledge to another person--it hurts and harms and is not acceptable to a good person. Therefore, pledges and oaths should not be taken or if taken, then one must know his capacities and intent in keeping them. Fourthly, If one wants an extended time for procreation and raising children, he or she must select very carefully and have a prenuptial legalized agreement. People inclined to dangerous drugs should never have children, unless such person has been clean for at least three years. Nothing is more harmful to children and society than mothers on drugs **b)** and the city streets filled with irresponsible and dead-beat dads. Likewise, because of the population explosion, no more than one child per person ought to be given life. Fifthly, good and fulfilling human intimacy does not depend upon approval by the State or the Church but upon the goodness and character of those sharing themselves with each other. Goodness makes one free and responsible. Human intimacy is a wonderful gift of God and should be fully enjoyed, and enjoyment is best between people who are good and care for each other. If people choose marriage, all forms of it can work, if the people themselves are good and capable. Yes, even monogamy. Many couples I know have been married 50 years and take great pleasure in each other and their children. But there are many paths to sexual intimacy and none should be condemned. The people themselves have the right to experience human intimacy in the way they choose.

Σ

ΣΙΓΜΑ

CHAPTER 18
THE ASCENT OF THE SOUL: FAITH, HOPE, LONGING AND MYSTICAL MEDITATION

I. FAITH, HOPE, AND LONGING

188a) From the writings of Plato himself, especially in the *Phaedrus* and the *Symposium* one can come to know his deeply felt and intense reaching out to the Eternal, the Good, and the Father and Maker of the cosmos. His entire philosophy is the drive towards that which is real, unchanging, and eternal as well as being pure, wondrous, beautiful, good and awe inspiring. All that is in its real and pure form finds its home in eternity and its meaning in being like God. More than any other man of his age he sought the beatific vision and life, becoming Godlike as much as possible that his soul might enjoy the love and friendship of God forever. It is that drive for the eternal that is the soul of Platonism and has given such power to the Platonic Tradition that has captivated and uplifted in its various forms all Western Spirituality since his death. He does not forsake the present life "in the cave", but uses his vision of the eternal to lead humanity to a blessed life here, and afterwards, to the eternal world of absolute bliss. For all the blessings of the earthly life he encouraged mankind to use numbers, higher mathematics, logic, and science to cultivate the laws of nature and life man to the highest peaks **b)** possible for his time in the material world experience: so that this life could imitate the absolutely real in as much as it is possible, and being as real as possible in this world of becoming, the world of constant change, mankind would be able to incarnate, as much as possible, the eternal forms of goodness and happiness, human harmony, and human advancement. Yes, he was an idealist, absolutely. For he could not conceive of wise men desiring anything less. For he believed that God instilled in man such a love for this absolute existence, both here and in eternity. That love, Eros, was a divinity within man that pushed him towards the Absolute Beautiful and Eternal, not letting him feel comfortable with any less blessing. Earlier the dialogue he presented in the *Symposium* between "Socrates" and "Diotima" was given in length, but here, as a reminder for this chapter I will give a much shortened adaptation of that dialogue.

c)

"When the love which is implanted into our soul seeks to behold Absolute Beauty, it starts its ascent upwards by acknowledging the beauties bound into this world's order, but perceiving that they are not the ultimate fulfillment, puts them to the side temporarily, and resumes its quest for Ultimate Goodness, and stepping upwards, one step by one, seeks that which is the Eternal Good and Absolute Beauty, knowing that what it has left behind will never fully satisfy it. When it finally meets Beauty itself, face to face, that Beauty that never decays or changes or fades, but gives it goodness to all reality, always and never wavering, then that soul knows it has become a Friend of God, beloved and uplifted by the Same to the vision of his eternal home."

d) Such is the faith and longing that Plato had and has encouraged the similar faith of men throughout history to let their souls also ascend in thought to the eternal, where they will receive the joy and power to enhance and beautify their present lives in a changing world in the great anticipation of being part of the eternal. Imitate the eternal and live that blissfulness now and here, as much as possible. Many men and women since have exclaimed the same deeply rooted faith and longing for the eternal in their lives, especially those who acknowledge the Platonic Tradition that has implanted itself into their thoughts and hopes in life. The person after Plato who absorbed this element in Plato most completely was Plotinus, and he will be presented at length in the next section of this chapter: Mystical Meditation. But, like Plato, it is very evident that Plotinus shared his intensity and longing for the Eternal. Some even called him the Second Coming of Plato.

189a) Augustine, who later became a bishop of the Christian Church, and a rather intolerant one at that, at first from the influence initially from Ambrose and then by his own reading of Plotinus, was a very tolerant and deeply spiritual person, as can be seen from this statement made in his famous "Confessions" (Book Seven):

"You [God] procured for me certain books of the Platonists, that had been translated from the Greek into Latin. In them I read, not indeed in these same words, but much the same thought, enforced by many varied arguments, that 'In the beginning was the Word [Logos in Greek, meaning Logic or Reason], and the Word was with God, and the Word was God. The same was in the beginning with God. All things were made by him, and without him nothing was made What was made in him, is life, and the life was the light of men. And the light shines in darkness, and the darkness did not comprehend it.'"

b)

One can see how the Christians made of Logos, Reason, into a personified being who became incarnate in the person of Jesus, who then later was seen as an eternal person with God and also, eventually, the Holy Spirit also became personified as a being, and the "Holy Trinity" was born. But the Platonists when they used the terms always used them as virtues or natural features of the One God. Word was with God in the creation only meant to them that God used reason and logic in making the universe and without them he made nothing. As to the "incarnation of logos" among the Platonists, it simply meant that God had given every man the gift of numbers, or reason, or logic and that was the "divinity" in him: a divinity because it was a most godlike virtue. For at the very top of God's qualities is that He is a God who has intellect and reason, and to imitate Him man is to use that "divinity" within himself, if he reasons as best as he can, then he himself would imitate God's goodness as much as possible. Augustine, being Christian, thought that this was a "prolegomena" or a type of prophecy of the coming of Jesus, whose incarnation he did not find among the Platonic writings. As Christians distorted the teachings of the Hebrew Prophets to find Jesus "prophesied" so also they distorted the Platonic writings as well to come up with the doctrine of the "Holy Trinity". The personification of Greek virtues was a way in which Plato lowered the traditional Greek Gods to become lower gods, but the personification of these virtues moved those virtues in the opposite direction towards deification: both Philo of Alexandria and the author the Gospel called the Gospel of John were the great influential propagators of this and in Christianity it ultimately deified Jesus of Nazareth into a person of the illogical three-in-one God, after a period of two-in-one God, with the "Holy Spirit" being added later.

c) But in other ways the younger Augustine was truly more Platonist than Christian. Philip Schaff listed the following works of younger Augustine that are purely Platonic, not yet infected with the foreign element of the developing Christian doctrines.

Contra Academicos libri tres (386 CE) - against skepticism
De Vita Beata (386) - perfect knowledge of God gives true happiness
De Ordine (386) - evil and the divine order of the world
Soliloquia (387) - a discourse with his soul about God, the highest good, knowledge of truth, and immortality
De Immortalitate animae (387) - about the immortality of the soul
De Quantitate Animae (387) - thoughts about the soul
De Musica Libri (387-389) - about music
De Magistro (389) - about the importance of the "Word" of God
De Anima et Eius Origine (419) - the origin of the soul

d)
They are all basically commentaries on Plato's teachings. Not listed by Schaff, but also an almost all Platonic work was his work *True Religion.*

Boethius was a proclaimed Christian, but he never set aside his Plato and maybe for that reason he was put into prison and executed by torture to death at the age of 44. But in his tragic punishment he produced a beautiful Platonic work called the *Consulation of Philosophy*, and in it Plato is called the son of Philosophy herself who now comes to rescue him from depression, while Christianity and its doctrines are never mentioned. Lady Philosophy saw he had fallen away from the wisdom of Plato and came to restore him to faith and the longing for the Eternal which he had forgotten.

190a) The works of the *Pseudo-Dionysius,* even though he often referred to and quoted the Judeo-Christian Bible, was well nourished on Platonic and Neoplatonic theology, including the most beautiful passages. He, as Plotinus before him wrote about the God who is absolute Beauty Itself. His words seem as if they were copied directly from Plotinus, but in the year 500 CE it was best not to mention the fact that you were quoting a pagan when the "Holy Scriptures", which "contained all spiritual truth" was available to you. Nevertheless, Plato was quoted, despite his being condemned as a pagan. The One, The Good, The Beautiful, Plato's God was also the God of the author of the *Pseudo-Dionysius*.In his work called *The Names*, he tells of the man who is illuminated from above and is drawn to praise and love The Good. He is also called The Beautiful, Beauty, Love, and The Beloved. "Beauty draws all things to itself"... "From this Beauty comes the existence of everything, each exhibiting its own way of beauty. For Beauty is the cause of harmony, of sympathy, or community. Beauty unites all things and is the source of all things."... "This--the One, The Good, The Beautiful--is in its uniqueness the Cause of the multitudes of the good and the beautiful"... "To put the matter briefly, all being drives from, exists in, and is returned toward The Beautiful and The Good."... "Each bestirs itself and all are stirred to do and to will whatever it is they do and will because of the longing for The Beautiful and The Good...The divine longing is good seeking good for the sake of The Good."(701c-708b).

b) And thus the beauty of Platonic thought is plundered and taken captive by the Church before placing him in hell, because he was neither Jew nor Christian. Speak of arrogance, ingratitude and judgmentalism! The Church perfected these attitudes.

Cicero, who studied at the Academy, reflects his Platonic feelings in his *Old Age and Death* in not seeing death as termination, but rather a journey away from the smallness of his earthly surrounding to a divine assembly of parted spirits. For this world was not designed as a permanent abode for him, and leaving it is like leaving an inn and going out to a greater scene. For he will see Cato again, a beloved friend whom he had buried, for he believes Cato in his present happy mansions awaits him. Cato himself had read Plato's *Phaedo* before his sentenced suicide by Caesar. That *Phaedo* is obviously recognized by Cicero for it also teaches that man goes directly after death to the company of the good and wise Gods, and the company of also the good and wise men. Thus Plato's Phaedo, comforted Cato before death and then comforted his close friend when he wrote and expressed his views about death.

c) Martin Luther loved the *Theologia Germanica* by an unknown author, probably written in the century before Luther. It was a form of

Platonism christianized, but, probably for safety, the author did not come forth to claim the work. Yet its rich and beautiful words were celebrated by Luther who then popularized it. Strange again, that a devoted Christian could unknowingly praise Platonic thought without even considering it a possibility that Plato himself would be present with the Christian saints before God, but would be in hell suffering. Nevertheless, in Chapter Ten there are these thoughts from the Platonic Tradition.

d)

"Therefore they renounce all desire and choice, and commit and commend themselves and all things to the Eternal Goodness; that is, to come to a clearer knowledge, and warmer love, and more comfortable assurance...So that every enlightened man could say: 'I would fain be to the Eternal Goodness, what His own hand is to a man.' And he...longs...And such men know well that this desire is not of man, but of the Eternal Goodness...seeing that it belongs to the Eternal Goodness only...that the Eternal Goodness is ever most graciously guiding and drawings us."

Ficino of Florence was in the same depth of immersion into Plato as was Plutarch and Plotinus, and his longing for the eternal Goodness and Beauty was constantly presented in his works. In the first paragraph of his massive work on *Platonic Theology* he stated:

191a)

"I pray that as celestial souls longing with desire for our celestial home we may loosen ourselves from our terrestrial bonds; as quickly as possible, so that, uplifted on Platonic wings and with God as our leader, we may fly unhindered to our ethereal abode, where the excellence of our generated nature will be happily seen."

He continues to encourage the souls who long for The Good to ascend strongly to it, leaving behind in thought the matter they so easily see and experience, then the animate physical life of the body, to the intellect of the mind of reason, on to the Good Itself. For it is to the very Principle Being that we long to see and imitate, for all things about us are in their own ways pointing us in that direction: where there is unity, truth, and goodness. For Plato tried to lead his listeners and students to this one principle of all things, which is The One, The True, and The Good, God himself.

In a written prayer Ficino prayed:

b)

"O Eternal fount of all that is good, we thirst for You everywhere. And so our thirst is not quenched by this good or that good, or by both together, if we really see that goodness itself is above them both. And may You, our God, may You alone quench this burning thirst... O best Father... By your gift may we one day share Your Bliss...most tender Father, have pity upon your children...You alone can satisfy our mind and heart by your pure truth and goodness."18.1

John Tauler in his *Sermon for the Second Sunday after the Epiphany* about 1350 CE expressed the Platonic longing in the following words:

c)

"When the Holy Ghost enters a soul, that soul feels a fire of love; indeed, a very conflagration of love burns in that soul, causing a fiery thirst after God; that is to say, an interior longing to possess Him. And it often happens that such a soul is mystified and cannot account for its condition, knowing only that it suffers interior emptiness and anguish, and that it loathes all created things."18.2

The slight variations from Platonism are that the Holy Ghost is substituted for the Daimon Eros and that the loathing of all created things is substituted for Plato's putting all material things secondary. It is evident that all the deeply spiritual teachings of Christianity are borrowed from Platonism and often twisted and corrupted thereby to fit into Church doctrine. Yet, here in John Tauler, and virtually all Christian mystics, the base of longing for assimilation to the Eternal God is from Platonic theology. This Platonized spiritual desire of God, the Beautiful, is clearly shown in *A Sonnet to Heavenly Beauty* by Joachim du Bellay who lived during the Renaissance:

d)

"If this our little life is but a day
In the Eternal--if the years in vain
Toil after hours that never come again--
If everything that has been must decay,
Why dreamest thou of joys that pass away,
My soul, that my sad body does restrain?

192a) Why of the moment's pleasure art thou fain?
Nay, thou hast wings--nay, seek another stay.

There is the joy whereto each soul aspires,
And there the rest that all the world desires,
And there is love, and peace, and gracious mirth;
And there in the most highest heavens shalt thou
Behold the Very Beauty, whereof now
Thou worshippest the shadow upon earth."

Thomas Browne in his *Religio Medici* feels that man must return, as his duty, a devout and learned admiration to God for his Beauty, the Beauty of the Cosmos, and also of all his creatures. Therefore, man must liberate his reason that it might search out the great beauty of all things.

"Search while thou wilt, and let thy Reason go,
To ransom Truth, even to th' Abyss below;
Rally the scattered Causes; and that line,
Which Nature twists, be able to untwine.
It is thy Makers will, for unto none
But unto Reason can He e'er be known.
b) ...
Give thou my reason that instructive fight,
Whose weary wings may on Thy hands still light.
Teach me to soar aloft, yet ever so
When neer the Sun, to stoop again below.
Thus shall my humble Feathers safely hover.
And, though near Earth, more than the Heavens discover.
And then at last, when homeward I shall drive,
Rich with the Spoils of Nature, to my Hive,
There will I sit like the industrious Flie,
Buzzing The Praises, which shall never die,
Till Death abrupts them, and succeeding Glory
Bid me go on in a more lasting story."18.3
c)
Rudolf Otto's great work *The Idea of the Holy* is read with much a reward given, and in it he refers to some words of frustration expressed by the Mystic Suso, whose following words he reprinted for his readers:

" Loving, tender Lord! My mind has from the days of my childhood sought something with an earnest thirst of longing, Lord, and what that is have I not yet perfectly apprehended. Lord, I have now for many a year been in hot pursuit of it, and never yet have I been able to succeed, for I know not aright what it is. And yet it is something that draws my heart and my soul after it, and without which I can never attain to full repose. Lord, I was fain in the earliest day of my childhood to seek it among created things, as I saw others before me do. And the more I sought, the less I found it; and the nearer I went, the further I wandered from it...Now my heart rages for it."18.4

d) Jeremy Taylor, a Cambridge Platonist, speaks reminiscent of Plato's dictum that one would not ever say something about God that one would be ashamed of saying about a good man--one of his critiques against Homer, when he stated in his *Holy Living*: "To believe nothing concerning God but what is honorable and excellent, knowing that belief is no honor to God if it entertains dishonorable thoughts about Him."18.5

In defining the word faith, Immanuel Kant wrote the following:

"We shall now take belief in the sense that, if we do our best, if we do what lies in our power, we may hope that God, in His wisdom and goodness, will make up our shortcomings. Faith, then, denotes trust in God that He will supply our deficiency in things beyond our power, provided we have done all within our power. Humility and modesty, combined with resignation, are the characteristics of such belief. The only demand it makes upon us is to do our duty to the best of our ability and for the rest to hope, without defining our hope more closely. This form of belief may be described as absolute, it is practical. Practical faith does not consist in saying: 'If only I trust implicitly in God He will do what I want'; but rather in saying; 'I will myself do all I can, and if I then leave myself in God's hands, He will strengthen my weaknesses and make up my shortcomings as He knows best.'"18.6

193a) Martin Luther, always somewhat inconsistent, but likewise penetrating of thought, declared this about faith, not the faith alone that stands by itself, but the living faith. "Lo, thus from faith flow forth love and joy in the Lord, and from love a joyful, willing and free mind that serves one's neighbor willingly and takes no account of gratitude or ingratitude, of praise or blame, of gain or loss." (*On Christian Liberty*).

George Santayana presents Platonism in the Italian poets of the Renaissance, and says this about Michael Angelo's poems:

"We find in Michael Angelo's poems a few recurring ideas, or rather the varied expression of a single half aesthetic, half religious creed. The soul, he tells us in effect, is by nature made for God and for the enjoyment of divine beauty. All true beauty leads to the idea of perfection; the effort toward perfection is the burden of all art, which labours, therefore, with a superhuman and insoluble problem. All love, also, that does not lead to the love of God and merge into that love, is a long and hopeless torment."18.7

b)

Santayana then quotes two of Michael Angelo's "in which the Platonic theory of beauty is clearly stated:"

"For faithful guide unto my labouring heart
Beauty was given me at birth,
To be my glass and lamp in either art.
Who thinketh otherwise misknows her worth,
For highest beauty only gives me light
To carve and paint aright.
Rash is the thought and vain
That maketh beauty from the senses grow.
She lifts to heaven hearts that truly know,
But eyes grown dim with pain
From mortal to immortal cannot go
Nor without grace of God look up again."

c)

And another of Angelo's poems:

"My love's life comes not from this heart of mine.
The love wherewith I love thee hath no heart,
Turned thither whither no fell thought incline
And erring human passion leaves no smart.
Love, from God's bosom when our souls did part,
Made me pure eye to see, thee light to shine,

And I must needs, half mortal thought thou art,
In spite of sorrow know thee all divine.
As heat in fire, so must eternity
In beauty dwell; through thee my soul's endeavour
Mounts to the pattern and the source of thee;
And having found all heaven in thine eyes,
Beneath thy brows my burning spirit flies
There where I loved thee first to dwell for ever."18.8

d)
This longing for the Eternal Beauty and the Eternal Good is found in all the Italian Renaissance poets, for Plato was the spiritual and artistic soul of that which was "reborn" in the Florentine Renaissance as well as the rest of Italy. Gabriel Marcel in *The Mystery of Being* has an entire chapter titled "The Need for Transcendence" for it is the innate longing and yearning for all: which he called "the urgent inner need for transcendence." In the conclusion of his work, Marcel gave a testimony of his own need for transcendence.

"The spirit of truth is nothing if it is not a light which is seeking for the light; intelligibility is nothing if it is not at once a coming together and the nuptial joy which is inseparable from this coming together. The more I tend to raise myself towards this Uncreated Light, without which I am left in the dark--which would mean that I have no being at all--the more I in some way advance in faith."

194a) Pierre Teilhard de Chardin, in his delightful *Hymn of the Universe*, stated:

"Yet in the very depths of this formless mass you have implanted--and this I am sure of, for I sense it--a desire, irresistible, hallowing, which makes us cry out, believer and unbeliever alike: 'Lord, make us one.'" ("The Offering")

And again he declared:

"Little by little, through the irresistible development of those yearnings you implanted in me as a child, through the influence of gifted friends who entered my life at certain moments to bring light and strength to my mind and through the awakenings of spirit I owe to the successive initiations, gentle and terrible, which you caused me to undergo: through all these I have been brought to the point where I can not longer see anything, nor any longer breathe, outside that milieu in which all is made one." ("Fire in the Earth")

b)

In the Islamic world the Platonized ones are the Sufis, who are saturated into Neoplatonistm. Rumi (*Birdwings*), warning that the more beautiful people on the path towards God are those in which each person is drawn by His love and beauty, and not by doctrines, stated:

"There are two types on the path.
Those who come against their will,
The blindly religious people,
And those who obey out of love.
The former have ulterior motives,
They want the midwife near,
Because she gives them milk.
The others love the beauty of the nurse.

The former memorize the proof texts of conformity,
And repeat them.
The latter disappear into whatever draws them to God."

c)

Thus there are two types upon the path, those who study doctrines and proofs of their positions and the other who are brought to God by being drawn to Him because of His Beauty, and by that Beauty seek to ennoble themselves by loving It.

Karl Jaspers in his *Way to Wisdom* speaks of faith as a direct feeling of experience with God, and that it has no need of doctrines, sacraments, or any other type of mediators. It is man or woman alone in the presence of God that authenticates their existence. He stated:

d)

"Hence the climax and goal of our life is the point at which we ascertain authentic reality, that is, God. This reality is accessible to existence through the orientation toward God that lies at its source. Hence faith in God, springing as it does from the source, resists any mediation. This faith is not laid down in any definite articles of faith applicable to all men or in any historical reality which mediates between man and God and is the same for all men. The individual, always in his own historicity, stands rather in an immediate, independent relation to God that requires no intermediary."18.9

He continued:

195a)

"If I meditate in these three forms--self-reflection, transcending meditation, contemplation of my task--and open myself to unlimited communication, an imponderable presence which can never be forced may come to me: the clarity of my love, the hidden always uncertain imperative of the godhead, the revelation of being--perhaps bringing with it peace of mind amid life's constant turmoil, a trust in the foundation of things despite the most terrible catastrophes."18.10

Concerning meditation, Thomas Merton in his *Spiritual Direction and Meditation* defined religious meditation this way:

"From the very start it must be made clear, however, that reflection here does not refer to a purely intellectual activity, and still less does it refer to mere reasoning. Reflection involves not only the mind but also the heart, and indeed our whole being. One who really meditates does not merely think, he also loves, and by his love--or at least by his sympathetic intuition into the reality upon which he reflects--he enters into that reality and knows it so to speak from within, by a kind of identification."18.11

He continued and ended the section on "What is Meditation:" with these words.

b)

"Let us never forget that the fruitful silence in which words lose their power and concepts escape our grasp is perhaps the perfection of meditation. We need not fear and become restless when we are no longer able to 'make acts.' Rather we should rejoice and rest in the luminous darkness of faith. This 'resting' is a higher way of prayer."

When any religion including Christianity is no longer based on the individual seeking and longing for his God, to love Him and adore Him and by that to be lifted up within his longings to experience the

Eternal and the Good, and thereby be warmed and made a living presence of the Eternal's love and virtue among his fellow man, then he is no longer a light in the darkness, but an emptiness of value, worth, goodness, and lost in a maze of the sheer temporal and material universe that by constant changes dies in all its forms, and being so attached to it man dies with it. That is faith only that longs for assimilation with the Eternal and the Good beyond Being. Without Platonic wings to carry a man's soul and hopes to the celestial realm, man is spiritually dead. He may confess doctrines, perform "sacred" rites, attend community worship services and even sing along with them, give money and be patriotic and still be spiritually dead. This decaying to death happens then to religions also: Aldous Huxley certainly felt that it happened to Christianity, which he condemned with the following words from his *The Prerennial Philosophy*:

c)

"In the past the nations of Christendom persecuted in the name of their faith, fought religious wars and undertook crusades against infidels and heretics; today they have ceased to be Christian in anything but name, and the only religion they profess is some brand of local idolatry, such as nationalism, state-worship, boss-worship and revolutionism. From these fruits of (among other things) historic Christianity, what inferences can we draw as the nature of the tree?...These wrong beliefs had one element in common--namely, an overvaluation of happenings in time and an under-valuation of the everlasting, timeless fact of eternity."18.12

If Christianity ever had a truly Platonic soul, then they lost it somewhere in history, most likely by 325 CE, and beyond question in 529 CE. Paul Tillich speaks of waiting in expectation within time for eternity in his Shaking of the Foundations:

"Our time is a time of waiting; waiting is its special destiny. And every time is a time of waiting, waiting for the breaking in of eternity. All time runs forward. All time, both in history and impersonal life, is expectation. Time itself is waiting, waiting not for another time, but for that which is eternal."18.13

d)

In this Tillich reflects Plato's two worlds: the world of becoming, the material creation in which time was born, and the world of being that is outside of time and in eternity. In our present state we are in a period or time of expectation, not of another time, but of the world of being which is eternal and beyond time. This waiting and expectation is faith and hope and longing. He reflects much the same thought with these word from his *Dynamics of Faith*:

"Human potentialities are powers that drive toward actualization. Man is driven toward faith by his awareness of the infinite to which he belongs, but which he does not own like a possession. This is in abstract terms what concretely appears as the 'restlessness of the heart' within the flux of life. The unconditional concern which is faith is the concern about the unconditional. The infinite passion, as faith has been described, is the pass for the infinite."18.14

II. MYSTICAL MEDITATION

196a) In the *Phaedrus,* Plato speaks of the beauties of the earth that stir the soul into a form of love that looks upon the visible and earthly beauties and finds his heart warmed with joy, but also upon a period of enjoyment finds an uneasiness in his soul that wants a higher beauty, beyond vision and unchangeable and eternal. For what they can see in the material world seem to be copies of something much more beautiful and permanent.

b)

"And they, when they behold here any image of that other world, are rapt in amazement; but they are ignorant of what this rapture means, because they do not clearly perceive. For there is no light of justice or temperance or any of the higher Ideas which are precious to souls in the earthly copies of them: they are seen through a glass dimly, and there are few who, going to the images, behold in them the realities, and these only with difficulty...But of beauty, I repeat again that we saw her there shining in company with the celestial forms; and coming to earth we find her here too, shining in clearness through the clearest aperture of sense. For sight is the most piercing of our bodily senses; though not by that is wisdom seen; her loveliness would have transporting if there had been a visible image of her, and the other idea is they had visible counterparts, would be wholly lovely. But this is the privilege of beauty, that being the loveliest, she is also the most palpable to sight"(250a-d)

Then Plato continued with the soul, after its first initiation in seeing earthly beauty, beginning to grow wings and it seeks to take flight to Beauty Itself, but it is not that easy. Then he compares the soul to a charioteer that has two steeds (wings) that must pull up the soul to the Eternal Beauty. For the soul seeks to, anthropomorphically speaking, "bath herself in the waters of beauty, have her constraint loosened, and be refreshed, and be released from all pangs and pains; to experience this **c)** sweetest of all pleasures, and understand why the soul of the lover will never forsake his Beautiful One, whom he esteems above all; and has forgotten mother, brothers and companions, and he thinks nothing of the neglect and loss of his property; the rules and proprieties of life, on which he formerly prided himself, he now despises, and is ready to sleep like a servant, wherever he is allowed, as near as he can to his Desired One, Who is the object of his worship."(251-252) This is the state of love for the Eternal, the Good, and Beauty Itself.

Plotinus' *Tractate 1.6 Beauty* is by far the best known of his and also the most beautiful. Yet in its essence it offers not much new, but extends and enhances Plato's concept of the longing of the soul for the Absolute Good and Beauty Itself. It likewise applies it to the self-improvement that is needed for beauty to be incorporated into the essence of the believer and to make a semblance of the like to like, beauty seeking Beauty Itself. It would be beneficial for those of the Platonic Tradition to make the reading of this tractate at least an annual event. Some of it is presented below:

d)

"And it is just to say that in the Soul's becoming a good and beautiful thing is in becoming like to God, for from the Divine comes all the beauty and all the good in being.....Therefore we must ascend towards the Good, the desired of every soul. Anyone that has seen This, knows what I intend when I say that it is beautiful. Even the desire of it is to be desired as a good. To attain it is for those that will take the upward path, who will set all their forces towards it, who will divest themselves of all that we have put on in our descent....Let us flee then to the beloved Fatherland...The Fatherland to us is there whence we have come, and there is The Father....And this inner vision, what is its operation?...Withdraw yourself and look. And if you do not find yourself beautiful yet, act as does the creator of a statue that is to be made beautiful; he cuts away here, he smoothes there, he makes this line lighter, this other purer, until a lovely face has grown upon his work. So do you also; cut away all that is excessive, straighten all that is crooked, bring light to all that is overcast, labor to make all one glow of beauty and never cease chiseling your statue, until there shall shine out on you from it the godlike splendour of virtue, until you shall see the perfect goodness surely established in the stainless shrine...and never can the Soul have vision of the First Beauty unless itself be beautiful. Therefore, first let each become godlike and each beautiful who cares to see God and Beauty...[Plotinus then describes the ascent towards Beauty Itself and, being draw up by The Good radiating beauty to it and how it finally reaches...] The realm of ideas which constitutes the Beauty of the Intellectual Sphere, and The Good, which lies beyond, is the Fountain and at the same time the Principle of Beauty: the Primal Good and the Primal Beauty have the one dwelling-place and, thus, always, Beauty's seat is there."

197a) So much of Plato is incorporated into this tractate: know yourself, an unexamined life is not worth living, work at your virtues in the process of the soul's beautification as a sculptor would when making a beautiful statue, imitation of the Ultimate Beauty, being attracted by Beauty Itself Who sends to those ascending visions of the radiating beauty he is seeking, the Good is always the Good, the Good is beyond being, and when one arrives he knows he has come home to his Father's land. There beyond Being, the Good dwells in eternity, and those who come to him come to know this to be their Eternal Fatherland for which they were made. Then the soul finds peace and fulfillment. All Western mystical meditation is founded in these thoughts. The element of self-improvement is important, and Meister Eckhart explained it this way:

b)

"The more he regards everything as divine--more divine than it is of itself--the more God will be pleased with him. To be sure, this requires effort and love, a careful cultivation of the spiritual life, and a watchful, honest, active oversight of all one's mental attitudes toward things and people. It is not to be learned by world-flight, running away from things, turning solitary and going apart from the world. Rather, one must learn an inner solitude, wherever or with whomsoever he may be. He must learn to penetrate things and find God there, to get a strong impression of God firmly fixed in his mind."18.15

This ascent of the soul to the Good and the Beautiful God takes place with the help of philosophy and logic and the Daimon Eros who compels the soul from within. But this, most beautiful spiritual experience of the soul of man does not need an organized religion, relics, creeds and dogmas; all that is necessary is to listen to the Daimon within and fix one's spiritual eyes upon Beauty Itself and the joy of the eternal blessing that awaits it. But one must be able to set aside the earthly passions and the desires of the body that, although blessings in themselves, they must not impede one's journey to the Ultimately Real and Eternal. The earthly beauties are good, but they are not ultimate, and are to be used as stepping stones that the soul can use on his journey to his Real Fatherland, the Eternal Home. The mystics of every religion have realized this truth and used such a path to find spiritual experiences that are not recognized as possible for those who have not taken the journey.

c) Evelyn Underhill in her comprehensive work *Mysticism*, stated:

"Mysticism, then, is not an opinion: it is not a philosophy. It has nothing in common with the pursuit of occult knowledge. On the one hand it is not merely the power of contemplating Eternity: on the other, it is not to be identified with any kind of religious queerness. It is the name of that organic process which involves the perfect consummation of the Love of God; the achievement here and now of the immortal heritage of man. Of, if you like it better--for this means exactly the same thing--it is the art of establishing his conscious relation with the Absolute. The movement of the mystic consciousness towards this consummation, is not merely the sudden admission to an overwhelming vision of Truth: though such dazzling glimpses may from time to time be vouchsafed to the soul. It is rather an ordered movement towards ever higher levels of reality, ever closer identification with the Infinite."18.16

d)

Underhill realized and put forth the truth that not all of mysticism is in a grand and extensive contemplative state, for she stated: "Not only the act of contemplation, the vision or state of consciousness in which the soul of the great mystic realizes God, but many humbler and dimmer experiences of prayer, in which the little human spirit truly feels the presence of the Divine Spirit and Love, must be included in it."18.17 For this also included the "one-sided" mystical Quakers, "who hold that all truth is revealed directly by the Inner Light of God in the soul, or the Quietists, who try to wait in a blank state of passivity for His message." Again Underhill reminds us that mysticism has been defined as "the science of the Love of God" and "the life which aims at union with God." The three stages of the mystic way are purgation (a cleansing of the earthly passions), illumination (either from within or without), and union (or assimilation to God) and these three were borrowed from Neoplatonism. Love and joyous intimacy of God are included in the final beatific vision in which the soul "meets" God, face to face. For those who are stiff in their faith in doctrines and creeds and are prone to judge the mystics of being out of step with "true religion", let them remember that among the mystics one does not find warriors, violence, witch or heresy hunts, hatred, greed, and human fraud. If it is true that one can judge the value of another's religion by the fruits of love, compassion, justice, all forms of human kindness, honesty, charity, and gentle human understanding of the fallen, then the mystics have no need to feel secondary to any body. The Hindu mystics speak of four sublime states: benevolence, compassion, sympathetic joy, and peace of mind. And Jami the Sufi, reflected the *Timaeus* of Plato when when he wrote:

198a)

"From all eternity the Beloved unveiled His beauty in the
        Solitude of the Unseen;
He held up the mirror to His own face,
        He displayed His loveliness to Himself.

...

...

Though He beheld His attributes and qualities as
        A perfect whole in His own essence,
Yet He desired that they should be displayed
        To Him in another mirror,
And that each of His eternal attributes should
        Become manifest accordingly in a diverse form.
Therefore He created the verdant field of Time and Space
        And the life-giving garden of the world,

That every bough and fruit might show forth
His various perfections.
The cypress gave a hint of His comely stature,
The rose gave tiding of His beauteous countenance.
Wherever Beauty peeped out,
Love appeared beside it;
Wherever Beauty shone in a rosy cheek,
Love lit his torch from the flame.
Wherever Beauty dwelt in dark tresses,
Love came and found a heart entangled in their coils.
Beauty and Love are as body and soul;
Beauty is the mine and
Love the precious stone.
They have always been together from the first:
Never have they traveled but in each other's company."18.18

b) Dante, in the last lines of his Divine Comedy are the words of one who has reached the beatific vision of the Eternal:

".....'and, in that depth,
Saw in one volume, clasped of love, what'er
The universe unfolds, all properties
Of substance and of accident, beheld
Compounded, yet One Individual Light
The whole. And of such bond methinks I saw
The Universal Form."18.19

Rumi, the great Sufi, spoke of the longing of his soul for the Eternal and the Good, and he presented it as a thirsty fish within him:
c)
"I have a thirst fish in me
that can never find enough
of what it's thirst for!
Show me the way to the ocean!
Break these half-measures,
these small containers."18.20

And speaking of God, Rumi said:

"In your light I learn how to love
In your beauty, how to make poems.

You dance inside my chest,
where no one sees you.
but sometimes I do,
and that sight becomes this art."18.21

d)

The Sufis are Islamic Neoplatonists, although they sometimes, as Christian mystics, are reluctant to admit the Neoplatonism in which their thoughts are swimming and their minds are breathing. But the beauty of Plato's *Phaedrus* and *Symposium* (sometimes called the *Banquet*), Plutarch's deepest thoughts, Plotinus' and Porphyry's works shines too brightly to be disguised. One sees it also in Petrarch's works, especially his beautiful *Triumphs* which is a work, much like Plato's Symposium, that shows man's longing and ascent of being until he finally reaches the Eternal. However, it is a more passive approach by man than Plato's *Symposium*, for man's thoughts and hopes must be triumphed by his six destinies until he finally reaches the Eternal. In Plato man himself must rationally climb from the temporal and corruptible to the Eternal. But the steps and the direction of both Plato and Petrarch are the same. Petrarch's first Triumph is earthly love, which is conquered or triumphed by earthly chastity (his childhood sweetheart and love of his life, Laura, married someone else--rich bankers make more money than struggling poets--and she always remained faithful to her husband and stayed with him until her sudden death in the Black Plague of 1348); thus her chastity triumphed over his love for her; and yet, in turn her chastity was conquered by the Third Triumph, the Triumphant Death which conquers all earthly life. Petrarch, in honor of her memory and to show his everlasting love for her, wrote many sonnets and other works so that at least her fame would live on, and in that way fame can outlast and conquer Death. But late in life, only four years before his own death, he realized that Time conquers and triumphs over all earthly fame. Yet, time itself is finally conquered by God's eternity. His words were:

199a)

"Your fame is nothing than a sunlit day.
Or a doubtful winter: clouds may end it all.
Great length of time is poisonous to great names.
Your grandeur passes, and your pageantry,
Your lordships pass, your kingdoms pass; and Time
Disposes willfully of mortal things,
And treates all men, worthy or not, alike:
And Time dissolves not only visible things,
But eloquence, and what the mind hath wrought.
And fleeing thus, it turns the world around,
Nor ever rests nor stays nor turns again
Till it has made you nought but a little dust.
Many indeed are the horns of human pride,
Nor is it strange if some of them remain,
Outlasting others, more than the common wont:
But whatsoever men may think or say,
If the span of this life of yours were not so brief,
You soon would see them fade away in smoke."18.22

b)

But God's Eternity conquers time and give life and beauty that will never fade.

"Five of these Triumphs on the earths below
We have beheld, and at the end, the sixth,
God willing, we shall see in heaven above.
Time, ever ready to destroy all things,
And Death, so greedy in her evil power,
One and the other, shall together die.
And those who merited illustrious fame
That Time had quenched and countenances fair
Made pale and wan by Time and bitter Death,
Becoming still more beauteous than before
Will leave to raging Death and thieving Time
Oblivion, and aspect dark and sad.
In the full flower of youth they shall possess
Immortal beauty and eternal fame." 18.23

Ficino spoke of the "climb" rather simply but to the point:
c)
"Let us climb into the high watchtower of the mind,
    Leaving the dust of the body below;
Then we will gaze more closely at the divine and
    View the mortal from a distance.
The former will seem greater than usual,
    And the latter smaller.
So, cherishing the divine,
    And discarding the mortal,
We will no longer be foolish or miserable,
    But indeed wise and happy."18.24

d) Jacob Boehme, who, as a mystic, could not understand how Christians who called themselves children of God could fight, argue, and even kill each other and still claim to have known God. He said that even the flowers of the field share the sun and earth together giving their beauty to each other and the entire earth without conflict. Each grew according to its own essence and characteristics. So, he claimed, it should also be among the children of God, and of the true children of God that it is so. The mystics were accepting of others, not just tolerant of them, but open in heart and arms to others seeking God. He then had this to say about those who preferred arguing and condemning to loving and accepting each other.

"Therefore those people who argue about knowledge and about God's will, and therefore despise one another, are more foolish than the birds in the forest and the wild beasts who have no proper reason. They are of less use before the Holy God than the meadow-flowers that are silent before the Spirit of God and let Him reveal divine wisdom and power through them. Yes, those who argue and despise each other are worse than the thistles and thorns among the beautiful flowers that are silent. They are as the ravenous beasts and birds in the forest that frighten other birds out of their singing and praise of God."18.25
200a)
The "official" Church and its theologians and inquisitors are the beasts, and those mystics are the flowers and singing birds who were condemned

by the beasts of the Church. The mystics proved that the closer one is to God the more he will love and accept others, while those who have never been warmed or enlightened by God's love will judge, condemn, curse and kill others and even pride themselves for bringing the influence of the now dead "heretics" to an end. Abraham H. Maslow in his *Religions, Values, and Peak-Experiences* speaks this way of those who have had mystical experiences:

"The empirical fact is that self-actualizing people, our best experiencers, are also our most compassionate, our great improvers and reformers of society, our most effective fighters against injustice, inequality, slavery cruelty, exploitation (and also our best fighters *for* excellence, effectiveness, competence). And it also becomes clearer and clearer that the best 'helpers' are the most fully human persons."18.26

b)

From Henry More, a Cambridge Platonist, we have these fine verses:

"Collect thy Soul into one sphear
Of light, and 'bove the Earth it rear.
Those wild scattered thoughts that erst
Lay loosely in the World disperst
Call in: thy Spirit thus knit in one
Fair lucid orb; those fears be gone
Like vain impostures of the night
That fly before the morning bright,
Then with pure eyes thou shalt behold
How the first goodness doth infold
All things in loving tender arms:
Thus deemed mischiefs are no harms
But sovereign slaves; and skillful cures
Of greater woes the world endures;
That man's stout soul may win a state
Far rais'd above the reach of fate."18.27

In Speaking of man's ascent, Ralph Waldo Emerson declared:

c)

"The heart which abandons itself to the Supreme Mind finds itself related to all its works, and will travel a royal road to particular knowledges and powers. In ascending to this primary and aboriginal sentiment, we have come from our remote station of the circumference instantaneously to the center of the world, where, as in the closet of God, we see causes, and anticipate the universe."18.28

There is where the unity of all virtues gather, in God's closet. The closer to God, the more open and tolerant we are to others. Ficino's famous expression of tolerance was:

"We can enjoy the divine mind through various Ideas,
Seek it through various traces,
Travel toward the goal by various paths.

God so disposed the intellectual eyes and
Tendencies of various souls in different manners,
In order that we may approach the different possessions
Of the manifold divine goods by different paths."18.29

d)

Yes! God himself made it so that humanity could see the variety of spiritual blessings by giving a variety of different men a variety of different paths to travel so that all the different possessions of the divine goods to mankind would be acknowledged and experienced by mankind. Each man in his soul can take on the wings of spiritual flight to the upper regions of God's beauty and see with the eyes of his spirit the wonder, beauty, and love of God. Thus each man incorporates that experience of the Divine and can live it and share the fruits of it with others.

T

TAY

CHAPTER NINETEEN
EDUCATION

I. PLATO'S VIEWS AND INSTRUCTIONS

210a) Plato taught that there is a symbolic relationship between the individual and the State and he developed this relationship in his *Republic*. As the State needed the three virtues of wisdom, courage and temperance knitted together for the sake of social harmony and justice, the fourth virtue, so also the individual needed the same in his tripartate soul: wisdom, courage, and self-control knitted together in the soul that the entire person, within his mind and soul would have harmony and justice. Those four virtues were the foundation of both political and personal justice and harmony, and that was then the goal of education, to make good and happy men by means of such virtues and a good and happy society by the same virtues. Knowledge led to goodness and goodness was the foundation of happiness and harmony. This knowledge was also a type of "Renaissance" knowledge in which every aspect of living well was developed, both the four cardinal or heavenly virtues, mentioned above, and also the four human or earthly virtues of health, comeliness, strength and wealth. The first four made men good of soul, of mind, and nature and were the force that in all situations could conquer and bring man the power to be good by rational, courageous and **b)** self-disciplined decisions. The latter four helped man to subdue the errant passions with which men were tempted by being in the body. If the needs of the body were taken care of: health, attractiveness, strength, and enough money not to be worried about finances, the bodily needs, directed by the four spiritual virtues would not succumb to any bodily passions, but would let wisdom take its course. Behind all this was always the advice of the two oracles of Delphi: "know yourself" (gnothi sauton - γνωθι σαυτον) and "nothing too much" (meden agan - μηδεν αγαν) *Protagoras* 343b. These basic ideas behind the educational system in Plato's mind were always to be present, from the time of infancy to the person's death. The following is taken from Plato's *Protagoras* (325c-326d).

c)

"Education and admonition commence in the first years of childhood, and last to the very end of life. Mother and nurse and father and tutor are vying with one another about the improvement of the child as soon as ever he is able to understand what is being said to him: he cannot say or do anything without their setting forth to him that this is just and that is unjust; this is honourable, that is dishonourable; this his holy, that is unholy; do this and abstain from that. And if he obeys, well and good; if not, he is admonished or punished. At a later stage they send him to teachers, and enjoin them to see to his manners ever more than to his reading and music; and the teachers do as they are desired. And when the boy has learned his letters and is beginning to understand what is written, as before he understood only what was spoken, they put into his hands the works of great poets, which he reads sitting on a bench at school; in these are contained many admonitions, and many tales, and praises, and encomia of ancient men, which he is required to learn by heart, in order that he may imitate or emulate them and desire to become like them. Then, again, the teachers of the lyre take similar care that their young disciple is temperate and gets into no mischief; and when they have taught him the use of the lyre, they introduce him to the poems of other excellent poets, who are the lyric poets; and these they set to music, and make their harmonies and rhythms quite familiar to the children's souls, in order that they may learn to be more gentle, and harmonious, and rhythmical, and so more fitted for speech and action; for the life of man in every part has need of harmony and rhythm. Then they send them to the master of gymnastic, in order that their bodies may better minister to d) the virtuous mind, and that they may not be compelled through bodily weakness to play the coward in war or on any other occasion....When they have done with masters, the state again compels them to learn the laws, and live after the pattern which they furnish, and not after their own fancies; and just as in learning to write, the writing-master first draws lines with a style for the use of the young beginner, and gives the tablet and makes him follow the lines, so the city draws lines, which were the invention of good lawgivers living in the olden time; these are given to the young men, in order to guide him in his conduct whether he is commanding or obeying; and he who transgresses them is to be corrected, or in other words, called to account...seeing that justice calls men to account. Now when there is all this care about virtue private or public, why, Socrates, do you still wonder and doubt whether virtue can be taught?"

202a)

Several points must be made:

1. Education is a life time project, from infancy until death.
2. All adults that influence the child are responsible to teach and be themselves a good example that they might be imitated.
3. To the very young, actions must be simple and clear: this is good, that is bad, etc.
4. Manners, like any other subject, are to be taught.
5. Reading and music are the first things taught by the teachers.
6. Writing comes next.
7. Reading of past heroes and the good deeds of great men, for the sake of imitation.
8. The playing of the lyre is taught.
9. They, or their teachers, are to compose the lyric poets and play and sing what they have composed.
10. The above teaches them harmony and rhythm in both thinking and creating.
11. After this the children go to the gymnasium to build up bodily strength and physical rhythm. Thus making it easier to be courageous and physically coordinated.
12. They, then, after being introduced to personal wisdom, courage, self-control (manners) which brings internal rhythm (justice), are then to learn the laws of the State so that they also harmonize with the rest of society.
13. Then there will be virtue, both private and public.

b)

It is upon such virtue that happiness is built, and the main goal of all education in Plato is to make men and their societies good ones that are blended together in harmony and rhythm with each other and thus give birth to both personal and social happiness. Plato himself, by founding the Academy, created in reality the first permanently located university in the history of mankind. This was that man might ask the great questions of life, of the laws of nature, and the ultimate meaning of life, and in so learning they could advance men in knowledge, science, mathematics, calendar making, ship building, and every other art which depends upon advanced thinking. Plato did believe that the greater the knowledge, the **c)** greater the goodness and then the greater the happiness. Plato often interchanges the words good and beautiful, and the Greek word kallos (καλλος) means both. As a quest for the ideal, the words beautiful (καλλος) and good (αγαθος) were often combined as German words are today (καλλοκαγαθια – meaning being a man both beautiful and good). Then, to the above, a sentence from the *Republic* is appropriate: "The end goal and consummation of culture is the love of the beautiful."(403c). Plato has much more in his writings about education, but what is to be especially noted is that in all training the child and then the young person, and later all adults are to be very knowledgeable of and trained in the arts: writing, poetry, music, singing, and all creative activities so that they themselves can express what they are doing or thinking in the most beautiful ways. Likewise, gymnastics to give their bodies both strength and beautiful form. Greek art of antiquity always sought to make something as beautiful as possible, and Plato applied that to not only the human body but to the soul, mind and spirit of man. He also cared deeply for the city or state in which men lived, and that is why in his *Republic* he wanted the best and most wise people to lead the direction in which the city would exert itself. For men might live like a **d)** motley horde of wild emotional animals "unless either philosophers become kings in our states or those whom we now call our kings and rulers take to the pursuit of philosophy seriously and adequately."(*Republic* 473d) For building a state is to be pursued like an artist making a statue as beautiful as possible. If the statue has an ugly leg, or arm, or head or even an eye, then it lacks the beauty of artistic harmony, and the same is true of the state or city. Thus the cultivation of the beauty and goodness of the state is a work of art and can only be effected by one who loves wisdom, a philosopher. Therefore, the end and goal and consummation of education is knowledge of goodness and beauty, that they might be incarnate in the leaders and applied to all the workings of men and women. Also, as mentioned earlier in a preceding chapter, both men and women are to be totally educated for the purpose of building the best state possible, and the best people possible.

203a)

II. THE CHILDREN'S HOUR

From the time of their birth children begin the process of learning by various means: the affection of the mother and others in the household, the actions that the child first observes and tries to mimic, from simple stories, from nursery rhymes, fables, mythological and exciting stories, and proverbs. Many of these can be effective even after the maturity years and even through adolescence. The younger the age, the more often the story or myth must be explained clearly, but as the child grows he becomes aware of the hidden lessons in fairy tales and myths. He learns how to use words, simply at first, but then his verbal communications become more complete and expressive. In this they should be encouraged, some more than other others. Often little ones almost too much enjoy talking, but that is far better than the ones who are stumble and are hesitant to speak.

b)

A. Nursery Rhymes

"I like little kitty, her coat is so warm,
And if I don't hurt her, she'll do me no harm.
So I'll not pull her tail, nor drive her away,
But kitty and I very gently will play."

This and other related rhymes about animals give the child a sense of tenderness and also a feeling of friendship with the animal world. I remember myself when I was quite young on the farm having a pet goat. The greatest feeling in the world it was. I fondly look at the one picture I have of my arm draped around its neck. A child who is blessed with an animal friend receives a great pleasure and a life time lesson.

"Little Bo-Peep has lost her sheep,

And did not know where to find them;
Leave them alone, and they'll come home,
Wagging their tails behind them."

c)

"Hey diddle diddle,
The cat and the fiddle,
The cow jumped over the moon;
The little dog laughed
To see such a sport,
And the dish ran away with the spoon."

Of course some of the them do not make a lot of sense, but they can be entertaining and imaginative. Such rhymes, if possible, should be illustrated with pictures. Likewise with parent and child saying and acting them out together it bonds the relationship with fun and gaiety.

d)

"One, two, Buckle my shoe;
Three, four, Shut the door;
Five, six, Pickup sticks.
Seven, Eight, Lay the straight;
Nine, ten, A big fat hen."

As the children become older, some of the rhymes can be used to help with articulation and the mistakes can cause much laughter.

"Simple Simon met a pie-man
Going to the fair;
Says Simple Simon to the pie-man,
Let me taste your ware."

"Peter Piper picked a peck of pickled pepper;
A peck of pickled pepper Peter Piper picked;
If Peter Piper picked a peck of pickled pepper,
Where is the peck of pickled pepper Peter Piper picked?"

B. Fables

204a)

The most popular fables of the ancient Greeks are the ones attributed to Aesop, most of which were preserved by Babrius and Phaedrus. A fable incorporates and makes alive all nature, even rocks and trees as well as animals can speak to humans. They are good for, once again, teaching the children about the vastness of the world, and how much humans and animals are alike, and how pleasant and beautiful nature can be. Babrius introduced his book of fables with these words:

"T'was a race of just men who lived first on the earth, Branchus my boy, the race that men called Golden. After them there came, they say, a different generation, the one of Silver; and we are third in descent among these, and ours is the generation of Iron. Now in the Golden age not only men but all the other living creatures had the power of speech and were familiar with such words as we ourselves now use in speaking to each other. Assemblies were held by these creatures in the midst of the forests. Even the pine tree talked, and the leaves of the laurel. The fish swimming about the sea chatted with the friendly sailor, and quite intelligibly, too, the sparrow conversed with the farmer. Everything grew from the earth, which made no demands on men, and good fellowship prevailed between even those of heaven and those of earth. That this is so, you may learn and fully understand from wise old Aesop, who has told us the fables."

b) The setting is then set for the child to feel quite at home in the loveliness of nature and all its plants, flowers, trees, as well as with all the animals and birds. It helps the child to visualize mentally the ideal that could be, and when she or he has a pet or raises a flower, such will find a gentle unity of life between herself and other living things. The child will truly feel that he has a soul mate in a family pet, sibling, or parent that can share love and tenderness with him or her. The following are some adaptations of Aesop's fables.

Strength in Unity

"A wise old man once brought his children together to teach them a lesson before he died. He asked them to bring him some slender pieces of wood, and the bound them together and asked each to try to break them.

None could, but then he separated them and the children easily broke them one by one. Thus he said, 'Children if with one mind you stay together as a family, you will remain strong and unbreakable. But if you part from each other and do not care for each other, you will easily be broken down in life. Stay together and value each other with love."

c) This is, of course, a way to let the children know of the blessings they have within the family, which is a bond of love and of strength. Parents themselves must show this by example, for that is the best way to teach the young.

The Two Signs

"An ancient story tells of Promethius, a heavenly helper of God, making two signs for each man in order to teach men a lesson about humility and judgmentalism. A small sign was hung from his neck and covered his chest and on it were his own virtues. So the man could always look down and see his good habits.. But the other sign which was much larger was hung so that it was on his back, where he could not see it, but all other people could see it. On this sign were his own faults that everyone else could see. That is why it is easy to see our good habits and everyone else's bad habits, but we can not see our own bad habits. Each person is unaware of his faults, but he can see and talk about everyone else's faults."

d) This is a good opportunity for the parents to talk about not judging someone else, and instead to try to get to know their own character much better. Otherwise people will see their faults and laugh at them. If possible speak of the oracle of Delphi here: Know yourself! Making such signs for the family and hanging them on each person's front and back could even be done, and the child would understand how difficult it was to see what was written on his back, but how easy it is to read what is on someone else's back.

The Lion and the Mouse

"A big lion caught a little mouse and decided to eat him. But the little mouse begged for his life, saying "I am so small I am not enough food for you, and if you let me go I will be your friend.." The lion laughed at the idea that a little mouse could be a friend: he was so little. But the lion let him go. However some weeks later a group of humans captured the lion and tied it up with strong ropes, and the lion was miserable and feared dying soon. But then one day the mouse saw his friend all tied up, and sneaked up close to him and with his sharp tiny teeth he cut into the strong rope until at last after much biting, the rope broke and the lion ran away to his freedom."

No person is too small or too poor to be a good and faithful friend, and each child should be taught how to treat all people with kindness and helpfulness, because a friend made is a great blessing in life.

205a)

The Shepherd's Dog and the Sheep

"A sheep who was jealous of the shepherd's dog because he was fed good food directly by the shepherd, complained that the dog was favored when they were the ones who produced all the wool, and the milk and the cheese that come from the milk, while the dog did not produce anything. The shepherd then had to explain that if the dog was not there to protect the sheep, thieves would come and take them for food or the wolves would kill them for food. It was the dog who was saving their lives."

Children, sometimes not seeing the "whole picture of life" often misplace their envy when they see the blessings that some one else gets of which they themselves are deprived. Perhaps they see a toy or a newer type telephone that a friend receives, but do not acknowledge the fact that the parents are thriftly saving money for their college or even a car at graduation. They must be taught to see the "entire picture", so that they can understand the temptation of being envious of something when they are actually receiving something of much more value for themselves.

b)

From Phaedrus receive the following fables of "Aesop".

The Peacock's Complaint

"A peacock came to Juno complaining with injured pride that she had not given him the tuneful voice of a nightingale, whose song was admired by all who heard it, while he himself was laughed to scorn the moment he tried to sing but one note. Then to console him the goddess said: 'But in beauty you surpass the nightingale; you surpass her in size. The brilliance of the emerald glitters on your neck, you spread a tail bedecked with jewels and gaily painted feathers." But the peacock still was not happy because he felt that beauty was not enough if he were humiliated by his voice. So Juno answered him that is was by the will of the Fates that the respective gifts had been assigned. To the peacock, beauty; strength to the eagle; to the nightingale melody; to the raven prophecy; and unfavorable omens to the crow. All birds are to be contented with their own peculiar gifts; and each is not to strive for that which has not been given it, otherwise each will be upset and fall into self-pity."

c) Children are to be shown the blessings of their own particular talents, and not to fret because someone else is taller or has a cute nose or is strong athletically, or is good at a musical instrument or more inclined to learn foreign languages or have a love of mathematics. Likewise by wisdom the parents are to spot those talents the children have by nature and encourage them to develop them and appreciate them. For many different stones are needed to build a wall, and many different talents are necessary to build a human society. Each has a place and each is to be honored.

The Hunter's Dog becomes Old

"A dog who had helped the hunter for many years when he was very fast and could catch food for the hunter, became old, and one day he just was too old to catch anything. The hunter was upset and blamed and scolded the poor dog. But the dog told the hunter: 'I tried with all my spirit to serve you as I was able in the past, but my body is weak now with age. It is now your duty to remember me for all the good years that I served you and helped you to get food.'"

d) The child must understand the aging process of pets, and with the same love and gentleness to care for them when they are old, as they would a dearest friend, for, in reality, that is what they have been. They should try to remember the joy their pets gave them while they were young. This will also be a good lesson for them when their parents become old and need a loving caretaker.

These few fables will suffice as examples of how children can learn by means of them. There are many books available that illustrate the fables as well. As the children grow older there are more developed folk tales, fairy tales, and myths by which the children can get the moral and ethical lesson. The Grimm brothers, Hans Christian Anderson (especially his "Sea Maiden" or "Mermaid"), and even Ovid are full of stories for older as well as younger children. Parents themselves might learn from them also and thus ought to be well read in all such types of literature, for the amount of wisdom buried in them is enormous.

206a)

III. ADOLESCENTS AND YOUNG ADULTS

From ages 15 to 25 the young mature into adults, and this decade is also enormously important. Much of what will follow from the Platonists of the past will apply to them and also all adults who, if honest enough, know that all of life is a learning experience. The goal is knowledge that leads to usefulness and goodness and happiness.

Persius who satirized the culture of his day, Nero's age, levels his criticism at those

"Who mock all science, all her laws despise,
Insult the good, and ridicule the wise;
Hence too, that mushroom race of beardless fools,
An annual crop, the produce of our culture;
Who hear unmoved the sage's warning tongue,
To mark his shoe ill form'd, or gown ill hung;
Whose noisy laugh, whose plaudits still are heard,
When the pert wanton plucks the cynic's beard.
Yet thoughtless fools, for greater things unfit,
The paths of vice for those of dulness quit:
There kill the time--there linger out your day,
Grow weakly men, and dream your lives away."(I.225-238)

b) Persius despairs over a culture that has schooled fools who remain beardless, that is, they never grow up into adulthood or wisdom, and never appreciate the advances of science or the importance of laws for justice and harmony. They can not enter reality because they are in spirit and mind weakly men, who live in fantasy all their days. To him education has failed.

Epictetus believes the central core of education is getting to know ourselves and what is in our power and what is not. Education is a type of wisdom that enables us to make sound decisions: (Discourses I.22)

"What then is education? Education is the learning how to adapt the natural precognitions to the particular things conformable to nature; and then to distinguish that of things some are in our power, but others are not; in our power are will and all acts which depend on the will."

c) Epictetus also stresses the moral need and claimed that if a man loses his virtues, he will perish. Virtue keeps man balanced and in harmony with himself, with others, and with the universe.

Plutarch directs man to a mature and adult form of education that comes only by the divine leadership of reason and philosophy (from his essay *On Listening*):

"So bear in mind that for intelligent people the passage from childhood to adulthood is not an abandonment of rules, but a change of ruler: instead of someone whose services are hired and bought, they accept in their lives the divine leadership of reason -- and it is only those who follow reason who deserve to be regarded as free. For they alone live as they want, since they have learned to want only what is necessary; but undisciplined and irrational whims and actions signify an inferior caste, and there is little freedom of will in often changing one's mind... You ought to approach philosophy, which is the only thing that invests young people with the manly, perfect and orderly attire that truly stems from reason...It goes without saying that a young man who is denied all instruction and never tastes any rational discourse not only remains barren and unproductive of virtue, but also might become marred and perverted towards vice, producing plentiful mental weeds from his unturned and unworked soil, as it were. The reason for this lies in the tendency towards pleasure and the tendency to have reservations about hard work, which are not external tendencies implanted by words, but are native sources of countless pathological conditions; if these tendencies are allowed to roam free along the paths they naturally take, if their nature is not disciplined by using good arguments to eradicate or divert them, then there is no wild beast which would not appear tame compared to a human being."19.1

d)

In such words one is reminded of the same sentiment in both Plato's *Republic* and his *Laws*. In his essay *On Parentage*, he related that the same format of instruction be applied to arts, sciences and virtues. Three factors must participate and contribute to the growth of the youth in all three areas of knowledge: the nature of the subject, reason, and habit or practice. "In the degree that any of these factors are lacking, in that degree virtue (or art or science) is lame. Nature without learning is blind, learning apart from nature is fractional, and practice in the absence of both is aimless."19.2 As is well known Plutarch was a moral philosopher and historian, and, following Plato, the goal of all education is to make good and intelligent adults: wisdom and goodness are the basis of success and happiness. Plutarch spoke of, what we would call role models, and warned his readers that children ought not to be influenced by the shallow and immoral people who are only looking for fame or glory. "The young must be kept at the furthest remove from the silly display of carnival orators. To please the mob is to displease the wise. " For Plutarch, the love of wisdom, philosophy, was the absolute key to a good education and the happiness of the soul:

207a)

"Hence it follows that philosophy must be made the prime object of education. For the care of the body men have discovered two sciences, medicine and gymnastics, of which the one bestows health and the other robustness. But for the diseases and distempers of the mind philosophy is the sole remedy. Through philosophy, and with it, a man may understand what is noble and what is base, what is just and what unjust, what, in a word is to be chosen and what is to be avoided; how he should demean himself to the gods, to his parents, to his elders, to the laws, to strangers, to magistrates, to friends, to women, to children, to servants; that he should revere the gods, honor his parents, respect his elders, obey the laws, defer to the magistrates, love his friends, be chaste towards women, affectionate towards children, not lord it over servants; and most important, not to be overjoyed in prosperity nor over dejected in adversity, not to be dissolute in pleasures nor uncontrolled and brutish in anger."19.3

b) Plutarch also stressed complete honesty in people, for "lying is a slavish habit, despicable in the eyes of all." He warned of anger and unjust profit. He believed in strong discipline but also reminded his readers that just as they tolerate one's friends shortcomings they are to likewise tolerate, out of love, the shortcomings of their children, and by loving instruction help them to outgrow those shortcomings.

Iamblichus in his *Life of Pythagoras* stressed that education in using reason separates one man from another more than any other thing. And, according to Iamblichus, Pythagoras was responsible for laying down the different subjects for study that included: medicine, science, music, mathematics, astronomy, virtue and stressed the beauty of nature, peace and the harmony of the soul. However, not that much is really known about Pythagoras and by the time of "Neopythagoreanism" he is presented with perhaps too much originality and his image has been somewhat platonized. Nevertheless, such subjects were basic certainly from the time of Plato onwards. In a list of Pythagoreans, Iamblichus named 218 famous ones who had followed his convictions and teachings to the time of Iamblichus who wrote about 300 CE, which was about 750 **c)** years after the ministry of Pythagoras. Of note, of the 218 famous followers, 17 were women. That is not a high number, but still, considering the age, it shows Pythagoras' open mindedness towards women.

After the Christian takeover of classical culture, and the schools of philosophy as well as all other "pagan" schools were shut down, scientific education was severely hindered until the rebirth (Renaissance) took place in Italy in the 15th Century. Francois Rabelais in 1532 CE wrote *Gargantua's Advice to Pantagruel* in which Gargantua said:

"Now all the branches of science have been re-established and languages have been restored: Greek, without which it is a crime for anyone to call himself a scholar...The world is now full of scholarly men, learned teachers, and most ample libraries; indeed, I do not think that in the time of Plato, of Cicero, or of Papinian there ever were so many advantages for study as one may find today....Things have come to such a pass that, old as I am, I have felt it necessary to take up the study of Greek, which I had not condemned, like Cato, but which I never had had the time to learn in my youth...And I take a great deal of pleasure now in reading the *Morals* of Plutarch, the beautiful *Dialogues* of Plato, the *Monuments* of Pausanias, and the *Antiquitites* of Athenaeus, as I wait for the hour when it shall please God, my Creator, to send for me and to command me to depart this earth."

d) Of course it was true, for Johann Gutenberg invented the press with movable type and printed the Judeo-Christian Bible in 1456.

Aferwards books abounded and Plato and the other Greeks were brought to Italy from Greece which was being pressed by the Turkish Empire, and eventually the Platonic Academy of Florence was established under the sponsorship of the Medicis, and history was changed. By 1532 when Rabelais wrote the above words, the Western World did have greater opportunity than ever before for study in all areas of human interest.

Erasmus who was quite disturbed that the "Christian" Europe could not keep the peace among its own people, and broke out in many needless wars because of the stupidity, arrogance, and greed of the kings and princes, wrote a book in 1516 called *The Education of a Christian Prince* and dedicated it to a young Prince Charles who later became the Habsburg Emperor Charles V. Erasmus wanted them to forget inherited "nobility" and think in terms of quality and goodness when choosing a king or prince.

208a)

"Similarly, a kingdom is best entrusted to someone who is better endowed than the rest with the qualities of a king: namely wisdom, a sense of justice, personal restraint, foresight, and concern for the public well being. Family trees, gold and jewels are no more relevant to governing a state than they are pertinent to a sea-captain in steering a ship."

One can easily notice that three of Plato's four cardinal virtues appear in the statement: wisdom, justice, and self-control. And this is normal for Erasmus who was a Platonist and three paragraphs earlier had referred to Plato's educational plan for the "guardians" of his *Republic*. Erasmus goes on to ridicule the princes for hiring experts to train a horse, a bird, or a hound, but do little research in finding a good tutor for their own children. As a result the young prince-to-be often chooses the worst of counselors who often are greedy and mislead him for their own personal gain. Such counselors ought to be severely punished.

b)

"Just as someone who poisons the public fountain from which everybody drinks deserves the severest punishment, so someone who implants in a prince's mind perverted ideas, which will eventually be the ruin of a great many people, is the most vicious of men. Given that anyone who debases the prince's coinage is punished with death, how much more deserving of that punishment is someone who corrupts his mind?"

All parents are to take Erasmus' advice for training a prince for the training of their own children: set a good example themselves, look for the best schools or best teachers as they would a good personal physical trainer or trainer for their pets, and be sure that the training includes training in ethics and goodness as well as artistic expertise to avoid the poisoning of their mind. Likewise, he will help the child to grow into a pious and rational adulthood if the parents themselves show some philosophical wisdom both in their own lives and in the lessons they themselves teach their children. He also recommends for children serious reading as they grow, and it is a crime to have them read foolishness and childish literature when they are capable of so much more.

c)

"But today we see a great many people enjoying the stories of Arthur and Lancelot and other legends of that sort, which are not only tyrannical but also utterly illiterate, foolish, and on the level of old wives' tales, so that it would be more advisable to put one's reading time into the comedies or the myths of poets rather than into that sort of drivel."

How relevant! Look at the books that even older adolescents love to read today --silliness and magic and fantasy that takes them away from rational thought that demands a sense of true wonder and the imagination to intelligently create solutions to real problems. He recommended books of proverbs, Plutarch's *Apophthegms* and his *Moralia*, then Seneca, and finally to the level of Plato. Whether princes or parents, one who himself does not become wise by exchanging thoughts with the great thinkers of the past, will be able to act "smart", but in reality they are not, and they simply poison the well of the child's mind and intellect. Wisdom within the family must start with the parents. Finally from Erasmus' *The Education of a Christian Prince*, I quote:

d)

"Whenever the prince takes a book in his hands, let him do it not for the purpose of enjoyment but in order that he may get up from his reading a better man."

Of course, comedy and enjoyment can be good and entertaining, and help man bring his natural playfulness to the intellect, and this is a good thing. But to limit one's reading simply for pleasure, is a surrender to a life-time of ignorance. One must remember, as Plato's words at the beginning of this chapter declares that education is a life-time quest, and growth in knowledge can help growth in goodness and that can add growth in happiness.

Steven Ozment in his very good book *The Age of Reform 1250-1550: An Intellectual and Religious History of Late Medieval and Reformation Europe*, said this about Philip Melanchthon, who followed Luther in the reformation and was given the head of the task of educating Germany, and thus was known as the Praetor (leader) of Germany:

209a)

"Philip Melanchthon, the great-nephew of Reuchlin, who earned the title "Teacher of Germany," developed the new curriculum for the university. Melanchthon came to Wittenberg on August 25, 1518 as professor of Greek and within days of his arrival delivered stirring inaugural speech, "On Improving the Studies of the Young." In the name of good letters and classical studies he criticized 'those in the schools who ...are truly barbarians practicing barbarous arts,' identifying them as the progeny of Thomas Aquinas, Duns Scotus, Durandus, and Bonaventura. To these scholastic theologians he traced contempt for the Greek language, the neglect of mathematics and sacred studies, and the corruption of classical rhetoric and dialectic. Melanchthon further associated the fall of piety with the loss of good letters and the broken alliance between the humanities and divinity; curricular reform promised to be the key to a revival of piety. In place of the traditional scholastic authors, he endorsed the study of classical philosophers, rhetoricians, and poets, especially Plato, Homer, Virgil, Horace, and 'the true historical Aristotle'."19.4

b) With Luther's encouragement the curriculum was restructured at Wittenberg's university, and later with the help of Jonas and Bugenhagen a curriculum for all the children of Germany was established and that was the foundation of the modern German school system. Melanchthon truly was the Praetor of Germany. One can trace all public education back to this movement in Germany encouraged by Luther and led by Melanchthon. Kant, a Platonist, was also a very moral philosopher as Plato and Plutarch, and his advise was, at the very earliest age possible, to install such a sense of personal honor within the child that he would despise doing wrong because it was beneath his dignity and would shame his self-image. Kant stated in his *Lectures on Ethics*:

"From its earliest infancy we ought to instill in the child an immediate hate and disgust of hateful and disgusting actions; an immediate, not a mediated abhorrence, which has only a pragmatic usefulness; an action should, therefore, be represented to the child not as forbidden or harmful but as in itself detestable."19.5

c) How that is done is a difficult thing. Kant recommends not punishing a child for telling lies, but that he should be shamed, and, eventually that sense of shame for doing wrong things would be so implanted in his mind and soul that he simply would detest lowering himself to do such wrongs. For Kant felt that punishment does not work, for if a child could do bad things and escape punishment then he would have no barriers within to stop the bad actions, but he could never escape an implanted sense of dignity and shame of doing wrong. Schiller, who claimed to be "totally Kantian", felt that the child must be taught to love and serve the idea of beauty above all else. In beauty he saw the power to uplift to another level the loveliness of life in man's hopes and quests. Thus Schiller wrote his *On The Aesthetic Education of Man*, and more of it will be discussed in the chapter "The Arts". If, throughout man's life, starting in childhood, he can experience the sense of beauty in the moon, the sunset, the flowers, a butterfly, an act of kindness, a loving touch from his mother, and the laughter of himself and others, he will be headed toward a moral and beautiful life. The ideal of beauty will lift up his mind and soul to a new level and his life will truly be adorned with the graces.

d) Horace Bushnell (1802-1876) said in a sermon: "The child must not only be touched with some gentle emotions towards what is right, but he must love it with a fixed love, love it for the sake of its principle, receive it as a vital and formative power."19.6 From Alfred North Whitehead's book *The Aims of Education* are the following statements:

"Culture is activity of thought, and receptiveness to beauty and humane feeling. Scraps of information have nothing to do with it. A merely well-informed man is the most useless bore on God's earth. What we should aim at producing is men who possess both culture and expert knowledge in some special direction. Their expert knowledge will give them the ground to start from, and their culture will lead them as deep as philosophy and as high as art." (the first paragraph of the book)

"Education is the acquisition of the art of the utilisation of knowledge."
210a)
"The essence of education is that it be religious. Pray, what is religious education? A religious education is an education which inculcates duty and reverence. Duty arises from our potential control over the course of events. Where attainable knowledge could have changed the issue, ignorance has the guilt of vice. And the foundation of reverence is this perception, that the present holds within itself the complete sum of existence, backwards and forwards, that whole amplitude of time, which is eternity."

"The life of man is founded on Technology, Science, Art and Religion. All four are inter-connected and issue from his total mentality. But there are particular intimacies between Science and Technology, and between Art and Religion. No social organisation can be understood without reference to these four underlying factors." [This statement is in fact a brief condensation of Plato's view of education and is taken from an essay called *The Place of Classics in Education* produced in 1923]
b)
"It is the function of the scholar to evoke into life wisdom and beauty which, apart from his (effort), would remain lost in the past. A progressive society depends upon its inclusion of three groups--scholars, discoverers, and inventors."

Whitehead, in these series of statements taken from his various lectures, posits the main aims of Plato when he established the Academy, and why Plato attracted Eudoxos of Knidos, the foremost mathematician of the day, and Timaeus who was thought to be the greatest astronomer of the day. All areas of life, science, mathematics, music, poetry, dialogue and rhetoric, ethics, the nature and nurture of the body, education, politics, the acquisition of knowledge, psychology, theology and philosophy were to be examined and re-examined, ordered, taught and discussed that man in every part of his being would be harmonized and fulfilled. Thought was to be free and imaginative, posited and reproved, examined and tried, that truth could be attained. It was the complete exercise of reason and intellect for the sake of utility, goodness, and beauty. That is Platonic Education.

Υ

ΥΨΙΛΟΝ

CHAPTER TWENTY
SCIENCE

211a)

The great Greek desire to know how everything works in the cosmos began escalating rapidly in the 5th century BCE, as the Greeks sought as much knowledge as possible and from as many peoples of the earth as possible. They went to the land of the Vikings, "where the sun never set during the summer solstice." They sailed down the west coast of Africa, and even earlier had traveled to the Indus River. They drew maps, examined the climates, studied the stars from different locations on the earth, learned things about how others solved certain problems, and all this they brought back to Greece and discussed them. By the 4th century the study of the stars and planets were serious and all questions were asked about earth's relation to them. Herklides of Pontus, a student of Plato, taught that the earth turns on is axis, and suggested that some of the planets may circle the sun. Eudoxos of Knidos was another student of Plato and at the time probably the foremost scholar in mathematics of his day. Some have said that Socrates and Plato ruined scientific philosophy because they put so much emphasis on virtue, goodness, happiness, and quite a bit on politics. But that is quite incorrect, as would be known to one who knew who these people were at the Academy and in what subjects they excelled. Aristotle, another student of Plato for twenty years, established the Lyceum where he studied all forms of animal life and plant life as well, zoology and botany flourished at the Lyceum. Those who heeded Plato and learned their mathematics did great wonders in the years after Plato, even teaching that the sun was the center **b)** of our planetary system and all planets including the earth circled it. Aristarchus of Samos (310-239 BCE) so taught and his followers

continued to teach until the second century BCE, when Hipparchus, as brilliant as he was opposed Seleucus who had followed the solar system of Aristarchus, and Hipparchus was considered so brilliant--he had invented trigonometry and calculated the year to exactly 365 and ¼ days--that people believed him rather than the school of Aristarchus. Copernicus reexamined Aristarchus's theory and brought it back to life 1700 years later. Eratosthenes, a geographer, calculated the circumference of the earth to 252,000 stades, which is 24,662 miles, within 195 miles of the correct figure 24,857, all without knowledge of the Western Hemisphere or the vastness of the Pacific Ocean, and using only mathematics and ancient instruments. Posidonius calculated the size and distance of the sun within 3/8 and 5/8 of the correct figures, amazingly close figures for that time--a time in which the Jewish people, Enoch Chapter 78, believed the sun and the moon were the same size and **c)** that there were holes in heaven through which the hail and rain came down from waters above the earth. The Greeks knew that the sun was enormous and believed it to be from 300 to 600 times larger than the earth. All these people used mathematics and lived after Plato, in his shadow, who taught that mathematics was next to the divine world itself in being absolutely perfect, eternal, and trustworthy. From Plato's Academy students went to the rest of the Mediterranean world and established similar schools in Antioch, Pergamum--who had the second largest library in the Greek world, Rhodes, Smyrna, Cos, Tarsus, Syracuse, Apamea, Miletus, some others and the greatest of all of them, with the largest library, was at Alexandria, Egypt. The Mediterranean world was united in Greek thought and to be educated meant to know Greek and its culture. Listed below are some of those who lived at the time of Plato or after him and taught humanity in their various locations.
d)
From Italy and Sicily

Archimedes of Syracuse: mathematician and inventor, 287-212 BCE
Aristoxenus of Tarentum: musicologist, Fourth Century BCE
Callias of Syracuse: historian, c. 300 BCE
Deodorus Siculus of Sicily: historian, c. 50 BCE
Leonidas of Tarentum: epigrammatist, Third Century BCE
Moschus of Syracuse: poet, Second Century BCE
Nossis of Locri: poet, Third Century BCE

Pilemon of Syracuse: poet, c. 360-270 BCE
Theocritus of Sicily: writer of Idylls, c 270 BCE
Timaeus of Sicily: historian, c. 350-260 BCE

212a)
From the Aegean, the Black Sea Area and Thrace

Andronicus of Rhodes: philosopher, First century BCE
Apelles of Cos: painter, fl. 330 BCE
Aristarchus of Samos: heliocentric astronomer, fl. Third Century BCE
Aristarchus of Samothrace: commentator and head of library at
Alexandria, c. 215-144 BCE
Ariston of Ceos: philosopher, Late Third Century BCE
Aristophanes of Byzantium: librarian, Third Century BCE
Asclepiades of Samos: epigammatist, c. 330 BCE
Bion of Olbia: philosopher, born c. 325 BCE
Chares of Mytilene: historian, Fourth Century BCE
Conon of Samos: astronomer, Third Century BCE
Diogenes of Sinope: philosopher, Fourth Century BCE
Diphilus of Sinope: new comedy, Late Fourth Century BCE
Duris of Samos: historian, 340-270 BCE
Erasistratus of Ceos: physician, Third Century BCE
Eudemus of Rhodes: philosopher, Fourth Century BCE
Hecataeus of Abdera: historian, 315-285 BCE
Hercleides Ponticus of Heraclea (Black Sea), philosopher, 390-310 BCE
Hermarchus of Mytilene: philosopher, Third Century BCE
Panaetius of Rhodes: philosopher 185-109 BCE
Philinus of Cos: physician, Mid-Third Century BCE
Philitas of Cos: sophist, Fourth Century BCE
Scopas of Paros: sculptor, Mid-Fourth Century BCE
Simis of Rhodes: poet, c. 300 BCE
Sphaerus of Bosporus: philosopher, Late Third Century BCE
Theophrastus of Lesbos: philosopher, 370-286 BCE
Theopompus of Chios: historian, 377-320 BCE

From Central and Eastern Turkey

b)

Aratus of Cilicia: poet and astronomer fl. Early Third Century BCE
Asclepiades of Bithynia: physician, Early First Century BCE
Crantor of Cilicia: philosopher, c. 325-275 BCE
Dio Chrysostom of Tithynia: sophist, 40-112 CE
Epictetus of Phrygia: philosopher, 55-135 CE
Flavius Arrian of Bithynia: historian, 95-135 CE
Strabo of Pontus: grammarian, First Century BCE
Tyrannio the Elder of Pontus: grammarian, First Century BCE
Zeno of Citium (Cyprus): philosopher, c. 335-265 BCE

c)

From Syria and Palestine

Antiochus of Ascalon: head of Plato's Academy, Mid-First Century BCE
Antipater of Sidon: epigrammatist, Mid-Second Century BCE
Archias of Antioch: poet, c. 118-60 BCE
Diogenes of Seleucia (on the Tigris): grammarian, c. 240-152 BCE
Herodian of Syria: rhetorical moralizer, fl. 225 CE
Isidore of Charas: historian (about Parthia) fl. 25 CE
Libanius of Antioch: teacher of many "Cappadocian Fathers" Mid-Third Century CE, and friend of Emperor Julian
Meleager of Gadara, poet, 140-70 BCE
Menippus of Gadara: satirist, Early Third Century BCE
Nicolas of Damascus: philosopher and historian, Late First Century BCE
Nicomachus of Gerasa: mathematician, Mid-Second Century BCE
Numenius of Apamea: philosopher, Second Century CE
Poseidonius of Apamea: philosopher and historian, 135-50 BCE
Seleucus of Babylon, astronomer, follower of Aristarchus of Samos, who also taught heliocentric planetary system, c. 150 BCE

d)

From Asia Minor

Agatharchides of Cnidos: grammarian, fl. C 116 BCE
Alexander Polyhistor of Miletus: historian, Mid-First Century BCE
Apollodorus of Pergamum: rhetorician, 100-22 BCE

Apollonius Molon of Caria: rhetorician, Mid-First Century BCE
Aristides of Miletus: writer of tales, Second Century BCE
Artemidorus of Ephesus: geographer, fl. 100 BCE
Bion of Phlossa: poet, c. 100 BCE
Cleanthes of Troad: philosopher, c. 330-235 BCE
Crates of Pergamum: philosopher, Early Second Century BCE
Critolaus of Lycia: philosopher, Second Century BCE
Ephorus of Cyme: historian, Fourth Century BCE
Herophilus of Chalcedon: physician, Third Century BCE
Ephorus of Cyme: historian, Fourth Century BCE
Herophilus of Chalcedon: physician, Third Century BCE
Phoenix of Ciolophon: poet, Early Third Century BCE
Straton of Lampsacus of the Troad: philosopher, Third Century BCE
Xenocrates of Chalcedon: philosopher, head of Academy, 395-314 BCE

213a)
From Alexandria in Egypt

Apollonius Rhodius: poet, Third Century BCE
Appian: historian, 155-235 CE
Chaeremon: philosopher, Mid-First Century CE
Cleitarchus: historian, c. 350-300 BCE
Ctesibius: inventor, Third Century BCE
Didymus: commentator, Mid-First Century BCE
Dionysius Thrax: grammarian, Second Century BCE
Diophantus: mathematician, Late Third Century CE
Dioscorides: epigrammatist, Third Century BCE
Euclid: geometer, c. 300 BCE
Heron: mathematician and inventor, c. 100 BCE
Manethon: historian, Early Third Century BCE
Philo(n): Jewish philosopher (Judaeus), c 25 BCE -CE 50
Zenodotus: librarian, Late Fourth Century BCE

b)
From North Africa

Callimachus of Cyrene: poet, Late Third Century BCE
Carneades of Cyrene: philosopher, c. 213-129 BCE

Cleitomachus of Carthage: philosopher, 186-109 BCE
Eratosthenes of Cyrene: scientist. Third Century BCE
Herillus of Carthage: philosopher, Second Century BCE

c)
From Greece and Rome

It is well that the first people recognized were the more permanent disciples that studied under Plato at the Academy. Diogenes Laertius lists the following:

Speusippus of Athens (Plato's nephew). Succeeded Plato as leader of the Academy
Xenocrates of Chalcedon, Succeeded Speusippus as head of the Academy
Aristotle of Stagira, who, after Plato's death, started his own school, the Lyceum also in Athens
Philippus of Opus, probably the final editor of the unfinished Laws, which was most likely Plato's final sarcastic spoof on the Athenians. Possible author of the Epinomis.

d)
Hestiaeus of Perinthus
Dion of Syracuse
Amyclus of Heraclea
Erastus of Scepsus
Coriscus of Scepsus
Timolaus of Cyzicus
Euaeon of Lampsacus
Python of Aenus
Heraclides of Aenus
Hippothales of Athens
Callippus of Athens
Demetrius of Amphipolis
Heraclides of Pontus
Lastheneia of Mantinea--female
Axiothea of Philius--female

Also it is possible that Theophrastus, Hyperides, Lycurgus of Athens, Demosthenes, and Polemo.

214a) His faculty at the Academy included: Menaechmus, Theaetetus, Philippus of Opus, Hestiaeus, Heraclides, and Hermodorus (who wrote some of Plato's lectures, known a "agapha" because they were not written by Plato--unfortunately Hermodorus' works are left only in fragments).

Others who came to the Academy to study after his death included Philon of Larissa, Antiochus of Ascalon (both of whom became heads of the Academy), Zeno of Citium who after about 9 years at the Academy left and established the Stoic school, also in Athens. Aratus, Clitomachus, and even some of the Romans like Cicero, and others who were greatly influenced by him included Cato the Younger, Seneca, and Marcus Aurelius, and the Emperor Julian. Also all those who were from Aristotles' Lyceum and Zeno's Stoic school absorbed much of Plato because their founders had spent so much time being nourished at the Academy. Panaetius, Posidonius, and Epictetus and many others were nourished on the teachings of Plato. It should be noted of the 19 listed by Diogenes Laertius above, only 3 were from Athens. Plato attracted them **b)** from all of Greece. They wanted to "go off to college". The Academy continued in existence until 529 CE when it was forced to close by the Christian Emperor Justinian. Nevertheless, its 915 years of existence exceeds the time of operation of any other "university level" school in the history of mankind. And it certainly had more influence that any other school that has ever existed.

I. SCIENCE IN GENERAL

The word science derives from the Latin words related to *scio*--to know. *Sciens* is knowing something and *scientia* is more of a philosophical knowing of something. It is the Latin word for the Greek words related to gnosis (γνωσις) -- inquiry or seeking to know, and gignosko (γιγνωσκω) or ginosko (γινωσκω) to know by observance or reflection. Such are the base concepts of science: the seeking by inquiry, observance and logical reflection of knowledge. Aristotle added that to know something is to know 1) that it is, 2) why it is, 3) how it is as it is, and 4) that it can not be otherwise. If these are not all conclusively proved, then one has what Plato called opinion, doxa (δοξα), not knowledge. Thus science was greatly advanced by Platonic reasoning and **c)** mathematics and Aristotle's gathering of many different species and classifications of them; both plants and animals. But it was Platonic reasoning and mathematics that ultimately were the basis of all experimental investigations of the laws of nature that helped the Greeks and those trained in Greek schools to open up the secrets of the cosmos for future humanity. Plato's religion did not oppose science, it helped to create it, further it, adorn it, and praise it, for it was of that same quality of knowledge that ethics and virtue were: for knowledge was one as all other virtues. One's faith would be opened to new realities and each generation of scientific advancement would further beautify reality and the awe of time and eternity and space and allow men to see the true magnificence of God and the utterly transcendent. Plato himself pointed out how very distant and how enormous in size were the stars of the sky. Aristarchus would show us the heliocentric system of our planet and the other planets of the sky. Boethius would proclaim that earth is only a pinpoint in the vastness of the cosmos. Darwin would show us how very close we are to our animal brothers and sisters. Modern science gives us a new "*Timaeus*" by which to speculate on how the entire system of the reality we can perceive may have started. Teilhard de Chardin taught us how to sing the *Hymn of the Universe* and feel so much a part of it.

d) Unfortunately, so much of this progress has been made despite the Church's strong and deadly opposition to it. Frankly, the Church, which claimed to have all truth, was deeply fearful of truth, and waged war upon it. But the innate desire to know could not be repressed. J. Bronowski in his *Science and Human Values* stated:

"Independence, originality, and therefore dissent: these words show the progress, they stamp the character of our civilization as once they did that of Athens in flower. From Luther in 1517 to Spinoza grinding lenses, from Huguenot weavers and Quaker ironmaster...and from Newton's religious heresies to the calculated universe of Eddington, the profound movements of history have been begun by unconforming men. Dissent is the native activity of the scientist, and it has got him into a good deal of trouble in ...(the past). But if that is cut off, what is left will not be a scientist. And I doubt whether it will be a man. For dissent is also native in any society which is still growing."20.1

Bronowski then quotes from Albert Schweitzer the words:

215a)

"Rationalism is more than a movement of thought which realized itself at the end of the eighteenth and the beginning of the nineteenth centuries. It is a necessary phenomenon in all normal spiritual life. All real progress in the world is in the last analysis produced by rationalism. The principle, which was then established, of basing our views of the universe on thought and thought alone is valid for all time."20.2

The religious ideal and the power of the spiritual life should in no way be limited in man's quest to find and experience happiness on the highest level conceivable to man. But if he uses those personal experiences to try to empower himself and maybe his followers to retard and hinder the development of man, his wisdom, and his knowledge of the material realm, then he has forsaken the Good Itself and excluded himself from the reality of hope and human kindness. To reject medical care for a loved one, and insist on prayer and the laying on of hands as the only way to treat a serious disease, is an action of self-centeredness and human cruelty disguised as some sort of piety and faith. In all realms of science the religious man is not only to permit science to go forward for the benefit of man, he is, as the followers of Plato, to praise it, encourage it, and participate in it in every area of his life and the lives of his loved **b)** ones. The Platonic doctrine that knowledge is the basis of goodness and goodness is the basis of happiness, can not be undermined by the less rational among humanity. Inebriated by revelations and dreams and myths, the religious man can be, and has been so very often in human history, a cruel hindrance to the happiness of mankind. If such scientific discoveries are destructive to religions then those religions were built upon falsehoods, myths, and legends that were actually chains that bound man's spirit, mind, and soul. From shackles let us be liberated and may our souls take flight on Plato's wings to the joy of truth and knowledge.

By sheer mathematics, Leverrier's calculations in 1846 pointed him to the idea that there was a large planet that had not yet been identified. So he then measured the volume, projected a certain orbit and set a time and place and looked at it with his telescope, and exclaimed "Look There." as Neptune appeared within one degree of his projection. Reason and mathematics gave to man a joyous new discovery for our knowledge of the heliocentric planetary system.

c) Archytas, an acquaintance of Plato, and a famous mechanic of his day, stated: "It is necessary that you should become scientific, either by learning from another person, or by discovering yourself the things of which you have a scientific knowledge." Eunapius spoke highly of the medical arts of Oribasius for he was so famous that he was taken in by the Emperor Julian as a personal physician. But after Julian's death, the Christian emperors persecuted him and he fled to the borders of the Empire and served the "barbarians". (Eunapius 498). Galen, c.129-199 CE, almost two hundred years before Oribasius, had warned others that the Christian were dangerous for those who practiced medicine and the other sciences. Now they were in power and proved Galen's prophecy and warning to be true. Taken away was the previous age of delight in science and the arts which Plutarch expressed at the time when the first Gospels of Christianity were being written.

d)

"Nor does Thamyras break out into poetic raptures upon any other accord; nor, by Jove, Euxodus, Aristarchus, or Archimedes. And when the lovers of the art of painting are so enamoured with the charmingness of their own performances, that Nicias, as he was drawing the Evocation of Ghosts in Homer, often asked his servants whether he had dined or not, and when King Ptolemy had sent him threescore talents for his piece, after it was finished, he neither would accept the money nor part with his work; what and how great satisfactions may we then suppose to have been reaped from geometry and astronomy by Euclid when he wrote his Dioptrics, by Philippus when he had perfected his demonstration of the figure of the moon, by Archimedes when with the help of a certain angle he had found the sun's diameter to make the same part of the largest circle that that angle made of four right angles, and by Apollonius and Aristarchus who were inventors of some other things of the like nature? The bare contemplating and comprehending of all these now engender in the learners both unspeakable delights and marvelous height of spirit."

216a)

This was taken from an essay of Plutarch's called *That it is not Possible to live Pleasurably According to the Doctrine of Epicurus*, for to Plutarch a life of leisure without the joy of scientific and artistic discovery and expression could not be pleasurable, at least in the highest sense of the term. Man was made to think, to reason logically, and to create, and in those activities he would find happiness. Plutarch was simply following Plato's formula that knowledge leads to usefulness and goodness and they to happiness. To the Platonists, Logos (Reason) was incarnate in every man, and that was his divinity, and to take away its creativity for the sake of some "inspired doctrine or book" was to take away the "castle" of his humanity and his spiritual source. Plutarch continued in the same Essay:

b)

"But we find ourselves in one and the same ecstasy with Eudoxus, Archimedes, and Hipparchus; and we readily give assent to Plato when he said of the mathematics, that while ignorance and unskilledness make men despise them, they still thrive notwithstanding by reason of their charmingness, in despite of contempt."

Plutarch, one of the greatest of all Platonists, certainly reflected Plato's joy and thrill with science and mathematics and the development of all the arts of which man's intellect could conceive. That was life at its fullest, and it was ecstasy. To suppress the sciences and the arts was the greatest cruelty and an ultimate destruction of man's highest spirits and blessings. And that the Church did for a thousand years. Timaeus taught for the first time that woman was pregnant, not ten months, but nine. Philo Judeus had taught that it was seven months. Likewise, Plutarch had no problem with the theory of evolution and presented the teachings of Anaximander, Empedocles, and Pythagoras and Plato. He declared in his essay *Of the Generation of Animals and How Animals are Begotten:*

c)

"Anaximander's opinion is, that the first animals were generated in moisture, and were enclosed in bark on which thorns grew; but in process of time they came upon dry land, and this thorny bark with which they were covered being broken, they lived only for short space of time. Empedocles says, that the first generation of animals and plants was by no means completed, for the parts were disjoined and would not admit of a union; the second preparation and for their being generated was when their parts were united and appeared in form of images; the third preparation for generation was when there was no longer a mixture of the elements, but a union of animals among themselves......Pythagoras and Plato, that the souls of all those who are styled brutes are rational; but by the bad constitution of their bodies, and because they have a want of discoursive faculty, they do not conduct themselves rationally. This is manifested in apes and dogs, which have inarticulate voice but not speech. (from *How Many Species of Animals There are, and Whether all Animals Have the Endouwement of Sense and Reason)."*

d)

The above clearly expressed a beginning of life in moisture, a gradual development of each species, an adjustment to living on land, and their ultimate growth to having a rational mind, although less obvious than man's by the limitations of their construction and bodies. Humanity, of course, is the climax of that evolution. A doctrine condemned by the Church and not revived until Darwin. "Science is the critique of myths," was a statement made by W B Yeats in a letter to Sturge Moore. Those who believe the myths will obviously fight against science that they might continue to live by superstition and fantasy. A scientific mind must be both open and investigative. Leibniz sounds like Plato when he stated the following from his *On Method* under the section "On Wisdom":

"Wisdom is a perfect knowledge of the principles of all the sciences and of the art of applying them. But principles I mean all the fundamental truths which suffice to enable us to derive any conclusions we may need .....to preserve one's health, to perfect one's self in any sort of things we may need, and finally, to provide for the conveniences of living. The art of applying these principles to situations includes in it the art of judging well or reasoning, the art of discovering unknown truths, and finally, the art of recalling what one knows on the instant and whenever needed.... We must never recognize as true anything but what is manifestly indubitable... We must avoid prejudices and attribute to things only what they include. But we must also never be dogmatic. When there does not seem to be any means of arriving at such an assurance, we must be content with probability, while waiting for greater light. But we must distinguish degrees of probabilities." 20.4

217a) Man in his very finest element is by his power of reason a scientific creature, stunned by the wonder of the universe and his own existence, curious as to how it all works, filled with inquiry, investigative by the stimulus of his intellect, creative as he seeks to solve natural, material, and personal problems, filled with longing and hope for the eternal, and joyous when he recognizes his successes. Philo shows his

Platonic coloring with these words about the nature of man: "He has capacities for science and art, for knowledge, and for the noble lore of the several virtues". (*On Creation* 83) Diogenes Laertius declared of Herillus (fl c 260 BCE): "He declared the end of action to be knowledge, that is, so to live always as to make the scientific life the standard in all things." (165).

II. THE COSMOS: THE HEAVENS AND THE EARTH

b) Plato speaks of the beginning of the heavens and the earth in his Timaeus, and because it was beyond knowledge he called his account a myth (μυθος): the actual phrase in Timaeus 29d is (εικοτα μυθον) that can be translated iconic myth or a reasonable or probable account or story. He introduces Timaeus to the group to make his account and that to be followed by discussion as to its probability. There is no dogma to be laid out, but with the best astronomers and mathematicians they are to discuss the beginning of the Cosmos or Kosmos (κοσμος). Plato was not putting forth a "revelation" or any such thing, but he was proposing to have the best discussion possible with the most capable men of his day about the existence of heaven and earth. That is science as inductive reasoning. His words in Timaeus 27a-b were as follows: Critias is speaking:

"Consider now, Socrates, the order of the feast as we have arranged it. Seeing that Timaeus is our best astronomer and has made it his special task to learn about the nature of the Universe, it seemed good to us that he should speak first, beginning with the origin of the Cosmos and ending with the nature of mankind. After him I am to follow, taking over from him mankind, already as it were created by his speech, and taking over from you a select number of men superlatively well trained. Then, in accordance with the word and law (λογον και νομον) of Solon, I am to bring these before ourselves, as before a court of judges."

c)

Thus the discussion would take place: by a likely account by Timaeus, followed by Critias, and then others of expertise would act like judges in critically reviewing the logic and probability of the "creation story". This format is exactly what scientists do today: present a theory by an expert, put it up for discussion, and be open to the critical analysis and judgment of the other scientific experts in that same field of study. For us today, we are to be more impressed with Plato's approach, or modus operandi, that with the answers that he is able to present in his day and age, limited as he was without knowledge of the cosmic gravitational pull, no understanding of the atmospheric pressure to stabilize the air about the moving earth, and no telescopes. His conclusions were:

d)

1. There had to be a First Cause who initiated the ordering of the cosmos.
2. The cosmos is a beautifully ordered work.
3. Life on earth is beautiful and good, and therefore the First Cause must be Good.
4. Because this beautiful work of the cosmos still has natural happenings that defy order, The Maker, and First Cause were limited in power by the laws of nature, called necessity or ananke (αναγκη).
5. However the Maker of the cosmos was without fault because the pattern in his mind that he followed was perfect, but the materialization of it was hindered by the laws of nature which He could not change.
6. Because of the laws of nature, the materialized world was in a constant flux and change, and therefore was called by Plato the world of "becoming", not the world of being which is the ideal and eternal world.
7. The "Father and Maker" was delighted at his first attempt, and being so encouraged, sought to make the material world even better.
8. The "Father and Maker" that is, the First Cause, was happy with his ordering of the elements and called it the Cosmos or **218a)** his child, made in the image of his thoughts.
9. Then The Maker made all species and especially man, and endowed man with reason (logos -- λογος), by which man could, as did God himself, rationalize with his intellect and utilize the gift of numbers. God then had

made something akin to himself, indeed, like children in whom he could rejoice and whom he could love.

10. Man's body was made by the "lower gods" that is those elements of the cosmos that seemed to be eternal: sun, moon, earth etc. But which were also material and thus the material or temporal part of man reflected also its maker. But the soul of man, wherein logos or reason dwelt, was the divinity of man and that element of man God made to be eternal and to be in communication with its Maker forever. Thus man dies in the body because of the law of nature and the limits of the material body. He does not die because of sin or because God had exercised his wrath. There is no wrath of God in Plato that visits mankind with death, and there is no eternal hell for his children, and while Plato presents many different and conflicting ideas of man's soul's immediate fate after death, he is convinced that ultimately all will live in eternal bliss with the blessings and joy of God.

b)

When one considers the teaching that was before Plato and taught by Empedocles, which presented an evolutionary process, and that Plato taught that man's body was created by the sun and moon and earth, one can see that he was thinking along almost modern lines. He also states that the stars are evidently too distant to make any calculations about them and their "revolutions have not been discovered by men". He does say that they are very misleading: they appear to be so small, but due to their great distance they are really enormous in size and can not be computed (at least in his day). But what we have in Plato's Timaeus is a formula for good science: gather all the information we can by the most competent people in that field, present it to others, have discussions and judgments be made, review the critical analysis and then try to posit a theory that will be held until new knowledge prompts a renewed process of evaluation. In the world of becoming, we are always dealing with opinion and not ultimate knowledge, but, as Plutarch said, we must have degrees of probability so that we can function with the best knowledge that we do have.

c) In Galileo's defense of the heliocentric planetary system in his *Dialogue Concerning the Two Chief World Systems*, he defended his proof by mathematics and stated: "Plato himself admired the human understanding and believed it to partake of divinity simply because it understood the nature of numbers. I know very well; nor am I far from being of the same opinion." And this basically was the entire nature of the Renaissance: pitting Plato against the Church and the Papacy. Plato and Science eventually won, at least in the eyes of the intellectual and scientific community. It is time for the Churches, Orthodox, Catholic, and Protestant to try to understand that their calling was to give hope and joy to mankind, and not try to rule it by force, inquisition, interdict, excommunication, and control of elections in matters of personal freedoms and the advancement of science. They can learn much from the Platonic and Scientific Greeks whose work they destroyed and whose teachings they burned and whose spiritual devotion they condemned. If they cannot so learn, they have made themselves not only obsolete, but will continue being a heavy burden upon the shoulders of the rest of mankind. Those who have followed Plato in the past have "put up with fools" at great expense. Praise be to Roger Bacon, Copernicus, Paracelsus, Galelio, Darwin and to many others who have lifted mankind out of superstitious ignorance, for they are the incarnations of the Eternal Logos.

Φ

ΦI

CHAPTER TWENTY ONE
THE FINE ARTS

I. THE ARTS IN GENERAL

219a)

By the time of Plato the Greeks had already developed a sense of beauty in everything they did and all that they created. But Plato insisted that there were three essential components to all the fine arts as well as the mechanical arts: useful function, beauty, and for the sake of goodness. Whatever was made needed to work, display beauty in itself or the beauty of its operation, and educate the user into goodness. Rhetoric, if well done and formed in the most flowing of words, yet misled the people or was dishonest, while popular among some sophists, was scorned by Plato. A statue that was impressive and declared goodness, but did not appear in beautiful form and in harmony with the nature it was trying to express was defective. The arts, in a way, reflected Plato's tripartate soul of wisdom, courage, and self-control: if any of the three were missing, there could not be harmony or justice within the soul. Likewise in art the three elements supplemented each other to form a unit of harmony. Whether or not this had to do with Plato's love of geometry and the triangle can be debated. But his desire for balance, mathematical harmony, beauty, goodness, and usefulness may seem to be part of his "If **b)** you do not know geometry, do not come in." at the entrance of his Academy. He was, without doubt, seeking to idealize the earthly life as much as possible by following he "heavenly pattern" of the world of forms. To him life and all of its adornments and creative activities can be perfected by its unifying the basic principles of function, beauty, and goodness. Such were to appear in rhetoric, poetry, sculpture, architecture, painting, pottery, the human body and all the mechanical inventions as well. Then, if a man did the same thing with his soul, man could in every aspect of his life enjoy balance and harmony. Then he would also be imitating the heavens which showed every day and night the same harmony and beauty of its own. Kosmos (Cosmos) in the Greek mind meant "organized beauty". Thus it was proper to name those substances that ordered the beauty of a woman's face "cosmetics".

c) The art of living a beautiful, useful and good life was, of course, the greatest of all the arts, and to have a teacher that would be able to mold a student into such a life would be a gift of God. Eunapius described the education and development of Porphyry this way:

"Tyre was Porphyry's birthplace, the number one city of the ancient Phoenicians, and his ancestral fathers were not insignificant. He was given a liberal education, and advanced so rapidly and made such progress that he became a hearer of Longinus, and in a short time was an ornament to his teacher. At that time Longinus was in his person a living library and a peripatetic museum; and moreover he had been entrusted with the function of critic of the ancient writers, like many others before him, such as the most famous of them all, the Carian Dionysius, Porphyry's name in the Syrian town was originally Malchus, "King", but Longinus gave him the name "Porphyry" (purple) which was the color of royalty. With Longinus he attained to the highest culture, and like him advanced to a perfect knowledge of grammar and rhetoric, though he did not incline to that study exclusively, since he really preferred philosophy. For Longinus was in all branches of study by far the most distinguished of the men of his time, and many of his books are in circulation and are greatly admired. Whenever any critic condemned some ancient author, his opinion did not win approval until the verdict of Longinus wholly confirmed it." (Eunapius' *Life of the Philosophers*, 456)

Longinus was a living example of Plato's "Renaissance" man, fully developed in all the arts and sciences of his day. His writing *On the Sublime Writing* will be referred to later in the chapter.

d) The Renaissance in Italy gave birth to the beauty of art in all its forms, beauty that had been lost in the public realm after the destruction of ancient pagan culture. But again it came alive from 1200 CE onwards and all art, including church art which itself borrowed from the pagan society in which it was born. The Jewish heritage of the church, other than in writing and some singing, forbad most arts, especially those of the plastic or material arts: no sculptures, no paintings, no beautiful decorations, no replicas of animals or humans and especially no images of God. But the Church inherited from the pagan culture, which it condemned, the beauty of many arts. But all such arts were to glorify the teachings and heroes of the Church and nothing else. But in the Renaissance Plato, Cicero, the Caesars, Homer and many other myths and legends of the pagan culture were revived. When the Reformation took place, some of the Protestants wanted to return to the Tanak which forbad all works of art and all images of the abstract concepts and of God. Luther opposed them and made a stand for the power of artistic beauty in spiritual matters. It is in German, but a beautiful book, with first class pictures and photographs of German and Lutheran Protestantism is *Luther und die Folgen fuer die Kunst* by Werner Hofmann. When Christians enjoy the beautiful works of the Church and fellow Christians, they must remember that such beauty is from a Platonic-Christian heritage and not a Judeo-Christian heritage. In the West it was the Greeks, without parallel, that taught Europe the concept of beauty in all forms of art. If one compares a work of Periklean Athens **220a)** with the art from Babylonia or Egypt one will be aghast at the incalculable gap between them. But it was not until the person of Friedrich Schiller that Platonism in its fulness was reborn in the aims and substance of art: he brought back the three vital elements of art; function, beauty, and education for the sake of goodness. Schiller wrote a series of letters to Denmark's Prince, Friedrich Christian, *On The Aesthetic Education of Man*, as compiled and translated by Reginald Snell, and from it are the following quotations.

He begins the first letter with these words:

"So you are willing to allow me to lay before you, in a series of letters, the results of any inquiries into Beauty and Art. I am keenly sensible of the importance, but also of the charm and dignity, of such an undertaking. I shall be speaking of a subject which is closely related to the better portion of our happiness, and not far removed from the moral nobility of human nature."

b) Here Schiller immediately brings together beauty, art, happiness, charm, dignity, and the moral nobility of human nature. Function: happiness and dignity; beauty and charm; and goodness is moral nobility. He is totally Platonic in his concept, however much he received it through Kant not withstanding. Again, in his Fourth Letter he speaks as if he is quoting Plato:

"Every individual man, it may be said, carries in disposition and determination a pure ideal man within himself, with whose unalterable unity it is the great task of his existence, throughout all his vicissitudes, to harmonize."

In his Sixth Letter his gives praise to the ancient Greeks in general.

c)

"Our reputation for culture and refinement, which we justly stress in considering every mere state of Nature, will not serve our turn in regard to the Greek nature, which united all the attractions of art and all the dignity of wisdom, without, however, becoming the victim of them as does our own. The Greeks put us to shame not only by their simplicity, which is alien to our age: they are at the same time our rivals, often indeed our models, in those very excellencies with which we are wont to console ourselves for the unnaturalness of our manners. Combining fullness of form with fullness of content, at once philosophic and creative, at the same time tender and energetic, we see them uniting the youthfulness of fantasy with the manliness of reason in a splendid humanity."

d) It is the fine arts that ennobles mankind amidst barbarous times and historical changes, for it presents man with truth and beauty and thus the eternal which stabilizes his soul. It is beyond and superior to one's own time period. "No doubt the artist is the child of his time; but woe to him if he is also its disciple, or even its favorite...but his form he will borrow from a nobler time--nay, from beyond time."(Ninth Letter). It is so pure and moral and "The pure moral impulse is directed at the Absolute" and one must "elevate its thoughts to the necessary and the eternal." "Live with your century, but do not be its creature; render to your contemporaries what they need, not what they praise." One can see the same push towards the Eternal, the Good, and the Absolute that was in the mind-set of Plato: the Absolute and Eternal Ideal. Art, proclaimed **221a)** both Plato and Schiller, has that power to lift up men to the ideal and even infuse that ideal into the artist's life. A lost society or man "must be restored by means of Beauty." Education must nourish its students in this power of art lest man remain more beastly than angelic. Art takes man's emptiness and fills it, his personality and builds it towards wholeness, and his scattered impulses and unites them into unity. Art breaks all material and bodily fetters and liberates the soul to ascend to godliness. Art is a way of incarnating beauty itself into matter that matter itself can participate in the spiritual realm. Art brings together imagination, creativity, wonder and gratitude. In his Twenty First Letter he stated: "It is then no mere poetic license, but also philosophical truth, to call Beauty our second creator." To be born again, is to be baptized into Beauty. That baptism brings a deeper joy and bliss into the mind and soul of man. He does not depreciate reason, but Schiller felt that reason is helped by aesthetics. Noble and absolute virtue and duty to which reason calls us, is helped by the beautiful and the aesthetical. Schiller was greatly influenced by Goethe, also in spirit claimed to be totally Kantian, and by admission was baptized into the same spirit of the arts that they ancient Greeks had, and was a soul-mate to Plato.

b) Georg Wilhelm Friedrich Hegel, a contemporary of Schiller also had much to say of the arts and their role in lifting man's spirit from the material to the transcendental world. Hegel presented a triad: art, religion, and philosophy or science. Art expressed the spirit of man, in religion spirit became a living thing, and philosophy was the logical and scientific aspects of the spirit. He was well acquainted with Kant who preceded him a few years, and even, in 1795, composed a Life of Jesus in which Kantian morality became incarnate, but it was never published. But it was a major step in his interest in religion, not only of Christianity but of all the world religions and unfolded itself in his *Lectures on the Philosophy of Religion* which he gave later in life. The following words are from his *Introductory Lectures on Aesthetics*:

c)

"It is well known that Plato was the first to require of philosophical study, in a really profound sense, that its objects should be apprehended, not in their particularity, but in their universality, in their genus, in their own nature and its realization: inasmuch as he affirmed that the truth of things did not consist in individual good actions, true opinions, beautiful human beings or works of art, but in goodness, beauty, truth themselves." 21.1

d) Hegel believed that art replicates man's spiritual self, thus expressing his inner being:

"The universal need for expression in art lies, therefore, in man's rational impulse to exalt the inner and outer world into a spiritual consciousness for himself. He satisfies the need of this spiritual freedom when he makes all that exists explicit for himself within, and in a corresponding way realizes this his explicit self without, evoking thereby, in the reduplication of himself, what is in him into vision and into knowledge for his own mind and for that of others. This is the free rationality of men, in which, as all action and knowledge, so also art has its ground and necessary origin." 21.2

222a) If art is perfect, according to Hegel, then one can see the character and spirit of the artist, for it is a replication of what he actually is, expressed in a material way. Therefore, the true aim of art is to bring forth one's feelings, his deepest inspirations, and all things significant in the mind of man. It is in art that man can represent what he believes to be splendid and noble and do it in a rational, delightful, and even emotional way. Thus a religious work of art will tell much of the spirit of religion within the artist. Even though the art is by an individual it is a representation of the universal spirit: for in art as well as life, every man is both an island and not an island unto himself. As to the functional value of art, it can be didactic if not used as a mechanical instrument. Perfect art according to Plato does all three: beauty, education to goodness and function. For instance, the beautiful Greek vases of antiquity served the function of carrying water or storing oil, beautifying the space it occupied and taught a lesson by the story told by the painting upon it. That is perfect art. The windows of a cathedral likewise, served its function by keeping out the rain and letting in the light, by adorning with its beautiful colors the interior of the nave, and by its pictures teaching a story of Jesus or of certain saints. Therefore, if art is to be perfect it also needs to have a didactic utility, and the personal expression of the artist himself is to incorporate the expression of his own spirit in such a way that beauty is expressed and a lesson presented to the person **b)** seeing the art. The more the art is able to express the absolute beauty, the depth of goodness, and also be used as a material function then the greater the art, and the more innate spiritual power it radiates. This can be in the fine arts and also arts like buildings and architecture, how a bridge or house is built, or how a poem is written and the ideas of the words illuminated to the mind, and how music can give pleasure, and beautiful harmony and also moralize a soul. At a temple the ultimate purpose of art is to bring God and His Beauty and Goodness into the community and thus lift up the spiritual desires and passions of the people. Also, speaking Platonically, man's need to produce such art is symbolic of the Daimon within that longs for the presence of God even now within the present realm.

c) William Ralph Inge stated it well in his *Platonic Tradition in English Religious Thought:*

"Plato would banish all poets who are not edifying; his test of good music is its effect on the character; and so on. This canon is now rejected with contempt; but I venture to think that a firm faith in the ultimate identity, or perfect harmony, of the Good, the True, and the Beautiful, will help a critic far more than it hinders him. Plato's famous Ideas would now be called absolute and eternal Values; and Values are for the Platonist not only ideals but creative powers."21.3

Inge goes on to quote Westcott's words:

"Religion in its completeness is a harmony of philosophy, ethics, and art, blended into one by spiritual force, by a consecration at once personal and absolute. The direction of philosophy is theoretic, and its end is the true; the direction of ethics is practical, and its end is the good; the direction of art is representative, and its end is the beautiful. Religion includes these several ends, but adds to them that in which they find their consummation, the Holy."21.4

d) A quotation from Ovid (Epistulae Ex Ponto II. Ix. 47) stated:

"Note too that a faithful study of the liberal arts humanizes character and permits it not to be cruel."

II. MUSIC

Music and its beauty and joy and symbol of harmony was very important to Plato and his Academy of friends. At the banquets of feasts there was always singing and often females who played the lyre, danced, and sang. They would sing first together a song and then sang around one by one, and teachers were likewise to teach children how to play the lyre and helped them to compose their own ȿongs. Music to them as well as to millions after them was the breathing of the soul. A teacher of Pericles by the name of Damon said that when the modes of music change in society, the laws also change. Music is so flexible it can address any situation and Aristotle addressed the question of why people who are grieving as well as those enjoying themselves both like the sounds of the flute. Also was addressed by Aristotle was the reasons we from childhood like to dance to the sounds of music while delighting in rhythm and melody. The sweetness of music was always a part of Athenian social gatherings and entertainments. It gave the body a relaxing rest and gave the mind a quite time of peace.

223a) Pythagoras is said by Iamblichus to have had the opinion that music contributed greatly to health, if it was used in an appropriate manner. Certain melodies were used to alleviate despondency and lamentation, and he used music with dancing to ignite the spirits of those who seemed spiritless. Nicomachus credited Pythagoras with inventing the octave using a ratio according to numbers. The myths surrounding Orpheus included those in which he and his lyre created such beautiful music that the wild animals came to him and were charmed. Evagrios the Solitary had his students control their passions by means of music and prayer.

Plato believed there was music from the heavenly bodies, but because of their distance we are unable to hear it, but he talked without any doubts of the heavenly chorus. Baldassare Castiglione in his *Music and the Courtier* presented this part of a conversation of the words of the Count as he defends music and its power:

b)

"I shall enter into a large sea of the praise of music and call to rehearsal how much it has always been renowned among them of old time and counted a holy matter; and how it has been the opinion of most wise philosophers that the world is made of music, and the heaven in their moving make a melody, and our soul framed after the very same sort, and therefore lifts up itself and revives the virtues and force of itself with music...I shall tell you that grave Socrates, when he was well stricken in years, learned to play upon the harp. And I remember I have understood that Plato and Aristotle will have a man that is well brought up to be also a musician; and declare with infinite reasons the force of music to be to very great purpose in us, and for many causes ought necessarily to be learned from man's childhood, not only for the superficial melody that is heard, but to be sufficient to bring into us a new habit that is good and a custom inclining to virtue, which makes the mind more apt to the conceiving of felicity, even as bodily exercise makes the body more lusty, and not only hurts not civil matters and warlike affairs, but is a great stay to them. Also Lycurgus in his sharp laws allowed music. And it is read that the Lacedaemonians, which were valiant in arms, and the Cretenses used harps and other soft instruments; and many most excellent captains of old time (as Epaminondas) gave themselves to music; and such as had not a sight in it (as Themistocles) were a great deal the less set by.....Therefore let our courtier come to show his music."

c)

Ficino likewise shared this sacred and Platonic view of music, and he declared:

"Indeed, since pleasure generally arises on account of some likeness, it necessarily follows that he who takes no pleasure in concordant sound in some way lacks concord within. Let me say, if I may, that this man has not been formed by God, for God forms all things according to number, weight, and measure. Moreover, I would say that such a man is no friend to God, for God rejoices in harmony to such an extent that he seems to have created the world especially for this reason, that all its individual parts would sing harmoniously to themselves, and to the whole universe; indeed the universe itself should resound as fully as it can with the intelligence and goodness of its Author. Let us add that He has so arranged the spheres and regulated their movements in relation to one another, as the Pythagoreans and Platonists teach, that they make a harmony and melody beyond compare."21.5

d)

Friedrich Schleiermacher in his *Christmas Eve: Dialogue on the Incarnation* the following parts of a dialogue: "It is precisely to religious feeling that music is most closely related....music attains its perfection only in the religious sphere." The reason for this is simple, music itself is the breathing and rejoicing of the spirit within that drives us towards beauty and harmony and felicity. Even without any religious representation music is sacred in itself.

224a) John Milton wrote this lovely *At a Solemn Music:*

"Blest pair of Sirens, pledges of Heaven's joy,
Sphere-born harmonious sisters, Voice and Verse,
Wed your divine sounds, and mixed power employ
Dead things with inbreathed sense able to pierce,
And to our high-raised fantasy present
That undisturbed song of pure consent,
Aye sung before the sapphire-colored throne
To him that sits thereon
With saintly shout and solemn jubilee,
where the bright seraphim in burning row
Their loud uplifte angel-trumpets blow,
And the cherubic host in thousand choirs
Touch their immortal harps of golden wires,
With those just spirits that wear victorious palms,
Hymns devout and holy psalms
Singing everlastingly;
That we on earth with undiscording voice
May rightly answer that melodious noise;
.....
O may we soon again renew that song,
And keep in tune with Heaven, till God ere long
To his celestial consort us unite,
To live with him, and sing in endless morn of light.

b) Nietzsche did have this right: "Without music life would be a mistake." (*The Twilight of the Idols*) Finally a word from Paul Tillich: "In the state which we call faith, sound and vision are united and perhaps this is the reason why the 'holy' likes to be expressed in music more than in any other medium. Music gives wings to both, word and image, and goes beyond both of them."21.6

III. A FEW COMMENTS ON OTHER ARTS

A. Rhetoric

The art of speaking well, beautifully, and with the power of persuasion was called the art of rhetoric. This was one of the arts which the sophists came to the different cities of ancient Greece to teach to those who hoped to be political leaders in the future as well as those who needed to defend themselves in court, for the ancient Greeks did not permit lawyers to be involved with the justice system. Each man was on his own and if he could not speak well and with the power of persuasion, he could never be a politician and he would be in trouble if he were to have to defend himself in court. It was an essential element of the Greek higher educational system, and, even through the Middle Ages, it was one of the Seven Liberal Arts, being part of the Trivium (the primary three).

c) Demosthenes is a prime example of the importance of rhetoric in ancient Athens. He wanted to become a political leader but had a weak voice and could not be heard over the crowd, so he went to work on his voice. He attacked his problem with a discipline and courage that only a few would have. He constructed a subterraneous study in a cave, trying to hear his own voice from the echoes it produced. He exercised both his voice and his body vigorously, and would practice his gestures before a mirror to see how he appeared when he spoke with enthusiasm. He exercised his mouth muscles by speaking loudly with small pebbles in his mouth, and ran up steep hills while speaking loudly to build up his breathing stamina and did the same while running along the seashore. He committed to memory entire speeches, and finally he became a great orator and became one of the most influential politicians of ancient Athens. Rhetoric or a great speaking voice would have also been necessary for the actors in the ancient plays and dramas which were so very popular and powerful.

B. Poetry and Writing

d) Until Plato virtually all writing in ancient Greece was in the form of poetry, but his prose was so beautiful and powerful that it gained immediate recognition as a proper was of expressing oneself in writing.

Poetry itself is the wording of thoughts in a rhythmic, metered, expressive, harmonious, and pleasant sounding way. Those thoughts were of glorious national epics, which aroused the nationalistic feeling and loyalty of the hearers, or of tales, myths, and stories of personal tragedy or comic experience. They had the potential of being educational, devotional, and inspirational acoustical pleasures. They could be recited, sung, or presented on stage, and the more beautifully constructed the poetry was, the more effective was both its message and pleasure. Until historical and philosophical prose became established, poetry was the main source of education to the young: Homer's *Illiad* and *Odyssey* were the basic text books for the education of the Greek until challenged by Plato and his Academy. Contemporary to Homer, there was Hesiod who wrote both the *Theogony*, a poem about the Greek gods and the origin of things and *Works and Days*, which was a mixture of myths and a type of Farmer's Almanac of basic wisdom.

225a) Lyric poetry was very popular and during the period between the middle of the Seventh Century BCE and the Fifth Century BCE, there were numerous writers of such: Archilochus, Tyrtaeus, Solon, Alcman, Alcaeus and Sappho of Lesbos, Anaceon, Simonides, and Pindar. The entire Greek speaking world was filled with poetry that was sung to the joy of many audiences, both large and small. Those barbarians who saw and heard such rhythmic beauty made up of words, were astonished, and even more so with the powerful dramas in which the poetic tragedies of Aeschylus, Sophocles, and Euripides were presented. It was no wonder that the non-Greeks sought eagerly to know the Greek language, for to see a comedy of Aristophanes without being able to understand and join in the laughter was a frustration. For these poetic writers put into words the deepest questions and feelings of mankind and of the human dilemma, not always with the answers, but with the power to make each hearer feel and think more deeply about being human than any words they have previously experienced. The music of the harmonized chorus that went with the drama added the acoustical pleasure that even more heightened the experience. Man contemplated deeply as he saw, felt, and heard the human drama played out in all the passions, fears, joys, and perplexities that befell his mortal race. The dramas were both a philosophical and existential experience. This power of art made him pause to "Know Himself". This heritage was left for all of mankind.

Longinus a Platonist and teacher of Porphyry wrote *On the Sublime Writing,* in which he had the following comments:

b)

"Two things are required from every specialized treatise: it should clarify its subject and, in the second place, but actually more important, it should tell us how and by what methods we can attain it and make it ours."

"...great passages have a high distinction of thoughts and expression to which great writers owe their supremacy and their lasting renown. Great writing does not persuade; it takes the reader out of himself. The startling and amazing is more powerful than the charming and persuasive, if it is indeed true that to be convinced is usually within our control whereas amazement is the result of an irresistible force beyond the control of any audience."

"Five sources most productive of great writing

1. Vigor of mental conception
2. Strong and inspired emotion
3. Adequate fashioning of figures
4. Nobility of diction
5. Dignified and distinguished word arrangement"

c)

"For I would make bold to say that nothing contributes to greatness as much as noble passion in the right place; it breathes the frenzied spirit of its inspiration upon the words and makes them, as it were, prophetic."

"Sappho, for example, selects on each occasion the emotions which accompany the frenzy of love."

"Xenophon gives us in this way an impressive picture of the anatomy of man's bodily dwelling, and later Plato does the same even more divinely. He calls the head the citadel, the neck an isthmus between it and the body. The vertebrae, he says, are fixed under it like pivots; pleasure is a bait of evil for men; the tongue is the assayer of tastes; the heart is the knot of the veins and the source of the blood which courses violently round, and it is established in the guardhouse; the passages of the ducts he calls the straits." [This is a partial example, for Plato speaks this way about the entire body in his Timaeus 69c ff)

d) For someone wanting to be great writer today, he would do well to read Longinus' *On Great Writing*; it is 58 pages filled with creative thoughts. Plutarch reminded his students that words are verbal intimations of the minds and judgments of the writers and, if the writers are good, they will be easily understood and hopefully observed.

Plato was renowned above all others at least in prose by those of antiquity and from the Renaissance forth: Ficino declared of his writing:

"If you hear the celestial Plato you immediately recognize that his style, as Aristotle says, flows midway between prose and poetry. You recognize that Plato's language, as Quintilian says, rises far above the pedestrian and prosaic, so that our Plato seems inspired not by human genius but by a Delphic oracle. Indeed the mixing or tempering of prose and poetry in Plato so delighted Cicero that he declared: 'If Jupiter wished to speak in human language, he would speak only in the language of Plato.'"21.7

226a)

Hegel stated about the arts:

"Painting, music, and poetry are more inward, they are not bound in the same way to three-dimensional external existence as their inescapable medium, as are architecture and sculpture. Painting deals in the 'abstract visible', . Music is in sound which is already more ethereal; and poetry in words where sound rises to the spiritual reality of sign."21.8

W R Inge liked Shelley's Platonized verse:

"Shelley turns Plato and Plotinus into exquisite music, as in the stanza:

'The One remains, the Many change and pass;
Heaven's light for ever shines, Earth's shadows fly;
Life, like a dome of many-coloured glass,
Stains the white radiance of Eternity.'"21.9

W R Inge also liked this quotation from Hegel:
b)
"The Divine is the centre of all the representations of art; and great poetry may be likened to a statue whose pedestal is upon the dark earth, but her face, emerging from the shadows into a loftier air, is turned towards that divine centre, and reflects the glory of God." 21.10

C. Sculpture

Another great artistic development into which Plato was born was the art of sculpture, and one of tragedies of the history of mankind is the loss of so much original Greek sculpture. Never before, and perhaps never since, has such beautiful work been done in the field of the plastic arts. Whether a statue was presented as a perfectly balanced and harmonious ideal of man or anthropomorphic god or it was an expression of man's deepest emotions, it projected reality with extreme care and delicacy. A non-Greek, seeing such statues, might think that it was actually a painted man, and would look for it to move, but perhaps in many cases, would wonder why it was naked. The nude was in fact an art form invented by the Greeks, and both gods and men were often presented in the nude, although among the goddesses only Aphrodite was ever formed in the total nude, and very seldom were human women presented totally naked.

c) Some of the great known sculptors were Scopas, Praxiteles, Phidias, Lysippus, Apelles, and Myron, all of whom used strict mathematical proportion. If the statue were presented in an activity like running, fighting, or throwing a discus, then every muscle was formed according to the bodily change that would take place for such an activity. Even the muscles on a horse's face would be in accordance with his facial activity; nothing was overlooked, as reality had to be perfectly presented. For truth in art was beauty, and beauty was the attraction for the Greeks in every creative activity. Even in the Early Classical Period (480-450 BCE) of Greek sculpture one can see that the Greeks had far excelled their contemporaries in style, perfection, and beauty; a Poseidon (or Zeus) bronze set to throw a spear, the head of a Mourning Woman, A Mourning Athena, and Diskobolos by Myron. The Head of the Athena Lemnia by Pheidias, Portrait of Perikles possibly by Kresilas, and Nike by Paionios are examples of the carefully developing perfection which was to continue to be present in future Greek sculptures. Eirene and Ploutos by Kephisodotos, three works by Praxiteles (The Aphrodite of Knidos, Apollo Saurokronos, and Hermes with the infant Dionysos), and many more wonderful creations changed sculpture forever. The portrait busts of Plato, Herodotus, Sophokles, and Euripides we can take to be near identical to the great men themselves.

d) Philostratus in his *Lives of the Sophists* speaks of one Onomarchus of Andros who wrote a lovely poem of a man who fell in love with a statue of a female for it reached perfection of female form. The words were:

"O living loveliness in a lifeless body, what deity fashioned thee? Was some goddess of Persuasion, or a Grace, or Eros himself the parent of thy loveliness? For truly nothing is lacking in thee, the expression of the face, the bloom on the skin, the sting in the glance, the charming smile, the blush on the cheeks, signs that thou canst hear me. Yea and thou has a voice ever about to speak. And one day it may be that thou wilt even speak, but I shall be far away. O unloving and unkind! O faithless to thy faithful lover! To me thou hast granted not one word." (599).

When something is made perfect, it is hard not to love it, and in the form of a woman was just too much to bear for the created lover, Onomarchus. And I am sure that few men wanted to be seen naked immediately after their women had seen a perfectly sculptured Apollo. Beautifully idealized form was hard to be matched by humans in their own bodies, yet that was the Greek quest; to set the ideal and then try to actualize it in their own lives. Thus Plato's quest to be as much like God as possible set the highest moral ideal possible for mankind.

227a)

D. Architecture

When a non-Greek landed his ship at the Piraeus (Athen's seaport) and looked up at the acropolis with its beautiful buildings shining in the sun, he knew something special awaited him there. Atop the Acropolis was the majestic temple, the Partheon, its metope, pediments, and frieze decorated by the splendid sculptures of Phidias and others. It has been called the most perfect expression of the spirit and civilization of ancient Greece. The beauty of the building itself is enhanced by the magnificent art scenes depicting myth, history, religion, and heroes. Dione and Aphrodite on the east pediment, a battle between Centaurs and Lapiths on the metope, a Heifer being led to sacrifice on the frieze as well as a discussion between Poseidon, Apollo, and Artemis and many other scenes used to edify and educate the visitors. Surrounding the Partheon, on a slightly lower level, were many others structures which illustrated the Athenian spirit to beautify life: the altar and Temple of Athena, the Erechtheion with its unbelievably miraculous karyatid porch, the Sanctuary of Artemis, other structures, and the stately Propyleia which served as the entrance to this sacred area. Greek established cities throughout the entire Mediterranean World had high places made sacred by such buildings in order to unify and inspire the city.

b) Not only the temples of Greek cities were built on the basis of harmonic proportion and beauty, but the altars, city treasuries, tholoi, propyleia, and all such assembly places like the stoai, bouleuteria, and prytaneia were constructed in such ways that men felt themselves surrounded by architectural beauty. Likewise the gymnasia and palaestras as well as the huge theaters were designed to promote the pleasure of living. The conbination of function and beauty also was evident in the building of the lighthouses. The lighthouse Pharos built in Alexandria reached a height of 440 feet, and was classified as one of the seven wonders of the world, as were four other Greek constructions: the Statue of Zeus by Phidias in Olympia, the Colossus of Rhodes, a colossal statue of the Sun, was the work of Chares the Lindian, a pupil of Lysippus; no less than 105 feet in height. It was, unfortunately, destroyed 56 after its completion by an earthquake. The Temple of Artemis at Ephesus, and the Mausoleum of Halicarnassus designed by Pythius and the beautified by the sculptures of Scopas and Praxiteles are the two other Greek made wonders of the world. Such beauty did the Greeks give to their works of art, any of which were dedicated to spiritual thoughts and their gods. But

c) that was part of their horrible fate: beauty and worship. For when the Christians came into power, they destroyed these "pagan" temples, first looting them for their precious metals, tearing off their doors to use for their own churches, and destroying what was left after the looting. They were proud of stomping out pagan temples and gave thanks for their

actions to their God. Only Julian as Emperor put a brief end to it, brief because he died in battle after only three years in office, and then the Christians were again empowered to destroy what they were incapable of appreciating, and Julian was condemned as an "apostate" and referred to as such until this very day.
d)

E. Painting and Pottery

Painting is an art at the mercy of time and weather, and most of the Ancient Greek painting has all but disappeared from the walls, metropes, stellai, plaques and tombs. However, it is with the beautifully painted pottery that the brilliance of Greek painting is preserved for us to behold. While this section will focus on the painted pottery, the glorious vases, two other painters shall be mentioned. Apollodoros (c 430-400 BCE) presented form, color, and shading so effectively that his paintings appeared to be reality in miniature, as the perspective of distance brought the viewer into the scene; and Apelles who works included famous portraits, including one of Alexander the Great, who had a preference for his paintings. Perhaps in no other activity of creativity did the Greeks combine beauty and function more magnificently than in their pottery. The exquisite way in which they could paint the stories, activities, geometric figures, myths and history of their people on pottery was far beyond the imagination of the non-Greek people of the world. The common activities of smiths, pot makers, miners, men voting, the chariot races, a youth dancing and men and women mourning are all represented in vase paintings. The more dramatic events of men running in the games and soldiers at war, the actions of well known historical figures like Sappho and Alcaeus, and the national myths such as Theseus' slaying the **228a)** minotaur, the birth of Athens, Hercales slaying Nessus, and Ajax carrying the body of Achilles all were represented on the pottery and served as educational aids. Instead of just pottery to carry water, wine, and olive oil, they were objects of beauty to decorate the house, and instruments of education for the children as the parents would explain the subjects of the painting; subjects inspiring also religion and patriotism.

F. Mechanical Arts

The great advances that had been made by the Greek mathematicians aided in the construction of many mechanical devises that other cultures did not even think possible. There are two great men who towered over all the others in this field: Archimedes of Syracuse (ca 287-212 BCE) and his contemporary Ctesibius of Alexandria (287-222 BCE). Their great works seem to be totally independent of each other because of the great distance between them, one in western Italy and the other in Egypt.

b) Although Archimedes' main interest and specialty in which he showed his brilliance was mathematics, he used his knowledge of the exact measurement of the circle, the sphere, the cone, conoids, spheroids, and the cylinder to construct many mechanical things and thus is known as the "Founder of Mechanics and Hydrostatics." Botsford and Robinson's *Hellenic History* lists some of his achievements:

"Archimedes invented a planetarium, the compound pulley, and the so-called Archimedean drill--an endless screw used to pump water from ships and to drain Egyptian fields after the flood of the Nile..He invented engines for hurling great missiles with which his fellow citizens long kept at bay the besieging Romans, the helix for launching great ships and conveying other heavy weights, and other useful machines. In the application of power Archimedes and other ancient mechanics made use of water, compressed air (pneumatics), with levers, screws and cogged wheels." 21.11

c)

Benjamin Farrington presents Ctesibius as the "Founder of the School of Mechanics" at Alexandria, Egypt and the creator of the musical instrument known as the water-organ, an ingenious water-clock with hours varying in length so that at all times of the year there would be 12 hours of daylight, pieces of artillery working by compressed air, and a double-action pump for raising water which was used in fire-engines. Ctesibius' younger contemporary, Philo of Byzantium wrote nine books on mechanics which survive in fragments and deal with some social uses of artillery, and the defense and siege of towns. 2.12

Just in 2006 CE an astrological calculator to the Greeks of the First Century BCE was, after a century of study, finally recognized as a "complex and uncannily accurate astronomical computer" which could "predict the positions of the sun and planets, show the location of the moon and even forecast eclipses."(LAT 11/30/2006) The mechanism had a complex arrangement of wheels that was not to be seen again until the 14th Century: the name of the device is The Antikythera. Again a sad reminder how this brilliant Greek culture was bruised by the Roman conquests and buried by the Christian Church.

d)

G. The Art of Living the Beautiful: in Body and Soul

The human body was also to become a work of art for the Greeks: the molding of the human form to its utmost beauty and most efficient function. The Greeks seeking perfection in the physical body, and competitive by nature to be the best, developed the Greek games. Virtually every city had its own competitive games, the Panathenaea being the most recognized. But to be best within the city was simply not enough if one were seeking perfection, and in the year 776 BCE the all-Greek festival at Olympia was inaugurated to determine the best of all Hellas. These games, their language, and Homer's works were the great unifying forces to give the Greeks, naturally divided by mountains and water throughout the Mediterranean world, a sense of uniqueness, their difference from all other peoples of the earth. Started originally as a running contest, many other events were gradually introduced into the Olympic games in order to develop the completeness of a perfect physical man: running different distances, throwing various objects (discus and javelin), jumping, boxing wrestling, boxing and wrestling combined (Pankration), and running in full armor. The victors were treated like national heroes with many benefits and often being immortalized by the poets, especially Pindar, for, after all, they reached closer to the ideal physical man than any other that year (every four years at Olympia). The quest for the beautiful was an essential part of a Greek's life: his speaking, his writing, his dramas, his music, his architecture and fine arts, his decoration of even his pottery, and the building of strong and well shaped physical bodies. His life was an imitation of what Plato's God was: Absolute Beauty and Goodness.
229a) The spiritual element of beautiful living was the continual growth of the mind and the soul into knowledge and goodness as much as

possible that man would be happy. The happy soul was the good soul, and the man of wisdom was the beautiful mind. The good mind, good soul, and good body gave man a type of happiness completion. And this expressed itself in many ways. One was play.

The play life, so essential to what man is, was expressed in child's games, like knuckle bones, and sports, like the community games, as well as mind games and dialogues. Dancing and song played a big role in play. Imagine a banquet in which all had to sing, some must have been quite off note, especially after a meal and an adequate supply of wine, yet each was to sing after the common initial song in which all participated like a chorus. Phaedrus tells a tale he took from the legends of Aesop's fables that indicated quite early on the thinking Greeks needed, as all men need, the simpleness of mind relaxation even if it becomes playful and silly at times. Laughter is good and mind games help it to happen. The story was:

b)

"A certain Athenian, on seeing Aesop in a crowd of boys playing with nuts, stopped and laughed at him as though he were crazy. As soon as Aesop perceived this he placed an unstrung bow in the middle of the street and said: 'Here now, Mr. Philosopher, interpret my symbolic action.' The people gathered round, and the man racked his brains for a long time and could see no point in the problem put to him. At last he gave up. Thereupon, Aesop, the winner of the battle of wits said: 'You will soon break your bow if you keep it always bent; but if you unbend it, it will be ready to use when you want it.' So it is. You should let your mind play now and then, that it may be better fitted for thinking when it resumes its work." (III.14)

As the body, which needs rest and relaxation, so also the mind. Johan Huizinga wrote a book called *Homo Ludens* (Man the Playful) and he said so many things about play being necessary to human life that it is a good read for all, especially those who are filled with tension and high strung, for they then will realize that playfulness, like the unstrung bow, is a refreshing rest period for the mind. Platonism sees play as a gift of God as a blessing for both mind and body. Huizinga reminds us of many things:

c)

1. Play is older than culture. Animals play just like men.

2. "Wish play" as a fiction is designed to keep up the feeling of personal value. One can have fancy day dreams: it is a form of mind play that is good for the soul--as a break from the duties of reality.
3. Nature gave us play, with its tension, its mirth, and its fun.
4. Play is a special form of significant activity and as a social function.
5. Genuine and pure play is one of the main bases of civilization.
6. Play to be play is a voluntary activity, for the freedom of it is vital to its very nature.
7. In its higher forms play belongs to the sphere of festival and ritual -- the sacred sphere.
8. All forms of competitive play forbid any cheating, for then it is no longer play. [This is so important today: children cheat to win a game and adults even cheat at cards: and that is a sacrilege, a blasphemy against the sacred sphere of play itself, and destroys the entire value of play itself-- it also corrupts the soul by its dishonesty]
9. Play in its purity is a type of mystic unity among those playing.
10. Playfulness is even important in intimacy; sporting or playful sexual activity gives it a human freshness and even purity..

d)

As I said above, Huizinga's book is well worth reading.

The ancient Greeks, which he pointed out, used a suffix which they added to words to indicate that the action described implied a playfulness. That suffix was "inda"; thus to play king of the castle one would play basilinda (basil = king), and a throwing game would be streptinda, and playing with a ball would be sphairinda. All ages and both sexes could "inda" at many things. For it is man's nature.

Schiller in one of his letters on aethetics declared:

"For, to declare it once and for all. Man plays only when he is in the full sense of the word a man, and he is only wholly man when he is playing. This proposition, which at the moment perhaps seems paradoxical, will assume great and deep significance when we have once reached the point of applying it to the twofold seriousness of duty and of destiny; it will, I promise you, support the whole fabric of aesthetic art, and the still more difficult art of living. But it is only in science that this statement is unexpected; it has long since been alive and operative in Art, and in the feeling of the Greeks, its most distinguished exponents."21.13

230a)

"Let us play!" is as important as "Let us pray!"

H. Humor, Joyfulness, Celebration and Cheerfulness

Because humor, joyfulness, celebration and cheerfulness are so interrelated they will all be discussed under one heading. Humor is actually a playfulness of the mind using common or understood knowledge by which to relate incidents to each other that make a funny combination. The mind is delighted and laughter often follows even among large groups. Both the playfulness of the mind and the soul's laughter are good for the human spirit and body. In the feasts and banquets good humor was always welcomed, even if it were somewhat personal, to laugh at oneself is just as important as laughing at others' funny ways or certain happenings that would normally be unimaginable and harmless. Plutarch stated about well timed and appropriate humor and jests: "Those who know how to time and apply a jest confirm Plato's opinion, that to rally pleasantly and facetiously is the business of a scholar and a wit."21.14

b) In commenting on Plato's *Banquet (Symposium)* Plutarch stressed the fun and games of the mind and the good humor of the situation, in the very midst of a serious philosophical discussion, he stated:

"And Plato brought in Aristophanes' discourse of love, as a comedy, into the entertainment; and at last, as it were drawing all the curtains, he shows a scene of the greatest variety imaginable, -- Alcibiades drunk, frolicking, and crowned. Then follows that pleasant raillery between him and Socrates concerning Agatho, and the encomium of Socrates....These men, having such a pleasant way of discoursing, used these arts and insinuating methods, and graced their entertainment's by such facetious raillery."21.15

These are some of the words to answer the critics of the Banquets of the Greeks for having flute-girls to entertain a gathering of philosophers: of course they would have flute-girls entertain them with music and dance and probably some rather heavy and even romantic flirtations. That was the Greek way of social delight even among, or perhaps, especially among the philosophers. For even the most serious "debates" of politics and philosophy were to be entertaining with an open spirit to all points of view, and they added to the banquets or feasts among friends. Friendship among the Greeks was valued, and friendly humor only enhanced the occasion for all. Plutarch again gives reference to Plato: "Plato admits two principles of every action, the natural desire after pleasure and acquired opinion which covets and wishes for the best; one he calls reason and the other passion."21.16 And all had to participate and each had to deliver his opinion.

c) Philostratus in his *Lives of the Sophists* tells of a story that is to teach that one under criticism, if he is witty enough, can playfully turn the criticism towards the critic himself. A certain Cynic, Proteus, at Athens attacked Herodes and insulted him in a "semi-barbaric" fashion. Finally Herodes simply turned around and said: "You speak ill of me, so be it, but why in such bad Greek?" acting as if the true insult was to be near a ranting mouth that was in itself an insult to the Greek language. Rather than get angry, use humor, it lifts a person about the ugly passion and sets a pleasant tone to a difficult situation.

The prince of Renaissance humor was Desiderius Erasmus who, in his *Praise of Folly* ridicules the religious and political situation of those proclaiming themselves either at the right hand or the left hand of God, the theologians and the kings and princes. Folly, the art of fools, was talking about his birth proudly, his one parent was drunkedness and the other ignorance, and also he was boasting proudly about his family and relatives and companions: self-love, flattery, laziness, pleasure, madness, wantonness, and intemperance. But the biggest element of pride was that Folly's ancestors and posterity include kings and bishops, **d)** princes and popes. Folly is also proud of how he can stir up mankind by promoting wars, making parasites, panders, thieves, and cut-throats. On the lighter side he instills hope in gamesters so that their heart runs rampant with every throw of the dice. He is active in the Church also and motivates the papal counterfeit pardons bought with money, magical charms -- called sacraments, paid for short prayers prayed by a spiritual

impostor, and the creation of patron "saints", and an entire "ocean of superstitions". Folly also panics the spiritual leaders when free choice of belief is expressed by an individual so that they are driven mad that this one thought would destroy all of Christendom unless suppressed immediately. A man accidentally swallows a gnat and is accused of stealing and entire herd of cattle, for Folly can make them seem like the same thing. Folly also convinces the Church leaders that their ceremonies and petty traditions are so great that God will have to reward them more than one heaven. But one of the greatest achievements of Folly is to convince people living on one side of the river that all their problems would cease if they could kill everyone on the other side of the river with an act of war. He, Folly, can make men of the Church so wicked that the Church will have absolutely no agreement with Christ. Erasmus felt later that he laid the egg to the Reformation and Luther hatched it. There is little doubt that the humorous ridicule of the evils of the kings and the Church leaders did much to, not only help spark the Reformation, but also supported it when it happened.
231a) Two Greeks of late antiquity, Hierocles of Alexandria and Philagrios the Grammarian, collected many witticisms in Greek and called the collection φιλογελως (Friend of Laughter). One of them is: "A Scholastic who wanted to swim was nearly drowned. He swore never again to go into the water until he had learned to swim."

Marsilio Ficino spoke of the joy and warm experienced in life because God imparts such into our souls. In fact, the soul recognizing its eternalness overflows with joy that there is life without death. Just as God has given the sun to pierce the darkness with life and warmth, so has he given spiritual light a "life-giving warmth and joy, thus bestowing life, free from death" for such light from God infused into the mind that feeling of its being beyond the limits of time and a flowing of currents of eternal stillness. That feeling is clothed in beauty and goodness and thus is drawn by its very nature to God himself. "Thus Infinite Goodness and Beauty, the source of innumerable forms of goodness and beauty, equally attract and fulfill the mind in eternity."21.17 Teilhard de Chardin reflects the same thought with the words: "For what exhilarates us human creatures more than freedom, more than the glory of achievement, is the joy of finding and surrendering to a Beauty greater than man, the rapture of being possessed."21.18

Paul Tillich in his *The New Being* made the following statements:

b)

"No conflict is necessary between the joy of God and the joy of life".p.144

"Do joy and pleasure exclude each other? By no means! The fulfillment of the center of our being does not exclude partial and peripheral fulfillments. And we must say this with the same emphasis with which we have contrasted joy and pleasure...Man enjoys eating and drinking, beyond the mere animal need of them. It is a partial ever-repeated fulfillment of his striving for life; therefore, it is pleasure and gives joy of life. Man enjoys playing and dancing, the beauty of nature, and the ecstasy of love. They fulfill some of the most intensive strivings for life: therefore they are pleasure and give joy of life. Man enjoys the power of knowledge and the fascination of art. They fulfill some of his highest strivings for life;...Man enjoys the community of men in family, friendship, and the social group." Pp.147-148

c) Alfred Adler in his *Understanding Human Nature* had this to say about the happy and cheerful person:

"The talent for bringing pleasure to others makes a man more interesting. Happy people approach us more easily and we judge them emotionally as being more sympathetic. It seems that we sense these traits as indicators of a highly developed social feeling, quite instinctively. There are people who appear cheerful, who do not go about forever oppressed and solicitous, who do not unload their worries upon every stranger. They are quite capable, when in the company of others, to radiate this cheerfulness and make life more beautiful and meaningful. One can sense that they are good human beings, not only in their actions, but in the manner in which the approach, in which they speak, in which they pay attention to our interests, as well as in their entire external aspect, their clothes, their gestures, their happy emotional state, and in their laughter." (p.199)

d) People who enjoy celebrating happy remembrances and birthdays and holy days give themselves and those who celebrate with them a spirit of joyous life. Platonists celebrate the birthdays of Socrates on the traditional day of May 6 and Plato's traditional birthday on May 7 and that gives them a chance for a two day festival of celebration. At the back of this book there is a calendar of birthdays and events that can be celebrated and the truly wonderful people of the past can be remembered for their contributions to human society in jubilation. While, of course, everyday for the happy man can be considered a jubilee, nevertheless for group festivals and community gatherings certain people and events are joyously remembered for their gifts to all humanity.

232a) The Greeks loved to celebrate the Dionysos festivals and there were four major ones in Greece: the Athesteria festival in the Ionic-Attic area where wine drinking is definitely very popular; the Agrionia festival in the Dorian and Aeolic territories which perhaps is the most energetic (wild) of the four; the Dionysia in which fertility and sexuality are celebrated; and the Katagogia in Athens where wine flows freely. Dionysus was the god of wine and vegetation, and we think of our Thanksgiving Day, in thankfulness for the harvest that is brought in at the end of the fertility season. But Dionysus incorporated many festival activities including much music, dance and drama. Likewise, in the more mythical way it was in gratitude of the eternal harvest in which the souls stepped into eternity. It seems to be the most beloved and celebrated of all festivals of ancient Greece. Plutarch has an essay entitled *Contentment* and it ends with the theme that life is a festival using a quotation from Diogenes who had said: "Isn't every day a festival in the sight of a good man?" Plutarch, however, does go on to the other festivals and makes the two following statements:

"Life is an initiation and consummation of these mysteries and should therefore be filled with contentment and joy.

b)

"...recall the past with gratitude, and face the future without apprehension or misgivings but with hope and glad shining."

One caution about popular holidays is that they can become burdens with both time and money being consumed. Seneca raved a little about the commerciality of December, which ought to sound rather familiar, which was involved with the Satrunalia festival of ancient Rome. Families prepared the travel plans, spent money on gifts, and decorated their houses for friends and relatives. Because it was a custom to give gifts to each other, much was spent. The substance of the form of celebration was borrowed by the Church so that the Christians too would be celebrating something in late December, and so they gave to Jesus the traditional birthday of the 25th. The following complaint by Seneca could be applied to both celebrations.

"The month of December, and the whole city is in a sweat. Public luxury is given license, everywhere there is the noisy bustle of elaborate preparation--as if there were any difference between the Saturnalia and a business day. The saying that 'December was once a month but now it's a year'." (*Letter on "Holidays"*)

But in this, Seneca missed the deep rooted joy of the day when families got together, forgot all their troubles, gave each other gifts and hugs, sang songs and feasted in the company of their most beloved ones. It was by far the most popular celebration of the year, and the Roman spirit of joy would have died had the festival died.

c) But returning to the idea that every day is a festival, why not each family or communal group who lives together imitate the ancient Greek banquets. Sing together, eat, tell stories and discuss questions of value and even personal problems or challenges that some of the members face. Take a couple of hours together and forget outside evening activities. Well, maybe at least once or twice a week.

Plotinus reminded us all that the life of man itself could be the most joyous and beautiful element of his existence, and that each virtue with which we adorn ourselves we radiate both happiness to others on the outside and increase the beautiful and happy nature of our soul on the inside. That to him was the ultimate art of beauty, the incarnation of beauty and the attending joyousness that came with it. Kant in his *Observations on the Feeling of the Beautiful and Sublime* encourages his readers to note the beauty in creation in all of its various forms and try to absorb the elements of those beautiful objects into one's own soul and life so that one's life itself becomes, by absorption and imitation, a beautiful life that glows and radiates such beauty to others, and thus the feeling of the beautiful and the sublime will enhance the goodness and morality of the soul that itself becomes the source and center of power of another form of beauty for the human race. That would be the supreme peak of the experience of the art of living.

X

XI

CHAPTER TWENTY TWO
PROVERBS--MAXIMS--ADAGES--SATIRES

233a)

Short and wise sayings have been part of every culture's common and basic wisdom, for they are easy to remember and bring with them advice and insight that is usually universal in nature and application. The following are those sayings that are part of the Platonic Tradition or, at least, not contrary to the same. Those words taken from Plato's writings were all written by Plato himself and then put into the mouths of the speakers: Plato is probably the creator of most all the thoughts expressed, even though they are put into the mouth of Socrates or Timaeus or any other speaker. The exact words themselves to express the thoughts are almost assuredly from the mind of Plato.

Oracle of Delphi: (Plato's *Protagoras* 343b)
"Nothing in excess" (μεδεν αγαν)
"Know yourself" (γνωθι σαυτον)

Plato:

(Phaedo speaking) "It never occurred to me to feel sorry for him (Socrates), as you might have expected me to feel at the deathbed of a very dear friend. The master seemed quite happy, Echecrates, both in his manner and in what he said; he died so fearlessly, and his words and bearing were so noble and gracious, that to me he appeared blessed. I thought that in going to the other world he could not be without a divine call, and that he would be happy.." (*Phaedo* 58e)

b)

(Socrates speaking) "Now to you, my jury, I want to explain to you how it seems to me natural that a man who has really devoted his life to philosophy should be cheerful in the face of death, and confident of finding the greatest blessing in the next world when his life is finished...Ordinary people seem not to realize that those who really apply themseves in the right way to philosophy are directly and of their own accord preparing themselves for dying and death." (*Phaedo* 63e-64a)

(Socrates speaking) "Whence come wars, and fightings, and factions? Whence but from the body and the lusts of the body? Wars are occasioned by the love of money, and money has to be acquired for the sake and in the service of the body; and by reason of all these impediments we have not time to give to philosophy." (*Phaedo* 66c)

c)

(Socrates speaking) "No, this soul secures immunity from its (body's) desires by following reason and abiding always in her company, and by contemplating the true and divine and unconjecturable, and drawing inspiration from it, because such a soul believes that this is the right way to live while life endures, and that after death it reaches a place which is kindred and similar to its own nature, and there is rid forever of human ills." (*Phaedo* 84a-b)

(Socrates speaking) "When I have drunk the poison I shall remain with you no longer, but depart to a state of heavenly happiness." (*Phaedo* 115d)

Plato continued:

d) (Socrates speaking) "Is what is holy holy because the gods approve it, or do they approve it because it is holy?" (*Euthyphro* 10a).

(Socrates speaking) "It is there (a place beyond the heavens) that true being dwells, without color or shape, that cannot be touched; reason alone, the soul's pilot, can behold it, and all true knowledge is knowledge thererof." (*Phaedrus* 247c)

(Socrates speaking) "In my opinion, it (justice) belongs in the fairest class, that which a man who is to be happy must love both for its own sake and for the results." (*Republic* 358a)

(Socrates speaking of the citizens of the proposed ideal city) "Reclined on rustic beds strewn with yew or myrtle. And they and their children will feast, drinking the wine which they have made, wearing garlands on their heads, and hymning the praises of the gods, in happy conversation with each other. And they will take care not to have offspring beyond their means, lest it lead to poverty and war." (*Republic* 372b-c)

234a)

(Socrates speaking) "But as to saying that God, who is good, becomes the cause of evil to anyone, we must contend in every way." (*Republic* 380b)

(Socrates speaking) "People think him to be their worse enemy if he tells them the turth."(*Republic* 426a)

(Socrates speaking) "Those who love the truth in each thing are to be called lovers of wisdom [philosophers] and not lovers of opinion [doxophilists]." (*Republic* 480)

(Socrates speaking to Charmides, a noble and attractive youth) "Fix your attention more closely and look within you." (*Charmides* 180d)

b)

(Socrates speaking) "For children are your riches, and upon their turning out well or ill depends the whole order of their father's house." (*Laches* 185a)

(Laches speaking) "But a man whose actions do not agree with his words is an annoyance to me, and the better he speaks the more I dislike him." (*Laches* 188e)

(Socrates speaking) “Are both friends, if only one loves?” (*Lysis* 212b)

(Socrates speaking) “And so it is because it is holy that it is loved; it is not holy because it is loved.” (*Euthyphro* 10d)

(Socrates speaking) “To do wrong is the greatest of evils.” (*Gorgias* 469b)

c)

(Socrates speaking) “The happiest of men is he who has no evil in his soul.” (*Gorgias* 478d)

(Socrates speaking) “The pleasant as well as everything else should be done for the sake of the good, not the good for the sake of the pleasant.” (*Gorgias* 500a)

(Socrates speaking) “This is the best way of life--to live and die in the pursuit of righteousness and all other virtues.” (*Gorgias* 527e)

(Timaeus speaking) “He (God) was good and The Good can never have any jealousy of anything. And being free from jealousy, he desired that all things should be like himself as much as possible. (*Timaeus* 29e)

(Timaeus speaking) “Time, then, and the heaven came into being at the same instant in order that, having been created together, if ever there was to be a dissolution of them, they might be dissolved together. (*Timaeus* 38b)

d)

(Athenian speaking) “There is another thing of which any Greek should be aware. We Greeks enjoy a geographical situation which is exceptionally favorable to the attainment of excellence...But we may take it that whenever Greeks borrow anything from non-Greeks, they finally carry it to a higher perfection.” (*Epinomis* 987d)

(Plato speaking) "The human race will not see better days until either the stock of those who rightly and genuinely follow philosophy acquire political authority, or else the class who have political control be led by some dispensation of providence to become real philosophers." (*Letter Seven*)

235a)

(Socrates speaking) "But you cannot buy the wares of knowledge and carry them away in another vessel; when you have paid for them you must receive them into the soul and go your way." (*Protagoras* 314b)

(Protagoras speaking) "The life of man in every part has need of harmony and rhythm." (*Protagoras* 326b)

(Socrates speaking) "The Lacedaemonians met together and dedicated in the temple of Apollo at Delphi, as the first-fruits of their wisdom, the far-famed inscriptions, which are in all men's mouths, -- "Know yourself", and "Nothing too much" (*Protagoras* 343b)

(Socrates speaking) "No man voluntarily pursues evil, or that which he thinks to be evil. To prefer evil to good is not in human nature; and when a man is complelled to choose of two evils, no one will choose the greater when he may have the lesser." (*Protagoras* 358c)

b)

(Socrates speaking) "But now, as you think that wisdom can be taught, and that wisdom only can make a man happy and fortunate, will you not acknowledge that all of us ought to love wisdom, and you individually will try to love her?" (*Euthydemus* 282c)

(Socrates speaking) "If we knew how to convert stones into gold, the knowledge would be of no value to us, unless we also knew how to use the gold...Nor would any other know-ledge, whether of money-making, or of medicine, or of any other art which knows only how to make a thing, and not how to use it when made, be of any good to us." (*Euthydemus* 289a)

(Socrates speaking) "I must first know myself, as the Delphian inscription says; to be curious about that which is not my concern, while I am still in ignorance of my own self, would be ridiculous." (Phaedrus 230a)

c)

(Socrates speaking) "We ought always to do good, not to the most virtuous, but to the most needy; for they are the persons who will be most relieved, and will therefore be the most grateful; and when you make a feast you should invite not your friend, but the beggar and the empty soul; for they will love you and attend you, and come about your doors, and will be the best pleased, and the most grateful, and will invoke many a blessing on your head." (Phaedrus 233d)

(Socrates speaking) "But of the heaven which is above the heavens, what earthly poet ever did or ever will sing worthily? It is such as I will describe, for I must dare to speak the truth, when truth is my theme. There abides the very being with which true knowledge is concerned; the colourless, formless, intangible essence, visible only to mind, the pilot of the soul. The divine intelligence, being nurtured upon mind and pure knowledge and the intelligence of every soul which is capable of receiving the food proper to it, rejoices at beholding reality, and once more gazing upon the truth, is replenished and made glad." (Phaedrus 247d)

(Socrates speaking) "For there is no light of justice or temperance or any of the higher ideas which are precious to souls in the earthly copies of them: they are seen through a glass dimly; and there are few who, going to the images, behold in them the realities, and these only with difficulty." (Phaedrus 250b)

d)

(Socrates speaking) "The unexamined life is not worth living." (Apology 38a).

(Socrates speaking) "The knowledge at which geometry aims is knowledge of the eternal, and not of aught perishing and transient." (Republic 527b)

(Socrates speaking) "At any rate, we are satisfied, as before, to have four divisions; two for intellect and two for opinion, and to call the first division science, the second understanding, the third belief, and the fourth perception of shadow, opinion being concerned with becoming, and intellect with being; and so to make a proportion--

As being is to becoming, so is pure intellect to opinion.
And as intellect is to opinion, so is science to belief,
and understand to the perception of shadows."

(Republic 533e-534a)

236a)

(Socrates speaking) "In the first place the tyrant is always stirring up some war so that the people may be in need of a leader...And so that being impoverished by war taxes they may have to devote themselves to their daily business and be less likely to plot against him." (Republic 566e-567a)

(Socrates is giving an example of what tyranny is) "From individual wealthy private citizens in our states who possess many slaves. For these resemble the tyrant in being rulers over many, only the tyrant's numbers are greater." (Republic 578d)

(Socrates--talking about the tripartate soul: wisdom, courage, and temperance) "Then when the entire soul accepts the guidance of the wisdom-loving part and is not filled with inner dissension, the result for each part is that it in all other respects keeps to it own task and is just." (Republic 586e)

b)

(The words of Plutarch about Plato's prayer of gratitude to God as he saw death approaching)

"Plato, when he saw his death approaching, thanked the Guiding Providence and Fortune of his life, first, that he was born a man and a Grecian, not a brute or a barbarian, and next that he happened to live in the age of Socrates" (Plutarch: Life of Caius Marius)

Aristotle:

"It promotes health to reduce one's diet and increase one's exercise." (865a)

"Sexual intercourse is the most pleasant of all things to animals." (878b)

"The fat is consumed in those who exert themselves." (880b)

"Man who of all animals has the advantage of most education, yet is the most unjust of all."(950b)

c)

Persius:

"Rely not always on the general voice;
Nor place all merit in the peoples' choice;
Let your own eyes be those with which you see;
Nor seek in others what you yourself should be. (I.11-15)

"Think not, when well, if ever well I write,
I feel from praise no genuine delight:
But praise ought not to be the only end
For which our morals or our lives we mend;
For which our virtue struggles to excel,
And seeks pre-eminence in doing well." (I. 77-82)

"Let Truth's fair form confess'd before them rise,
And virtue stand reveal'd to mortal eyes,
Astonish tyrants by her placid mien,
And teach them, dying, what they might have been." (III.59-62)

d)

[Persius 34-62 CE: died at age 28 after his attacks were recognized to be against Nero, possibly during the prosecution by Nero against his Stoic critics]

Publius Syrus (c. 50 BCE)

"As you treat a neighbour, expect another to treat you."

"Love your parent, if he is just: if not, bear with him."

"Others' possessions are plenty to us, ours to them."

"Hasty judgement means speedy repentance."

"Misfortune reveals whether you have a friend or only one in name."

"Rule your feelings lest your feelings rule you."

"No gain satisfies a greedy mind."
"Good ideas may fail but are not lost."
"With the good man anger is quick to die."
"From a neighbor's fault a wise man corrects his own."
"To shun desire is to conquer a kingdom."
"The end always passes judgment on what has preceded."
"What can't be changed you should bear, not blame."
"Man is only lent to life, not given."
"The spiteful mind has hidden teeth."
"You may spare even the bad, if the good is to perish along with him."
"Do not despise the steps which raise to greatness."
"Youth must be mastered not by force but by reason."
"For a fool it is wisdom to hold his tongue."
"By testing everything even the blind walk safely."
"Goodness means the inability to do a wrong."

237a)

Seneca:

"Each day acquire something which will help you to face poverty, or death, and other ills as well. After reflecting over a lot of different thoughts, pick out one to be digested thoroughly that day."

"Since I have mentioned the gods I might propose that the ideal to which a prince might best mold himself is to deal with his subjects as he would wish the gods to deal with him." [The "prince" of Rome at that time was Nero] (From *On Clemency)*

"Treat your inferior as you would wish your superior to treat you."

b)

Plutarch:

"To return to Cleopatria; Plato admits four sorts of flattery, but she had a thousand." (*Lives*: Antony)
"It is both more noble and delightful to do than to receive a kindness." (*That a Philosopher Ought Chiefly to Converse With Great Men*)

Cicero:

"Socrates was perfectly right when he declared that there is a direct short-cut to winning a reputation: 'Make yourself the sort of man you want people to think you are.'" (*On Duties II*)
"Friendship is only possible between good men." (*Laelius: On Friendship*)

"As Ennius rightly said, a friend in need is a friend indeed." (*Laelius: On Friendship*)

c)
Epictetus:

"It is circumstances which show what men are. Therefore when a difficulty falls upon you, remember that God, like a trainer of wrestlers, has matched you with a rough young man." (I.24)
"He meets with a man as a man, who learns his opinions, and in his turn shows his own. Learn my opinions: show me yours; and then say that you have visited me." (III.9)
"Can we abolish the acropolis (logos-reason) which is in us and cast out the tryants (passions) within us, whom we have daily over us, sometimes the same tyrants, at other times different tyrants?" (IV.1)
"I indeed would rather that a young man, who is making his first movements towards philosophy, should come to me with his hair carefully trimmed than with it dirty and rough, for there is seen in him a certain notion of beauty, and a desire of that which is becoming."(IV.11)
"What then? is it possible to be free from faults? It is not possible, but this is possible, to direct your efforts incessantly to being faultless." (IV.12)

d)
Stobaeus (*Pythagoric Ethical Sentences*):

"The grace of freedom of speech, like beauty in season, is productive of greater delight...Neither the sun to be taken from the world, nor freedom of speech from erudition."
"The rabble is a bad judge of a good thing."
"Those that do not punish bad men, wish that good men

may be injured."

Sextus the Pythagorean:

"Such as you wish your neighbor to be to you, such also be you to your neighbors."

"Before you do any thing think of God, that his light may precede your energies."

"The greatest honor which can be paid to God, is to know and imitate him. There is not any thing, indeed, which wholly resembles God; nevertheless the imitation of him as much as possible by an inferior nature is grateful to him."

238a)

Evagrios the Solitary: *On Prayer.*

"If you patiently accept what comes, you will always pray with joy."

Mark the Ascetic: *On The Spiritual Law.*

"Never reject criticism uncritically."

Attributed to Antony the Great:

"When people come to an inn, some receive beds; others, having no bed, sleep on the floor, and these too snore just as much as those who sleep on beds. But when, after their night's stay, they leave the inn early next morning, all set off alike, each taking with him only what belongs to him. In the same way, all who come into this life, both those who live modestly, and those who enjoy wealth and ostentation, leave this life like an inn: each takes with him none of its pleasures and riches, but only his own past actions whether good or bad."

b)

Thalassios the Libyan:

"An all-embracing and intense longing for God binds those who experience it, both to God and to one another."

"Love alone harmoniously joins all created things with God and with each other."

"The true ruler is he who rules over himself and has subjected soul and body to the intelligence."

Rumi: (In expressing the idea that it is love between God and man that binds them together in joy: not doctrines or asceticism)

"The fearful ascetic runs on foot, along the surface,
Lovers move like lightning and wind.
No contest.
Theologians mumble, rumble-dumble,
necessity and free will,
while lover and beloved
pull themselves into each other."

(In speaking of one's spiritual journey towards the eternal)
"Your 'real' country is where you're heading,
not where you are."

c)

"There was once a man
who inherited a lot of money and land.
But he squandered it all too quickly.
Those who inherit wealth
do not know what work it took to get it.
In the same way, we do not know the value of our souls,
which were given to us for nothing!"

"The wine God loves,
is human honesty."

Meister Eckhart:

"Whether you like it or not,
whether you know it or not,
secretly all nature seeks God
and works toward him."

d)

"Let whoever wishes to be the best loved of all people,
be the best of all people."

Ficino:

"We, the family of Plato, know nothing except what is bright,
joyful, celestial and supreme."

Thomas Browne:

"Calculate thyself within, seek not thyself in the moon, but in thine own orb or microcosmical circumference."

Benjamin Whichcote:

"The good nature of a heathen is more Godlike than the furious zeal of a Christian."

239a)

"The proud man has no God.
The unpeaceful man has no neighbor.
The distrustful man has no friend.
The discontented man has not himself."

Erasmus' *Adages*

"Make haste slowly" (σπευδε βραδεως -- festina lente).
"A wise promptness together with moderation, tempered with both vigilance and gentleness, so that nothing is done rashly and then regretted."

"The Sileni of Alcibiades" (Σειληνοι Αλκιβιαδου — Sileni Alcibiadis).
"Used either with reference to a thing which in appearance seems ridiculous and contemptible, but on closer and deeper examination proves to be admirable, or else with reference to a person whose looks and dress do not correspond at all to what he conceals in his soul. For it seems that the Sileni were small images divided in half, and so constructed that they could be opened out and displayed; when closed represented some ridiculous, ugly flute-player, but when opened they suddenly revealed the figure of a god."

b)

The use of this concept comes from Plato in his Symposium and is part of the speech of Alcibiades praising Socrates as the Eros incarnate. It reads: "What he (Socrates) reminds me of more than anything is one of those little sileni that you see on the statuaries' stalls; you know the ones I mean-- they're modeled with pipes or flutes in their hands, and when you open them down the middle there are little figures of the gods inside." The point that Alcibiades was making was that Socrates' physical body's oldness and unattractiveness were very deceptive because inside of him was an inner divine beauty that far excelled his outer appearance.

"War is sweet only to those who have not experienced it." (Γλυκυς απειρω πολεμος -- Dulce bellum inexpertis)

c)

Immanuel Kant: (From *Observations on the Feeling of the Beautiful and Sublime*)

"He who perpetually chatters is silly."

"He whose words or deeds neither entertain nor move one is boring."

"Subduing one's passions through principles is sublime. Castigations, vows, and other such monks' virtues are grotesque."

"Among moral attributes true virtue alone is sublime."

"A certain tender heartedness, which is easily stirred into a warm feeling of sympathy, is beautiful and amiable, for it shows a charitable interest in the lot of others, to which principles of virtue likewise lead."

"In summary of the basic principle, I say that it is the feeling of the beauty and the dignity of human nature. The first is a ground of universal affection, the second of universal esteem."

d)

"A vain and frivolous person is always without strong feeling for the sublime, and his religion is without emotion, for the most part only a thing of fashion, which he attends with all politeness while remaining cold."

Francis Bacon: (from the Novum Organum)

"There are four classes of idols which beset men's mind.
To these for distinction's sake I have assigned names --
calling the first class, idols of the tribe;
the second, idols of the cave;

the third, idols of the market-place;
the fourth, idols of the theatre."

240a)
Ralph Waldo Emerson:

"Be a gift and a benediction. Shine with real light and not with the borrowed reflection of gifts. (*Spiritual Laws*)

"There are not in the world at any one time more than a dozen persons who read and understand Plato:--never enough to pay for an edition of his works; yet to every generation these come duly down, for the sake of those few persons, as if God brought them written in his hand." (*Spiritual Laws*) [Things are better now, Ralph, but, unfortunately, not that much better]

"The good soul nourishes me and unlocks new magazines of power and enjoyment to me every day. I will not meanly decline the immensity of good, because I have heard that it has come to others in another shape." (*Spiritual Laws*)

"But (if) the man and woman of seventy assume to know all, they have outlived their hope, they renounce aspiration, accept the actual for the necessary and talk down to the young. Let them then (however) become organs of the Holy Ghost; let them be lovers; let them behold truth; and their eyes are uplifted, their wrinkles smoothed, they are perfumed again with hope and power. This old age ought not to creep on a human mind. In nature every moment is new; the past is always swallowed and forgotten; the coming only is sacred." (*Circles*)

b)
JDE:

"Test the Idols and "Spiritual Giants": are their teachings of the highest spiritual nature? Do their lives match their teachings? Do their high spiritual natures live on in their followers? Are such powers for all people? Are their principles universally valid? Are they of perpetual truth and a reflection of eternity?

Or are they temporary, localized, shortsighted, unhistorical, unscientific and confined to irrelevant and obsolete mythical thinking?"

Julian Huxley: (*Religion Without Revelation*)

"So it is with the religious feeling, the sentiment of sacredness. No one expects a child of four to have the same kind of religious life as a boy of sixteen, or either of them as a man of thirty.... The history of religion is the history of gradual change in the situations which, with increase of experience and changed conditions of life, are felt as sacred. It is in the main (like the history of humanity as a whole, or the history of science as a whole) a history of progress."

c)

Dag Hammarskjold: (*Markings*)

"Don't be afraid of yourself, live your individuality to the full--but for the good of others. Don't copy others in order to buy fellowship, or make convention your law instead of living the righteousness. To become free and responsible: for this alone was man created."

"Is life so wretched? Isn't it rather your hands which are too small, your vision which is muddled? You are the one who must grow up."

"God does not die on the day when we cease to believe in a personal deity, but we die on the day when our lives cease to be illumined by the steady radiance, renewed daily, of a wonder, the source of which is beyond all reason."

d)

"When he saw them all flee,
The skunk decided
He was King of the Beasts."

Hammarskjold's last recorded thoughts before he was killed in a plane crash on September 18, 1961 are the following words about a dream during the night:

> "Is it a new country in another world of reality than Day's?
> Or did I live there before day was?....But it is the same land.
> And I begin to know the map and to get my bearings."

Ψ

ΨI

CHAPTER TWENTY THREE
PLATONIC LOVE

241a)

Love to Plato is more than an emotional passion, it is a daimon placed by God into the hearts of men; a daimon that is passionate about beauty and by beauty it is strongly attracted. But the purpose of this attraction to beauty has manifold aspects based ultimately on man's loving desire for that which is perfect, never wavering, always present--not coming and going, eternal and good, Beauty Itself. However, every form of beauty is a reminder to the daimon of love of this one final purpose, and helps to initiate its quest for the Abstract and Eternal Beauty. Even a rose or a butterfly has a participation in the form of Perfect Beauty, and they are there to draw man back to the God who implanted the Daimon of love in the first place. That is why men and women are so restless in life, for they have within their minds and souls the desire for the Eternal Beauty and their quest is always innately reminding them not to be satisfied with the material and temporary participants in beauty but to seek that Good Beyond Being, Beauty Itself. The great dialogue, the *Symposium*, sometimes called the *Banquet,* takes the reader through various steps of the soul's ascent from one physical material aspect of the attraction of beauty to the Eternal and Absolute Beauty. It starts by trying to define love, and each participant in the dialogue puts forth his definition of love; one after the other. Each speech gives an element of a certain aspect of love and what it seeks, but each speech seems to spin its wheels without rising to the fulness of that which love ultimately seeks. Yet, the truths put forth are valid, although insufficient, and are not to be lightly discarded. Those ideas will also be presented below before the final definitive climb of the soul to Beauty Itself takes place. The quotations following are set forth in the order in which they are presented in the *Symposium*. Many of the quotations have been condensed and paraphrased to save the statements from undue length.

b)

Phaedrus speaks first the following:

"Love is the oldest of the divinities for even Hesiod declared:
'From Chaos rose broad-bosomed Earth, the sure
and everlasting seat of all this is, and afterwards, Love...'
In other words, after Chaos and the Earth, came love....and the antiquity of Love is universally acknowledged....For nothing but Love, nothing, not kindred, not honor and not wealth, but only Love can be that radiant light which a person must follow when he desires to experience the better life."

"Nothing but Love will lead a man to give his life for another -- and it not only motivates men to do so, but women also."

"I conclude then that Love is both the most noble and oldest of the gods, for He is the mightiest of the gods, and the chief author and giver of virtue in life, and of happiness after death."

c)

Pausanius speaks second:

"There are basically two types of love: the earthly and the heavenly. The earthly is physical and passionate, but the heavenly is more vigorous because it is intellectual and heavenly bent....Base is the vulgar lover who loves the body rather than the soul, inasmuch as he is not even stable, because he loves a thing which is in itself unstable, and therefore when the bloom of youth which he was desiring is over, he takes wing and flies away, in spite of all his words and promises; whereas the love of the noble disposition, a person's soul, is life-long, for it becomes one with the everlasting [the soul]."

"Love is also base when it is given for the sake of money or political prestige, or gives in to fear or ill-treatment...but if it is given in a desire for tender virtue and for the purpose of wisdom, that is, to know the other deeply, then it is the heavenly love."

Eryximachus is the third to speak, and stated:

d)

"Love is medicinal to the body, for medicine is the science of what the body loves and needs to be healthy, and that medicine itself is totally under the direction of the god of love. Love brings a healthy harmony to the body as well as to society, and directs our feelings of love to parents and towards all the divine things. It also nurtures decency, reverence, and friendship that they exist in a healthy state of body and mind."

Aristophanes, the comedian, speaks next:

Aristophanes is a comic break in the ongoing dialogue, jesting about man's three fold inclinations towards romantic and physical love: male to male, female to female, and male to female. He proposes that all human animals at one time were hermaphrodites in a sense: they were the union of two people: male with male, female with female, and male with female. They had four arms and four legs and proved to be rather pesky for the gods to handle and so the gods decided to cut them all in half. But ever since each has longed for the separated one: male for his lost male, female for her lost female, and male and female for each other. That, to Aristophanes, was the cause of the deep longing that some people had for each other, and it was perfectly natural. This presentation by Aristophanes was not to ridicule any of the three groups, but, since it was a reality in human, especially Greek, culture, this was the way he light heartedly explained it. "When the work of bisection was complete it left each half with a desperate yearning for the other, and they ran together and flung their arms around each other's necks, and asked for nothing better than to become one again." One thing the Greeks did accept, which was difficult for the Judeo-Christian tradition, was the naturalness of each of the three loves, each having a "desperate yearning for the other." Thus they let love take its course and honored it.

Agathon speaks of Love Himself:

242a)

"The previous speakers have focused their comments on the actions and blessings of Love, but seem to have forgotten to praise Him for Himself alone. They have not shown much of the nature of Love Himself...We ought to praise Him for what He is, and only after that, for what He has given to us...Love of all things is the loveliest and most blessed of all the gods."

"Love has such a high moral excellence He has never caused harm to anyone, and is himself never injured by anything. He never works by force, for those who meet Him accept Him gladly. Both weaker and stronger in virtue are mastered by Him. Also, even above his self-control and great virtue, He is a genius of a special sort, filled with wisdom. He, Love Himself, brings

'Peace upon earth, the breathless calm
That lulls the long-tormented deep,
Rest to the winds, and that sweet balm
b) And solace of our nature, sleep.'

He unites and brings friendship into gatherings such as we are now enjoying; in fact he is leading us in singing and dancing, cultivating courtesy and dispersing brutality. He is kind, gracious and tenderly loving. He brings the sense of wonder to the wise, and to him in despair He brings encouragement. His charm and grace present us with a delightful elegance and gives us a longing for the good. He, the very richest ornament in heaven, is our helper and pilot, directing us how to follow the good things of life, and He gives our songs a type of divinity that causes joy among us. Love, indeed, charms both our mortal and immortal natures."

c) Socrates then speaks and refers to a conversation he had with a woman of Mantinea, one whose name was Diotima (one who honors God). He learned from her that love is born of both poverty and wealth, for those were his parents, and he was therefore in the middle, neither poor nor wealthy. And as he recollects his father, he longs for that of great value which he believes to be the quality of beauty, but each time he experiences a type of beauty, even though it is delightful, he still senses something lacking and then continues to seek out the beautiful on progressively higher levels. He leaves the physical beauties, and searches the mental beauties and finally he reaches for the beauty of the eternal realm. During his search, he finds much satisfaction, but it is never totally fulfilling and it always ends up being a momentary experience. Diotima speaks of his ever rising spiritual ascent until he finally comes to Beauty Himself, face to face, that eternal and never ending Beauty, and then for the first time he realizes his friendship with God, who is Absolute and never changing Beauty. The following is from 210e-212a of the *Symposium.*

d)

Diotima speaking to Socrates:

"'He who has been instructed thus far in the things of love, and who has learned to see the beautiful in due order and succession, when he comes toward the end will suddenly perceive a nature of wondrous beauty (and this, Socrates, is the final cause of all our former toils) -- a nature which in the first place is everlasting, not growing and decaying, or waxing and waning; secondly, not beautiful in one point of view and foul in another, or at one time or in one relation or at one place beautiful, at another or in another relation or at another place foul, as if beautiful to some and foul to others, or in the likeness of a face or hands or any other part of the bodily frame, or in any form of speech or knowledge, or existing in any other being, as for example, in an animal, or in heaven, or in earth, or in any other place; but Beauty Absolute, separate, simple and everlasting, which without diminution and without increase, or any change, is imparted to the ever-growing and perishing beauties of all other things. He who from these ascending under the influence of true love, begins to perceive that beauty, is not far from the end. And the true order of going, or being led by another, to the things of love, is to begin from the beauties of earth and mount upwards for the sake of that other beauty, using these as steps only, and from one going on to two, and from two to **243a)** all beautiful bodily forms, and from beautiful bodily form to beautiful institutional practices, and from beautiful practices to beautiful knowledgeable concepts, until from these conceptual beauties, he arrives at the knowledge of Absolute Beauty, and at last knows what the essence of beauty is. This, my dear Socrates', said the stranger of Mantinea, 'is that life above all others which man should live, in the contemplation of Beauty Absolute; a beauty which if you once beheld, you would seek after the measure of gold, and garments, and beautiful youths, whose presence now entrances you; and you and many a one would be content to seeing them only and conversing with them without meat or drink, if that were possible--you only want to look at them and to be with them. But which if a man had eyes to see the True Beauty--the Divine Beauty, I mean, pure and clear and unalloyed, not clogged with the pollutions of mortality and all the colors and vanities of human life--thither looking, and holding converse with the True Beauty simple and divine? Remember how in that communion only, beholding beauty with the eye of the mind, he will be enabled to bring forth, not images of beauty, but realities (for he has hold not of an image but of a reality), and bringing forth and nourishing true virtue to become the friend of God and be immortal.'" (*Symposium* 210e-212a).

b)

Plotinus in his *Enneads*, III.5, says the following about love:

"It is sound, I think, to find the primal source of Love in a tendency of the Soul towards pure beauty, in a recognition, in a kinship, in an unreasoned consciousness of friendly relation."

"For every soul is striving towards The Good, even the mingling Soul and that of particular beings, for each holds directly from the divine Soul, and is its offspring."

"This indwelling love is no other than the Spirit which, as we are told, walks with every being, the affection dominant in each several nature. It implants the characteristic desire; the particular Soul, strained towards its own natural objects, brings forth its own Eros, the guiding spirit realizing its worth and the quality of its Being."

c)

"We understand, now, why good men have no other Love - no other Eros of life -- than that for the Absolute and Authentic Good."

Proclus believed that the Maker filled the intellect of man to make fine distinctions and differences among things, but also filled all men with love by which all the differences would be brought together in unity. "The Demiurgus is refulgent with intellectual sections, manifest that power of him which is effective of difference. But he fills all things with love through the power which is effective of sameness."(*The Commentaries of Proclus on the Timaeus of Plato: Book III)* He continued:

c)

"The One Demiurgus imparts friendship to the world...this greatest and most perfect of bonds, which the Father on all sides throws round the world, as being effective of the friendship and harmonious communion in it...The paternal self-begotten intellect understanding his works disseminated in all things, the bond of love heavy with fire...That all things might remain loving for an infinite time, woven together intellectually in all the light of the Father. For account of this love, all things are adapted to each other, that the elements of the world might remain running in love...The Demiurgus likewise possesses in himself the cause of Love. For he is the First Generator and much-pleasing Love Itself." (Book III)

d) Plato taught it simply that Eros, Love, was the mediator between God and man and that was what built a bridge between the divine and the mortal. Love itself brings a type of divinity between friends and unites them. Diadochos of Photiki stated that: "When a man begins to perceive the love of God in all its richness, he begins also to love his neighbour with spiritual perception...for the sweetness of God completely consumes (their differences)." (*On Spiritual Knowledge*) Marsilio Ficino who created the idea of "Platonic Love" made the following statements:

"I have followed the divine Plato from my youth. But you will easily distinguish my own writings from others in this way: in my letters, as far as in me lies, there is always a purpose relating to morals, natural subjects, or theology. But if occasionally there is anything in them in some way relating to love, it is certainly Platonic and honorable."23.1

244a)

"In that happiness the joy surpasses the vision. For as we find more merit with God in this life by loving Him than by searching for Him, so the reward in the next life is greater for loving than searching. We find far more merit by loving than by searching for many reasons. First, because no one in this life truly knows God."23.2

In his Platonic Theology, book 14, Ficino stated the following:

"Love unites the mind with God more quickly, more closely, and more firmly than does knowledge, because the force of knowledge consists more in distinction; that of love more in union...We are united more closely with God though the joy of love, which assimilates us to the beloved God, than through knowledge...Furthermore, recognizing God, we contract His amplitude to the capacity and concept of our mind; but loving Him, we enlarge the mind to the immense amplitude of divine goodness. There, so to speak, we lower God to our level; here, we lift ourselves to God. For we know as far as we can comprehend; but we love both what we see clearly and what we expect as the remainder of the divine goodness beyond our clear sight."

b)

Jeremy Taylor, one of the Cambridge Platonists, wrote the following:

"But once we have entered and tasted the goodness of God, we love the Spring for its own excellence, passing from feeling to reason, from thanking to adoring, from sense to spirit, from consideration of ourselves into a union with God. This is a reflection and small foretaste of heaven. It is a picture of blessedness, the beginnings of glory. We need no incentives by way of special mention to move us to the love of God, for the excellence of anything we love for any reason is found infinitely greater in God. Only two things can create love: perfection and usefulness. Our response to them is admiration and desire, and both of these are centered in love. Perfection in God is infinite, eternal, without limit or change."23.4

c)

Peter Sterry another Cambridge Platonists reflects his reading of Plato's *Symposium* in his work *A Discourse of the Freedom of the Will:*

"Study the love of God, the nature of God, as he is love, the work of God, and the perfection of his work....That love is the bond of perfection. It is love then, which runs through the whole work of God, which frames, informs, unites all into one masterpiece of divine love...Study and practice that great command of love, as the lesson of your whole life, with which alone you are to entertain yourself, and all the heavenly company, both here and in eternity...Be yourself in your whole person, the sacrifice of a whole burnt-offering, ascending in a sacred flame of heavenly love to God, the only and Eternal Beauty...So let his heavenly love of the Divine Beauty, which is the Beauty Itself, descending in a pure and sweet flame upon you, by consuming you, convert you into one spiritual flame with itself."

d)

Leibniz framed love with these words:

"To love is to be led to take pleasure in the perfection, well-being or happiness of the beloved object. And for this reason we do not consider or demand any other pleasure for self than just that which is found in the well-being of pleasure of the one loved." (*Knowledge And Metaphysics: Chapter Twenty).*

"A good man moreover is one who loves all men as much as reason permits. Justice, therefore, which virtue is the mistress of the affection the Greeks call love of mankind (φιλανθρωπια -- philanthropy), will be defined, most properly, unless I am mistaken, as the love of the wise man (*caritatem sapientis),* that is, love according to the dictates of wisdom." (*On the Notions of Right and Justice).*

245a)

Ascanio Condivi wrote these words of Michelangelo Buonarroti, and one can immediately see the Platonic love of the beautiful theme in his description of Michelangelo:

"I have often heard Michael Angelo reason and discourse of Love, and learned afterwards from those who were present that he did not speak otherwise of Love than is to be found written in the works of Plato. For myself I do not know what Plato says of Love, but I know well that I, who have known Michael Angelo so long and so intimately, have never heard issue from his mouth any but the most honest of words, which had the power to extinguish in youth every ill-regulated and unbridled desire which might arise. But this we may know that no evil thoughts were born in him. He loved not only human beauty, but universally every beautiful thing--a beautiful horse, a beautiful dog, a beautiful country, a beautiful plant, a beautiful mountain, a beautiful forest, and every place and thing beautiful and rare after its kind, admiring them all with a marvelous love;

thus choosing the beauty in nature as the bees gather honey from the flowers, using it afterwards in their works, as all those have done who have ever made a noise in painting."23.5

b)

The Renaissance in Italy especially but elsewhere also was immersed and even baptized into Plato, and it was not only because of the Florintine Academy sponsored by the Medici and led by Ficino. Rather the Academy was necessitated by the power of Plato, as well as all Greek culture, which reappeared slightly after the revival of ancient Roman culture, but carried a more powerful soul and impact within the Renaissance in its natural and universal nature. John Colet felt strongly the Platonic Tradition, in Plato and also in Plotinus, and it is evident in his words:

"God pours forth abundantly his sweet goodness that it may return again to him...who, though stationary in himself, yet marvelously extends himself to others, that by his fragrant grace he may draw them together to himself...(God can) communicate bountifully...to others...his own divinity...without in any wise departing from himself, or lessening his own majesty."23.6

c)

Colet as did many others during the Renaissance, such as Ficino and Erasmus refer to Plato as the Divine Plato and the Divine Philosopher, as did those ancient Platonists of the Greco-Roman world. Emanuel Swedenborg in his Divine Love and Wisdom (28) made them the two ultimate sisters of the spirit of man:

"Sum up all things you know and submit them to careful inspections, and in some elevation of spirit search for the universal of all things, and you cannot conclude otherwise than that it is Love and Wisdom. For these are the two essentials of all things of man's life; everything of that life, civil, moral, and spiritual hinges upon these two, and apart from these two is nothing. (29) Love together with wisdom in its very essence is in God... (30) It is because the Divine Essence itself is Love and Wisdom that man has two capacities for life; from one of these he has understanding, from the other will... (31) It is because the Divine Essence itself is Love and Wisdom, that all things in the universe have relation to good and truth; for everything that proceeds from love is called good, and everything that proceeds from wisdom is called truth... (39) But so far as a man does from love what wisdom teaches, he is an image of God."

d)

From the Theologia Germanica:

"Hence it follows, that in a truly Godlike man, his love is pure and unmixed, and full of kindness, in so much that he cannot but love in sincerity all men and things, and wish well, and do good to them, and rejoice in their welfare." (Chapter 33)

"Some may ask, 'What is it to be a partaker of the Divine Nature, or a Godlike man?' Answer: he who is imbued with or illuminated by the Eternal or Divine Light, and inflamed or consumed with Eternal or Divine Love, he is a Godlike man and a partaker of the Divine Nature; and of the nature of this True Light we have said somewhat already. But you must know that this Light or knowledge is worth nothing without Love. This you may see if you call to mind, that though a man may know very well what is virtue or wickedness, yet if he does not love virtue, he is not virtuous." (Chapter 41)

246a)

"But true Love is taught and guided by the true Light and Reason, and this true, eternal and divine Light teaches Love to love primarily the One true and Perfect Good, and that simply for its own sake, and not for the sake of a reward, or in the hope of obtaining anything, but simply for the Love of Goodness, because it is good and has a right to be loved. And all that is thus seen by the help of the True Light must also be loved of the True Love. Now that Perfect Good, which we call God, cannot be perceived but by the True Light; therefore He must be loved whenever life is seen or made known." (Chapter 42)

b)

"When the true Divine Light and Love dwell in a man, he loves nothing else but God alone, for he loves God as Goodness and for the sake of Goodness, and all Goodness as One, and one as All; for, in truth, All is One and One is All in God." (Chapter 47)

Auguste Sabatier from his *Outlines of a Philosophy of Religion*, p.133:

"The Father who lives in me lives equally in my neighbor; He loves him as much as He loves me. I ought therefore to love Him in my neighbor as well as in myself. This paternal presence of God in all human souls creates in them not only a link but a substantial and moral unity which makes them members of one body, whatever may be the external and contingent differences which separate them. From the Fatherhood in heaven flows the brotherhood on earth. From a relation of righteousness and love towards God springs a similar relation between men."

c)

From Walt Whitman's *Leaves*, 1855 edition:

"Swiftly arose and spread around me the peace and joy and
knowledge that pass all the art and argument of the earth;
And I know that the hand of God is the elder hand of my own,
And I know that the spirit of God is the eldest brother of my own,
And that all the men ever born are also my brothers,
....and the women my sisters and lovers,
And that a kelson of creation is love."

From G.E. Moore's *Principia Ethica*, p.178:

d)

"The ethics of Plato are distinguished by upholding, far more clearly and consistently than any other system, the view that intrinsic value belongs exclusively to those states of mind which consist in love of what is good.."

From Josiah Royce's *Religious Aspect of Philosophy* (paraphrased and versed by William James and JDE) (pp. 157-162):

"What then, is our neighbor?
Thou has regarded his thought, his feeling,
as somehow different from thine.
Thou hast said, 'A pain in him is not like a pain in me,
but something far easier to bear.'

He seems to thee a little less living than thou;
his life is dim, it is cold, it is a pale fire beside
247a) thy own burning desires....
So, dimly and by instinct has thou lived with thy neighbor,
and hast known him not, being blind.
Thou hast made of him a thing,
no self at all.
Have done with this illusion,
and simply try to learn the truth.
Pain is pain, joy is joy,
everywhere, even as in thee.
In all the songs of the forest birds
in all the cries of the wounded and dying,
struggling in the captor's power;
in the boundless sea where the myriads of
water-creatures strive and die;
amid all the hordes of savage men:
in all sickness and sorrow;
in all exultation and hope, everywhere,
from the lowest to the noblest,
the same conscious burning willful life is found,
endlessly manifold as the form of living creatures,
unquenchable as the fires of the sun,
real as these impulses that even now
b) throb in thine own little selfish heart.
Of thy neighbor thou has made a thing,
no Self at all.
When thou hast loved, hast pitied,
or hast reverenced thy neighbor,
then thy feeling has possibly raised
for a moment the veil of illusion,
Then thou has known what he truly is,
a Self like thy present Self.
But thy selfish feeling is too strong for thee.
Thou hast forgotten soon again what thou hadst seen,
and hast made even of thy beloved one
only the instrument of thy own pleasure.
Lift up thy eyes, behold that life,

c) And then turn away, and forget it as thou canst;
But, if thou has known that,
thou hast begun to know thy duty.

William James from his essay *What Makes a Life Significant?*

"If you say that this is absurd, and that we cannot be in love with everyone at once, I merely point out to you that, as a matter of fact, certain persons do exist with an enormous capacity for friendship and for taking delight in other people's lives; and that such persons know more of truth than (other whose hearts are not so big)."

d) From the above one can realize that the good life of loving others is an impartial energy that glows to all, and is universal by nature. The love of the beautiful will find, in a kind and gracious way, beauty in all beings and will, by love, create in those beings the motive to become worthy of it. It is passing on the love that one has received from Beauty Itself, for the longing love towards Beauty itself, when assimilated then becomes a participant of that beauty and its power that also creates love in others by drawing them to the person participating in the Absolute Beauty. Being a beautiful person in mind and soul will create love in those beholding that very incarnate beauty. For it is the nature of Beauty to attract love and also love's nature to long for beauty. The two create a mutual compliance and promotion of each other. It creates a system of harmony and order that becomes a triumph over diversity. Such a creative life-energy comes from the exertion of love itself. And this energy cohabitates with both goodness and happiness.
248a)
John Smith, the Cambridge Platonist stated:

"Goodness and virtue make men know and love, believe and delight in their immortality. When the soul is purged and enlightened by true sanctity, it is more capable of those divine irradiations, whereby it feels itself in conjunction with God. It knows that almighty Love, by which it lives, is stronger than death. It knows that God will never forsake His own life, which He has quickened in the soul. Those breathings and gaspings after an eternal participation of Him are but the energy of His own breath within us."23.7

Pierre Teilhard de Chardin stated in his *Building the Earth*:

b)

"Love is a sacred reserve of energy,
and the very blood stream of spiritual evolution;
that is the first discovery we can make
from the Sense of Earth."

"One only--Love:
Love the supreme form and the totalizing principle
of human energy.
Picture a man who has become conscious
of his personal relations with a supreme Person
with whom he is led to merge
by the whole interplay of cosmic activity.
In such a man, and starting from him,
a process of unification is launched,
marked by the following stages:
-- the totalization of every operation in relation to the individual;
-- the totalization of the individual in relation to himself;
--and lastly, the totalization of the individual in the collective

c) Man.

All these so-called 'impossibilities' come about under the influence of love."

Gabriel Marcel: *The Mystery of Being, V 2*: pp 50-51.

"I think that we must all, in the course of our lives, have known beings who were essentially creators; by the radiance of charity and love shining from their being they add a positive contribution to the invisible work which gives the human adventure the only meaning which can justify it."

Gabriel Marcel in his *Sketch of a Phenomenology and Metaphysic of Hope*, stated:

d)

"By this I mean a reference to a certain spiritual interconnection at the heart of which my existence can preserve its meaning and its value. We are not dealing here with an abstraction, an impersonal order: if I inspire another being with love which I value and to which I respond, that will be enough to create this spiritual interconnection. The fact of the reciprocal love, the communion, will be enough to bring about a deep transformation in the nature of the bond which unites me to myself."

Paul Tillich stated in his *Theology of Culture*, p.145:

"Love includes justice. Love without justice is a body without a backbone. The justice of love includes that no partner in this relation is asked to annihilate himself. The self which enters a love relation is preserved in its independence. Love includes justice to others and to oneself. Love is the solution."

Daniel Day Williams in his *The Spirit and the Forms of Love*, made the following statement:

249a)

"Among the many issues we follow one clue to the relation of the divine and the human loves. This is that all the loves work within the history of the self's becoming. No love, whether it be the ethical love of neighbor, or the love in the sexual life, or the love of God for man, is a 'thing', a static pattern or form. It is a spirit at work in life and taking form in the process of becoming."

Douglas N Morgan in his *Love: Plato, the Bible & Freud* proclaimed: p 5

"Before Plato, no conception of love had ever been even remotely adequate to the depth and scope of human love. Since then, every philosopher and psychologist of love--and, indeed, every thoughtful human--has been in Plato's debt. Platonic love is not what most people think it is. It is not a cold and sexless friendship, or a dreamy, rococo thinking of beautiful thoughts together. It is not inhibited chivalric sentimentality....Platonic love is a disciplined, passionate commitment to all that is good and true and beautiful, and through these things, to the Goodness, Truth, and Beauty that make them so. As a psychological genius, Plato was both sensitive and tough-minded. As a hard-boiled moralist, his mind was disciplined. As a poet, he sought vivid clarity of thought, feeling and expression. As a philosopher, he dared to triangulate the universe."

Ω

ΩΜΕΓΑ

CHAPTER TWENTY FOUR
CONCLUSION

There are certain ways to judge the value of a religion:

250a)

1. What is actually known of the "founder" of the religion?
2. How is he or she presented in the religion's writings and teachings? Is there factual truth about his existence and the stories about him, or is he presented as a myth or legend?
3. Is the founder presented in such a way that he opens the hearts of the universal in mankind or does he speak only to his own tribe, race or nation and show a partiality of how his blessings are distributed?
4. How does the founder and his followers present the nature of God?
5. Are the claims by or about the founder rational or historically possible?
6. Have the ideals and ethics of the founder become actualized in the lives of his followers?
7. Have the Holy Scriptures or Canons of the religion become outdated and a hindrance to the advancement of humanity's welfare?
8. Is there any closemindedness towards those who are different or to scientific discovery?
9. Does the religion seek to control others by political, financial, psychological, or judicial power?
10. Does the religion breed love, peace and unity among humanity or does it sponsor hatred, judgmentalism, exclusivity, snobbishness and separation?
11. How do its followers treat the young, the weak, and the old?

12. How are man's kindred, the animals, and man's home, the earth, treated?
13. Are the "believers" of the religion both happy and ethical?

b)

These and other aspects of a religion are to be thought through by any person looking for spiritual nourishment, guidance and fellowship. Also it is necessary to remind oneself that "**An unexamined faith is not worth believing**". One should be as intelligent and logical about the way of life and worship that is selected as one would be about buying a new house or looking for a new job or about having children. Last of all is a personal introspection asking if one is richly and deeply happy and fulfilled with his faith and whether or not it gives him a joy in being ethical and moral.

In this present study of the value and history of the two holy scriptures of two different Abrahamic based religions, Judaism and Christianity have been analyzed and declared to be wholly inadequate for modern humanity, and, in fact, in many ways have been a hindrance to its personal growth and happiness as well as hindering scientific development for the enhancement of humanity's benefit and pleasure. Because Christianity has claimed so many people and so much power it has been the leader of all earth's religions in hypocrisy, cruelty, and desire to control absolutely all human culture. The third Abrahamic based religion, Islam, has not been discussed because its hold on the Western man has been insignificant, nevertheless, it too has shared in its own region an equal amount of divisiveness, cruelty, and judgmentalism toward "the infidel", and certainly has shown an inability to bring peace and mutual acceptance within itself.

c) The failures and cruelties of the Abrahamic religions have been and continue to be absent from those within in the Platonic Tradition, whose teachings have been put forth in this thesis for those seeking a philosophical religion that puts reason before myth, science before magic and superstition, openness of thought before closed and cemented creeds, piety before ritual, universality of God's love rather than elected or chosen people, no mythical apotheosis of its heroes that makes them idol gods without whom no one is pleasing to the Eternal Father of all, no guilt enforcement upon the natural pleasures, goodness as the basis of happiness and friendship, and does not need to frighten people into faith by teaching the fear of hell and the existence of Satan. It also presents a

God who, with delight and cheerfulness, made all men and women to have an eternal soul to enjoy the eternal realm of reality forever, and also taught that men and women are equals in both politics and priesthood. It has always scorned slavery comparing a slave owner to a petty tyrant, and tyranny was considered the absolute worse form of government. A fair sense of human rule, governed by the people of philosophical and ethical acumen, men and women equally, was always the goal of Plato's political ideal state.

d) Human goodness and happiness adorned with love and friendship, are, and have always been, the goals for those following the Platonic Tradition Education in the mechanical arts, mathematics, science, the fine arts, and the art of beautiful living as the means proposed for the sublime human life that each can experience the absolute beauty and joy of the human existence. It instills the wonder of life and the joy of pursuing truth. Its great virtues are the foundation of this sublime experience: justice, wisdom, courage, temperance, and holiness for the heavenly virtues and health, comeliness, strength, and wealth for the earthly virtues. These united in simplicity, honesty and love empower the human soul to live and enjoy the "divine" life, both here and now, and after the death of the body, forever. Such is the Platonic Faith.

CALENDAR

Of Things & People to Honor and Celebrate

January	1	New Year's Opening to the Future
	8	Axiothea: Female Student at Plato's Academy
	14	Albert Schweitzer's Birthday: Philosopher and Humanitarian
	25	Eudoxus: Professor of Mathematics at Academy
February	1	Immanuel Kant: Platonist, Embodiment of Reason
	9	Hypatia: She embodied Nobility and Philosophy
	21	Ammonius Saccas: Teacher of Plotinus & Origen
March	1	J. W. Von Goethe: Platonic Scientist, Poet, Politician, & Philosopher
	10	Festival of the Fine Arts
	20	Spring: Earth Day: Greek Anthesteria Festival
	21	Johann Sebastian Bach's Birthday
April	1	Antiochus of Ascalon: Influenced Scipio's Circle
	8	Honoring Science
	15	Zeno of Citium, Founder of Stoic School
	23	Socrates' Diotima & Boethius's Lady Philosophy
May	6	Socrates' Birthday: Traditional
	7	Plato's Birthday: Traditional
	15	J C F Schiller: Ode to Joy, Alle Menschen werden Brueder (All Men are Brothers)
	20	Aratus: Mapped the Heavens
June	1	Aristarchus:Taught the Heliocentric Planetary System 250 BCE
	8	Friede, Freude, Freiheit (Peace, Joy, Freedom)
	15	Hipparchus: invented Trigonometry
	21	Honoring the Animal Kingdom

CALENDAR

July	5	Longinus: The Platonic "Living Library"
	12	The Florentine Academy: The Medicis and Ficino
	20	Francis of Assisi: Love of Earth and its Animal Children
	20	Plutarch: The Greatest of the Middle Platonists
August	3	Celsus: Platonic Apologist & Defender of the Faith
	10	David Friedrich Strauss: Critic of Judeo-Christian Bible's Historical Accounts and teacher of Plato
	16	Festival of Friendship and Family
	25	Eunapius: Platonic Apologist
September	1	Plotinus: First Major Neoplatonist
	8	In Honor of the Mechanical Arts
	15	Greek Karneia: A Three Day Festival of Games, Music, Dancing, and Feasting
	22	Nicholas Copernicus: Revived Aristarchus
October	5	Libanius of Antioch: Educator
	18	Porphyry: Edited Plotinus & Platonic Apologist
	27	Birthday of Desiderius Erasmus: Example of Wisdom and Peacefulness
November	1	Julian: Platonist Emperor of Rome
	10	Martin Luther: An Example of Courage
	18	Boethius: Consolation of Philosophy
	25	F E D Schleiermacher: Translator of Plato into German
December	1	Benjamin Jowett: Translator of Plato into English
	8	Nicholas of Cusa: Rescuer of Platonic Manuscripts from the East
	15	Michaelangelo Buonarroti: Painter & Poet
	25	Traditional Celebration of Birthday of Jesus of Nazareth, an Example of Courage
	31	Day of Thanksgiving for the Year

"Plato, when he saw his death approaching, thanked the guiding Providence and Fortune of his life, first, that he was born a man and a Grecian, not a brute beast or a barbarian, and next, that he happened to live in the age of Socrates." (Plutarch: Life of Caius Marius)

GLOSSARY

Academy	The philosophical school established by Plato, 386 BCE.
Adiaphoria	Issues or actions that are insignificant morally.
Aition	Cause.
Arche Aition	First Cause.
Arete	Virtue or the excellence of function.
The Banquet	Another name for Plato's Symposium.
Corpus Hermeticum	Sacred books by the Platonically influenced Gnostics attributed to a Hermes Trrismegistus, but in reality written at different times by different people.
Cosmos	(Gk KOSMOS) The ordered material universe.
Daimon	(Daemon or Demon) A spirit within man: in Plato it is used for the spirit of love, Eros, that focuses upon and desires beauty, but especially Absolute Beauty Itself, that is, God, and continually drives man by desire back to God and keeps his soul restless until seeing Beauty Itself face to face.
Eros	Love, driven by its own nature to Ultimate and Eternal Beauty.
Doxa	Opinion or belief, contrasted and inferior to knowledge, Gnosis.
Gnosis	Knowledge.
Gymnasium	A center of Hellenistic learning within a city: multiple forms of education offered; rhetoric, music, mathematics, and athletic development.
Hubris (Hybris)	A Greek word meaning inordinate pride or arrogance, especially of man's haughty attitude before the gods.
Kallos	Beautiful and good
Know Yourself	Delphi Oracle: (γνωθι σαυτον - gnothi sauton: or sometimes γνωθι σεαυτον – gnothi seauton).
Koine	The Greek language that was spread throughout the OIKOUMENE and was its common language for all the peoples: the "lingua franca" of the Mediterranean World.
Logos	The reasoning element of the intellect (NOUS): but was used in various ways. Was personalized in Middle Platonism by the Alexandrian Platonists. Often used to

	mean a spoken saying that was a logical expression. Often translated "word", and it was the source of the word logic.
Lyceum	The philosophical school established by Aristotle, and stressed the biological studies as well as all other forms of philosophy.
Metanoia	Change of mind, conversion, repentance. Plato used it to denote man's change from focusing on the temporal world to focusing on the eternal world, which gave men a completely new and deeper meaning to life.
Mimeomai.	Imitation, to imitate. A theme within Plato was to focus upon the good and beautiful (Virtues of God), and seek to imitate them as much as possible.
Moira	A Greek word: the force of destiny or fate.
Myth	(Μυθος) Myth, story, or account
Nike	The Greek Goddess of victory.
Nous	The intellect or mind, often used of God.
Oikoumene	"Household administration" is referred to as a concept denoting the administration of the entire Eastern Mediterranean World by the Greeks, who considered the territory their own "household." Economy is derived from it.
Ortho-doxa	Correct belief or opinion.
Paideia	The Greek form of education that ended at our high school level. Plato established the first University level school with his Academy.
Pankration	Greek game made by combining boxing and wrestling: the most brutal contest of the games.
The Piraeus	Athens' seaport.
Psyche	Plato's word for man's eternal soul.
Q	Quelle (German word for source) symbolizing a literary source from which both Matthew's gospel and Luke's gospel received saying of Jesus.
Septuagint	"Work of the Seventy": thus abbreviated LXX, based on a legend that seventy translators of the Hebrew Scripture into Greek, working separately, all had the exact same translation. But this legend and historical reality differ greatly.

Stromata	Miscellanies.
Tanak(h)	Term used for the Hebrew Scriptures: an acronym: T for Torah-the Law, N for Nevi'im-the Prophets, and K for Kethubim-the Sacred Scriptures.
Theophiles	"One whom God loves" or "Beloved of God" or "Friend of God."
To Agathon	The Good.
Torah	Hebrew name for the first five books of the Bible, attributed to Moses, thus the books of Moses, or The Law.

NOTES

CHAPTER THREE

3.1 Der Spiegel. On The New Testament, pp 180-181
3.2 Ibid, p 95
3.3 Ernst Kaesemann, Exegetische Versuche und Besinnungen, vol.2
3.4 Ernst Kaesemann, Essays on the New Testament Themes, p.188
3.5 Martin Niemoeller, Eine Welt order keine Welt, p 120
3.6 "Wundergeschicten der Bibel in der Grundschule". Evangelische Unterweisung, Febr. 1966, p 44.
3.7 A H M Jones, Constantine and the Conversion of Europe, p 189
3.8 Hermann Doerries, Constantine the Great. p 227
3.9 Carolly Erickson, The Records of Medieval Europe, p 95
3.10 Aldous Huxley, The Perennial Philosophy, pp 133-134
3.11 Jerry Dell Ehrlich, The Joy of Embracing God, p 92
3.12 J.B. Bury, History of the Later Roman Empire, 2 vols., pp 360-361
3.13 Harold Mattingly, Christianity in the Roman Empire, pp 93-94

CHAPTER FIVE

5.1 Kurt Seligman, Magic, Supernaturalism and Religion, pp 182-183

CHAPTER SIX

6.1 A E Taylor, Plato: the Man and his Work, p 5
6.2 LCL (tr. R G Bury)

CHAPTER SEVEN

7.1 Barry Gross, Great Thinkers on Plato, p 94
7.2 Constantin Ritter, The Essence of Plato's Philosophy, p 308
7.3 The Autobiography of Giambattista Vico, tr. Fisch & Bergin, p 138
7.4 Jaroslav Pelikan, The Growth of Medieval Theology (600-1300) p 100

NOTES

CHAPTER NINE

9.1 Plutarch, Sentiments Concerning Nature with which Philosophers were Delighted: Book One, Chapter 7: "What is God?"
9.2 The Essential Plotinus, tr. O'Brien, p 78
9.3 Rudolf Otto, The Idea of the Holy, p 154
9.4 Leland Miles, John Colet and the Platonic Tradition, p 35
9.5 The Philokalia, vol 2, tr. Palmer, Sherrard, Ware, p 228
9.6 Iamblichus, Life of Pythogoras, p 148
9.7 F C Happold, Mysticism, p 217
9.8 Paul Tillich, Theology of Culture, p 23
9.9 Julian Huxley, Religion Without Revelation, p 33
9.10 Walter Burkert, Greek Religion, p 275
9.11 Iamblichus, Life of Pythogoras, p 192
9.12 Plutarch, Essays, vol 3, p 34
9.13 John M Rist, Eros and Psyche, p 82
9.14 Constanitn Ritter, op cit., pp 373-374
9.15 Pseudo-Dyonysius, p 114
9.16 The Philokalia vol 2, p 88
9.17 Ibid. p 181
9.18 Marsilio Ficino, Platonic Theology, vol 1, p 195
9.19 Aldous Huxley, The Perennial Philosphy, p 169
9.20 Iamblichus, op cit., p 144
9.21 Marsilio Ficino, Meditations of the Soul, p 65
9.22 R W Emersion, Self Reliance and Other Essays, p 55

CHAPTER TEN

10.1 Iamblichus, Life of Pythagoras, 161
10.2 Seneca, Letters from a Stoic, pp 122-123
10.3 Ibid., 130
10.4 Jacob Boehme, The Way to Christ, p 98
10.5 The Portable Renaissance Reader, p 390
10.6 Leibniz, Selections, p 526
10.7 Ibid., pp 526-527
10.8 Teilhard de Chardin, Letters From a Travelor, p 164
10.9 Plutarch's Essays, Penguin Classics, p 348

10.10 Longinus, On Great Writing, p 47
10.11 C K Barrett, The New Testament Background: Selected Documents, p 65
10.12 Iamblichus, Life of Pythagoras, p 179
10.13 The Philokalia vol. I, p 338
10.14 Leibniz, Selections, p 369
10.15 Ibid., p 397
10.16 Cambridge Platonist Spirituality,, p 170
10.17 Auguste Sabatier, Outlines of a Philosophy of Religion, p 1
10.18 Teilhard de Chardin, Hymn of the Universe, p 91
10.19 Abraham H Maslow, Religious Values, and Peak-Experiences, p 18
10.20 Henry A Murray, Myth and Mythmaking, p 61
10.21 Anne Fremantle, Christian Conversation, p July 4

CHAPTER ELEVEN

11.1 Cambridge Platonist Spirituality, p 95-96
11.2 Hegel, Lectures on the Philosophy of Religion, pp 75-76, 116, 196
11.3 August sabatier, op. cit., p 40
11.4 W R Inge, Platonic Tradition in English Religious Thought, p 40
11.5 Rudolf Bultmann, Jesus Christ and Mythology, pp 63, 81
11.6 Plutarch, Essays and Miscellanies, vol. 3, p 324
11.7 The Letters of Younger Pliny, p 230
11.8 Seneca, Letters from a Stoic, p 212
11.9 Iamblichus, op. cit., p 145
11.10 Ibid., pp 192-194
11.11 Paul Tillich, Christianity and the Encounter of the World Religions, p 63-64
11.12 The World Treasury of Modern Religioous Thought, ed. by J. Pelikan, p 492
11.13 Erasmus, The Handbook of the Militant Christian, p 36
11.14 Hegel, Lectures on the Philosophy of Religion, p 193
11.15 Charlest Taylor, Hegel, p 482
11.16 Schleiermacher, On Religion, p 7
11.17 Ibid., p 16

11.18 Ibid., p 36
11.19 Ibid., p 40-41
11.20 Ibid., p 63
11.21 Freemantle, op. cit., April 21
11.22 Iamblichus, op. cit., p 52
11.23 The Philokalia, vol. 1, p 355
11.24 Jeremy Taylor, Holy Living, pp 24-25
11.25 George Santayana, Interpretations of Poetry and Religion, pp 136-137
11.26 R W Emerson, Self-Reliance, p 33
11.27 Jacob Boehme, op. cit., p 98
11.28 August Sabatier, op. cit., p 107
11.29 Thomas Browne, Religio Medici, pp 85-86

CHAPTER TWELVE

12.1 Seneca, Letters From a Stoic, p 120
12.2 Walter Burkert, Greek Religion, pp 84-86
12.3 Long and Sedley, The Hellenistic Philosophers, p 330
12.4 Marcus Aurelius, Meditations, p 78
12.5 Plutarch, Essays and Miscellanies, vol. 3, p 168
12.6 Commentaries of Proclus on the Timaeus of Plato, p 286
12.7 Freemantle, op. cit., Janurary 25
12.8 Ibid., May 18
12.9 Teilhard de Chardin, Letters from a Traveller, pp 67-68
12.10 Pliny, Natural History, p 102
12.11 Ibid, p 123
12.12 Pliny's Letters, vol 2, LCL, pp 255-257
12.13 Kant, Vorlesungen, Ethica, pp 579-582
12.14 Iamblichus, op. cit., p 90
12.15 Michel de Montaigne, Selected Essays, pp 63-64
12.16 Jeremy Taylor, Holy Living, pp 25-26

CHAPTER THIRTEEN

13.1 Plutarch, Essays, tr. Robin Waterfield, p 27

13.2 Ficino, Meditations of the Soul, p 84
13.3 Ibid., p 188
13.4 Thomas Browne, Religio Medici, p 15
13.5 Cambridge Platonist Spirituality, p 137
13.6 John Dewey, The Living Thoughts of Thomas Jefferson, p 96
13.7 G E Moore, Principia Ethica, p 181
13.8 Richard McKeon, Selections froom Medieval Philosophers, p 317
13.9 Michael Grant, Cicero on the Good Life, p 54
13.10 Cicero, Nature of the Gods, pp 71-72
13.11 Seneca, Letters from a Stoic, p 151
13.12 Plutarch, Essays and Miscellanies, vol. 3, p 49
13.13 Ficino, Meditatins of the Soul, pp 82-83
13.14 Charles Taylor, Hegel, p 505
13.15 Seneca, Letters From a Stoic, pp 77-78
13.16 Moses Hadas, The Stoic Philosophy of Seneca, p 182
13.17 Gabriel Marcel, The Mystery of Being, vol 1, pp 173-175
13.18 Moses Hadas, On Love, The Family, and the Good Life: Selected Essays of Plutarch, p 32
13.19 Saint Basil, Letters, vol 1
13.20 The Essential Gandhi, p 152
13.21 Ibid., pp 160-161
13.22 Ibid., p 236

CHAPTER FOURTEEN

14.1 Moritz Schlick, Problems of Ethics, p 192
14.2 Plutarch's Lives, GBWW, pp 353-354
14.3 Epictetus, GBWW, p 122
14.4 Ibid, p 181

CHAPTER FIFTEEN

15.1 Hans J Hillerbrand, Fellowship of Discontent, p 82

NOTES

CHAPTER SIXTEEN

16.1 Frederick Ungar, Friedrich Schiller, p 76
16.2 Immanuel Kant, Lectures on Ethics, pp 207-208

CHAPTER SEVENTEEN

17.1 Bertrand Russell, Marriage and Morals, p 190
17.2 Benjamin Karpman, The Sexual Offender and His Offences, p 466
17.3 The Ancient Near East, ed. James B Pritchard, pp 170-172
17.4 C K Barrett, The New Testament Background, pp 37-38
17.5 Plutarch's Lives, GBWW, Cato the Younger
17.6 Jessie Bernard, The Future of Marriage, p 305

CHAPTER EIGHTEEN

18.1 Ficino, Meditations on the Soul, p 148-149
18.2 Carolly Erickson, The Records of Medieval Europe, p 283
18.3 Thomas Browne, Religio Medici, pp 15-16
18.4 Rudolf Otto, The Idea of the Holy, pp 115-116
18.5 Jeremy Taylor, Holy Living, p 110
18.6 Immanuel Kant, Lectures on Ethics, pp 95-96
18.7 George Santayana, Interpretations of Poetry and Religion, p 132
18.8 Ibid., pp 134-135
18.9 Karl Jaspers, Way to Wisdom, p 47
18.10 Ibid., pp 124-125
18.11 Thomas Merton, Spiritual Direction and Meditation, p 43
18.12 Aldous Huxley, The Perennial Philosophy, p 242
18.13 Paul Tillich, The Shaking of the Foundations, p 152
18.14 Paul Tillich, The Dynamics of Faith, p 9
18.15 Meister Eckhart, tr. R B Blakney, p 9
18.16 Evelyn Underhill, Mysticism, pp 81-82
18.17 Evelyn Underhill, The Mystics of the Church, p 10
18.18 F C Happold, Mysticism, pp 252-253
18.19 Ibid., p 264

18.20 Rumi, Coleman Barks, p 19
18.21 Ibid., p 122
18.22 The Triumphs of Petrarch, tr. E H Wilkins, pp 99-101
18.23 Ibid., p 112
18.24 Ficino, Meditations of the Soul, p 32
18.25 Jocob Boehme, op. cit. p 106
18.26 Abraham H Maslow, op. cit. p. xii
18.27 Cambridge Platonist Spirituality, pp 167-168
18.28 R W Emerson, Self-Reliance, p 55
18.29 Leland Miles, John Colet, pp 23-24

CHAPTER NINETEEN

19.1 Plutarch, Essays, tr R Waterfield, pp 27-29
19.2 Plutarch, On Love, The Family, and the Good Life, tr M Hadas, pp 102-103
19.3 Ibid., pp 111-112
19.4 Steven Ozment, The Age of Reform, p 311
19.5 Immanuel Kant, Lectures on Ethics, p 46
19.6 Vergilius ferm, Classics of Protestantism, p 352

CHAPTER TWENTY

20.1 J. Bronowski, Science and Human Values, p 61
20.2 Ibid., p 69
20.3 Iamblichus, op. cit., p 181
20.4 Leibniz, Selections, pp 77-78

CHAPTER TWENTY ONE

21.1 G W F Hegel, Introductory Lectures on Aethetics, p 25
21.2 Ibid., p 36
21.3 William Ralph Inge, Platonic Tradition in English Religious Thought, p 98
21.4 Ibid., p 108

21.5 Marsilio Ficino, Meditations of the Soul, p 59
21.6 Paul Tillich, The New Being, p 131
21.7 Marsilio Ficino, Meditations of the Soul, p 79
21.8 Charles Taylor, Hegel, p 478
21.9 W R Inge, op. cit. P 83
21.10 Ibid., p 89
21.11 Botsford and Robinson's, Hellenic History, p 449
21.12 B. Farrington, Greek Science, pp 201-205
21.13 Friedrich Schiller, The Aesthetic Education of Man, p 80
21.14 Plutarch, Essays, vol. 3, p 153
21.15 Ibid, p 259
21.16 Ibid, p 309
21.17 M Ficino, Meditations of the Soul, p 45
21.18 Teilhard de Chardin, Hymn of the Universe, p 119

CHAPTER TWENTY THREE

23.1 M Ficino, Meditations of the Soul, p 1
23.2 Ibid., p 128
23.3 Leland Miles, John Colet, pp 133-134
23.4 Jeremy Taylor, Holy Living, p 122
23.5 Ascontio Condivi, Michaelangelo Buonarrote, The Portable Renaissance Reader, pp 509-510
23.6 Leland Miles, op. cit., p 95
23.7 Aldous Huxley, The Perennial Philosophy, p 212

BIBLIOGRAPHY

Adler, Alfred. Understanding Human Nature. Tran. W B Wolfe. Greenwich, CT: Fawcett Pub., 1961.
Ady, C.M. Lorenzo dei Medici. New York: Collier Books, 1962.
Amselm: Proslogium, Monologium, Cur Deus Homo. Tr. S N Deane. La Salle, IL: Open Court, 1951.
Aratus. Phaenomena. LCL.
Archer-Hind, R.D. The Timaeus of Plato. New York: NY Times Company, the Arno Press, 1973.
Aristotle. Politics. Edited and Translated by Ernest Barker. Oxford: Oxford U. Press, 1969.
Athanasius. In Controversy with the Arians. Translated by John Henry Parker. London: Oxford, 1853.
Augustine. The City of God. Translated by Marcus Dods. New York: Random House, the Modern Library, 1950.
The Confessions. Translated by J.K. Ryan. Garden City, NY Doubleday, Image, 1962.
The Greatness of the Soul. Translated by J.M. Colleran. Maryland: The Westminster Newman Press, 1950.
Of True Religion. Translated by J.H.S. Burleigh. Chicago. Henry Regnery Company, 1959.
Babrius. Tran. B. E. Perry. LCL, 1965.
Bacon, Francis. Ed. S. Warhaft. N Y: Odyssey, 1965.
Baiton, Roland H. The Travail of Religious Liberty. NY: Harper, 1958.
Baldwin, John W. The Scholastic Culture ofthe Middle Ages 1000-1300. Lexington MA: D C Heath, 1971
Barker, John W. Justinian. Madison, WI: Wisconsin U. Press, 1977.
Barnstone, Willis. Editor. The Other Bible. San Francisco: Harper & Row, 1984.
Barrett, C.K. The New Testament Background. London: SPCK, 1958.
Barrow, John D. The Origin of the Universe. London: Phoenix, 1994.
Basil, Saint. Letters. Translated by Sister Agnes Clare Way. New York. The Fathers of the Church, Inc., 1955.
Bede. A History of the English Church and People. Baltimore, Penguin.
Benko, Stephen. Pagan Rome and the Early Christians. Bloomington, IN: Indiana U., 1986.
Bernard, Jessie. The Future of Marriage. N Y: World Pub., 1972.
Bigg, Charles. The Christian Platonists of Alexandria. Oxford: Clarendon Press, 1913.

BIBLIOGRAPHY

Bigg, Charles. The Christian Platonists of Alexandria. Oxford: Clarendon Press, 1913.

Boardman, John. The Greeks Overseas. Baltimore: Penguin Books, 1964.

Boas, Marie. The Scientific Renaissance 1450-1630. New York: Harper & Row, Harper Torchbooks, 1966.

Boehme, Jacob. The Way to Christ. Tr. Peter Erb. NY: Paulist, 1978.

Boethius. The Consolation of Philosophy. Translated by Whitney J. Oats. New York: Frederick Ungar Publishing Co., 1957.

Bornkamm, Guenther. Jesus of Nazareth. Tr. Irene & Fraser McLuskey. NY: Harper, 1975.

Botsford and Robinson's Hellenic History. Revised by Donald Kagan. London: MacMillan Co. 1969.

Bowder, Diana. Who was Who in the Greek World. New York: Washington Square Press, Pocket Books, 1984.

Brehier, Emile. The Hellenic Age. Translated by Joseph Thomas. Chicago: U. of Chicago Press, 1970.

Broderick, Carlfred & Bernard, Jessie. The Individual, Sex, & Society. Baltimore, 1969.

Bronowski, J. Science and Human Values. N Y: Harper & Row, 1956.

Brown, Peter. The World of Late Antiquity. London: Harcourt Brace Jovanovich, 1978.

Browne, Thomas. Religio Medici. New York: Dutton, 1965.

Buber, Martin. Eclipse of God. N Y: Harper, 1957.

Bucke, Richard M. Cosmic Consciousness. London: Penguin, 1901.

Bultmann, Rudolf. Theology of the New Testament, 2 Vols. Translated by Kendrick Grobel. New York: Charles Scribners Sons, 1955.

Primitive Christianity. New York: Meridian Books, Living Age Books, 1959.

Jesus Christ and Mythology. New York: Charles Scribners Sons, 1958.

"Gnosis." From Kittle's Theologisches Woerterbuch Zum Neuen Testament. Translated by J.R. Coates. London: Adam & Charles Black, Soho Square, 1952.

Kerygma and Myth. NY: Harper, 1961.

Burchhardt, Jacob. The Civilization of the Renaissance in Italy, 2 Vols. New York: Harper & Row, Harper Torchbooks, 1958.

BIBLIOGRAPHY

Burkert, Walter. Greek Religion. Tr John Raffan. Cambridge, MA: Harvard U. Press, 1985.

Burnet, John. Early Greek Philosophy. New York: World Publishing Co., Meridian Books, 1930.

Burn, A.R. The Pelikan History of Greece. Baltimore: Penguine Books, 1966.

Bury, R.G. The Symposium of Plato. Cambridge: W. Heffer and Sons Ltd, 1973.

Cambridge Platonist Spirituality. Ed. Taliaferro & Teply. NY: Paulist, 2004.

Campbell, James M. The Greek Fathers. New York: Cooper Square Publishers, 1963.

Campbell, Joseph. The Hero with a Thousand Faces. Princeton U. Press, 1972.

Can Christianity Survive? Ed. Joe David Brown. NY: Time-Life, 1968.

Cary, M. The History of the Greek World. New York: Barnes & Noble Inc. L965.

Catechism of the Catholic Church. N Y: Image (Doubleday), 1995.

Cawthorne, Nigel. Sex Lives of the Popes. London: Prion, 1996.

Charles, R.H. The Apocrypha and Pseudepigrapha 2 Vols. Oxford, Clarendon Press, 1913.

Christianity: Some Non-Christian Appraisals. Ed. David McKain. NY: McGraw-Hill, 1964.

Cicero. The Nature of the Gods. Translated by H.C.P. McGregor. New York: Penguin Books, 1984.

On The Good Life. Tr. Michael Grant. Baltimore. Penguin Books, 1971

On the Commonwealth. Tr. Sabine & Smith. NY: Liberal Arts Press, 1929.

Clark, Davis W. Child Labor and the Social Conscience. NY: Abingdon, 1924.

Clark, Gordon H. Hellenistic Philosophy. New York: Appleton-Century-Crafts, 1940.

The Classics of Protestantism. Ed. Vergilius Ferm. NY: Philosophical Library, 1959.

Clemen, Carl C. Primitive Christianity and its Non-Jewish Sources. Edinburgh: T. & T. Clark, 1912.

Cook, Joseph. Marriage. Boston: Houghtn, Osgood & Co., 1879.

Copleston, Frederick. A History of Philosophy, Vols. 1-3., 6 NY: Newman Press, 1966.

Cornford, F.M. Before and After Socrates. Cambridge: Cambridge U. Press, 1972.

From Religion to Philosophy. Mineola, NY: Dover, 2004.

Cudworth, Ralph. Cudworth. A Treatise Concerning Eternal and Immutable Morality. CTHPH, 1996.

Culver, Elsie Thomas. Women in the World of Religion. Garden City, NY: Doubleday, 1967.

Daniel-Rops, Henri. Israel and the Ancient World. Garden City, N.Y. Image, 1964.

Dante. The Divine Comedy. Translated by Charles E. Norton. GBWW, 1952.

Debs, Eugene V. Eugene V Debs Speaks. Ed. Jean Y Tussey. NY: Pathfinder Press, 1970.

Dewart, Leslie. The Future of Belief. NY: Herder & Herder, 1968.

Dewey, John. The Living Thoughts of Thomas Jefferson. Greenwich, CT. Fawcett Publications: Premier, 1957.

Dickinson, G. Lowes. The Greek View of Life. Ann Arbor, MI: U. of Michigan Press, Ann Arbor Paperbacks, 1958.

Dillon, John. The Middle Platonists. Ithaca, New York: Cornell U. Press, 1977.

Diogenes Laertius. Lives and Opinions of Eminent Philosophers. Translated by F.H. Colson and G.H. Whitaker. LCL.

Doerries, Hermann. Constantine the Great. Tr. Roland Bainton, NY: 1972.

Drees, Ludwig. Olympia. New York: Frederick A Praeger, 1968.

Dunham, Barrows. Heroes and Heretics. N Y: Delta, 1963.

Eckhart, Meister. Tr. Raymond B. Blakney. NY: Harper, 1941.

Ehrenberg, Victor. From Solon to Socrates. London: Methuen & Co., 1973.

Ehrlich, Jerry Dell. Plato's Gift to Christianity: The Gentile Preparation For and the Making of the Christian Faith. San Diego: Academic Christian Press, 2001.

Building a Life by Carpenter Jesus: The Divine Teacher's Seven Steps to Wholeness with Supplementary Wisdom from both Western classical and Eastern Sages. San Diego: Academic Christian Press, 2003.

The Joy of Embracing God: Humanity's Longing for the Eternal. San Diego: Academic Christian Press, 2005.
Ehrlich, Paul. The Population Bomb. NY: Sierra Club/Ballantine, 1971.
Ehrman, Bart D. Misquoting Jesus. San Francisco: Harper, 2005.
Einstein, Albert. The World As I See It. NY: Wisdom Library, 1949.
Eliade, Mircea. Rites and Symbols of Initiation. NY: Harper, 1965.
Emerson, R W. Self-Reliance. NY: Dover, 1993.
Representative Men. Elibron Classics, 2005.
Essays. Random House. 1944.
Enoch, Book of. tr R H Charles. London: SPCK, 1960.
Epictetus. Discourses. Tr George Long, GBWB
Erasmus, D. The Education of a Christian Prince. CTHPT, 1974.
Ten Colloquies of Erasmus. Tr. C R Thompson. NY: Liberal Arts Press, 1957.
The Praise of Folly. Tr 1668. Ann Arbor: U of Michigan Press, 1960.
Christian Humanism and the Reformation. Ed. John Olin. NY: Harper, 1965.
Erasmus, the Essential. Ed. John Dolan: NY: New American Library (Mentor), 1964
Erickson, Carolly. The Records of Medieval Europe. Garden City, NY: 1971.
Eunapius. Lives of Philosophers. Tran. W C Wright. LCL, 1921.
Eusebius. Ecclesiatical History Vols. 1-2. Translated by Roy J. Deferrai. FC, 1955.
Fairweather, William. Jesus and the Greeks: Early Christianity in the Tideway of Hellenism. Edinburgh: T & T Clark, 1924.
Farrington, Benjamin. Greek Science. Baltimore: Penguin Books, 1961.
Ficino, Marsilio. Platonic Theology, vol. 1: Tr. M. Allen. Cambridge MA: Harvard U. Press, 2001.
Meditations on the Soul. Rochester, VT: Inner Traditions, 1996.
Feibleman, James K. Religious Platonism. Westport, CT: Greenwood Press, 1958.
Finlan, Stephen. Proablems with Atonement. Collegeville, MN: Liturgical Press, 2005.
Finley, M. I. The Ancient Greeks. New York: Viking Press, 1969.

Forrest, W.G. The Emergence of Greek Democracy. NY: World University Library, McGraw-Hill Co., 1975.

Fox, Matthew. Breakthrough: Meister Eckhart's Creation Spirituality in New Translation. NY: Doubleday, Image, 1980.

Friedlaender, Paul. Plato. Translated by Hans Meyerhoff. Princeton: Princeton University Press, 1969.

Frost, Frank J. Greek Society. Lexington, MA: D.C. Heath & Co., 1971.

Galileo. Tr. Stillman Drake: Berkeley: U of California Press, 1967.

Gamble, Harry Y. The New Testament Canon. Philadelphia: Fortress, 1985.

Gandhi. The Essential Gandhi. Ed. Louis Fischer. NY: Vintage, 1963.

Gardner, Helen. Art Through the Ages. New York: Harcourt, Brace, & Co., 1948.

Gerson, L.P. God and Greek Philosophy. New York: Routledge, 1990.

Gilson, Etienne. Reason and Revelation in the Middle Ages. New York: Scribner Library, Charles Scribner's & Sons, 1938.

Grant, Frederick C. Roman Hellenism and the New Testament. New York: Charles Scribner's Sons, 1962

Grant, Michael. Jesus. New York: Charles Scribner's Sons, 1977.

From Alexander to Cleopatra. New York: Charles Scribner's Sons, 1982.

The History of Ancient Israel. New York: Charles Scribner's Sons, 1984.

Grant, Robert. Early Christianity and Society. San Francisco, CA: Harper, 1977.

Greek Philosophers of the Hellenistic Age. Trans. by Gregory Woods. New York: Columbia U. Press, 1993.

Green, Peter. Ancient Greece. London: Thames & Hudson, 1984.

Gregory of Nyssa. Ascetical Works. Translated by Virginia W. Callahan. FC, 1967.

Gross, Barry. Great Thinkers on Plato. New York: G.P. Putnam's Sons, 1968.

Gruen, Erich S. Heritage and Hellenism:The Reinvention of Jewish Tradition. Berkeley, CA: University of California Press, 1998.

Guignebert, Charles. The Jewish World in the Time of Jesus. New Hyde Park, N.Y. University Books, 1968.

Guignebert, Charles. The Jewish World in the Time of Jesus. New Hyde Park, N.Y. University Books, 1968.
Guthrie, W.K.C. The Greek Philosophers. New York: Harper Torchbooks, Harper & Row, 1960.
Hadas, Moses. On Love, Family, Good Life: Selections from Plutarch. New York: Mentor, New American Library, 1957.
Hellenistic Culture. Morningside Heights, New York: Columbia U. Press, 1959.
Ancilla to Classical Reading. New York: Columbia U. Press, 1954.
Haeger, Knut. History of Sürgery. NY: Bell Pub. Co., 1988.
Hamilton, Edith. The Greek Way. New York: W.W. Norton Co., The Norton Library, 1964.
Hammarskjold, Dag. Markings. Tr. Sjoberg & Auden. NY: A. Knopf, 1964.
Happold, F C. Mysticism. London: Penguin, 1963.
Hardy, W.C. The Greek and Roman World. Cambridge, MA. Schenkman Publishing Company, 1962.
Harenberg, Werner. Der Spiegel On the New Testament. London: Macmillan Co., 1966.
Harnack, Adolf. What is Christianity? Translated by T.B. Saunders. New York: Harper Torchbooks, Harper & Row, 1957.
Heer, Friedrich. The Medieval World. Translated by J. Sondheimer. New York: Mentor Book, New American Library, 1961.
Hegel, G W F. Introductory Lectures on Aethetics. N Y: Penguin, 1883.
Phenomenology of Spirit. Tr. AV Miller. Oxford: Oxford U. Press, 1977.
Lectures on the Philosophy of Religion. Tr. P C Hodgson. Berkeley, CA: U of California Press, 1988.
Hengel, Martin. Jews, Greeks, and Barbarians. Philadelphia: Fortress Press, 1980.
Hesiod. Theogony and Works and Days. Translated by Dorothea Wender. Baltimore: Penguin Classics, 1973.
Hesiod. Theogony and Works and Days. Tr. Hugh Evelyn-White, LCL, 1974.
Hillerbrand, Hans. A Fellowship of Discontent. NY: Harper & Row, 1967.
Hippolytus. Kessinger Reprints.

BIBLIOGRAPHY

Hofmann, Werner. Luther und die Folgen fuer die Kunst. Prestel-Verlag, 1984.

Hoffmann, R. Joseph. The Origins of Christianity. Buffalo, NY: Prometheus Books, 1985.

Julian's Against the Galileans. Amherst, NY: Prometheus Books, 2004.

Porphyry's Against the Christians. Amherst, NY: Prometheus Books, 1994.

Horst, Pieter W. Van der. Hellenism-Judaism-Christianity. Kampen, The Netherlands: Kok Pharos Publishing House, 1994.

Hough, Lynn Harold. Great Humanists. NY: Abingdon-Cokesbury, 1952.

Huizinga, Johan. Home Ludens. Boston: Beacon Press, 1950.

Hurtado, Larry W. How on Earth Did Jesus Become a God? Grand Rapids, MI: Eerdmans, 2005.

Huxley, Aldous. The Perennial Philosophy. NY: Harper, 1944.

Huxley, Julian. Knowledge, Morality, & Destiny. N Y: Harper, 1957

Religion Without Revelation. NY: Mentor, 1957.

Iamblichus. Life of Pythagoras. Tr Thomas Taylor. Rochester, VT: Inner Traditons International: 1986.

Inge, W R. Platonic Tradition in English Religious Thought. London: Longmans, Green & Co., 1926

Jaeger, Werner. Early Christianity and Greek Paideia. Cambridge, MA: Harvard U. Press, 1961.

Jaspers, Karl. Socrates Buddha Confucius Jesus. N Y: Harcourt, Brace etc., 1962.

Way to Wisdom. Tr. R. Manheim. London: Yale U. Press, 1962.

Jonas, Hans. The Gnostic Religion. Boston: The Beacon Press, 1963.

Jone, Heribert and Adelman, Urban. Moral Theology. Westminster, MD: Newman Press, 1951.

Jones, A H M. Constantine and the Conversion of Europe. NY: Collier, 1967.

Jones, W.T. A History of Western Philosophy: The Classical Mind and The Medieval Mind. San Francisco: Harcourt, Brace, & World, 1969.

Jorgensen, Johannes. St Francis of Assisi. Garden City, NY: Image,1955.

Kahane, P.P. Ancient and Classical Art. New York: Dell Publishing Co., 1968.

Kant, Immanuel. Religion within the Boundaries of Mere Reason. CTHPH, 1998.
_____ Observations on the Feeling of the Beautiful and Sublime. Tr. John T Goldthwait. Berkeley: U. of California Press, 1963.
_____ Lectures on Ethics. Tr. Louis Infield. NY: Harper, 1963.
_____ Gesammelte Schriften: Vorlesungen. Band IV. Berlin: Walter de Grunter, 1974.
Karpman, Benjamin. The Sexual Offender and His Offenses. NY: Julian Press, 1954.
Katchadourian, Herant and Lunde, Donald. Fundamentals of Human Sexuality. NY: Holt, Rineharrt & Winston, 1972.
Kinneavy, James L. Greek Rhetorical Origins of Christian Faith. Oxford: Oxford U. Press, 1987.
Kitto, H.D.F. The Greeks. Baltimore: Pelican Original, Penguin Books, 1951.
Koester, Helmut. History, Culture, and Religion of the Hellenistic Age. Berlin: Walter De Gruyter, 1995.
Kristeller, Paul Oskar. Renaissance Thought. San Francisco: Harper Torchbooks, Harper & Row,
_____ Eight Philosophers of the Italian Renaissance. Stanford U.Press, 1964
Lactantius. The Divine Institutes. Translated by Mary F. McDonald. FC.
Leibnitz. Ed. P P Wiener. NY: Scribner's, 1951
Lessing's Theological Writngs. Tr. Henry Chadwick. Stanford U. Press, 1957.
Lieberman, Saul. Hellenism in Jewish Palestine. New York: Jewish Theological Seminary of America, 1950.
Lloyd-Jones, Hugh. Editor. The Greek World. Baltimore: Penguin Books, 1962.
Lodge, Rupert C. The Philosophy of Plato. New York: The Humanities Press, 1956.
Lohse, Eduard. The New Testament Environment. Translated by John E. Steely. Nashville: Abingdon, 1976.
Long, A.A. and Sedley, D.N. The Hellenistic Philosophers. New York: Cambridge U. Press, 1987.
Longinus. On Great Writing. Tr. GMA Grube. Cambridge: Hackett Pub. 1991.

MacKendrick, Paul. The Greek Stones Speak. New York: Mentor, New American Library, 1966.
Malebranche, Nicolas. Dialogues on Metaphysics and on Religion. CTHPH, 1997.
Malinowski, Bronislaw. Sex and Repression in Savage Society. NY: World Pub. Co., 1963.
The Malleus Maleficarum. Kramer & Sprenger. NY: Dover, 1971.
Mannix, Daniel. The History of Torture. NY: Dell, 1964.
Marcel, Gabriel. Homo Viator. Translated by E. Cfraufurd. New York: Harper Brothers, 1962.
______ The Mystery of Being. Vols 1-2. Chicago, IL: Henry Regnery Co., 1949.
Marcus Aurelius. Meditions. Tr. M. Staniforth. Baltimore, MD: Penguin, 1970.
Marrou, H.I. A History of Education in Antiquity. Translated by G. Lamb. New York: Mentor, New American Library, 1964.
Marsilius of Padua. The Defendor of Peace. NY: Harper, 1956.
Maslow, Abraham H. Religions, Values, and Peak-Experiences. NY: Penguin, 1970.
Mather, Cotton. On Witchcraft. Mineola, NY: Dover, 2005.
Mattingly, Harold. Christianity in the Roman Empire. NY: Norton, 1954.
McLean, George F. and Aspell, Patrick J. Readings in Western Philosophy. NY: Appleton Century Crofts, Meredith Corp., 1970.
Medieval Reader. Ed. Ross & McLaughlin. NY: Viking Press, 1968.
Melling, David J. Understanding Plato. New York: Oxford U. Press, 1987.
Menn, Stephen. Plato on God as Nous. Carbondale; Southern Illinois U. Press, 1995.
Merton, Thomas. Spiritual Direction and Meditation. Collegeville, MN: Liturgical Press, 1960.
Metzger, Bruce M. The New Testament: its Background, Growth, and Content. Nashville: Abingdon, 1982.
Miles, Leland. John Colet and the Platonic Tradition. London: Allen & Unwin, 1962.
Mill, John Stuart. On The Subjection of Woman. Greenwich, CT: Fawcett, 1971.
Miller, Stephen G. Arete. Chicago: Ares Publishers Inc., 1979.
Minor Latin Poets. Vol. 1: Duff & Duff, LCL 1924.

Modern Religious Thought. Ed. Jaroslav Pelikan. Boston: Little, Brown, 1990.

Montaigne, Michelde. Selected Essays. Mineola, NY: Dover, 1996.

Moore, G E. Principia Ethica. Amherst, NY: Promethius, 1988.

More, Paul Elmer. The Religion of Plato. Princeton U. Press. Reprint from New York: Kraus Reprint Co., 1970 (originally 1921).

More, Thomas. Utopia. Tr. H V S Ogden. NY: Appleton-Century-Crofts, 1949.

Murphy, John L. General Councils of the Church. Milwaukee, WI: Bruce, 1959.

Murray, Gilbert. Five Stages of Greek Religion. Boston: Beacon Press, 1951.

Murray, Henry. Myth and Mythmaking. Boston: Beacon Press, 1959.

Muste, A J. The Essays of A J Muste. Ed. Nat Hentoff. NY: Simon & Schuster, 1970.

Nag Hammadi Library. General Editor, James Robinson. San Francisco: Harper & Row, 1981.

Neugebauer, O. The Exact Sciences in Antiquity. New York: Dover Publications, 1969.

Nicholas of Cusa. Tr. H. Lawrence Bond. NY: Paulist Press, 1997.

Nietzsche, Friedrich. Twilight of the Idols & The Antichrist. Tr. T. Common. Mineola, NY: Dover, 2004.

The Philosophy of Nietzsche. New York: Random House, Modern Library, 1954.

Nilsson, Martin P. A History of Greek Religion. Translated by F.J. Fielden. New York: Norton Library, W.W. Norton Co., 1964.

Oakesmith, John. The Religion of Plutarch: A Pagan Creed of Apostolic Times. NY: Longmans, Green, 1902.

O'Brien, Elmer. The Essential Plotinus. New York: Mentor, New American Library, 1964.

Ozment, Steven. The Age of Reform 1250-1550. New Haven: Yale U. Press, 1980.

Otto, Rudolf. The Idea of the Holy. Tr. J Harvey. Oxford: Oxford U. Press, 1958.

Ovid. Metamorphoses. Tr Rolfe Humphries. Bloomington: Indiana U. Press, 1955.

Paine, Thomas. The Age of Reason. Paris: Barrois, 1794.

Papahatzis, Nicos. Ancient Corinth. Athens: Ekdotike Athenon S.A., 1979.
Paracelsus. Tr. Nicholas Goodrick-Clarke. Berkeley: North Atlantic Books, 1999.
Patterson, Robert L. Plato on Immortality. Pennsylvania State U. Press, 1965.
Pelikan, Jaroslav. What Has Athens to Do with Jerusalem? Ann Arbor, MI: U. of Michigan Press, 1997.
Persius. FCL, 1831.
Peters, F.E. The Harvest of Hellenism. New York: Touchstone, Simon & Schuster, 1970.
Phaedrus. Tr. B E Perry. LCL, 1965.
Phaedrus. Tr. Philip Francis. FCL, 1831/
Phillips, M.M. Erasmus on His Times. Cambridge: U. Press, 1967.
Philo. Vols. 1-3. Tr. by F.H. Colson and G.H. Whitaker, LCL, 1929 & 1930.
The Philokalia: Nikodimos and Makarios. Tr. Palmer, Sherrard, & Ware. London: Faber & Faber, 1979.
Philostratus. Lives of Sophists. Tr. W C Wright. LCL, 1921.
Imagines. Tr. A. Fairbanks. LCL, 1960 .
Life of Apollonius. Tr. C P Jones. Baltimore, MD: Penguin, 1970.
Pico Della Mirandola, Giovanni. Oration on the Dignity of Man. Tr A.R. Caponigri. Chicago: A Gateway Edition, Henry Regnery Co., 1956.
Plato. The Republic. Tr by Francis MacDonald Cornford. Oxford: Oxford U. Press, 1973.
Plato. Edited by Edith Hamilton and Huntington Cairns. Bollingen Series LXXI, Princeton University Press, 1973.
The Dialogues of Plato. Translated by B. Jowett. In Two Volumes (1892 by Macmillan Co., and in 1920 by Oxford U.). Reprinted with introduction by Random House, N.Y. 1937.
Plato. LCL in 12 Volumes.
Pliny, The Elder. Natural History. Tran. L. Haberly. N Y: Ungar, 1957.
Pliny, The Younger. Letters. Tran. B Radice. Baltimore: Penguin, 1963.
Plotinus. The Enneads. Translated by Stephen MacKenna and Abridged by John Dillon. New York: Penguin Books, 1991.

The Essential Plotinus. Translated by Elmer O'Brien. A Mentor Book by The New American Library, N.Y. 1964.

Plutarch. The Lives of Noble Grecians and Romans. The Dryden translation. GBWW, 1952.

Plutarch. Essays. Tr. R. Waterfield. N Y: Penguin, 1992.

Plutarch: Essays and Miscellanies. Vol.3, Kessinger Publishing.

Porphyry. Letter to Marcella. Tr. Alice Zimmern. Grand Rapids, MI.: Phanes Press, 1986.

Prior, William J. Unity and Development in Plato's Metaphysics. London: Croom Helm, 1985.

Procopius. The Secret History. Baltimore, MD: Penguin, 1966.

Pseudo-Dionysius:The Complete Works. Translated by Colm Luibheid. New York: Paulist Press, 1987.

Randall, John Herman, Jr. Hellenistic Ways of Deliverance and the Making of the Christian Synthesis. New York: Columbia U. Press, 1970.

Ranke-Heinemann, Uta. Eunuchs for the Kingdom of Heaven. Tr. Peter Heinegg. London: Penguin, 1991.

Rankin, H D. Plato and the Individual. London: Methuen & Co., 1964.

Raven, J.E. Plato's Thought in the Making. Cambridge: Cambridge U. Press, 1965.

Reich, Wilhelm. The Murder of Christ. NY: Noonday Press, 1953.

The Invasion of Compulsory Sex-Morality. NY: Farrar, Straus & Giroux, 1971,

The Renaissance Philosophy of Man. Edited by Cassirer, Ernest; Kristeller, Paul Oskar; Randall, John Herman Jr. Chicago: Phoenix Books, U. of ChicagoPress, 1963.

Renaissance Reader. Ed. Ross & McLaughlin. NY: Viking Press, 1974.

Rexine, John E. Religion in Plato and Cicero. New York: Greenwood Press, 1968.

Richardson, Peter. Herod: King of the Jews and Friend of the Romans. U. of South Carolina Press, 1996.

Richter, Gisela. Greek Art. New York: Paidon, 1974.

Rist, John M. Eros and Psyche. Toronto: Phoenix, U. of Toronto Press, 1964.

Ritter, Constantin. The Essence of Plato's Philosophy. Translated by Adam Alles.New York: Russell & Russell, 1968.

Robinson, John M. An Introduction to Early Greek Philosophy. Boston: Houghton Mifflin Co., 1968.
Robotti, Frances Diane. Chronicles of Old Salem. NY: Bonanza Books, 1948.
Rose, H.J. Religion in Greece and Rome. New York: Harper Torchbooks, Harper & Row, 1959.
Rostovtzeff, M. Greece. Translated by J.D. Ruff. Oxford: Oxford U. Press, 1963.
Rudolph, Kurt. Gnosis. Translated by R.M. Wilson. San Francisco: Harper & Row, 1987.
Ruether, Rosemary R. Gregory of Nazianzus. Oxford: Clarendon Press, 1969.
Rumi, The Essenial. Tr. C. Barks, NY: Castle Books, 1995.
Russell, Bertrand. A History of Western Philosophy. NY: Simon & Schuster, 1945.
Bertrand Russell Speaks His Mind. NY: Bard Books, 1960.
Why I am Not a Christian. N.Y: Simon & Schuster, 1957.
Marriage and Morals. N.Y: Liveright Pub. Co., 1968.
Russell, D.S. Between the Testaments. Philadelphia: Fortress, 1989.
Sabatier, Auguste. Outlines of a Philosophy of Religion. NY: Harper, 1897.
Sahakian, W.S. & M.L. Plato. Boston: Twayne Publishers, 1977.
Sallustius. Tr. A D Nock. Chicago: Ares Pub., 1996.
Santillana, Giorgio. The Crime of Galileo. Chicago U. Press, 1955.
Santayana, George. Interpretations of Poetry and Religion. N Y: Harper, 1957.
Three Philosophical Poets. NY: Doubleday, 1953.
Saunders, Jason L. Greek and Roman Philosophy after Aristotle. New York: Free Press, 1966.
Schaff, Philip. History of the Christian Church Vols. 1-3. Grand Rapids, MI: Eerdmans, 1953.
Schiller, Friedrich. On The Aesthetic Education of Man. Tr R. Snell. New York: Ungar, 1965.
Schleiermacher, Friedrich. On Religion. NY: Harper, 1958.
Christmas Eve: Dialogue on the Incarnation. Tr. T. Tice, Richmond, VA: John Knox, 1952.
Schlick, Moritz. Problems of Ethics. Tr. David Rynin. NY: Dover, 1962.

Christmas Eve: Dialogue on the Incarnation. Tr. T. Tice, Richmond, VA: John Knox, 1952.

Schlick, Moritz. Problems of Ethics. Tr. David Rynin. NY: Dover, 1962.

Schuster, M. Lincoln. The Worlds' Great Letters. NY: Simon and Schuster, 1960.

Schweitzer, Albert. The Quest of the Historical Jesus. NY: MacMillan, 1968.

Scot, Regnald. The Discoverie of Witchcraft. NY: Dover, 1972.

Scott, Ernest F. The Varieties of New Testament Religion. NY: Charles Schribner's Sons, 1944.

The Literature of the New Testament. NY: Columbia U. Press, 1943.

Scott, Walter. Hermetica Vol. I. Boston: Shambhala, reprint in 1985 (Originally in 1924).

Seligmann, Kurt. Magic, Supernaturalism and Religion. NY: Pantheon , 1948.

Selections From Medieval Philosphers: Vols. 1-2. NY: Charles Scribner's, 1930,

Seneca: Letters From a Stoic. Tr. Robin Campbell. NY: Penguin Books, 1969.

The Stoic Philosophy of Seneca: tr. Moses Hadas, Garden City, NY: Doubleday Anchor Books, 1958.

Seneca Epistulae Morales. Tr. RM Gummere. Vols 1 & 3. Cambridge, MA: 1979 (Orig. 1917).

The Situation Ethics Debate. Ed. Harvey Cox. Philadelphia: Westminster, 1968.

Sparks, H.F.D. Editor. The Apocryphal Old Testament. Oxford: Clarendon Press, 1984.

Spencer, Herbert. Data of Ethics. NY: John Lovell Co., 1879.

Socrates and Sozomenus. Church Histories. NPNF. 1952.

Solmsen, Friedrich. Plato's Theology. Ithaca, New York: Cornell U. Press, 1942.

Spong, John Shelby. Resurrection: Myth or Reality? San Francisco: Harper, 1994.

Stendahl, Krister. Meanings: The Bible as Document and as Guide. Philadelphia: Fortress, 1984.

Stephanus, E.H. Thesaurus: Graecae Linguae. Graz: Akademische Druck, U. Verlagsamstalt, 1954.

Swedenborg, Emanuel. Divine Love and Wisdom. Tr. J C Ager. NY: Citadel, 1965.
Tabori, Paul. Secret and Forbidden. N Y: New American Library, 1966.
Tarn, W.W. Alexander the Great. Boston: Beacon Press, 1956.
Hellenistic Civilization. New York: Meridian Books, The World Publishing Co., 1969.
Taylor, Alfred Edward. Platonism and its Influence. London: George G. Harp & Co. Reprint by by the Plimpton Press, Norword, MA.
Plato: The Man and His Work. Meridian Books, NY: Reprint in 1957 (Originally 1926).
Taylor, Charles. Hegel Cambridge University Press, 1975.
Taylor, Jeremy. Holy Living. Brewster, MA: Paraclete Press, 1988.
Tcherikover, Victor. Hellenistic Civilization and the Jews. New York: Atheneum, 1974.
Teilhard de Chardin, Pierre. Letters From a Traveller. N Y: Harper & Row, 1962.
Building the Earth. Wilkes-Barre, PA: Dimension, 1965.
The Future of Man. NY: Harper & Row, 1964.
Theognis. Elegies. Translated by Dorothea Wender. Baltimore: Penguin Classics, 1973.
Theologia Germanica. Tr. S. Winkworth. Mineola, NY: Dover, 2004.
Thomas, Gospel of. Tr. Guillaumont, Puedch, etc. NY: Harper, 1959.
Thomas, Norman. Great Dissenters. NY: Norton, 1961.
Tillich, Paul. The Shaking of the Foundations. N Y: C. Scribner's Sons, 1948.
The New Being. N Y: C. Scribner's Sons, 1955.
Dynamics of Faith. N Y: Harper & Sons, 1957.
The Religious Situation. N Y: Meridian Books. Inc. 1960.
The Courage to Be. New Haven: Yale U. Press, 1963.
The Theology of Culture. N Y: Oxford U. Press, 1964.
Christianity and the Encounter of the World Religions. N Y: Columbia U. Press, 1961.
Tolstory, Leo. A Confession. Tr. Aylmer Maude. Mineola, NY: Dover, 2005.
The Kingdom of God is Within You. Tr. Leo Wiener. Noonday Press, 1961.
Trevor-Roper, H R. The European Witch-Craze. NY: Harper, 1967.

Tripp, Edward. The Meridian Handbook of Classical Mythology. NY: New American Library, 1970.
Underhill, Evelyn. The Mystics of the Church. NY: Schocken, 1964.
Mysticism. NY: Dutton, 1961.
Ungar, Frederick. Friedrich Schiller. N Y: Ungar Pub., 1959.
Van Buren, Paul. The Secular Meaning of the Gospel. NY: MacMillan, 1963.
Virgil. The Pastoral Poems. Translated by E.V. Rieu. Baltimore: Penguin Books, 1967.
Webster, T.B.L. Everyday Life in Classical Athens. New York: G.P. Putnam's Sons, 1969.
Whitehead, W N. The Aims of Education. NY: Mentor, 1955.
Process and Reality. NY: Free Press, 1978.
Williams, Daniel Day. The Spirit and the Forms of Love. N Y: Harper & Row, 1968.
Wind, Edgar. Pagan Mysteries in the Renaissance. New York: Norton Library, 1968.
Woodhouse, S.C. English-Greek Dictionary: Attic Greek. London: Routledge & Kegan Paul Ltd., 1954.
The Young Hegelians. Ed. L S Stepelevich. Cambridge: University Press, 1983.

INDEX